A Mob of His Own: Mad Sam DeStefano and the Chicago Mob's Juice Rackets

Copyright © 2008 Tony Dark

Published 2008 by HoseHead Productions

ISBN 978-0-615-17496-9

Library of Congress Control Number: 2008921543

First Edition 2008

Typesetting & Cover Design by **LRT**

Manufactured in the United States of America

A Mob of His Own

Mad Sam DeStefano and the Chicago
Mob's "Juice" Rackets

Tony Dark

Contents

Chapter One

His eyes would burn a hole in your soul as he informed you how you were going to be tortured and killed. Drool dripping from the corner of his mouth as he stabbed you over and over with an ice pick. The repeated "jab jab" in your stomach as you felt the steel blade pierce your skin over and over again. The last image your eyes could make out was the smile of a crazy man who was covered in your blood screaming and yelling, telling you what a piece of shit you are, a maggot, a nothing, a scum bag, a rotten vegetable. This was the image of a mad man, a mad hatter, a "juice" man, a killer. This was the image many had witnessed, the image of a sick man standing over them as the life poured out of their body. His actions gained him the nickname of "Mad Dog" for his vicious style and techniques, but many just called him "Mad Sam."

Mad Sam DeSefano

Sam DeStefano lived his life believing that he was a man above the rest. Cut from the same cloth as Caesar, King Arthur, or Jesus Christ. Believing his mind was superior to the average man, he could out-smart you at every turn. No one could match Mad Sam, NO ONE!

Belief of all these things made Sam DeStefano a very successful man. Rich, powerful, loved and hated, he covered all the angles. He knew who you were before you did. He was on top of his game and on top of the criminal world. EVERYONE knew who Sam DeStefano was in Chicago, EVERYONE!

His career in organized crime began in the 1920's when Al Capone was running the city of Chicago. Mad Sam was a natural and was noticed among his fellow criminals. He would use the thousand-year-old racket of loaning money and demanding it paid back with interest into an organized empire in Chicago. He was the juice man, the loan shark, the king of shylocking. When you didn't pay, you were done with, a nothing, something had to be done, pain or death, it didn't matter to Mad Sam.

What kind of man was Mad Sam DeStefano? Why is his name put in the ranks of Chicago's most terrible murderers? Did it bring joy and delight to him being linked to scores of murders, torturing hundreds or even thousands?

People close to him say he was a kind and gentle man who was just misunderstood. Those who worked for him, investigated him, and befriended him saying he was the sickest man alive in Chicago in the 1960's and 70's.

What kind of man was Sam? A man who saw dishonesty and betrayal around every corner. A man who had his wife Anita taste his food to make sure it was not poisoned without any regard for her life. Even the food that his wife cooked and prepared was suspect and tested before he would eat it. A man who in his leisure time would drive around in his car down lonely country roads for hours looking for new places to dispose of the bodies of his victims. He would give his loan shark victims presents like a gold watch with his name engraved on the back so if he had to kill his victim and the police came saying *"you killed him Sam"* he could say: *"No I didn't, look, I was his best friend, why would I kill my best friend? I even have my name on his watch."*

He was a man who insisted that every time he was in an automobile and driving down a four-lane road demanded that the car always be driven in the left lane so if someone was to pull up in another car to shoot him, he had more ways to escape. His dream in life was to own a pig farm so he could feed his victims to the pigs. He would drive to a pig farm and just watch them for hours. He wore thick black rimmed glasses making people believe he couldn't see without them but it was just another tool to him. When people saw him with his glasses off, they thought Sam couldn't see them or what they were doing but the truth was that he was watching everything going on, taking mental notes on how that person operated.

Sam told one of his collectors, Chuckie Crimaldi, that he put him in his will for $100,000 because he was like a son to him. But Crimaldi knew better; he found out that he was in Sam DeStefano's will and in case DeStefano had to kill Crimaldi, he could tell the police, "*Why would I kill him, look, I even put him in my will. Why would I have him killed, he's like a son to me?*"

His wife Anita had to endure his violent moods and spur-of-the-moment rants, which on many occasions almost cost Anita her life. According to Charles Crimaldi, one time Sam had had enough of his wife and wanted her dead. He made Anita take his gun, put the end of the barrel in her mouth, and demanded that she pull the trigger to kill herself. Anita pulled the trigger and was shocked when the gun didn't go off. Sam began to laugh and told her that he removed the bullets. That incident brought Mad Sam extreme pleasure and he would tell the story over and over again to his mob buddies for amusement.

Another time in 1961, according to Crimaldi, Sam once again had had enough and said Anita was to die. Sam and Crimaldi tied her up and placed her in the trunk of Sam's car. The plan was to drive her out to the country and kill her. As they placed her in the trunk of the car, the garage door began to open; Sam's kids had returned home and were unaware of what was happening. In a panic, Sam and Crimaldi rushed Anita back into the house freeing her and telling her not to say a word to the kids. Minutes passed as the kids came in and Sam finally had time to cool down. He then decided that Anita could live and cancelled his plans for disposing of her body. That didn't stop him from continuously beating Anita many times, striping her naked, and kicking her.

FBI agent William F. Roemer wrote in his book The Enforcer that he would go to Sam DeStefano's house to question him about mob business, often arriving in the early afternoon. His wife Anita would always have to wake her husband up. On a few occasions, he wrote, DeStefano would walk down the stairs in his pajamas exposing himself. Often Anita would ask the agents if they would like some coffee while they interviewed her husband. They were served the coffee and often commented to Sam that the coffee had a unique taste to it. Sam said the coffee was special Italian coffee beans that his wife brewed. Months later Roemer found out that Sam had been pissing in the coffee before it was served to the agents. Roemer wrote he could never drink coffee again in his life.

One well-known incident involving one of Sam's collectors showed that not even being a close and personal friend of Mad Sam's was a good thing. In 1964 one of DeStefano's men named Peter "Cappy" Cappelletti kept $25,000 he collected from a loan shark victim which belonged to DeStefano and fled to Milwaukee, Wisconsin, to hide out to avoid a beating by Sam and his crew. Cappy also took DeStefano's "sheets" containing all the names of his "juice" victims and the amounts owed to him.

DeStefano, very unhappy, went to, then top Chicago mob boss, Tony Accardo and asked for permission to have Cappy killed and his body mutilated. Accardo gave his blessing and the contract was ordered. Sam received word from Chuckie Crimaldi that Cappy had contacted him and wanted to talk to Sam to straighten this mess out. With an evil smile on his face, Sam summoned his brother Mario, Chuckie Crimaldi and another DeStefano hoodlum named Sam Gallo and went to Wisconsin to meet with Cappy. Once they found Cappy, Sam pistol-whipped him and then forced him into his automobile and brought him back to Chicago for his punishment. On the ride home, Cappy tried to explain to Sam that he had planned a bank messenger robbery, which would net him $75,000. He would give Sam his $25,000 back plus another $25,000 to forget this ever happened. Sam didn't want to hear anything about his money being paid back, it didn't matter; just the joy of cutting Cappy's head off with a dull knife filled his thoughts with joy.

Cappelletti was taken to the basement of Mario DeStefano's restaurant in Cicero where he was stripped of his clothes, chained to a radiator, and beaten over and over again for 3 days. He was chained to the radiator with a metal chain so when the radiator would heat up, the chain would heat up and burn his skin. Sam finally decided that Cappy was not going to die, so he decided he would accept the $50,000 from Cappy's planned robbery and teach him a lesson. As Gallo, Crimaldi, and Mario beat Cappy with their fists and feet, Sam sat at a table sipping wine and smiled.

Sam then arranged a party and invited Cappelletti's mother, his wife, his relatives, policemen, and judges on Sam's payroll and a few other mobsters and their wives that were friendly with Sam. After the party had been in progress for a lengthy period, DeStefano announced that Peter had been located. While Sam gave his energetic speech about how he was not as bad of a man as everyone thought he was, he had Mario, Crimaldi and Gallo carry the chair out into the middle of the dining room with Cappelletti still bound to it naked. Cappy was covered in his own blood, which oozed from the cuts and burn marks on his body. His hair and face were soaked with urine since the three pissed on Cappy just before they carried him out. Sam presented Cappy as the *"double-crossing, pig fucker Peter Paul Cappelletti."* It was even reported that DeStefano ordered Cappy's relatives to either urinate on him in unison or spit on him. Sam announced that he was a good man and was giving Cappy's life back to his wife.

FBI agents made contact with Cappelletti after they were informed of the story. Cappelletti presented himself at FBI offices for an interview. He admitted he knew Sam DeStefano and his wife Anita and that he was associated with DeStefano in a bail bond business but steadfastly denied that he had ever had any reason to flee from Sam DeStefano or that DeStefano had found him in Milwaukee and brought him back to Chicago. He also denied that there was any truth to the story of the situation as it was supposed to have occurred at Mario's Restaurant.

Weeks later Sam DeStefano received $50,000 from Cappelletti, and he was allowed to resume working for DeStefano.

The Family

Mad Sam came from a typical Italian family from Italy, finding its way in the new land known as America. An FBI investigation into the world of Sam DeStefano reported that Sam's father, Samuel DeStefano Sr., and his mother Rosalie "Rose" DeStefano, nee Brasco, were both born in Italy and came to America in 1903, heading straight for Chicago for a short stay before moving to Streator, Illinois. Samuel Senior worked on the streets of Chicago as a laborer with thousands of his fellow Italians from the neighborhood. Later in life, he went on to be a store grocer and real estate salesman before dying of natural causes around 1942 at the age of 77. His mother Rose was a stay-at-home mother, supported by the contributions of her various children. She died in October 1960. Both parents were listed as law-abiding people who became U.S. citizens. They had a very large family with four sons and six daughters.

Mad Sam DeStefano's parents (Author's Collection)

Sam DeStefano's family according to a 1947 report:

Josephine DeStefano (Josie Pignato) was married with four children and as of 1947 was residing in Cleveland, Ohio. Her husband was listed as a railroad employee.

Angeline DeStefano (Casale) was married with two children and was living at 4188 Adams Street, Gary, Indiana. Her husband Louis operated a shoe repair shop.

James DeStefano was married to his wife Caroline "Carrie," had a son James V. and a daughter Rosemary. James was listed as living at 668 Evergreen Avenue, Chicago. He was employed as a City of Chicago foreman in the Streets Department.

Michael DeStefano was single and crippled because of a spine injury as a result of a bullet wound. On Parole.

Catherine DeStefano (Milano) was married to Leo Milano with two children living in Chicago. Her husband was a railroad employee.

Mario Anthony DeStefano was single and confined to Illinois State Penitentiary serving 30 years for murder.

Jean "Minnie" DeStefano (D'Errico) was married with no children living in Chicago. Her husband Frank is a foreman in a radio factory. "She would later go on to marry Angelo Rossi."

Mary DeStefano (Storino) was married with one child, living in Franklin Park. Her husband Sam was a supervisor in a soft drink plant.

Rose DeStefano (Sommario) was married with three children, residing in Chicago. Her husband Thomas had a job working for the Sanitary District in Chicago and Rose was reported as working with radios.

Samuel DeStefano Junior was born on September 13, 1909, in Streator, Illinois and lived there for 2 months, then the family moved to Heron, Illinois. The family called Heron home for 14 years, with Sam Sr. working as a miner. In 1922, the entire family packed up and moved to Chicago, taking up residence on the near west side in the Italian immigrant community, which was at the time a low economic area known as the "Patch." The family moved into a second floor apartment at 3109 West 39th Street. The area produced a high rate of delinquents, which led the young Sam to join local gangs. Despite the surroundings, Sam attended public, school completing the ninth grade, before getting in trouble with the law. DeStefano's prison record listed the schools he attended as Westside School, Heron, Illinois, 1915 to 1918; Southside School, Heron, Illinois, 1918 to 1922; Andrew Jackson, Chicago, 1923 to 1924; and McKinley High School, 1924 to 1925.

Sam, his brothers Mike and Mario, all looked up to their big brother James and quickly became acquainted with many of his friends. James was listed as being born around 1907 and was arrested on December 22, 1928, for larceny. He ran out of a store with a suit without paying for it and was placed on probation for one year. While on probation he was found guilty of larceny of an auto and after many continuances, the case was dismissed.

At the age of 15, the young Sam was committed to the Cook County School for Boys in Chicago. It was at this time that he would join the notorious "42 Gang" that would set the structure for the rest of his life.

Chapter Two

The 42 Gang

The 42 Gang got its start in Chicago's Little Italy neighborhood around 1920. The name, "42 Gang," was to mean that there would be no more or no less than 42 members in the gang at one time. Though at times the number of young hoodlums in the gang varied, and if it did ever reach 42 members, it didn't remain that way for very long. The gang was made up of some of the toughest, youngest hoodlums Chicago produce at the time, it acted as a "minor league" for the Capone gangsters and other top gangs of the time. It was sort of scouting grounds for the syndicate. The best and most skilled members would wind up as the new blood in the top gangs, while the ones left behind would make up the small-time robbers and thieves that the gangs fed off. Once in the 42 Gang, you wore a white fedora hat to let others know you were a "42" Gang member and you should not be messed with-or else.

At the end of the 1920's, Chicago was under the control of one man, Al Capone, who used the alias of "Al Brown" and was given nicknames like "Scarface" and "Snorky" by the press and outsiders. The "42's" territory was the west side of Chicago operating on such streets as Taylor Street, Polk Street, Harrison Street, Aberdeen, Racine Avenue, Blue Island Avenue, Roosevelt Road, and many others around that area.

The gang situation in the city of Chicago at the time consisted of many gangs divided by territory. The breakdown of each gang and its territory is as follows, consisting of gang members and associates believed to be connected with each gang:

Known members of the 42 Gang

William Alioiso

Felix "Milwaukee Phil" Alderisio

Paul Ascoli

Mario Balsommo

Frank "Duke" Battaglia

Sam "Teetz" Battaglia

Eugene Beimont

Frank Berardi

John Bolton

Louis "The Barber" Briatta

Mike Briatta

Fiore "Fifi" Buccieri

Marshall Caifano

Fat Campanelli

Samuel Capise

Archie Capozzi

Alfred Carfagno

Joseph Carfo

Frank "Skids" Caruso

Joseph Catrina

Kasty Catrina

Ralph "Red" Ciangi

Joey "Babe Ruth" Colaro

Carlo Coliano

Philip Colonero

Sam Cozi

William "Potatoes" Daddono

Pasty DeAngelo

Johnny Draco "D'Arco"

Tony DeBartola

Louis "Cadoodles" DeChristoforo

Frank "Chudaback" DeLuca

Guido De Salvo

Sam "Mad Sam" DeStefano

Mario "Merle" DeStefano

Michael "Clumsy Mike" DeStefano

James "Babe Ruth" DiCola (Killed 1927)

Tony DiGiovanni

Frank D'Nordi

Joseph "Caesar" DiVarco

Sam Domico

Willie Doody

Charles "Chuckie" English

Sam "Butch" English

Anthony "Tony X" Esposito

Dan Fanello

Frank Fillichio

Pete "Mibs" Fillichio

John Fiore

Vito Fosco

Albert "Obbie" Frabotta

Michael Gadoto

Rocco Gallasi

Sam "Mooney" Giancana

Leonard Gianola

Michael Gilfone

Solly Goldsmith

John Guida (Killed 1930)

Alphones Gurriano

Sharkey Icola

Vincent "Saint" Inserro

James Kohinis

Mike La Goia

Joe Leopold

Sam Lewis

<u>Known members of the 42 Gang (cont.)</u>

Carmen Liuputa
Chickie Lombardo
Peter Longo
Daniel Luderrozzi
William Madden
Nick Maintanis
Bennie Maioni
Rocco Marcantonio (Founding Member)
Dominic Marzano
Vito Mascini
Mike Messino
Thomas Messino
Anthony "Pineapples" Mldorado
William Molone (Killed 1927)
Dominick Monaco
Joe Morando
Nicholas "Little Man" Muscato
Peter "The Ape" Nicastro (Killed 1930)
Charles "Chuckie" Nicoletti
James Nuzzo
Red O'Brien
Johnson Orlando
Ralph Orlando
Tony Panico
Pasty Pargoni
Joe Pape
Tony Papa
Joseph Parello
Hank Pargoni
Jit Pargoni
Joseph Pargoni (Killed 1928)
Vito Pellitiere

Joseph Perelto
Two Gun Pete
Frank PeTito (Killed 1930)
Hank Petitto
Alex Pope
Rocco Potenza
Monk Pupillo
Emil Quaglia
Diego Ricco
Fat Riccio
Joe Roberti
Ned Rooney
Paul Rossi
Angie Russo
Frank Russo
Tumpa Russo
Salvi
James Sassone
Isadore Scaramuzza
George Schiulo
Charles Seno
Pastsy Steffanelli
Sam Surdo
Pastsy Tardi (Killed 1931)
Tony Torrisello
Carlo Torrisello
Mike Tortorello
John Tossiello
Frank Tufano
Tony Vittulo

The Capone-Torrio Gang

Thomas Abbott

Tony "Joe Batters" Accardo

James Adduci (William Pion)

Joe Adduci (Colosimo-Torrio)

Sam Adler

Sylvester Agoglia

Gus Alex

Sam Alex

Mike Allegreffa

August "Genero" Annereno

Johnny "Peppi Ganero" Annereno

Albert Anselmi

Ted "The Greek" Anton

Julius Anixter

Tony Arasso

John Armoado

Nicky Arnstein

Dominick Ballo

Ned Bakes

Louis Barlo (Barko)

Bobby Barton

Sylvester Barton

Barney Bartsche

Joe Bartsche

Morris Becker

Frank Beige

John Began

James "King of Bombers" Belcastro

Rocco Belcastro

Tony Belcastro

Maurice Van Bener (Torrio)

Cesare Benvenuti

Julius Benvenuti

Leo Benvenuti

Frank Berman

Frank Biego (Perry)

Willie Bioff (Henry Martin)

Charles Blakely

Ike Bloom

Dom "Nags" Brancato

Harry "Frisco Dutch" Brown

Ralph Brown

Ralph Buglio

Fred "Killer" Burke

Mike Butero

Gerald "Cheese box" Callahan

Louis "Little New York" Campagna

Tony Campagna

Salvatore Canale

Anthony "Caps" Capezio

Al "Scarface" Capone

Frank Capone

John "Miami" Capone

Matt Capone

Ralph "Bottles" Capone

Mat Cappalario

Charlie "Coin" Carr

 (Carl Torraco)

Mike "Dago Mike" Carrozzo

Michael Castello

Santo Cellebron

Frank Chiaravalotti (Colosimo)

Tony Cifaldo

Nick Circella

Louis Clementi

Sam Cohen

Ernest "Butch" Cook

Dennis "The Duck" Cooney

The Capone-Torrio Gang (cont.)

Charles Castello
Michael Costello
Vincenzo Cosmano
Joseph Cota
John "Bathhouse" Coughlin
Freddy "The Cowboy"
Louis Cowen
Andy Craig
Frank Crimaldi
Tony Curingione (Tom Ross)
James Cusick
Frank Darrice
James DeAmato
Nick DeGrazio
Robert DeGrazio
Rocco DeGrazio
Tony DeGrazio
Bert Delaney
Rocco DeStefano
Frank Diamond (Maritote)
William Diggs
Fred Di Giovanni
Anthony C. D'Andrea
Phil D'Andrea
James Doherty (Torrio Gang)
Max Eisen
Morris Eller
William "Dutch" Emerling
Frank "X" Esposito
Gaetano Esposito
Joe "Diamond Joe" Esposito
Rocco Fanelli
Fred Farley
Joseph Ferrari

Joseph Ferraro
Joe Fiore
Charles Fischetti
Rocco Fischetti
"Bozo" Fogarty
Carl Fontana
Ernest Fontana
James Forsyth (Fawcett)
Earl "Big" Fraher
Joseph Fusco
John Genaro
Joseph "Peppy" Genero
Ralph Gillette
Charles "Cherry Nose" Gioe
Joe "Little Murphy" Glimco
Simon Gorman
Joe Grabiner "Jew Kid"
Joe Granata
Peter Granata
Alec Louis Greenberg
Barney Grogan
Martin Guilfoyle
Joe Guinta (Juno)
Harry Guzik
Jake "Greasy Thumbs" Guzik
Sam Guzik
Sam Hare (Torrio Gang)
Sam Harris
David Hedlin
Jack Heinan
Joe "Dutch" Heitler
Mike "De Pike" Heitler
Murry "The Camel" Humphreys
Sam "Golf Bag" Hunt

The Capone-Torrio Gang (cont.)

Charles Jackson

Dan Jackson

Nick Juffre

Marty Kane

Sam Kart

Julian "Potatoes" Kaufman

Frankie Kelly

Mike Kelly

Michael "Hinky Dink" Kenna

Tom Kerwin

Henry Kimmel

Phillip Kimmel

Alex Korocek

Louis LaCava

Al Lambart

Isadore Lazarus

Hymie "Loud Mouth" Levine

Harold Levy

Bill Lewis

Frank "Dago" Lewis

Joe Lewis

Joe Lolordo

Pasqualino Lolordo

Antonio "Scourge" Lombardo

Marcus "Studdy" Looney

Jack Lynch

Claude "Screwy" Maddox (John Moore)

Lawrence "Dago" Mangano

Sam Marcus

Frank Marino

Bill Marshell

Lester Martin

Louis Massessa

Robert McCullough

Jack "Machine Gun" McGurn

John McLead

Dave Miller

Harry Miller

Hirschie Miller

Joey Miller (Torrio Gang)

Max Miller

Jimmy Mondi

Joe Morici (Ferraro)

Jim Murphy (Torrio Gang)

Tim "Big Tim" Murphy

Tom "James" Nash

Ted Newberry

Frank "The Enforcer" Nitti

Dominic Nuccio

James Nuccio

Mike Nuccio

Nick Odine

Edward O'Hare

James O'Leary

Martin O'Leary

Steve Oswald

Joseph Palumbo (Parillo)

Frank Panio

Johnny "Boy Mayor" Patton

James Pelcere

Pete Penovish

Frank Perry

Nick Perry

Joe Pise

Mike "Cowboy" Pontelli, aka Fred DiGiovanni

Frank "West Side Frankie" Pope

Albert Prignano

The Capone-Torrio Gang (cont.)

Arthur Quinn
Frank Quirk
Martin "Sonny Boy" Quirk
Paul "The Waiter" Ricca
Fred Ries
Pete Rinelli
Frank "Kline" Rio
Rocco Rocuna
Ike Roderick
Frank Romano
Louis Romano
Robert Rose
Ernest Rossi
Bruno Roti
Frank Roti
Al Ruggio
James Russo
John Russo
Robert Ryan
Martin Sanders
Ralph Scala
John Scalise
William Schaaf
Abe Schaffner
Dan Serritella
Jack Sherman
William Skidmore
Jack Sopkin
Nick Sorella
Tony "The Chevalier" Spano (Joe Nerone)
Mike Spranze
Claude Stallings
Pollock Stanley

Danny Stanton
Walter Stevens
Frank Sullivan
Tom Sullivan (Tom Cullen)
Paul Swain
William "Billy Goat" Taglia
Tony Tagonti
Clement Tatton
Mont Tennes
Johnny "The Fox" Torrio
Nick Valeta
Danny Vallo
James Vinci
Ted Virgillo
Sol Vision
Ed Vogel
George "Legge" Vogel (Dutch)
Tony "Mops" Volpe
Matt Wallace
William White
Maxie Williams
Gus Winkler
Jack Zuta

Spike O'Donnell Gang, (South Side) Allied with Capone

Edward "Spike" O'Donnell
George "Spot" Bucher
Charles O'Donnell
Steve O'Donnell
Tom O'Donnell
Walter O'Donnell
Jerry O'Connor
George Meeghan

William "Shorty" Egan
Leo Gistenson
Henry Hasmiller
Thomas "Morris" Keane
John Rappaport
Pasquale Tolizotte
Percy O'Donnell
Johnny O'Donnell
Joe Larson

O'Donnell Gang (West side) allied with Capone

William "Klondike" O'Donnell
Myles O'Donnell
Bernard O'Donnell
George "Red" Barker
William "Three Fingered" White
James "Red" Doherty
Thomas "Red" Duffy
William "Rags" McCue
Harry Madigan
Mickey Wendel
Mickey Quirk
John "West Side Jack" Barry

James "Fur" Sammons
James Duffy
Eddie Tanel
Phillip Corrigan
Joseph "Humdinger" Corrigan
Frank Cawley
George Clifford
Tom McElligot
Michael Reilly
Frank Krueger

Saltis Gang (Southwest Side)

Joe (Polack Joe) Saltis
Danny Stanton (1929)
Willie Neimoth
Steve Saitis
Jack Geis
Earl "Big Earl" Herbert
John "Dingbat" O'Berta (O'Berta Gang)
Frank "Lefty" Koncil
Frank McErlane
George Kostenek (Darrow)

Charles "Big Hayes" Hubacek
George "Big" Karl
William Dickman
Sam Malaga
Frank Conlon
Peter "Three Finger" Kunshi
Paddy Sullivan (Patrick) (O'Berta Gang)
James Joyce

Genna Gang Became Allied with Capone

Samuzzo Amatuna
Angelo Genna
Tony Genna
James Genna
Mike Genna
Sam Genna
Pete Genna
Tony D'Andrea
Joseph LaCava
Lorenzo Algano
Diego Attlomionte
Ecola Baldelli
Vito Bascone
Giovanni Blaudins
Joseph "Little Joe" Calabrese
Dom Cinderella
Anthony Finalli
Alphonse Fiori

Phillip Gnolfo "Abbate"
Numio Jamericco
Agostino Moreci
Antionio Moreci
Andrew Orlando
John "Billiken" Rito
Henry Spingola
Orazio "The Scourge" Tropea
Joseph Lombardi
John Mangogna
Joe Mangogna
Peter Spingola
Joseph Spingola
Tony Ponetti
Conchas Lallone
Paul Battaglia
August Battaglia
Frank Battaglia

Saitis-McErlane Gang

Joseph "Polack Joe" Saitis
Frank McErlane
Joseph "Dynamite Joe" Brooks
John "Bingo" Alberto
Alfred Deckman
Ed "Big Hart" Herbert
George "Big Bates" Karl
Frank "Lefty" Koncil

Steven "Big Steve" Schultz
William Channel
Vincent McErlane
Dan McFall
Willie Niemoth
Peter Gusenberg
Walter Stevens
Red Golden

Circus Gang (West Side) Allied with Capone

Claude "Screwey" Maddox
Murray Humphreys
Anthony "Caps" Capezio
Ralph Pierce

Lawrence Cozzi
Edward "Casey" Konowski
Joseph Stopee
Edwrad Piranio a.k.a. Frank "Fatso" Estes

Amatuna Gang

Sam "Samoots" Amatune   John Scalice

Albert Anseline

Taddeo Gang (Melrose Park) allied with Capone

Aniello Taddeo	David Taddeo (Dave Brooks) (Dave Tadders)
Lazzaro Clemente	John Tuccello
Frank DeLaurentis	Leo Weiss
Carl Torraco (Charley Carr)	Paul Torraco
Jimmy Torraco	James DeGrazio
Sam Ariola	Alfonso Bracco
Joe Diamond	James Campanille
Harold Clifford	"Fat" Bishop
Joe Jacks	Carl Stepina
George Raymond	Joe Gugliuzzo
Tony Louis	Paseal Larry
Joe Aiuppa	Jimmy Scudally
Sam Aiuppa	Ralph "The Glass Man" Torraco
Angelo Torraco	Frank "Bones" Torraco
Angelo Coglionese	Fred DeAngelis
Nick DeGrazia	John Marzulla
Jerry Carusiello	Andrew DeGazio
Patsy Castardo	Sam Farino
Angelo Doglianest	Edward Schiller
Louis Giordgno	Pascal Walter
Henry Brandt	John "Short-Tall" Wyallos
Mickey Derico	Peter "Bananas" Santore
Thomas King	John Sakolowski
Peter Bronge	Anthony Vercillo
Carmen Salvatore	Frank Bernardi

Valley Gang (Westside)

Terry Druggan
Louie Alterie
John "Paddy the Cub" Ryan
Walter Quinlan
"Big Steve" Weisnewski
Frank Prazzo
Walter Gorney
Ben Applequist
James Farley
Heinrich Miller
"Fat" Watkins

Frankie Lake
Frank "Red" Krueger
"Bummy" Goldstein
Harry "The Schoolmaster" Schnider
Joe Symonds (Kline)
Harry Sers
Dan "Little Danny" Vallo
E. Applequist
William "Tootsie" Hughes
Johnny Barry

Gloriana Gang

Libby Nuccio

Ragen Colts Gang (South Side)

Ralph Sheldon
William "Gunner" McPadden
Michael "Bubs" Quinlan
Charles Kelly
Frank Ragen
Mike Ragen

Hugh "Stubby" McGovern
George Maloney
Danny Stanton
Danny McFall
James Ragen Sr.

Red Bolton Gang (Westside)

"Red" Bolton
Frank Wilson
Jimmy Farley

"Dinky" Quan
Heinie Miller

Moran-O'Banion Gang (Northside)

George "Bugs" Moran	Willie Marks
Frank Citro	William Skidmore
Frankie Foster	Leo Mongoven
Joe Aiello (Aiello Gang)	Tony Aiello (Aiello Gang)
Harry Beyer	Jack Zuta
Frank Gusenberg	Peter Gusenberg
Rinehart Schwimmer	John May
James Clark	Albert Weinshenk
Adam Heyer	Anthony "Red" Kissane
Ted Newberry	Dean O'Banion
Earl "Hymie" Weiss	Eugene "Red" McLaughlin
John "Boss" McLaughlin	Vincent "Schemer" Drucci
Louis Alterie	Maxie Eisen
Henry Finkelstein	Julian "Potatoes" Kaufman
Barney Bertsche	Bejamin Bennett
William Leathers	Angelo Lo Mantio (Aiello Gang)
Dan McCarthy	Hirschie Miller (Miller Gang)
Sam Monistero (Aiello Gang)	Patrick "Paddy" Murray
Sam Pellar	Peter Plescia (Aiello Gang)
Sam Rubin	Tony K. Russo (Aiello Gang)
Vincent Spicuzza (Aiello Gang)	Eddy Vogel
Max Wagman	

Ghetto Gang (West Side)

Sammy Kaplan	Johnny Armondo
James Belcastro	Abe "Humpy" Klass
Jules Portuguese	Benjamin "Buddy" Jacobson
Harry Portuguese	Teddy Stein
Louis "Big" Smith	Sam "Sammy the Greener" Jacobson
Sam "Samoots"	Sam Peller
Rocco Fanelli	Alex Portuguese

Vinci Gang (South Side)

Sam Vinci

Mike Vinci

John Minatti

Johnnie Genaro

Jimmy Vinci

Joe Annoreno

Peppy Genero

Joe "Machine Gun Joe" Granata

Ralph Sheldon Gang

Danny Sheldon

Hugh "Stubby" McGovern

Carl Mueller

Fred Ward

John Barry

Benjamin Butler

Frank DeLaurentis

"Stick Bomb" Donovan

Tom Foley

Charles Kelly

John Tuccello

Michael "Bubs" Quinlen

Mike McGovern

Arthur Schmidt

James De Mont

Karl Bates

Hillary Clements

William Dickman

John "Mitters" Foley

Tom Hart

Edward Lattyak

William Wilson

Cardinelli Gang

Frank Campione

Nick "The Choir Boy" Viana

Sam Cardinelli

Northwest Side Gang

Marty Guilfoyle

Al Winge

Leonard Boltz

Christ Madsen

Matt Kolb

Jimmy Barry

Sam Thompson

Louis Stryker

Touhy Gang

Edward "Father Tom" McFadden	Gustave "Gloomy Gus" Schafer
Willie Sharkey	Rodger Touhy
Joseph Touhy	James Touhy
Tommy Touhy	Edward Touhy
John Touhy	James Ryan
Matthew Kolb	LeRoy Marschalk
Jimmy La Marr	

The Guifoyle Gang (Guifoyle-Winge-Kolb syndicate)

Martin Guilfoyle	Matt Kolb
Al Winge	Joe Fisher

Maibaum Gang

Julius Maibaum	Charles Maibaum
Ed Weiss	Jackie Adler
Harry Hopkins	Jackie Wolfsohn

Summerfields Gang

Lewis Summerfield
Max Summerfield

Chapter Three

And It Begins. . .

The early years in Chicago for Sam DeStefano were filled with opportunity where very little could be found. The friendships and connections he would make in those poor and hopeless times would make DeStefano's future one of a humble millionaire.

One of the earliest reports found on Samuel DeStefano is from September 12, 1926, when he was arrested in Chicago and turned over to the Niles Police Department as a fugitive for breaking out of his jail cell.

On July 1, 1927, several hundred Westside gang members showed up threatening violence against a police sergeant for arresting Samuel DeStefano and shooting DeStefano's associate Harry Casgrovi. Then police sergeant John Leyendecker stated he suspected both DeStefano and Casgrovi had taken part in a gun battle earlier that night in which another policeman was injured by flying glass from his police car window, which was hit by a bullet. Both men were arrested at Canal and Bunker Streets. The sergeant searched DeStefano and found a revolver hidden in his pants. Knowing he, too, was in trouble, Casgrovi started to run from the policeman making his way down the street. The sergeant took Sam's gun, poked it into DeStefano's ribs, and forced him to run down the street while he gave chase to Casgrovi. As the three chased one another down Canal Street, sergeant Leyendecker began to fire the revolver at Casgrovi. By the time Casgrovi reached Roosevelt Road he had fallen, apparently shot, but before Leyendecker could take DeStefano to the spot, a crowd of locals had gathered and Casgrovi was rushed away to avoid being arrested by the police. Sergeant Leyendecker called for backup but it took more than an hour for any help to arrive. During that time, he had to fight off an angry mob with his revolver and blackjack club.

A month later on August 12, 1927, DeStefano was charged with carrying a concealed weapon. In DeStefano fashion, he never reported to his probation officer and did not inform the court as to his new address after moving.

In November 1927, once again Sam DeStefano was in court along with fellow gang member Ralph Orlando on charges of assaulting a 17-year-old girl. The allegation claimed that on August 19, 1927, the girl was taken from her escort while returning from the theater and was forced into an automobile by two men. The girl was driven to a garage where she was sexually assaulted by seven men.

Ralph Orlando, one of the original 42 Gang members was under indictment at the time for the March 12, 1927, robbery of the American Can Company plant and was out on $50,000 bail. Orlando, no stranger to crime, was arrested in September 1921 for attempting to rob a tailor shop with Frank Yario and Charles Gatuso. Once arrested, all three admitted to robbing the Stanlegh Hotel shop of $1,200 worth of cigars and liquor. Orlando had four other robbery charges listed between the years of 1922 and 1926.

After an all-night deliberation by the jury, Orlando and DeStefano were both found guilty of rape. Orlando was given 10 years in prison while DeStefano was given only 3 years. The reason for a lighter sentence was that the police arrived at the scene before Sam DeStefano could have his turn at raping the young girl. When the police arrived, only DeStefano and Orlando were caught while the others made a successful get away. Orlando was guilty of rape and DeStefano was guilty of being an accessory before the fact and punishable as a principal. It was also learned during the trial that Sam DeStefano was using the alias of Jack Napolean. As the judge read the guilty verdict, Ralph Orlando's sister, Margaret Constantino, became so hysterical that she had to be removed from the courtroom.

On December 24, the two were back in court one more time to see if they would be granted a new trial, at which time they were denied. The judge asked the two convicted men if they had anything to say. DeStefano remained mute while Ralph Orlando took full advantage of his opportunity telling the judge, *"Yes, I've got plenty to say. When I get out of the penitentiary, I'm going to commit murder by wholesale. The first men I'll get are Assistant State's Attorney Charles Dougherty and Policeman Daniel Madigan, the man that pinched me."*

Sam DeStefano entered Statesville Prison, otherwise known as Joliet State Prison in Joliet, Illinois, on July 12, 1928. There he would sit until his release three years later on January 10, 1931. DeStefano's and Orlando's Joliet Prison record gave the following information:

Ralph Orlando

Age 23
Weight 152
Catholic
Left home at age 14
Education 8th grade
Occupation: Chauffeur
Correspondents: Sister Margaret Constantino, 1222 Oregon Street, Chicago, IL

Previous Criminal Record

09-05-1924 Burglary

Discharged: October 11, 1934

Prison Punishment Record

12-08-1930	Playing cards and refusing to give them to the officer
04-11-1931	Throwing bread out of his cell and having cheese in his cell
07-16-1931	Refusing to enter his cell
02-15-1932	Laying down on the job
04-16-1932	Insolence to an officer
06-02-1932	Refusing to be transferred
06-30-1932	Insolence to an officer
11-21-1932	Back talk
12-21-1932	Refusing to obey orders
10-03-1933	Getting hair cut out of turn
10-19-1934	Refusing to obey officer's orders
02-01-1934	Insolence to officer

Sam DeStefano
Know as Jack Napolean
Age 19
Weight 120
Catholic
Left home at age 15
Occupation: Grocery clerk and chauffeur
Correspondents: Mother Rose DeStefano, 1506 Edgemont Ave., Chicago

Prison Punishment Record
11-05-1928   Being away from his place of work
10-22-1930   Throwing other inmates clothes out of cell

Once Sam was a free man it didn't take him long to get in trouble again. Three months later, on April 22, 1931, Sam DeStefano was arrested by the Chicago Police on a charge of general principles. After a few hours of questioning, he was released.

On June 24, 1931, he was arrested in the company of a 15-year-old girl named Clara Paprocki after registering in a hotel as man and wife. He was held to the Grand Jury on a charge of rape. On October 21, 1931, the case was Nolle Prossed on motion of the State's Attorney.

Nine days later on October 10, 1931, the Halsted Street National Bank located at 1929 South Halsted Street was robbed of $16,319 in a hold-up. Five armed gangsters pulled off the daytime robbery just blocks from the old Chicago Police "Scotland Yard" headquarters. Miss Geraldine Milsauskas was working in the bank at the time as a telephone operator when she said the leader of the gang pointed a gun into her face and said, "Get away from the switchboard and be quiet." The other robbers forced the rest of the customers and employees to lie down on the floor in a rear room while they robbed the place. The next day James Roti, Louis De Lucco, and John Rinella were standing on 31st Street and Wentworth Avenue when police surrounded them. All three were arrested and questioned in the robbery. The next day Sam DeStefano was picked up by police officers when he was walking down Taylor Street and brought into police headquarters for questioning. Once there, three of the bank employees identified Sam DeStefano as one of the armed robbers. DeStefano admitted participating in the robbery but refused to name the other men. He was held to the Grand Jury who returned a No Bill.

On May 7, 1932, Sam DeStefano, Dominick Monaco, and Frank Fiore were arrested and charged with disorderly conduct for allegedly threatening employees with a beating at a mortgage company on LaSalle Street in the Chicago Loop area unless a replevin for DeStefano's automobile was recalled. The arraignment was held at the municipal courtroom located at the police station at 11th and State Street in the city. DeStefano and Monaco were placed in a holding cell on the 11th floor of the building but everyone working there believed the two were placed in the cell adjoining the courtroom on the 9th floor. When the bailiff went to get the two on the ninth floor so they could be transported to the police jail, they were gone. This sparked an alarming search of the lower floors. Reports went out over the radio and teletype machines that

Mad Sam in 1932

DeStefano and Monaco had escaped from jail and were fugitives. While the search went on, DeStefano and Monaco sat in their 11th floor cell unaware of what was happening.

Three hours later, the bailiff came walking into the 11th floor lock-up pushing DeStefano and Monaco through the door. The bailiff claimed he found the two on the Westside of Chicago, to cover up his mistake, and hoped the charge of escaping would be added to their sentence. Both DeStefano and Monaco where flabbergasted at what was occurring, both denying that they escaped, and told the judge that they had been in a jail cell on another floor the entire time. Both were released.

On July 31, 1932, Sam DeStefano was arrested for robbing a cab driver with a gun. He was held to the Grand Jury and a No Bill was returned a month later. On August 22, 1932, Sam DeStefano was found shot and injured in a Chicago hospital and was arrested and charged for the burglary of a store. On December 6, 1932, the burglary charge was dismissed.

On May 17, 1933, DeStefano was arrested for violating a motor vehicle law and disorderly conduct. He was fined $5 for the disorderly conduct and $20 for the violation of a motor vehicle law.

The bad luck of fortune paid a visit to Sam DeStefano once again on July 11, 1933, when he was arrested in Mauston, Wisconsin, under the name of David Triner for robbing a bank. DeStefano participated in the robbery of $4,935.77 from the New Lisbon State Bank in Wisconsin. Shortly before noon on July 10, the New Lisbon State Bank was robbed by a bevy of three or four men, all carrying loaded revolvers. After they successfully completed their task, the bandits shot their revolvers in the air as they fled in an automobile to intimidate anyone from following them. As fortune had it, the get-away-car broke down a mile or so from the bank. With the sirens of the police in the distance and on the way, the bank robbers fled on foot. A chase ensued and DeStefano was caught halfway up a tree.

DeStefano was accused of being the driver of the car and acting as lookout man while the others were committing the holdup. Convicted with DeStefano were Lyall Wright, a former "boy sheriff" in Juneau County, Tony Pocevicz Sr., his sons Casimir Pocevicz, and Anthony Pocevicz Jr., Joe Burbatt, and William Roche. The senior Pocevicz owned the farm where the plot to rob the bank was hatched.

On September 29, 1933, Sam DeStefano was sentenced to 15 to 40 years in prison, a sentence he would serve in Waupun State Prison until December 30, 1942. That month Governor Julius Heil commuted DeStefano's original sentence to one of 10 to 20 years; he would be released and discharged from prison on December 26, 1944.

Several interviews were conducted by a psychiatric physician while DeStefano was in prison. The report says, "The examiner in April 1935 quoted DeStefano as saying, '*I was a stranger from Chicago, I carry a record and that's why I'm here.*' He denied complicity in the robbery. It was found that he had an intelligence quotient of 78, which reflects border-line defective general intelligence – this is a serious degree of retardation. The psychiatrist indicated that "delinquency is due to morbid impulsiveness, recidivistic type."

In January 1937, after renewing the original psychiatric diagnosis, the examiner called attention to DeStefano as "silly and maneristic in personality composition, absolutely indifferent to the asocial tendencies which he had portrayed, is a disciplinary problem in his prison environment, and even at the present time is subjected to escort and restraint of liberties as a result of his indisposition to accept institutional discipline. He minimizes the nature of his various asocial conflicts and attempts to picture himself as a victim of circumstances and malice on the part of others. His return to society will be followed by a repetition of his former mode of life, since no possibility of rehabilitation at the present time appears possible."

The examination conducted in June 1939 brought the following comments: "Intelligence of rather ordinary nature, no mental disease, flighty, tense, unstable and excessive in speech, gross impairment of judgment and reasoning faculties. Rejects all taint of guilt, save mistaken identity and conspiracy on the part of others."

The examination in 1941 reported DeStefano as "extrovert, superficial, impulsive, blustering, faulty in concentration, defective in logic and reasoning capability. He has retained affection for his wife. He had denied guilt on the 1927 rape charge. Because DeStefano is a second offender, no parole is possible for twenty years. A twenty-year commitment will minimize any rehabilitative possibilities."

The final report dated July 1943 reported DeStefano as "egotistical" and stated that parole for DeStefano was of doubtful value, since the man's cooperation would not be pleased to follow through on the matter.

Sam DeStefano's Waupun prison record contained the following information concerning his incarceration. During his time at the prison, DeStefano was disciplined thirty-six times for such offenses as arguing with authorities, throwing food, fighting with officers, fighting with inmates, lagging behind in line, failure to meet prison rules, leaving food on his plate, maintaining a sign system with other inmates and screaming and yelling in his cell. He was frequently punished by being placed in

29

solitary confinement three times, had restrictions of liberties enforced and was placed in detention three times, given only bread and water. He was described as being wild, profane, and threatening. He was considered a leader of prison inmates who followed him only out of fear.

In October 1942, the supervisor of a prison camp complained about DeStefano and requested he be returned to the prison. The reason was that DeStefano always demanded favors from the staff and could not remember that he was an inmate.

Other incidences concerning DeStefano during his prison stay were in October 1943 when he escaped from Madison General Hospital while a patient there but was caught a short time later. He was singled out as the leader in the serious riot, which occurred in 1943 at the prison. After failure to make parole in April 1944, he brought a habeas corpus action against the prison claiming he was being held illegally. It appeared that the Board of Parole had granted parole but the Governor had declined to sign the parole for DeStefano. At this time, DeStefano was denied the right to prosecute a writ of habeas corpus.

"I would consider Sam DeStefano as one of our sickest, agitators, and smooth trouble makers ever." John C. Burke, Warden Wisconsin State Prison June 20, 1947.

DeStefano's Wisconsin Punishment Record	
1933	Talking to inmate Garcia
1933	Fooling around
03-20-1934	Talking in shop
05-02-1934	Talking in dining room
01-07-1935	Passing food to inmate
03-08-1935	Talking in dining room
12-24-1935	Talking in line
02-25-1936	Talking during exercise
03-04-1936	Leaving food on his plate
03-24-1936	Violating dining room rules
05-09-1936	Fighting in the yard
05-27-1936	Making signs in yard
05-27-1936	Refusing to leave cell
08-26-1936	Talking in line
11-07-1936	Yelling in cell
01-06-1937	Striking at an inmate
01-06-1937	Striking at officers
04-08-1937	Threatening waiter
02-24-1937	Disobeying officers
06-28-1937	Talking at exercise
12-13-1937	Talking in school
01-08-1938	Not at doors for inmate count
01-17-1938	Hollering in line
06-13-1938	Smoking a cigarette in the hospital
06-22-1938	Talking from cell to cell with Banks
07-10-1938	Throwing bread out for birds
08-22-1938	Talking in line
08-24-1938	Arguing with officers
03-14-1939	Talking while in line, talking in recreation yard
10-24-1939	Disobeying officers orders
10-17-1942	Using foul language to officer
07-12-1944	Talking to another inmate in another cell

Sam was released from prison and made his gallant return to Chicago. From November 1945 until March 1947, Sam DeStefano had a partnership in the Midwest Printing Company located at 841 West Roosevelt Road in Chicago. The majority of the printing at this location was for various lottery tickets, namely, The All-American Football Cards, the Double-Action Baseball Lottery Tickets, and certain sweepstakes books for special races like the Kentucky Derby and the Stars & Stripes. When the sports went out of season, the company would do small printing jobs for commercial business.

Mad Sam disclaimed any knowledge as to who gave the orders for the printing of the lottery tickets and advised that one of the partners named Mr. Greenholt made all of the arrangements for the printing. At first DeStefano had a one-third interest in the shop and he raised $2,500 for the firm when it was in bad financial condition. He then bought out Greenholt's interest for $1,500 and DeStefano discovered that Greenholt had been writing "bum" checks through the business. Also discovered was that Greenholt had mortgaged some of the equipment without the consent of the other partners. The other one-third interest of the company was owned by a Mr. Pascucci. DeStefano sold out his two-thirds interest to one Pat Fahey in March 1947 for $3,300 cash and $1,500 in payments. DeStefano stated that he cleared, as his share, about $7,000 in the months from November 1945 to 1947. DeStefano told the authorities that the printing of lottery tickets was considered legal by him and he had been so advised by his attorneys. However, the State's Attorney's Office advised that the printing of any lottery tickets was considered a misdemeanor and the penalty was a $100 fine.

When asked what jobs had Sam held he replied, "An operator of a hat cleaning and shoeshine shop, I participated in a trucking business, I was a newspaper truck driver for the Daily Times, I went to Cleveland, Ohio, to operate a fruit and vegetable business for several months; I gave it up after a hand injury, then went to Columbus, Ohio, where I worked for several months in a Commission House operated by an uncle. I was a business agent for a Teamsters union there and was "on the bum" and "on the prowl" for a considerable period of time."

Sam's official list of jobs as of 1947 are as follows:

1925 to 1927 Proprietor of truck, peddling fruit & vegetables
1927 to 1930 Illinois State Prison, water boy
1930 to 1933 Hat cleaning & shoe shining parlor at Taylor Street and Oakley Blvd.
1933 to 1944 Wisconsin State Prison, inmate cook
1945 to 1945 Newspaper truck driver for Chicago Times, Wacker Dr. & Wells St.
1945 to 1945 Proprietor of fruit & vegetable store, Cleveland, Ohio.
1945 to 1947 Business agent for Local 440 of the Commission Horse Drivers Union.
1945 to 1947 Proprietor of Midwest Printing
1947 to 1947 Member of Newspaper Deliverers Union

Mad Sam loved to strike up a conversation and give his opinions as how to "fix" the world. When detectives would, show up to question Sam for a variety of crimes, Sam never had a problem talking to them. On one occasion, the authorities became interested in Sam's wife and how they met. Sam indulged in the conversation and told them that he married an Italian girl named Anna Anita Pisciotta in Crown Point, Indiana, on June 10, 1933, by the justice of the peace. However, when law enforcement officials went to investigate this claim they were unable to find any record of this marriage. The U.S. Probation office reported that DeStefano was married in a church ceremony at the Holy Family Catholic Church on February 15, 1945, to a woman of Italian descent, who was listed then as 32 years of age, who worked for fifteen years at a dress company as a trimmer.

However, his Leavenworth prison record lists a Mrs. Christine Caltro as his mother-in-law living at 913 S. Miller Street in Chicago who was married to a carpenter contractor. It was not known if this was her first or second marriage. Anna or "Anita," as she was called, was described as a rather meek type of person who had unquestioning faith in her husband.

In 1946, Sam and his family occupied a four room flat on the third floor rear of an old three-story tenement building located at 1062 Polk Street in Chicago's "Little Italy." The declining neighborhood stood as a shadow of its hey-days back in the 1920's. The building was a stove-heated flat in a poor state of repair. Sam paid $12 per month for rent when they moved into the building in December 1945. DeStefano said that due to an acute shortage of unfurnished flats it was the best housing he and his wife could find when he was released from prison. He also added that they had resided in this particular neighborhood for most of their life and it was not uncommon to find that persons of some means continued to reside there in the neighborhood. A number of professional people and businessmen of Italian descent who were reared in that area continued to remain there.

During this time, Sam DeStefano was listed as being arrested on only two occasions. On August 1, 1946, he was arrested for speeding and was discharged with a fine. On April 11, 1947, he was booked when he was wanted by the Chicago FBI for questioning as to information concerning a fugitive bank robber; not named, he was released.

Back to prison 1947

In January 1947, Sam DeStefano was arrested in Burlington, Wisconsin, by the office of Price Administration Agents. DeStefano entered a local grocery store in Burlington, Wisconsin, and attempted to receive payment for counterfeit sugar stamps. Records from the prison are as followed:

Prison Records

File number 64185-L at Leavenworth Penitentiary, Kansas, gives the following information on Sam DeStefano:

The file reflects that Sam DeStefano was sentenced on May 29, 1947, in U.S. District Court, Eastern District of Wisconsin, at Milwaukee, to serve one year and a day for "possessing and forgery, counterfeited sugar ration coupons." He was received at the U.S. Penitentiary on June 14, 1947, and given a conditional release on May 4, 1948. When released, DeStefano was furnished transportation to Chicago, Illinois, where he was to reside with his wife, Anita, at 1062 West Polk Street.

Associate Warden's Report

DeStefano entered a plea of not guilty to an indictment charging him with possession and forgery of counterfeiting sugar ration coupons. He was found guilty by a jury and sentenced on May 29, 1947. The report states that on January 7, 1947, DeStefano sold 6,000 counterfeit sugar ration coupons for $3,600 to a Lester Fritz. He was suspected of being closely connected with counterfeiters who print coupons and when questioned about the stamps he refused to divulge where he got the coupons he sold to Fritz. He was engaged in printing lottery tickets also in Chicago and was known to be a close friend of people engaged in a gambling syndicate. The Alcohol Tax Unit Investigators believed that DeStefano had furnished stamps to a "still operator" named Frank Ciccino, who was arrested in Kenosha, Wisconsin, for running an illegal "still" operation. DeStefano was taken into custody in January 1947 and was free under a $20,000 bond. DeStefano advised that $8,000 of this bond be posted by his sister, Mrs. Rose Sommario, $8,000 by his mother-in-law, and $4,000 by his aunt-in-law, Mrs. Hildred Wolande.

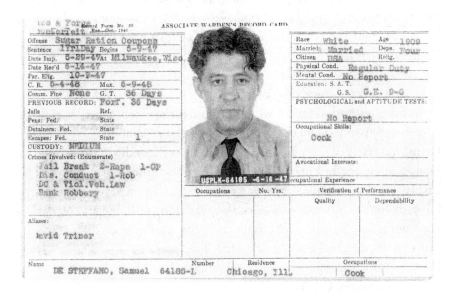

When the authorities contacted the Warden at Juneau, Wisconsin State Prison in 1947 about DeStefano's past, he and his staff were greatly relieved that DeStefano's offense was not a state matter, since everyone dreaded the possible return of DeStefano to Wisconsin State Prison. The warden wrote in a letter in 1944 concerning DeStefano that, *"Sam DeStefano has among the poorest records of any inmate. Thirty-six reports for misconduct. It would be difficult to put into words all the annoyance and difficulties that officers have been placed in concerning DeStefano. Because of DeStefano's trouble, many incidents were glossed over which under ordinary circumstances would have been written up as infractions of prison discipline."*

Inmate's own statement

Sam DeStefano stated, *"I plead not guilty and was found guilty by a jury. I had come back to Chicago after doing time in Waupun prison. My wife couldn't get soap and other scarce groceries we needed for the children, so I began getting some from a grocer across the Wisconsin line. One day some agents stopped me as I was coming out of the store and took the grocer and me into custody. Later the grocer claimed I had given him stolen stamps for sugar. There was no proof that I had ever given him any stamps."* He stated he was framed and convicted based on false testimony and his previous criminal record.

Adjustment – Previous Incarcerations:

DeStefano had served two state penitentiary sentences. He made a poor adjustment at the State Penitentiary, Waupun, Wisconsin, having received 35 disciplinary reports for misconduct, those reports being mostly for talking and refusing to obey orders, and violation of institutional regulations. He was made a trustee on several occasions, but only for short periods, as he did not get along well. He was listed as a cook while imprisoned. DeStefano takes his finding of guilty by the jury rather hard, and had been hopeful for an acquittal.

Information from US Attorney

Assistant United States Attorney Howard W. Hilgendorf furnished the following information about DeStefano and his arrest. Hilgendorf advised that DeStefano caused all kinds of problems when he threatened that he would *"bash in the head"* of the United States Commissioner and that *"if the United States Attorney was not careful"* he would take care of him too. He also threatened a witness that he would take care of the witness and his wife and that they had better not testify against him. Hilgendorf advised that according to the wife of the grocer with whom DeStefano was dealing, her husband told her that he was afraid of DeStefano and that he was forced to sell the stamps even though he did not want to because DeStefano was a "pretty tough guy" and that he figured that he had people behind him in Chicago. According to the grocer, DeStefano was a gangster and hoodlum from Chicago and was working with an old bootlegging gang belonging to the Capone syndicate.

Sam DeStefano's Police Record as of 1947

In his prison interview, Sam DeStefano stated that he had been arrested "at least one hundred times" and had been arrested for suspicion by various police departments and always was released without formal charges. His police record is as follows:

Date	Place and Offense	Disposition
Sept.12, 1926	Niles, IL - Broke out of jail, Re-arrest	
Jan, 23, 1927	Rape,	
Sept. 23, 1927	Rape, Chicago,	Committed 3 years
Apr. 22, 1931	General Principles,	Chicago
June 24, 1931	Rape, Chicago,	Charge *nolle prossed*
Oct. 13, 1931	Robbery, Chicago,	No billed
May 7, 1932	Stolen Auto, Disorderly conduct,	Fined $200.
July 31, 1932	Robbery, Chicago,	No billed
Aug. 22, 1932	Burglary,	Discharged
May 17, 1933	Disorderly conduct, Oak Park, IL,	Fined $5.00
July 11, 1933	Bank Robbery, Juneau, Wis.	Sentenced to 40 years
Aug. 1, 1946	Speeding,	Discharged
Apr. 11, 1947	Investigation,	Released

The Chicago PD "Name Card Files" shows an additional 20 arrests between 1931 and 1933 for investigations and charges of disorderly conduct. All cases were discharged.

MARTIN H. KENNELLY
EDWARD KELLY
MAYOR

JOHN C. PRENDERGAST
COMMISSIONER

CHICAGO POLICE DEPARTMENT
OFFICE OF THE
BUREAU OF IDENTIFICATION
1121 S. STATE STREET
CHICAGO, 5 ILL.

June 20, 1947 _____19__

Record of Sam De Stefano

N.G.	Mike De Stephuno	- Sept. 12, 1926 arr. by Sergt. Jenner & Sq. 14 A,D.B. & turned over to Niles City, Ill Police. Fugt. - jail break.
As	Sam De Stefano	- Jan. 23, 1927 arr. by Off.Quinn & Co., 16th Dist. & turned over to Sheriff of Cook Co. Rape. Dec. 23, 1927 sent. to Joliet, Ill. Pen. #2089. 3 yrs. Rape. Judge Mc Goorty. Disch. Jan. 10, 1931.
C-29190	" "	- Apr. 22, 1931 arr.G.P. Offs. Joyner & Hoffma, 24th Dist. Rel.
C-30347	" "	- June 24, 1931 Judge Hartigan held to C.C. on $5000. bond. Rape. Offs. Seery & Kelly, 22d Dist. Oct. 21, 1931 nolle prossed rape. Judge P. Sullivan.
As	" "	- May 7, 1932 $200. & costs.V.S. 4210 (dis. cond.). Judge Green. Off. Breitenreiter, D.S.A.
C-32834	" "	- Oct. term, 1931, no bill, robb. gun. Off. O'Donnell & Co., 22d Dist.
C-41069	" "	- July 31, 1932 robb. Aug. term, 1932, no bill, robb. Of.'s. O'Connell & Hartnett, 22d Dist.
As	" "	- May 17, 1933 Oak Park, Ill. Dis. cond. Fined $5. & costs. Motor Veh. Law Viol.
As	David Triner	- July 11, 1933 Manston, Wis. Bank robb. at New Lisbon, Wis.
"	Sam De Stefano	- Sept. 29, 1933 S. P., Waupun, Wis. #21284. Bank robb. 15 to 40 yrs.
D-48953	" "	- Apr. 11, 1947 turned over to Special Agent Frank Staub, F.B.I. Intimidating a federal Judge, Milwaukee, Wis. Offs. Smicklas & Alcock & Duffy, D.B.

TC

Ed Evans
Chief Identification Inspector

D 11 25M   rel 53

Initial Examination and Correlated History

General Status: General appearance good, weight 167 lbs., height 69 inches. Blood pressure 146/90.

Special Status: Eyes: 20/20, Appendectomy in 1943. Fracture with open reduction and fixation splint, 1st metacarpal 1943. Gunshot, right hip with bladder perforation and surgical repair, 1932. Foreign body retained, left thigh.

Psychiatric: Preliminary examination reveals no gross evidence of neurosis or psychosis. Subject was raised in an area of heavy delinquency and was frequently associated in gang activities as a youth. Several of his brothers have been imprisoned and he himself spent many years in confinement. His early prison adjustment was extremely poor, but he later stabilized and made an excellent institutional adjustment. In the 3 or 4 years that he has been out, he has made a satisfactory adjustment to society, but appears to have been involved in borderline activities. He is mature and fairly stable and makes a fairly good impression. He denies his guilt in the instant offense but realizes that he was quite lucky in getting such a light sentence when finally adjudged guilty. He expresses an excellent general attitude and appears sincere, but, in view of his background, he offers a guarded prognosis for future social rehabilitation.

Vocational: Subject states that he has driven a truck for 4 years. He operated a fruit and vegetable stand, a hat cleaning and shoeshine parlor, and he was also a member of a Union shop for 2 years.

Educational: Sam DeStefano attended the public schools of Illinois, entering at age 6 and completing the 8th grade at the age of 14. He attended 1 year of high school at Chicago, IL.

As of July 17, 1947, Sam DeStefano's work assignment in Leavenworth prison was that of a baker and cook. As of December 27, 1947, it was that of a window washer.

Cellmates of Sam DeStefano

The file contained information that Sam DeStefano was assigned to six different cells between June 14, 1947, and May 4, 1948. A list of his inmates was not kept; however, the files did contain a record, which indicates that a William Adley Carter was a cellmate on July 22, 1947. William Carter was sentenced on August 27, 1946, by the U.S. District Court at Omaha, Nebraska, to serve 2 years for violation of the National Motor Vehicle Theft Act. Carter was received in Leavenworth on August 30, 1946, and was discharged on April 4, 1948, by Mandatory Release.

List of Relatives and Approved Correspondents

James DeStefano	730 S. Laflin, Chicago
Mike DeStefano	730 S. Laflin, Chicago
Mario DeStefano	1900 Collins Street, Joliet
Rose DeStefano	730 S. Laflin, Chicago
Josephine Pignato	2178 Waterbury Road, Lakewood
Angeline Casale	4188 Adams Street, Chicago
Catherine Milano	810 S. Loomis Street, Chicago
Rose Semmario	1405 W. Fillmore Street, Chicago
Mary Storino	Franklin Park, Chicago
Jean D'Errico	Franklin Blvd., Chicago
Anna Anita Pisciotta	1062 W. Polk Street, Chicago
Phillip Collucci	772 W. Dekoven Street, Chicago
John Matassa	772 W. Dekoven Street, Chicago
Charles Yario	Cicero
James Pasccucci	3824 W. Madison Street, Chicago
Rose Pignato	2178 Waterbury Road, Lakewood

Leavenworth Punishment record

On September 15, 1947, Sam DeStefano was accused of taking a stick of bologna as he ducked into the bakery. The reporting officer stated that he observed DeStefano, as he was about to enter the bakery shop, grab a bag of rags from the implement room just outside the shop, then eluding the officer who was unlocking the door to the shop. DeStefano quickly stepped inside the bakery with the bag. He had no authority to enter the implement room and the rags were not properly in the implement room, inasmuch as the supply of cleaning rags is kept in another location. Mr. Zink immediately followed DeStefano into the bakery and in a large ragbag, just inside the door, he found the rags, which contained a stick of bologna, at which time he charged DeStefano with the violation. During the hearing, Sam DeStefano requested that he represent himself in the proceedings. He was asked to explain why he took the bologna. His response was as follows:

"From what I understand, Mr. Zink was supposed to have been thirty or forty feet away. Now I don't think I am charged with stealing it from the butcher shop. If I am not charged with stealing if from the butcher shop, it is obvious that this so-called bologna was stolen previous to the time I came in contact with it. If no, I don't steal any bologna at all from the institution. If I didn't steal bologna from the institution, then I couldn't be guilty of stealing bologna from the institution. If Mr. Zink says he saw me grab a sack of bologna, then it is obvious that Mr. Zink didn't know it was bologna in the sack. No one could tell that far away what was in it. If he knew there was bologna in it, he should have come over and examined it, but at no time did Mr. Zink find any bologna in my possession. I don't question the fact that Mr. Zink made a serious mistake. He may have seen some inmate grab for the bag. I assume that is the truth. I wasn't hungry enough to steal the bologna. In the next place, the bologna was obviously stolen long before I was supposed to have had it. If I assume that he did see me take it, he still didn't know that it was bologna in the bag. The bologna was not found in my possession, and Mr. Zink couldn't be true because he didn't know it was bologna in there. He was about forty feet away looking through a window, a very dirty window anyway, with an officer standing there letting me into the bakery, and then when he came in there he didn't find any bologna in my possession. I hadn't stolen any bologna from the butcher shop because I had not been in the butcher shop. My good time means a lot to me and I don't want to lose it. I am doing a year and a day and I have got three little children, one little girl 6 months old, and my 72 days good time means a lot to me. I am not complaining that I am being punished for this, I don't mind it because I figure you have got to have rules and regulations in here, but I say, think twice before you take my good time because it means a lot to me. I believe I have myself and my record speaks for itself. I have tried to live according to your rules and regulations. I am not blaming the office for thinking it was me, but I fail to see how it could have been me with an officer standing

41

there letting me into the bakery. I still say I didn't steal the bologna from the institution, and at that time, Mr. Zink did not know that it was bologna. It could have been a bag of rags and nothing else."

DeStefano was found guilty and his 72 days of statutory good time was taken away. However; due to the poor health of his wife and her surgery, 36 days of good time was restored.

Another prison sentence for Sam DeStefano was not a good thing; some could say his conviction in 1947 sent Mad Sam down another road concerning the way he looked at society and life in general. But as history has shown, his time at Leavenworth prison turned out to be the best break of his life and gave him a somewhat secure future. It was in Leavenworth that Sam DeStefano met the leader of the Chicago crime syndicate; it's where he met Paul DeLucia, otherwise known as Paul Ricca. Mad Sam had grown up with many of the top mobsters of his day and knew most of the gangsters in Chicago but he lacked that direct friendship with the top guys.

Meeting Paul DeLucia in prison turned out to be the best career move for Sam DeStefano. Because of their friendship that developed in prison, Sam was now under the protection of DeLucia and considered a distant member of the DeLucia faction.

Paul DeLucia's real name was Paul Maglio, but he is known in history as Paul "The Waiter" Ricca because when he arrived in Chicago in the 1920's he went to work as a waiter at a restaurant owned by the powerful Joseph "Diamond Joe" Esposito. From there he would rise through the ranks of the Capone gang and become top boss after the suicide of Frank "The Enforcer" Nitti in 1943.

With DeStefano under the protection of DeLucia, it was almost as good as being a "made" member of the mob. DeLucia sent the word out to the underground that anyone in need of fast cash should go to Mad Sam. Years later, Paul DeLucia could be seen arriving at DeStefano's house every Sunday at noon for brunch to talk and receive his envelope containing his cut from DeStefano's enterprises. On days when DeLucia couldn't make it, another DeLucia faction lieutenant like Felix "Milwaukee Phil" Alderisio would show up for the envelope of money.

DeStefano was known as a "stand-up-guy" and a man with integrity. If you went to DeStefano to "fix" a court case, he would always come through. If the defendant had to go to court and DeStefano couldn't deliver on his promise, he would pay all the court fees for the defendant as a "sorry" that he couldn't get the "fix" to stick. By the 1950's Sam had been making his money through his connections. His "clout" among judges, politicians, policemen, and labor leaders was at its highest and Sam would brag that he could fix anything. DeStefano charged around $20,000 to fix a murder case, half to Sam and the other half to the people who pulled off the fix. To fix cases such as assault or robberies the cost was around $1,500, $500 to the judge and the rest to Sam. He even had it that when certain policemen arrested a hood they would ask him if he knew Sam DeStefano. If the answer was yes, the policeman would drive right to Sam's house with the hoodlum and Sam would pay off the cop to let him go. His power was growing.

Chapter Four

Sam and the 1950's

One of the funnier stories attached to Sam DeStefano occurred in January 1950. Mad Sam decided to start the new decade by buying a new car. On January 28, DeStefano was pulled over by Chicago police officers and arrested. The police found Sam driving his new automobile down Aberdeen and Madison Streets bearing a sign written on the car "This is a lemon." To make sure everyone would notice this bold statement of his new car, DeStefano clustered his car in grapefruits. There were grapefruits across the rear widow, the front window, one on the antenna, and one replaced the hood ornament leading the car down the street. Once the police noticed this fruitful car, they arrested DeStefano taking him to the police station so the police could search the books, looking for any way to charge DeStefano for a crime. When the police came up empty, DeStefano was given a warning and told to wipe off anything that might obstruct his view while driving. DeStefano told the police he had bought the new car and thought he had bought a bad car and he wanted the world to know it. He also added that the car dealer offered to give DeStefano a new car to replace his bad one but DeStefano refused.

City Worker Sam

During the interview with DeStefano in November 1950, Sam was listed as a city of Chicago employee and the owner of a 21-room apartment building on the corner of Superior and LaSalle Streets. However, in 1952, the Chicago Tribune newspaper exposed ex-convicts that held city jobs and had been locked into civil service. His city job was a reward for his services while in Leavenworth. It came about after his release from prison in 1948 when Mad Sam headed back to Chicago to resume his life. Through the efforts of his new friend Paul DeLucia, he was sent to see some members of the DeLucia faction. The two people he was sent to see were Peter Fosco, who at the time was labor boss of the Hod Carrier's Union in Chicago, and one time committeeman of the old First Ward and his old friend, Frank "Frankie X" Esposito, union boss of the city laborers union. DeStefano was placed in a city job as a laborer.

In July 1949, Frank Esposito and the infamous West Side Bloc of legislators passed bill H.B. 633 which placed city workers with more than 3 years on the job into civil service status locking them into their city jobs. With this, DeStefano and other hoodlums were given a permanent job working for the City of Chicago, earning a pension. DeStefano, having to pass a civil service examination, lied and said that he had never been convicted of a crime.

When the story broke in March 1952, DeStefano became a major target of the media. With the headline *"Learn Rapist, Bank Bandit is City Foreman"* leading the way, it was reported that an ex-convict was locked into civil service working for the City of Chicago as a $3,900 a year garbage dump foreman. DeStefano's political sponsor for the job was listed as Peter Fosco.

DeStefano said to the press, *"I may not have listed my crimes. I've been strictly a working man, and now all this comes up. How do they expect an ex-convict to make a living?"* A few weeks later, Lloyd M. Johnson, then commissioner of streets and electricity in Chicago and DeStefano's ward boss, ruled that no charges were to be filed against DeStefano and that he was not going to be fired from his city job. Johnson stated that in his investigation it showed that DeStefano was doing reliable and creditable work for the city. Following this decision, DeStefano went on record as saying, *"This politician ordered me to quit. I wouldn't quit for him or anyone else. I earned my job. I'm going to keep it!"*

Others exposed in this scandal included Charles Kraft, an ex-convict working the public works division, and Max Berman, an old time burglar, bail jumper, and ex-convict having served 12 years in jail, who was a worker in the city's sewer department, being sponsored by then First Ward Alderman John D'Arco, Sr.

Another main figure to lose his job at that time was Benjamin "Buddy" Jacobson. Jacobson, a secretary for D'Arco and the First Ward, was on the city payroll at the same time as a $14-a-day laborer with the bureau of street traffic, a job given to him by John D'Arco. Other records show that Buddy had another city job since 1939 as a $4,200 a year house drain inspector. Jacobson's start came in the roaring 1920's when Al Capone and Johnny Torrio ruled the streets in the booze wars. His police record dates back to 1923 when he was arrested and charged with robbery with a gun. In 1926, he was known as a bodyguard for gangster bootlegger Earl "Hymie" Weiss who was later assassinated. In 1928, he was arrested for stealing votes during an election and in 1929 was arrested for kidnapping poll watchers trying to clean up the wards from corruption during election voting. His political career began as a fixer for Morris Eller, a onetime powerhouse in the old "bloody 20th" ward that later became Chicago's First Ward. Jacobson had also lied on his civil service application about having a police record, but because of his situation of being a member of the Democratic First Ward organization and being a director with the mob-controlled Anco Insurance Company, he was able to keep his position in the ward but was fired from his city job. Anco Insurance Company was the mob's company in the First Ward run by Alderman John D'Arco, Pat Marcy, and Frank Annunzio.

DeStefano was able to keep his city job until the end of the 1950's when the Chicago Tribune newspaper launched another investigation into the City of Chicago's payroll abuse of its city workers. The investigation was sparked by the killing of mobster Sam Gironda. Gironda, who was shot-gunned to death in the driveway of his home on November 2, 1959, was on the city payroll as a city sewer worker.

The investigation focused on men, either in or connected with organized crime in Chicago who had "no show" or "very comfortable" jobs working for the city. Among those exposed were John D'Arco who sponsored many ex-convicts and known hoodlums for their jobs, many being related to D'Arco through family and marriage. Most notable were the Briatta clan and the Roti clan.

With John D'Arco and Alderman Vito Marzullo acting as the political sponsors for these hoodlums, and with mob labor union boss Frank "Frankie X" Esposito in control of the city's street and sanitation workers, they were able to fill city jobs with whom they pleased. With John D'Arco's wife Antoinette being a Briatta, D'Arco placed her brothers in many city positions. Louis "Lou the Barber" Briatta was given a job as a city paving gang foreman and later a "no show" union position in the offices of Labor Local 1001. Joseph "Pep" Briatta, a former chief of the Cook County sheriff's police, was also given a job as a city street inspector. Tom Briatta was made a foreman for the laborers in the city electrical department and Michael Briatta, Sr. was made a paving gang foreman in the asphalt department. Louie Briatta was also related to Frank "Frankie X" Esposito through his first marriage to his late wife Sue De Luca. Sue's mother, May De Luca, was the sister of Mary Esposito, Frank Esposito's wife, making Sue Briatta Esposito's niece. Sue Briatta died from an illness in November 1946.

Frankie X Esposito

The Roti family got its start in the old First Ward from Bruno Roti who was listed in 1920 as a member of the Italian Black Hand in Chicago. Bruno's power was handed to his son Fred B. Roti, who would become a political powerhouse in the First Ward. Fred Roti would also become an Illinois state senator who was also receiving a paycheck for being a city sewer worker. Bruno Roti's son-in-law, Frank "Skids" Caruso, was placed on the payroll and his brother, Joe "Shoes" Caruso, was a no-show street sweeper working for the city. Other Roti's on the payroll at that time included two Frank Roti's, three Salvatore Roti's, two James Roti's, and two other Bruno Roti's.

John D'Arco's office secretary, Joseph Laino, and his family were all given city jobs. His brother, Dominic Lee Laino, an ex-convict who had spent time in prison for robbery with a gun, was given a job as an asphalt laborer. His father, Leonard Laino, was placed in the bureau of electricity as a watchman. Chicago Police reported that Joseph Laino was arrested with John "Miami" Capone, brother of gang boss Al Capone, in 1953.

Among others exposed were Jerry Cataldo, mob union boss of local 548 of the barbers union, who was given a job in the sewer department; Michael "Ike" Schivarelli, a convicted moonshiner; Anthony "Poolio" DeRosa, a mob muscleman and convicted cartage thief; Sidney Frazin, a gambling collector for Louie Briatta in the old First Ward convicted of gambling; Frank Miceli, convicted of looting cars; Sam Mesi, a mob gambling boss; Anthony Falco, brother-in-law to Frank Esposito, arrested for gambling; Phillip Catania, convicted of gambling; Sam "Bobo" Nuzzo, convicted syndicate gambler; Nick Cashia, outfit handbook operator; James Colletti, handbook operator; Anthony Gironda, syndicate hoodlum; Peter Maruca, listed as a Black Hand terrorist; George Trapp, listed as an associate within gang circles; Christopher Serritella, listed as a syndicate gambler; errand boy for mob chiefs and Sam "Mad Dog" DeStefano, rapist and bank robber.

During the investigation, it was determined that DeStefano was still on the payroll and was a no-show worker, never performing any work, yet receiving a regular paycheck. The fallout from the investigation lead to most of the names above being either fired or forced to quit. DeStefano was once again suspended from his job and in May 1960, he was forced to resign his job as a garbage dump foreman. The city job for DeStefano just showed a legitimate income to help hide the money coming in from all his other illegal operations. He didn't need the money; his "juice" operations would become his full-time passion.

Chapter Five

What Does "Juice" Mean?

It is believed that around 1955 Sam DeStefano decided to make the "juice" racket his full time job and main source of income. Below are official explanations from the FBI and Chicago Crime Commission as to what "Juice" means.

In the world of organized crime, one of its oldest and more lucrative practices was known as the "Juice Rackets." The "Juice Rackets" are usually run by organized criminals who act in sort as personal bankers who loan money to individuals who are in need of money fast without having to worry about credit checks, legal loans, and anyone knowing about the amount of the loan. These criminals lend the amount of money that is agreed on at a very high interest rate and in return, they are to be paid on a timely schedule. If late, the forms used to collect usually involve intimidation, beatings, and fear. In some cases the loan is written off as a "lose" and the person is killed.

This practice goes by many different names such as "Shylocking," "Loan Sharking," "The Arm," "Bleeding," and "Juice Loans." In the days of Sam DeStefano, it was this racket that made him "king" of the streets in lending money.

According to FBI documents, informants in the rackets explained that the term "juice" as a descriptive name for this activity is derived from the "squeeze" that is usually put on an individual in the repayment of money borrowed from the operators of this racket. The "juice" men figuratively "squeeze" the blood out of a person because of the exorbitant amounts of interest they charge, and it is said that the repayment of a loan is "blood money" in its truest sense. On "juice" loans in the amount of $10,000 to $15,000, the "juice" alone was high enough to bleed businessmen into bankruptcy and when a particular business is on the verge of bankruptcy, the individuals who loaned the "juice" money were in a position to take over the operation of the business. By these means, underworld characters have been said to be able to pry their ways into legitimate business such as nightclubs, automobile firms, restaurants, and taverns. In all, the loan sharking business connected with this racket is completely "under the table." Underworld characters rake in the money from the rackets and then turn the money in to their "juice" men. High interest loans are negotiated and these underworld characters usually receive a return of their original investment in less than 6 months.

The term "Shylocking" dates back to the days of William Shakespeare's "The Merchant of Venice." In this play, a central character named "Shylock" said to a person looking for a loan, *"If you repay me not on such a day, in such a place, let the forfeit be nominated for an equal pound of flesh, to be cut off and taken in what part of your body pleases me."*

Loan sharking came from the American adaptation of the word "Shylocking" unintentionally slurred by illiterate hoodlums coming out as "Sharks" giving the reference "loan shark" its base as the preferred phrase to be used to anyone engaged in the usurious money lending business. Before World War II, "loan sharking" was considered a low-level racket used by nothing hoodlums who earned a dishonest living. It was considered financially unproductive and undignified by most of the top hoodlums. After the World War, it was seen in a new light as potential tremendous profits were recognized if controlled and organized.

There are many types of loans, one where the borrower pays 10 percent weekly interest on the amount of the loan. When the principal loan is $100, weekly payment on that $100 loan is $10; however, that $10 payment represents just the interest on the $100 loan meaning that does not reduce the amount of the principal loan. Whenever the borrower wished to liquidate his loan, he must return the entire principal. If it takes the borrower a year to accumulate the amount of the principal, which didn't happen very often, he would have paid at the end of 1 year the amount of $520 in weekly interest and the principal of $100, more than four times the original $100 loan.

This is the situation that is most remunerative to the loan shark racketeers. The longer it takes the borrower to return the full principal, the greater the return on the original investment.

Another kind of method the loan shark operator stipulates is that should the borrower be able to pay back the principal within a specified period, say less than one year, he must still pay the interest for the entire year. A case in point would be a loan of $100 a week interest. After five weeks, he has paid $500 in interest. He now wants to liquidate the debt. However, he must pay the original principal of $1,000 and $4,700 in interest for the 47 remaining weeks. This represents a total payment of $6,200 on an original $1,000 loan.

The following set forth information as to the various types and methods of operation in connection with the "juice" loan activity. The information below is by no means all-inclusive regarding interest, and the "juice" man would always extract whatever interest rate he felt at the time was demanded, the circumstances surrounding the loan, the identity, and wealth of the borrower, and any other thoughts that the "juice" man may have concerning the borrower and the security of his loan.

Loan Company

In this type of operation a loan is made on a flat 20 percent annum (10 months constitutes a year) and payments are made over this period: for example, on an $800 loan the "juice" victim would repay $1,000 or $120 per month.

Six-for-Five Loan

This type of loan is utilized when the individual borrower is not a well-known person, when he is thought to be wealthy, or for any other person deemed feasible by the "juice" man. Here the interest, 20 percent, is payable weekly and the interest payment continues until such time as the borrower pays back the total amount of the loan plus 20 percent interest in one lump sum of cash. For example, an individual receiving a $400 loan pays $80 per week until the total cash payment of $480 is made. The "juice" man will, in some instance, reduce the interest rate to 10 percent or less at his discretion, depending upon many circumstances.

Ten Present Weekly

This is the most prominent type of loan utilized by "juice" men when they loan to regular customers, friends, and so forth. Here the operation is similar to the six-for-five loan, and payment is made in the same manner until such time as the total amount of the loan plus interest is paid in cash.

Gambling House "Juice"

This type of loan activity is found in gambling houses wherein individuals float from table to table, making loans to the player bettors. The interest charged here is usually 10 percent but may be 20 percent or five percent depending on the identities of the "juice" man and the borrower. The "juice" man keeps tabs on the outstanding loans and if the gambler is winning after utilizing the loan, the "juice" man will then immediately collect his loan plus interest on the spot. If the player borrower loses, the loan plus interest is due within 24 hours.

Structure of the Juice Gangs

In a 1970 report on the Juice Racketeers in the Chicago area, it stated the juice rackets were divided into four sections. The first was the syndicate leaders and juice financiers. The financers are the top hoodlums and top mobsters who have the financial resources to fund the operations. They often extend large loans up to $100,000 at a time to the second level of the juice gang hierarchy. They mostly handle short-term loans to the lesser hoodlum associates at the form of 1 to 5 percent interest. It's all based on high turnover for these leaders. These top hoodlums rarely, if ever, have contact with the actual juice customers. Most of the loans range from $10 to $19,999. Loans in excess of that amount are known as "classic loans." On some occasions the collectors, the men at the third level, will themselves make direct loans with money furnished by their superiors, those being the second level hoodlums.

The second level of the structure hierarchy is the juice racketeers who actually make the loans to the customers. They usually operate principally from taverns, restaurant, and other business establishments. Juice racketeers are appointed territories by the top hoodlums of the first level. Each faction is given a geographical area within which he has exclusive domain. Other members in organized crime may not encroach upon this territory. However, a second level man could get permission from the hierarchy to operate in another's territory. Permission must also be sought from the top leaders before criminal operations can be initiated in new territories where "juice" operations were not previously practiced. These are the characteristics of discipline that must be maintained by the outfit.

Significant independent juice racketeering activities are not tolerated. In rare instances where a person outside the organized crime establishment attempts to initiate his private criminal usury racket, he is immediately suppressed. A warning word from the gangster is sufficient to stop his operations.

The third and forth level of the juice operations hierarchy are the collectors, who receive the juice payments at regular intervals, and the enforcers, who deal out punishment when ordered.

In 1964, Chicago detectives released their findings on how the "juice" rackets work. It was as follows:

"A top mob figure who has made $200,000 from other illegal enterprises invests his money with the top loan sharks under the control of the outfit. The mob boss charges that hoodlum 6 or 7 percent interest on the loan, knowing that his identity would be protected at all cost and that the rate of return is guaranteed by his reputation for violent retribution. The second level hoodlum lends the $200,000 to five or six lesser hoodlums charging them an interest rate of 10 percent. Then at the third level of hoodlums working the juice rackets, the "juice" loans are made to the victims at rates ranging up to 5 percent a week. In return, the top mob bosses receive a good rate of return on their investment at no risk to them.

Any form of "juice" loans for the syndicate reaching from coast to coast across America remains a reliable source of income. In recent years, the "beatings" and "killings" from "juice" loans have declined tremendously among mobsters in the Chicago area but they are still known to happen. These days if you fall behind on a "juice" loan you're more likely to be "black listed" by organized crime and never allowed to be given a loan of any kind again."

> # The moſt excellent
> Hiſtorie of the *Merchant*
> *of Venice*.
>
> VVith the extreame crueltie of *Shylocke* the Iewe
> towards the ſayd Merchant, in cutting a iuſt pound
> of his fleſh: and the obtayning of *Portia*
> by the choyſe of three
> cheſts.
>
> *As it hath beene diuers times acted by the Lord*
> *Chamberlaine his Seruants.*
>
> Written by William Shakeſpeare.
>
> ※✻※
>
> AT LONDON,
> Printed by *I. R.* for Thomas Heyes,
> and are to be ſold in Paules Church-yard, at the
> ſigne of the Greene Dragon.
> 1 6 0 0.

Title page of the first quarto for *The Merchant of Venice* by William Shakespeare (1600)

Shylock After the Trial, describing Act II, Scene vii of William Shakespeare's play The Merchant of Venice (Painting by Sir John Gilbert, pre 1873

Chapter Six

He's Got the Gene!

In September 1959, twenty-five State's Attorneys' police officers led by then first Assistant State's Attorney, Frank Ferlic, raided the Dream Way building at 1312 S. Cicero Avenue with a search warrant on information that a gambling den was being run by Sam Giancana. Inside they found empty rooms with several dice tables and an elaborate handbook wall-sheet set-up. Finding no one there, they decided to raid the building next door at 1304 S. Cicero Avenue called Mario's Restaurant in search of their prey. With a sign on the window reading "closed for the holidays," the police smashed through the glass door, turned left thru another door, and headed down to the back of the restaurant. There they went through the back door and found an active mob handbook engaged in gambling. It was actually at Mario's Lounge next door at 1306 S. Cicero. There they found an array of hard cards and wall sheets used in the handbook. They also found a loud speaker to announce the results.

Mario DeStefano
(police photo 1964)

Among the 50 people arrested in the raid were Nick Marino, John Sparrow, Mike Bakes, Sam Pertrillo, Joe Angalone, Joe Neely, James Filisho, Joe Casha, Frank James, August De Merio, Tony Frieri, and Mario DeStefano.

Sam's brother Mario, held a special space in Sam's heart because he could be as sick and twisted as Sam. Sam always joked that the two had been made in the same mold and that Mario "understood" the way Sam operated and could grasp what Mad Sam was attempting to accomplish. Out of the three brothers Sam DeStefano had, Mario DeStefano was the one he trusted the most. Not only did he have his brother's trust, Sam could see that Mario had the "gene" like Sam did in understanding crime and that lifestyle.

Mario Anthony DeStefano was born on March 21, 1915, in Heron, Illinois. However, when the FBI contacted authorities in Heron they were unable to find any birth record for a Mario DeStefano. The FBI even went to Our Lady of Mount Carmel Church in Heron and searched for records but came up with nothing. Mario was the eighth child born out of ten siblings. He left Kelly Grammar School at the age of 15, completing the 8th grade, to assist his brother Jimmy DeStefano in the bootlegging trade. His adult arrest record dates back to March 1933, but his juvenile court record disclosed he was placed on probation and had been picked up by the police many times for alcohol difficulties. The amazing fact is that Mario DeStefano had been arrested over 100 times as a juvenile. He once told authorities that he had an insufficient childhood and began to engage in bootlegging activates which lead to armed robbery. During this time, he was in repeated contact with the police authorities and had become very familiar with the techniques of bribery and political manipulations. He at one time attempted to become a legitimate person by investing his bootlegging money in a tailor shop, but that venture didn't work out and he headed back into organized crime.

Some of Mario's arrests were as follows:

March 29, 1933, Mario was arrested for disorderly conduct and fined $100. On November 14, 1933, Mario was arrested for reckless driving and disorderly conduct and was sentenced to 6 months probation. On October 24, 1934, he was arrested on general principles and released.

On December 23, 1934, five hoodlums with handkerchiefs over their faces stormed into Michael Kilmartin's Tavern at 5601 South Halsted Street with the intent to rob the place. One of the bandits jumped behind the counter and forced the owner into a back room. The other robbers began herding the customers into another rear room. One of the customers was policeman Thomas Lydon who grappled with one of the hoodlums before pulling his pistol. In a split second, gunfire erupted between Lydon and the bandits. During the battle, four of the customers were wounded and one, a Benjamin Yoder, was shot and fell dead to the floor. Three of the robbers managed to make it out of the tavern with $105 taken from the cash drawer by jumping through the glass beside the front door while officer Lydon pointed his empty gun at two of the bandits on the floor making them surrender. The two were Mario DeStefano and Daniel Mirra. Officer Lydon had been shot in the hip but managed to take them into custody.

The next day, both confessed to the police that they had committed over 50 robberies in the past 3 months, robbing mostly meat markets, fruit stores, and 22 taverns and saloons. While Mario and Mirra were questioned about the attempted robbery, they admitted that the other robbers, David Cunningham, Joseph Orelli, and Joseph Milleta were members in their gang. All three were arrested along with Henry Chapman, a cab driver who acted as the getaway driver. Also arrested were two girls named Catherine Popenka and Wanda Satka, both believed to be companions of the robber's gang.

On December 31, 1934, a policeman was working alone on the 11th floor of the police lock-up at the police station at 1121 S. State Street when he had to move four prisoners in one cell to another cell to allow the prison's janitor to clean the cell walls. Once out of his cell, Mario made his break for liberty. He made his way to a ventilating window that was 1 foot high and 3 feet long, just large enough for him to squeeze through and crawled out before the policeman could grab him. Mario leaped onto an ice-coated iron bar wall brace hanging from the building three feet away. If he had missed the iron rung, he would have fallen to his death 11 stories down. He swung back and forth for a moment and with one great burst he swung onto the 10th floor landing, fleeing down the fire escape to freedom.

While the hunt for Mario was on, Daniel Mirra appeared before the grand jury to give his side of the story concerning the robbery of the tavern. Hours after the escape, Mario DeStefano's mother appeared at the offices of the state's attorney and was not aware that her son had escaped. Once told, she screamed, and then fainted, falling to the floor. Orders were issued to the patrolmen to "shoot to kill" Mario DeStefano by the then Chief of Detectives John L. Sullivan. Looking back on the incident there were signs that Mario was planning an escape. The night before his escape, Mario was being returned with other prisoners from the show-up area to the lockup area when he ran into an empty cell containing unbarred windows. Mario ran to the window and looked down the 11 floors to the street, taking a mental photo of the fire escape. A police officer grabbed and pulled Mario back into line. Mario told the policeman, *"I just wanted to look out the window. It would be better than the chair, if I did drop."* Later that night, a fellow inmate named Francis Punchard was in a cell near Mario's when he informed an officer that it would be in his best interest to pick up a fallen newspaper on the floor in the corridor next to DeStefano's cell. When the officer investigated, he lifted the newspaper and found several banana skins on the floor. Mario's plan was to have the guard walk on the newspaper and slip on the banana skins. Once on the ground in front of Mario's cell, he would reach out, grab the keys for his cell, and make his escape.

Mario DeStefano
(police photo 1935)

On January 14, 1935, three more men were arrested for their involvement in the robbery. Dr. Albert Bellini, Vito Laterza, and Henry Robarge were arrested when Joseph Aurelli confessed that after the shooting he was brought to the home of Joseph Robarge at 1128 S. Wood Street where he was treated for his gunshot wound that he received in the shootout. Once there, Vito Laterza went to get his brother-in-law Dr. Albert Bellini to fix the wound. Bellini told the grand jury that he treated Aurelli's wound and was paid $50 for his services and $20 for medicines. For this action, Bellini, Robarge, and Laterza were charged with being accessories to murder.

Twenty-five days after Mario's daring escape, police received a tip that Mario DeStefano was hiding out at the old Martha Washington Hotel at 3045 West Washington Boulevard. Six detective bureau squads surrounded the building from the roof to the basement and began to search each apartment with machine guns and shotguns. When they got to the top apartment, they found Mario swathed in blankets hiding beneath one of the beds. Mario surrendered peacefully begging the police not to shoot him as he came out from the blankets. Also arrested were Pasty Russo and his wife Mary for hiding DeStefano in their apartment. At that moment, Pasty Russo had been out on bond himself while awaiting his trial on a hijacking charge. Mary Russo, who held the lease on the apartment, was charged with accessory after the fact of murder.

On May 29, 1935, Mario DeStefano, Joseph Aurelli, and Daniel Mirra all plead guilty and were sentenced to 30 years in prison each. Patrolman Lydon was given a $100 hero award for his heroism.

DeStefano was received at Joliet Prison on June 13, 1935. Prison records reveal that until 1935 Mario DeStefano never had a reason to seek legitimate employment. His record contained this assessment:

"Mario DeStefano has highly developed delinquent attitudes and basic criminal patterns are apparent in this case. A well-steeped antisocial philosophy and criminalistic ideology are also present. This inmate's definition of values and objectives is on a delinquent level. He has pursued a consistent criminal career. The psychological examination indicates high average intelligence.

He denies his guilt of murder but acknowledges that he was an accomplice. "I had no part in the murder. I happened to be in the back when the shooting started, sir. I think I was crazy." His reaction would seem to indicate that he regards this crime as normal behavior. Mario did admit participation in 12 stick-ups over a period of several weeks. He complains that his numerous arrests were due to the records of his brothers who are now incarcerated at Waupun Prison.

We find this person to be rather egocentric and a hoodlum type. He is capable of leadership, is pleasant, capable of ingratiating himself into the good will of others, but also has highly developed delinquent attitudes and basic criminal patterns. The outlook in this case would seem to be guarded if not unfavorable, but he has some personality assets which might be utilized toward his rehabilitation."

After ten years at Joliet Prison, he was transferred to Menard State Prison in Illinois on February 20, 1945, for one year. He returned to Statesville on February 26, 1946, and back to the Joliet Division in August 1947. Mario spent his years in prison as a baker in the prison bakery and worked as a server in the dining room. His file contained the comment that Mario had become an excellent baker, fully capable of making any kind of pastry requested. The first few years he spent time in solitary confinement for minor offenses. In 1938, he was given ten days in solitary for being disorderly and attacking another inmate in the shop area. His report stated that Mario took several years to come to the full realization of what he had been missing on the outside by getting into trouble in the prison. After 16 years of imprisonment, he was paroled on May 15, 1950, and finally discharged on September 15, 1951.

On May 13, 1951, Mario DeStefano married Mary Davino in Chicago. The two would go on to have three children, his son Sam, and two daughters Carmine and Rosalie.

Mario once wrote in a letter, "*After my release from prison, I immediately went to work for the Fasano Pie Company as a baker, a trade I learned during my sixteen years of incarceration. After working for a while and saving a little money and with a little help from my Mother, I went into the restaurant business.*"

Mario's departure from prison ushered him into a different kind of organized crime that plagued the streets of Chicago. He went to work for his brother Sam and was picked up by the Chicago police on June 21, 1952, for stealing poultry; the charges were discharged. On July 24, 1952, he was arrested once again on a larceny investigation; however, no charges were filed. Between 1952 and 1958, he was only picked up for four traffic violations and arrested once on June 26, 1957, for an investigation.

CITY OF CHICAGO / DEPARTMENT OF POLICE   1121 South State Street   Chicago 5, Illinois   WAbash 2-474
IDENTIFICATION SECTION

ARREST RECORD OF   DESTEFANO, Mario A.   M/W   26 IOI (0
                                                                                  8 IOI

DATE   30 April 1964   66794

DATE OF BIRTH   21 March 1915   I.R.66794

NAME & ADDRESS	C.B. NO.	DATE OF ARREST · ARRESTING OFFICER & DIST. · CHARGE · DISPOSITION
Mario DeStefano	N.G.	-29 March 1933 $100 & costs V.S. 4210 (Dis. Cond.) Judge Gutknecht, Miller & Co. 24th Dist.
		-14 Nov. 1933 Prob. 6 mos. Reckless driving & Dis. Cond. Judge Gutknecht, Fitzgerald & Co. D.B.
	C 62352	-22 Oct. 1934 G.P. Morrison & Darr Sevick Sq. 5 B D.B.
		-29 May 1935 Judge Miller, Joliet Pen. #1557 30 yr Murder plea guilty
		-13 June 1935 received Joliet Pen. #1557
		-20 Feb. 1945 trans. to S.P. Menard Ill. #19092
		-26 Feb. 1946 Trans. to S.P. Joliet Ill. #23350
		-15 May 1950 Paroled
		-12 Sept. 1951 Disch.
3540 Congress St.	D 91606	-21 June 1952 Devereaux & Co. 26th Dist. G.P.
		-26 June 1957 Inv. Sgt. Allman & Co. C.O.
2613 S. Mayfair Westchester, Ill.	1506284	-30 April 1964 King B.I.S. Viol. of election laws
		- 18 May 64, Viol. Elect. Code, Nolle, Judge Ryan May 1964 Gr. Jury, Indictment #64-1440-41
		- 8 March 66, Ill. Vote (2), Fined $1000. (2), Judge Fitzgerald.
		- 2 May 66, Ill. Vote. Fine Vacated, New Sent, Fin $500. ea. Judge Fitzgerald.
Mario A. DE STEFANO 306 S.Meyers Rd. Oakbrook, Ill.	3151555	- 18 Nov 70 Willems Intell (CD) Consp. to Gamble 18 Nov 70, Released w/o Charging
Mario Anthony De STEFANO 2806 S. Meyers Rd. Oakbrook, Ill.	3625577	- 31 Aug 1972 Sgt. Motny IH/S#4(S.I.O.) Murder 31 Aug 72, G.J. IND#72-2309, Murder.
- ****** August 7, 1973	-Letter	-Off. Long Range Planning, Joliet, Ill -W Anderson

CPD-22.466 (REV.3/62)   mp

File Card

Mario DeStefano

AKA: Merlo
Born: March 21, 1915 (Herron, Illinois)
Died: August 8, 1975
Chicago P.D. IR # 66794
Height: 5'10"
Weight: 170 Pounds
Hair: Brown
Eyes: Brown

Known Addresses

2116 Taylor Street, Chicago (1935)
1900 Collins Street, Joliet (1947)
668 West Evergreen Avenue, Chicago (1950)
3540 Congress Street, Chicago (1952)
2236 South Northgate, North Riverside (1963)
2613 South Mayfair Avenue, Westchester (1964)
2806 S. Meyers Road, Oak Brook (1969)

Businesses

Mario's Restaurant 1300-1304 S. Cicero Avenue (Closed 1965)
Restaurant at 4830 W. 14th Street, Cicero (Opened 2-14-1966)
Tri-Cote Incorporated, Cicero (1969)
Décor-Cem Company 1310 S. Cicero Ave, Cicero (1970)
Metropolitan Bault Incorp. 1020 W. Pacific Avenue, Franklin Park (1972)

Chapter Seven

Little Brother, So What

Some say that family is everything and that "you never go against family," meaning nothing should get in between the relationships of family members. Sam DeStefano looked at "family" in a different way. When it came to his brother Michael DeStefano, the term "no mercy" comes to mind.

Mike DeStefano

On September 27, 1955, the body of Michael DeStefano was found shot to death in the trunk of a parked car. Five bullets brought an end to the young DeStefano's life and career as a hoodlum. Records show Mike DeStefano was born on March 7, 1908, and had the nickname "Clumsy Mike" because of the frequency with which he got into scrapes with the law.

Mike DeStefano attended Public school in Heron City, Illinois. A letter from the superintendent of the Herrin City Schools reads, *"Mike DeStefano graduated from our 8th grade in 1923. His record was very good in 1922-1923. We had trouble with Mike in 1921-1922 due to delinquency. He was retained in the 8th grade that year. His association and environment led to his delinquency in most cases. Mike was a gentleman in 1922-1923. He has visited our school every year since 1923 and from all appearances his environment may again get him into trouble."*

When Mike DeStefano was arrested, he told the police that he worked for the Sears, Roebuck & Company from 1925 thru 1927 and for two years as a foreman around 1928 at the old Curtis Candy Company in Chicago. When law enforcement officials checked that information, no records could be found that he ever worked there. He also said he was a truck driver for his brother James' trucking company.

His record begins back in the 1920's while he and his brother Sam were members of the "42 Gang." There are reports that Mike DeStefano was arrested in November 1926 for larceny and once again on February 2, 1927, for larceny with Robert DeAngelo. Both were sentenced to 60 days in the House of Corrections. However, law enforcement could not say for certain that it was the same Mike DeStefano in either case. On February 5, 1928, Mike DeStefano was arrested for disorderly conduct but the charges were dismissed by Judge Allegretti. There are five more arrests for a Mike DeStefano, most for disorderly conduct, but at each arrest, a different address was given. Only two of the addresses matched Mike DeStefano's at the time. In the 1930's DeStefano's family members were asked about the other addressed used; the family declared that they never lived at the addresses mentioned. The addresses given were 818 West Taylor, 3217 West 27th Street, 3217 27th Place, 3239 West 51st Street, and 1516 Laflin.

On November 8, 1930, Mike DeStefano, James Cozzi, and George Conrad were arrested and charged with larceny of a 1930 Ford automobile valued at $500 and owned by Joseph Hoditz.

Two years later in 1932, a crazy incident showed proof that Michael was Mad Sam's brother. Michael soaked a police squad car with gasoline and set it on fire. Michael showed up at the Maxwell Street police station and demanded that his brother Sam, who was sitting in a jail cell for driving a car with a fictitious license, be released. Michael even offered to take the place of his brother because he claimed his brother was too ill to sit in jail. When the police refused his request, Michael left the station only to return a few minutes later with some fellow gang members, Ambrose Russo, known as Tony Panico, and Mike Messino. The three drove their auto past a police squad car, emptied a two-gallon can of gasoline onto the upholstery of the police car, and applied the match, setting it ablaze. As the three sped off, the police quickly gave chase. All three were arrested and joined Sam in lock-up.

Michael made his bond and was released but that didn't stop him from getting in trouble. In April 1933 Mike DeStefano, Albert Bruno, Nick Greco, Anthony Pisciola "Russo," Charles Yario, and Anthony Taranto were arrested and questioned in the killing of Frank Holbrook.

Holbrook, a Chicago Loop circulation manager for the Daily Illustrated Times newspaper, was shot and killed in front of the old Ventee café at 3104 West Madison Street. While Holbrook lay dying on the ground, the group of killers, one wearing a deputy sheriff's star on his coat, kidnapped Holbrook's companion named Lillian Nance. Nance told police she was raped many times by the group and Holbrook was killed because he tried to save her from the killers. None of the men were charged when the witness refused to identify the killers. All were released except Pisciola, Yario, and Taranto; they were turned over to federal authorities after the police found 180 gallons of alcohol in Pisciola's home.

Six months later on June 3, 1933, Michael, Tony Panico, and Mike Messino were sentenced to one to three years in Joliet Prison for setting fire to the police car. However, once again, Michael was released on bond and this time he fled Illinois to escape his sentence.

A month after Michael was sentenced to Joliet, a coroner's jury ruled concerning the death of Emil Onesto, a onetime saloonkeeper who was shot to death in a saloon located on 1139 Taylor Street. Their ruling was that it was a "murder by persons unknown." It was reported that Michael DeStefano and William Madden set out on that day to raise defense funds for Michael's brother Sam who was sitting in jail. The two went to the saloon at 1139 Taylor Street to see Frank Laino, chauffeur for hoodlum labor boss Lawrence "Dago" Mangano, for the money; he refused. An angered DeStefano left and returned with guns ready to kill Laino. They drove by the saloon slowly as the two opened fire on Laino who was standing in the doorway. Seeing that they had missed Laino, DeStefano drove around the block so he could make another pass and fire another round of bullets. This time Frank Laino was shot in the chest, while a bartender, Emil Onesto, was shot and fell to the ground with 126 slugs in his body. Also wounded was Angelo Mozzone, an innocent bystander who lived in the neighborhood. More than 50 people witnessed the killing and word went out that DeStefano and Madden were the killers. The police hurried three of the victims to a hospital while the murder car returned one more time to make sure Lanio was dead. This time they saw the blood upon the street and sped off.

The next day, a hunt was issued for Michael DeStefano by the Chicago police. A police officer spotted the two and attempted to arrest them; a gun battle erupted while DeStefano and Madden made their escape. According to reports, both DeStefano and Madden were finally caught and arrested in Kansas City. Once back in Chicago, Madden was locked up while DeStefano managed to convince police that he was innocent, buying him his freedom. Once they discovered their mistake, DeStefano was nowhere to be found and reports had been gathered that he was on his way to Italy to hide out. However; DeStefano was not on his way to Italy; on July 10 of that year, Mike DeStefano and John Monaco, a lackey of Louis "The Louse" Clementi, were robbing the New Lisbon State Bank in Mauston, Wisconsin, of $5,000.

After the robbery, DeStefano fled Wisconsin and headed to Pittsburgh, Pennsylvania, where local police spotted him. According to reports, Pittsburgh Sheriff Morgan Rider and his deputies approached Michael. In Michael's desperation to get away, a struggle occurred between him and the police, and DeStefano was shot by one of the deputies. It was reported that DeStefano was paralyzed from the shooting with a spine injury. On April 5, 1934, Mike DeStefano and John Monaco were convicted of bank robbery and were each sentenced to 14 to 40 years at the state prison at Waupun, Wisconsin. Also convicted in connection with the robbery was Lyle Wright, a former "sheriff boy" of Juneau County.

It was there that Michael would serve his term until his parole on October 10, 1944, when he was turned over to the Cook County, Illinois authorities and brought to Joliet Prison to serve his one-to-three-year sentence on the 1933 conviction for arson of a police motor vehicle.

On April 23, 1947, Michael was released from prison and resurfaced in hoodlum circles in Chicago. At that time he started a family with his wife Josephine having a son, Michael Jr. and later two more kids, Eugene and Carol Joyce.

In 1949, like his brother Sam, Michael was placed in a City of Chicago job. Through the efforts of union boss and good friend Frank "Frankie X" Esposito, Michael was placed as a laborer in the city bureau of electricity and was given a Local 1001-A card of the AFL Asphalt Electrical Resurfacing Laborer, Carpenter Shop, and Vehicle Tag Union.

Records show that he was placed on the payroll on April 20, 1949, and was blanked into civil service on July 1, 1949, due to the efforts of Frank Esposito and the old West Side Bloc.

There is one report from November 1950 where Mike DeStefano was brought to Mother Cabrini hospital by two men for treatment of a gunshot wound to the forehead, DeStefano refused to tell the police how it occurred.

On September 27, 1955, the phone rang at a local police station informing the police that a body would be found in the trunk of a car parked in front of the McLaren Elementary School located at 1500 Flournoy Street in Chicago. At the same time, an anonymous telephone call was received at the offices of the Chicago American newspaper telling the reporter that a major story was developing at the same location. The reporter was the first to arrive at the scene. Curious, the reporter reached into the two-tone 1954 Buick, pulled out the ignition key and opened the rear trunk of the car. The reporter was amazed at the sight of the grotesquely sprawled body inside. The knees were drawn up and the head was twisted to the left. Dollar bills were sticking out from his right-hand pocket. The reporter left the body untouched and waited for the police to arrive from the Maxwell Street station. When police lieutenant Anthony Mulvaney arrived, he found the 1954 coupe had been opened and the trunk contained the murdered body of Michael DeStefano.

Reports indicate that he was shot five times in the chest, right side, and back, then wrapped in a quilted comforter and placed in the trunk to be found by the police. Detectives determined that Michael had been dead 12 to 15 hours before his body was found, and the absence of blood in the car meant he had been killed elsewhere and dumped in the car. Before the body was placed in the car, it appeared that it had been washed and dressed in clean clothes.

The day of the discovery, the police went to Michael's house at 726 S. Laflin Street to inform his wife about the murder. When they arrived, no one was to be found. The detectives then went to DeStefano's sister house, Mrs. Catherine Milano, and found out that Michael's wife Josephine had been ill and went to live with her mother taking their three children with her. Then the detectives went to Sam DeStefano's house to question him. Sam, who told the detectives that he was a retired real estate dealer and claimed to be also living at 1000 W. Polk Street, informed them that his brother Michael was *"quite quarrelsome when he had been drinking, he was a nasty drinker, but I don't know of any trouble he could have been in."*

The first suspicion as to why Michael was killed was due to his close association with Dominick F. Christiano. Christiano, an ex-convict, was found shot to death in his car on August 18, 1955. It was believed that DeStefano and Christiano were involved in a robbery ring and a dispute over disposition of the stolen goods led to their deaths. Another theory was that both had been implicated in passing Greenlease ransom money throughout Chicago. Bobby Greenlease of Kansas City was a 6 year-old boy who was kidnapped and found slain after the ransom money had been paid.

Mad Sam arriving to identify his brother

It was learned, after the murder, that Christiano was a suspect in a $54,000 robbery of the River Forest State Bank in March 1955. A year earlier in February 1954, both Christiano and DeStefano were suspected of taking part in the robbery of a jewelry store, netting over $35,000 in stolen jewelry. Along with DeStefano and Christiano was a third robber believed to be James Pampinella who at the time of DeStefano's murder was under indictment for that robbery. But at the time, the most likable theory was that DeStefano was suspected of being in a robbery gang that was robbing syndicate gambling dens and once his identity was found out, he was knocked off by the outfit.

The next day investigators said they believed that the killing was "personal" rather than a mob hit. Homicide detectives pointed out that Michael DeStefano was shot with a .32 caliber weapon instead of a .38 or heavier caliber weapon, usually used by outfit hit men. They also added that all of the bullet holes were in the body and not one in the head, which was a sort of calling card for syndicate executioners. Also, there was the fact that the killer or killers had intended to show consideration for the family of DeStefano by phoning the murder in so that a regular funeral and wake could be held before decomposition set in.

The day of DeStefano's murder, detectives said he showed up for work at a city storeroom located at 405 W. Chicago Avenue where he was a boiler maintenance man and had been "loaned" to the city purchasing department to work in the storeroom. When he showed up for work, he appeared to be drunk. At 11:00 a.m., his supervisor, Frank Reimann, urged him to go home, and DeStefano muttered, *"I have to go to Cicero."* On the way home, he was stopped by a west park district policeman for driving erratically; after a liquor test, the policeman let him go.

After the body was removed from the scene, an autopsy was conducted and it was confirmed that the body of Michael DeStefano had been washed and cleaned and dressed subsequent to his death. The murder was listed as unsolved and the investigation marked "pending investigation."

It wasn't until 1961 that detectives received some information that Michael DeStefano was killed by his own brother, Sam DeStefano. The reason given for this murder was that Michael had become addicted to morphine, which in Sam's eyes made his little brother a poor risk. For this, Sam killed his brother, cleaned him up, and stood by his casket mourning the death of his little brother with the rest of his family.

Sometime later Sam's collector Peter Cappelletti was questioned by the FBI regarding an incident involving Cappelletti being tortured by DeStefano. Shortly after Cappelletti left the FBI offices, the FBI supervisor received a phone call from Sam DeStefano. DeStefano stated he was extremely upset and in a very emotional and heated fashion threatened to go to the Attorney General in Washington with a complaint against the conduct of the FBI Agents for the method of their questioning. Cappelletti had told DeStefano that the agents accused DeStefano of having murdered his own brother Michael. The supervisor told Sam that he had no knowledge of the interrogation and suggested to him that he contact the two agents when they returned to the FBI offices that evening. DeStefano did as suggested and when he contacted the agents, he informed one of them that he should never attempt to come to his residence again and that he, DeStefano, would shoot the agent in the head. The other agents then suggested that they would come right out that evening to discuss this situation with him. However, within a minute after DeStefano hung up the phone, the agent received a telephone call from Sam's wife Anita who pleaded with the agent not to come to the residence because Sam was in such a violent temper that drastic action would result, and that either the agent or DeStefano would be the victim of this action. Therefore, the agent did not contact DeStefano and stayed away.

In the summer of 1963, the agents received a phone call from one of DeStefano's goons. The hoodlum made sure the correct agent was on the phone and handed the phone over to DeStefano. DeStefano advised that he had been waiting for the agent to appear so he could determine if the agents had said that he, DeStefano, had killed his own brother. The agent advised DeStefano that he had never informed anyone that DeStefano had killed his own brother, inasmuch as there was no actual proof of this. The phone call lasted approximately 45 minutes and was concluded on an amicable basis. Just prior to the conclusion of the telephone call, DeStefano was requested to arrange an interview with the FBI for his associate, William "Willie Potatoes" Daddono. DeStefano advised that he would do so on the condition that he would be allowed to be present as the attorney for Daddono. For one reason or another, arrangements were never perfected for that interview.

The investigation as to who killed Michael DeStefano remains open today with the Chicago Police department. However, the case file has not seen the day of light for decades. The only one who knows for sure who killed Michael DeStefano is Mad Sam, and he took it to his own grave

Michael DeStefano lies in section 37 of Mount Carmel Cemetery in Hillside, Illinois.

Author's Collection

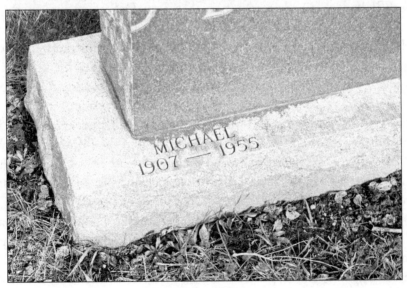

Author's Collection

71

Chapter Eight

A New Beginning on the Juice

At the start of the 1960's Sam DeStefano was out of a job, but more wealthy than the mayor of Chicago. DeStefano was the leading "juice man" in the Chicago area. The FBI's official listing on Sam DeStefano in 1960 read as follows:

"Sam DeStefano lends a great deal of money to individuals who do not have proper credit standing so that they can obtain money from legitimate money sources such as banks and lending institutions. The interest on these loans is usually "6 for 5" which means that the borrower must pay back an extra dollar for every five dollars which he borrows. This extra dollar is paid each week for the entire period that any amount of the principle of the loan is outstanding. It is believed that Sam DeStefano was the first hoodlum to discover this line of activity."

The FBI had obtained information that Sam DeStefano was in Rome, Italy, on July 29, 1960, and was heading to London, England. Wondering what Mad Sam was up to, FBI agents set out to uncover his motive. Among things learned, one was that Sam DeStefano had instructed his attorney to study existing extradition treaties between the United States and Brazil and to obtain a passport for Sam so he could go to Brazil to look it over as possible living quarters since he had become upset by the FBI's current investigation into his business dealings. A Chicago informant told the FBI that there was a possibility that DeStefano was considering the investment of a large sum of money in a business in Brazil and that he was considering leaving the United States for Brazil in this regard.

Also uncovered was that on June 1, 1960, a request by DeStefano was made to the passport agency for renewal of his passport for proposed travel to Brazil. Informants indicated that DeStefano had mentioned plans about traveling to France, England, Italy, Spain, Sweden, Switzerland, Germany, Denmark, Australia, Japan, and Beirut.

When Sam returned to the United States, FBI agents interviewed Sam DeStefano on August 24, 1960. DeStefano denied that he had any connections with organized crime in Chicago, which he referred to as "the outfit."

DeStefano told the agents that he was considered "dynamite" by the outfit and that he has always operated independently from the "big shots" in the outfit.

He recalled, however, that he had been called in by leaders of the outfit on several occasions and when asked to elucidate concerning this, he stated that in approximately 1948 he had a run-in with a close relative of one of the "big shots" in the outfit. He said that he slapped this individual in the mouth, and when the individual told him he would report him "out west," he informed this individual that he could *go west, go east, go north, go south, I don't give a fuck, just get the fuck out of my sight.*

Because of the above altercation, he said, he was called before the then ranking member of the outfit, who he refused to identify, and had to go to the "headquarters" of the syndicate which he said was in Cicero. He stated that the leader of the syndicate told him to sit down and asked him whether he wanted money. DeStefano said, *"Yea, give me three trunks full."* When told to get serious and told that he could be put on the "roll" for $200 or $300 a week, DeStefano said that he told this individual that he wanted no part of any connection with the outfit and he just wanted to be left alone. The syndicate leader then told him, he said, that he was the best gun in the City of Chicago and that this individual should get the best man that he has in the syndicate and they will go *"right out on 22nd Street and will put belly to belly and gun to gun and we'll see who's the tops."*

DeStefano stated that he advised this individual that he knew that the syndicate was too much for him and that they were too well organized and that if they wanted to, they could take him but that he was a better man than any one man in the Chicago crime syndicate.

There were many reports from FBI informants with information on Sam DeStefano that where contained in FBI files. They showed and explained the fear that many of these informants had towards DeStefano and being connected with him.

Another Chicago informant advised that DeStefano was perhaps the most ruthless and vicious killer in Chicago at that time. He said that DeStefano took a fiendish delight in torturing people who became delinquent in the repayment of loans he made to them. DeStefano also engaged in financing, not only for "juice," but also for the commission of other crimes and in hijacking, in particular. Chicago informants advised that DeStefano had a crew of several hoodlums working under his direction who hijacked trailer loads of merchandise and that DeStefano fenced the stolen goods after they were stolen.

One Chicago informant furnished information in 1961 that Sam DeStefano was not a member of organized crime in the Chicago. He was not a member of the organization controlled by Sam Giancana and did not operate under the supervision of Giancana or any other lieutenants of Giancana. This informant added that the only member of organized crime in Chicago who was closely associated with DeStefano was William "Willie Potatoes" Daddono Sr. This informant furnished information indicating that the leaders of organized crime allowed DeStefano to operate his "juice" activities in the Chicago area, but that he was not under the control of these individuals.

Mad Sam loved to tell people how powerful he was. One incident occurred when Sam explained to a reporter in 1961 that, "I loan money to friends, relatives, and some criminals and hoodlums. If a guy is a criminal, he really pays; those burglars and robbers, I sock them good. I'm not a 'juice' agent for William Daddono or Sam Lewis or any other gangster, I'm Sam De, the big guy, I work alone. Those 'juice' customers, who else can they go to for money but me? They don't have any money, friends, reputation or credit. They can't get money from a bank. So they come to me and I clip them. Some people are sent to me, see? They got a big proposition. They want a lot of money; they got a big venture. If a guy says he stands to make $5,000 on a venture, I'll handle it and take $1,000. That's just the way big business does business. They move in and take a part of your business if you can't keep up your payments, and so do I. Those guys who came to me for money always needed a police fix, too. Why, I used to get up in the middle of the night to go down to the police station to arrange things. I used to settle the case right inside the police station. But now, with all the police reform, I don't even go *inside those joints."*

During a June 28, 1961, interview with DeStefano and FBI agents, DeStefano became aware of the fact that Chicago police officers were taking movies of everybody entering his residence. He stated that he became quite excited over this and charged out into the street with his pistol threatening to kill the police officers. He stated that the police officers denied they were police officers and fled. DeStefano said that he then went down to Orlando Wilson's office and requested that he be advised if he is under investigation by the Chicago PD and asked whether the individuals taking movies of his residence were, in fact, police officers. He stated that when he was told that records of the Chicago PD showed he was not the subject of any investigation and that the individuals above were not known to be police officers, he informed the Police Commissioner's Office that under these circumstances, he must assume that the individuals involved in the above activities were interested in kidnapping his children and that he wanted to go on record at that time that if such occurrence should happen again, he will have no hesitation in killing the individuals involved. He stated that he informed the Police Commissioner's Office that he wanted it clearly understood and made a matter of record so that he would be fully justified in shooting anyone who engaged in similar activities in the future. However, on December 30, 1961, the Chicago PD advised FBI agents that the Intelligence Unit of the Chicago PD had been conducting daily surveillances during the recent months at the residence of DeStefano.

At the beginning of the 1960's, one report discussed the situation of Mad Sam and his control over Cicero concerning "juice" loans. That report, dated November 1961, reported that mobster Gustav "Gus" Kringas moved his gambling empire into the building at 4901 Roosevelt Road in Cicero from his old establishment called "Gus' Steak House." The new operation was set up by Kringas and two other mobsters, one named Frank "Sharkey" Eulo, listed at the time as an errand boy for mob boss Sam Giancana and boss of the 14th Street handbook and the other, Joe "Pepe" Giancana, listed as the "big wheel" in syndicate gambling in Cicero and brother to Sam. At the new location, you gained entry at the rear porch of the building by pressing a buzzer on the wall. Four syndicate hoodlum lookouts would decide if you were "ok" to enter. If so, a huge steel door would swing open and you were led to the gaming room. Once you lost all your money and needed to pay up, or needed more money to gamble, you were sent out to the pizzeria and pancake house at 13th and Cicero Avenue to see Mario for a "juice" loan. The area was designated "Sam DeStefano's" territory, charging 20 percent "juice" loans with a cut going to Sam Giancana.

As for Gus Kringas, he was exposed as a city of Chicago employee being listed as a $424 a month rat control expert. When Ted C. Epping, then deputy of street and sanitation, commented on the Kringas investigation, he said that, "He was checked by one of our best investigators and no connection to gambling was found. He isn't that smart, you have to be a sharpie to operate a place like that."

DeStefano, Crime Consultant

DeStefano proudly announced his 1960 income tax return to the public in an interview. He reported that he received more than $28,000 as a "consultant" to criminals. When Chicago detectives asked Sam about his claims on the tax return, DeStefano replied, "I never would think of cheating the government. I'm worth a lot of money, a whole lot of money."

He even called his two children into the room and ordered them to tell the police how he set up $13,000 in trust funds for each of them. He then went to a hiding place in his bedroom and pulled out a receipt book and payment records on one $4,000 borrower showing that his interest came to over $1,000. Because of this interview, federal and state officials opened an investigation stating that, "It is illegal for Sam DeStefano to function as a bondsman without a license. If we find that he had done that, we will prosecute him. DeStefano is facing a fine of $500 and a jail sentence up to a term of one year for each instance in which he posted bonds without a license."

The FBI learned that DeStefano was the actual owner of a bail bonds service, which was being fronted for him by one of his associates, Peter Cappelletti. The business was known as Cappy's Bail Bond Service, located at 26th and California in Chicago, right next door to the Cook

County Jail. An informant told the FBI that it was a legitimate bail bond company but that DeStefano's "juice" loan payments could be made there from his illegal enterprises.

When DeStefano was interviewed by agents in June of 1961 about his bail bond activities, he told them that at the present time he was financially behind a bonding company. He added that his name did not appear on any of the records of the company and it was being run for him as a front. He refused to identify the bonding company or the name of the person running it for him. He denied he charged a usurious rate of interest and stated that ordinarily an individual will come to him in need of money to invest in a business deal. He stated that he would listen to the details of the business deal and decide whether it appeared to stand a reasonable chance of being rewarded. If not, he refused to make the loan. If it appeared to be promising, he made the loans on the condition that he was reimbursed a certain percentage of the profits of the business venture.

He's Just Dumb

In April 1961, a war for control of a Chicago garbage scavenger business was under way and Chicago "juice" loan operations were caught in the middle. Some of the names mentioned in the war were mobsters William "Willie Potatoes" Daddono, Leo Rugendorf, and Sam DeStefano. It was called a clumsy move, by law enforcement agencies, when DeStefano entered the garbage strife. A squad of Chicago detectives followed DeStefano to a restaurant on the west side where mobsters were congregating for a meeting involving the garbage war. There he met with William Daddono, whose West Suburban Scavenger Service Company was in a fight for control with the members of the Chicago and Suburban Refuse Disposal association over the removal of lucrative garbage from Chicago's restaurants, nightclubs, and commercial stores.

After the meeting, Mad Sam and Daddono got into DeStefano's Cadillac and drove down Chicago Avenue. The detectives who had been following DeStefano decided to pull him over. They walked up to the driver's side window and knocked on the glass, motioning to DeStefano to roll down his window. While Daddono sat in silence, the detective asked DeStefano *"Who's your friend?"* DeStefano replied, *"Oh, he's just a dummy, he can't talk, he's deaf and dumb."* Playing along with DeStefano, the policeman stood there for half an hour while DeStefano made up sign language to try to communicate to Daddono as to what was happening. In return, Daddono wiggled his fingers back at DeStefano acknowledging his signs. Finally, the policeman gave up and told DeStefano, *"Tell Willie Potatoes we know who he is."*

Emotionally unstable in '62

While FBI agents continued to put pressure on the Chicago outfit, Sam DeStefano was labeled "emotionally unstable" and "most excitable" by FBI agent William F. Roemer. While Agent Roemer investigated another mobster named Ernest "Rocky" Infelice, he learned that Infelice was in big trouble with someone from the Chicago mob over money he owed to them. As a result, this person ordered and burned down Infelice's steak house located at 8500 West North Avenue known as the "North Avenue Steak House." During the investigation, a large outstanding "juice" loan was uncovered by Roemer; this loan was owed to Sam DeStefano. Roemer investigated DeStefano and reported that he, DeStefano, had a proclivity for setting fires in fits of rage over incidents, which he considered personal insults, or as a method of disciplining recalcitrant associates or customers who were delinquent in payments of "juice loans."

One such incident involving Mad Sam using fire as a weapon came on November 26, 1962, when there was a fire at the Café Chablis Restaurant, located at 6500 West North Avenue in Chicago. Chicago detectives stated that their investigation developed information indicating that possibly this restaurant was bombed and set ablaze due to the fact that Sam DeStefano was thrown out of the Café Chablis the night before the fire. According to an informant, it is possible that this restaurant was bombed by DeStefano through his hired "juice" collectors and muscle men due to the embarrassment caused to DeStefano by his eviction.

DeStefano was a main suspect in many of the Chicago fires connected to the Outfit. In June 1965, the Illinois Crime Investigation committee investigated two fires from March of that year where an apartment building, apparently owned by Sam DeStefano, burned down. The building at 152 W. Superior Street contained 21 apartments that were in a trust held in the names of Sam and Anita DeStefano. The investigation also discovered that the DeStefano's owned a truck stop restaurant, possibly taken over when the previous owner couldn't keep up with his "juice" payments. The fires were not listed as arsons and were originally determined to be caused by faulty wiring. The report stated that DeStefano had sold the building to his nephew, Angelo Milano, for $82,500 shortly before the fire but had never turned over the deed for the building.

Agent Roemer's official statement on DeStefano read, "*Sam DeStefano is emotionally unstable and most excitable. Many occurrences which would not disturb a normal person are said to put DeStefano into fits of rage during which time he is liable to commit crimes of violence far outweighing the reason for his anger.*"

Sam was duped

Another reason for Sam to get upset in 1962 was because of Carl Greene. Greene was known as a jukebox tycoon who drove a Rolls Royce and owned a stable of horses. Greene and his family disappeared at the beginning 1962. Reports came out that Greene was a friend to many syndicate gangsters at the racetracks and had taken "juice" loans totaling over $80,000 from Sam DeStefano, William Daddono, Sam Farrugia, and Morris Saletko, known as Maishie Baer. These loans were reportedly set up through mobsters Bill Gold and gang vice joint operator Vernon Fein. It was believed that Greene made the "juice" loans for as much as he could get, sold everything he could converting it into cash, then with over $500,000 in cash, packed up his family and headed for either Brazil, Cuba, or Argentina to live out his life. It was reported that the "juice" men had to accept that they were duped out of their money.

"I Ran the State"

In February 1962, a federal grand jury announced that it would be investigating the links between the Chicago syndicate and the Milwaukee syndicate. The focus was on Milwaukee, mob boss Frank Balistreri and Chicago hoodlums Felix "Milwaukee Phil" Alderisio, Albert "Obbie" Frabotta, Paul "Red" Dorfman, Jim "Don Vincenzo" De George, and Sam DeStefano. Frabotta, DeStefano, and Alderisio had a loan shark agreement between the two mobs that granted them money-lending rights in the Milwaukee underground.

Two of the reasons for DeStefano's name being focused on in the investigation was a result of his arrests in Wisconsin in 1947. The police found a little black book with many of his hoodlum associates names listed in it. Many of the names were those of Milwaukee gang figures. The other was when he was in prison in Waupum and he told the authorities that he "ran this state." No charges were ever filed against DeStefano; one informant said he had been told by Mad Sam that he would never have trouble in the state of Wisconsin again since they were scared to death to have him back as an inmate in their state.

The Beginning of the End

Mad Sam being escorted by the Rockford, IL Police Dept.

In October 1962, Sam DeStefano hopped into his Thunderbird auto and headed up state to Rockford, Illinois, to help a fellow hoodlum who had been arrested. One of DeStefano's boys was arrested and charged with forgery. Vito Zaccagnini and an Arthur Balaban were arrested in September 1962 for attempting to cash forged money orders. Balaban pleaded guilty to the charge and was sentenced to five years in prison while Zaccagnini was released on $10,000 bond awaiting his trial. DeStefano arrived at the Winnebago County Sheriff's office in downtown Rockford and announced himself as a "legal representative" of attorney Robert McDonnell and demanded an interview with Arthur Balaban.

DeStefano was told that he could only speak to Balaban with permission from the state's attorney William Nash. So, DeStefano went to see William Nash in his office and announced his name and stated the purpose of his visit. According to DeStefano, after a few minutes, Nash rose quickly from his chair and accused him of lying and told him to get out of his office, slamming the door immediately thereafter. DeStefano claimed he tried to reason with Nash and asked when he had lied to him. Nash said, *"You have already lied to me twice, now get out of my office."* DeStefano then stated that Nash came to his door, went into the hallway, and ordered DeStefano from the building telling him if he didn't leave, he would have him arrested. DeStefano said it was a public building and he was there to perform a chore for attorney McDonnell and that if Mr. Nash wanted him, he would be in the courtroom downstairs. DeStefano then headed down the stairs to the courtroom where another case was being heard. DeStefano sat down in the back of the courtroom refusing to leave. He was called back out into the corridor, at which time several deputies standing there ordered him from the building. When he refused to leave, they then placed him under arrest. DeStefano shouted, *"Get your hands off me. You hicks are talking to one million dollars in cash. You can't lock me up."*

DeStefano was searched, his money amounting to approximately $790 was taken along with his glasses, pills, and other personal property, and he was placed in a cell, charged with disorderly conduct. When they searched DeStefano, a piece of paper was found which contained the signature of Arthur Balaban in which Balaban exonerated Zaccagnini for any complicity in the forgery plot. DeStefano was then taken to be fingerprinted, at which time DeStefano asked the officer to call Mr. Nash. DeStefano was informed that Nash would come over after his fingerprints had been taken. DeStefano refused to sign his fingerprint card on the grounds that he was not required under the law of Illinois to sign anything. An assistant state's attorney by the name of Gene advised DeStefano that if he did not sign the fingerprint card he would not be let out of jail.

DeStefano then asked the sheriff to give him $200 of the $790 that had been taken from him so that he could post his bond. The sheriff refused.

DeStefano then received a phone call from one of his associates named Leo Foreman who was in Chicago and in the course of the conversation; he informed Foreman that the Rockford police were acting like the "Gestapo." The police immediately cut off the phone call and placed Sam back in his cell. To anger Sam further, the police refused to accommodate him in any way. When DeStefano asked the sheriff if he could have some lunch, he was told that lunch had already been served and he would have to wait until dinner for any water or food. Sam, disgusted with the lack of respect he believed he should have received, sat in his cell screaming and yelling about how they would regret their actions one day. Later in the day, Leo Foreman arrived with money. DeStefano posted a $200 bond and was released.

Mad Sam and Leo Foreman in Rockford, Illinois

DeStefano, Foreman, and another DeStefano associate walked out of the courthouse with Nash right behind them. Foreman urged DeStefano to ride home in his car and he agreed. The plan was to have Sam's other associate drive DeStefano's Thunderbird home for him. DeStefano and Foreman walked to Foreman's car, which was, parked about 50 feet away from the Thunderbird while Sam's associate opened the door to DeStefano's car, and sat down. Before either car could start its engines, eight or nine deputy sheriffs appeared and surrounded DeStefano's car. Noticing the commotion, DeStefano jumped out of Foreman's car and ran over to his car to see what was going on. The deputies noticed a two-foot long billy-club next to the driver's seat in DeStefano's car. DeStefano was once again placed under arrested for carrying a weapon. DeStefano, enraged, shouted, "Communist" as he was pulled away and carried back inside to his cell.

As he was being hauled back in, DeStefano begged and pleaded with them to let him go home because he was a sick, but they wouldn't do so. He was officially charged with possessing a bludgeon, a violation of Chapter 28, Section 24-1, of the Illinois Code and his bail was set at

$1,000. There he sat for 2 hours until a bondsman arrived with his $800 bond.

The next day DeStefano and Foreman went to D. Arthur Connelly, then chief of the criminal division of the U.S. Attorney's office, to file a complaint that his civil rights had been ignored. During the 80-minute meeting, DeStefano told Connelly his version of what happened step-by-step. He told him that two of the guards took turns at roughing him up. He even showed Mr. Connelly all of the bruises on his body and showed them his left arm, which was extremely bruised. He informed Connelly that, *"I do a lot of legwork for a Chicago lawyer, Robert McDonnell, who is in the hospital. But I didn't tell the sheriff that I was a lawyer. That would have been a crime."*

DeStefano said about the billy-club, *"The club is a Chicago police department billy. It belongs to my nephew, Robert Milano, a Chicago police officer. I don't know how Milano spells his name but he uses my car a lot. He must have left the club in the car."* Leo Foreman also told Connelley how upset they were that an FBI agent that he had known from a previous meeting was there at the courthouse watching their every step. After the meeting, both Sam and Foreman left Rockford.

On November 3, 1963, Leo Foreman appeared at the Chicago offices of the FBI, identified himself as a bail bondsman, and said he was active in a trucking business in Chicago. He stated that he had come to the FBI office to demand protection for Sam DeStefano who was to appear in the state court in Rockford on November 5. Foreman identified himself as a friend of Sam DeStefano and further identified DeStefano as a friend of Vito Zaccagnini. He then explained Zaccagnini's story and what happened to DeStefano the last time he was in Rockford. Foreman then said that the day before the arrest he and Sam DeStefano were sitting as observers in the courtroom in Rockford when the judge entered the courtroom, stood up and pointed at DeStefano, telling the bailiff to remove the two men from the court. Then the bailiffs or sheriff's deputies came forward and, even though DeStefano said that he would leave peacefully, they pushed and shoved him from the courtroom and continued to push and shove him when he was in the corridor outside the courtroom. Foreman said the officers looked as if they were going to push and shove him, Foreman, but he told them not to do so and they did not push him.

Foreman said that, *"Since the federal government is giving protection to the African Americans at the University of Mississippi, then good citizens like DeStefano and Foreman should be given protection by the FBI."* He subsequently requested that one or more FBI agents accompany DeStefano to the courtroom in Rockford and that the FBI agents observe the treatment that DeStefano would receive in this courtroom.

Later that day, a man called the FBI offices in Chicago, identified himself as Sam DeStefano, and said that he was calling to ask for the protection of the FBI when he appears at court. He related that he had sent Leo Foreman to the FBI offices and that Foreman had reported back to him. DeStefano said that this trouble started when he appeared on October 15, 1962, in the courtroom at Rockford for the purpose of getting a continuance for a friend, Vito Zaccagnini. He explained that he is not a lawyer nor was he a bondsman; however, his wife was a bondsman and had posted bond for Zaccagnini. He was merely acting, on this date, as a messenger or spokesman for his wife, the bondsman. He explained the situation, that Zaccagnini's attorney, Robert McDonnell, was in a sanitarium in New England and could not appear at court, and he merely requested that there be a continuance until the attorney could appear in court. He added that the judge ordered him to leave the courtroom and the sheriff's deputy at Rockford became angry because DeStefano stood on his constitutional rights and declined to sign his fingerprint card.

Mad Sam points at the press

DeStefano then read, to the agent on the phone, the newspaper article from the *Rockford Morning Star* telling the agent how right they got the story, adding various statements and observations. At that time, DeStefano went into a rage and spoke in a raving and incoherent manner. The agent said it sounded as if DeStefano were crying and made statements including, "*What am I to do, get a gun to protect myself? If I kill somebody, you'll send me to the electric chair, then I'll get some national publicity.*"

An attempt was made by the agents to reiterate to Sam DeStefano that his complaint had been received and referred to the Department of Justice and that the FBI does not furnish observers or the protection he requested. DeStefano stated, among other things, that he was an honest, law abiding citizen, but did not explain in detail. He also stated that he owned a large amount of property, all free and clear, and that he could produce large sums of money in cash if needed. He said that his government had let him down and was forcing him to get a gun to protect himself in court. He wanted to know the phone number of Attorney General Robert Kennedy or how to get in touch with him, and stated that he was either going to call the Attorney General or fly to Washington to see him.

When DeStefano appeared at his court date in Rockford, he served as his own lawyer once again. In normal Mad Sam fashion, he confused everyone in the courtroom when he approached the jury and asked, "*Have you ever seen an elephant?*" Moments later DeStefano suddenly changed his plea to guilty, telling the jury, "*Something had come to light that I had not known before.*" A confused jury found him guilty and fined him $100 on his disorderly conduct charge.

Traffic Court

On May 5, 1963, Chicago detectives sat outside Sam Giancana's Villa Venice restaurant in Northbrook, Illinois, watching all the Chicago mobsters arrive for the wedding of Ronald English and Diane Altieri. The two were the son and daughter of mobsters Sam "Butch" English and Cicero bookmaker Donald Altieri. As Sam DeStefano arrived at the gala affair, Chicago detectives welcomed him and shouted, "*Are you ready for traffic court Sam?*"

Three days later, Sam DeStefano arrived at traffic court for a traffic ticket he received on April 7 of that year. On that night, undercover detectives had been watching from their unmarked squad car, listing the hoodlums attending the wake of mobster Mike Spranze at the Montclair

Funeral home on Belmont Avenue. They noticed that a white 1962 Cadillac spun out of the parking lot, heading the wrong way on a one-way street. The undercover police placed their flashing light and siren on top of their auto and sped after the Cadillac. The Cadillac sped around the block heading back to the parking lot of the funeral home, stopping right in front of the main entrance. According to police, William "Potatoes" Daddono jumped out of the passenger side seat of the Cadillac and ran back into the funeral home screaming to anyone who would listen, *"I got nothing to do with this."* Then Sam DeStefano stepped out of the car and asked the police *"What's wrong?"* The officer commanded DeStefano to open the trunk of his Cadillac, DeStefano replied, *"I won't open it, there might be a body in there."*

Because the two officers were undercover police, they usually did not arrest people or carry routine arrest slips with them. They were forced to call for a marked police car and a uniformed policeman so they could issue a ticket to DeStefano for going the wrong way on a one-way street. When the police officer arrived, DeStefano pleaded his case, insisting the undercover policemen's eyes had mistaken DeStefano's Cadillac for the actual lawbreaker's auto. The cop didn't buy it and Mad Sam was issued a ticket.

Once again, DeStefano acted as his own lawyer, with attorney Robert McDonnell at his side. Mad Sam made sure the judge knew that he, DeStefano, was representing himself and that McDonnell was just there as an associate. DeStefano wore his trademark suit, which he had worn every time he defended himself in court. The suit was sincer-blue worsted, at the time eight years old, remodeled from an old double-breasted style suit. It was said he wore that suit for "effect" when he told the judges and jury how wronged he was and how defenseless and how nice he was.

When the case was called, DeStefano stepped up and asked the judge to exclude all the witnesses. The judge was not aware that the witnesses DeStefano asked to be dismissed included one of the policemen from that night. The judge then sent the undercover cop to the judge's chamber, unaware of the mistake he had made. DeStefano managed to win his case and have the ticket thrown out because DeStefano proved that the officer who wrote the ticket did not witness DeStefano drive the wrong way on the one-way street. After the case was dismissed, the judge said, *"I didn't know the policeman was in my chambers. If I had known that, I probably would have fined DeStefano."*

Mad Sam won his case but the police did manage to fine him $200 for contempt by the judge for the confusion he caused in courtroom.

In September 1963, the police were able to catch Sam once again when he was arrested in Lyons, Illinois, for speeding on Ogden Avenue. This time he was unable to win his case.

Sam DeStefano

Chapter Nine

The 1964 FBI Investigation

In March 1964 the FBI opened file Number, 92-7456 entitled "Sam DeStefano, Anti-Racketeering." This investigation focused on Mad Sam, where other investigations on Sam involved many other subject files. In the opening statement of the file it reads, *"This case is being placed in a pending inactive status in order that a control file will be maintained concerning other investigations opened in which Sam DeStefano is a principal. It is noted that at least three other cases are pending in the Chicago Office with DeStefano as a subject."*

That year would turn out to be a very active year for Sam with his name being mentioned almost weekly in the Chicago area newspapers.

The report began with what his immediate family was doing as of 1964. The report read, *"DeStefano's immediate family consisted of his wife Anita, whom he referred to as "Nita," his son John Eager Phillip DeStefano who was listed as attending Regis College in Denver, Colorado, a twin sister to John named Sandra Ann DeStefano and another daughter named Janice, both listed as attending St. Dominic College in St. Charles, Illinois. He and his family resided at 1656 Sayre in Chicago. During a 1961 interview with DeStefano, he advised FBI agents that he was thinking of selling his home at the time asking $72,000 for it. Information was received by the FBI in 1963 that a for-sale sign was on the front lawn of his house. DeStefano advised that he was considering moving from Chicago to DuPage County, Illinois."*

At the time of this investigation, attention was focused on his brothers and their involvement in Sam DeStefano's rackets. Mario was considered the right-hand man for his brother Sam, running most of his enterprises. With his brother Mike dead, reports on James DeStefano were explored. However, it could not be determined if the reports were of Mad Sam's older brother James or another hoodlum named Jimmy DeStefano. The reports on James DeStefano are listed as follows:

1) One report dated August 1938 concerned the murder of hoodlum Joseph LaPorte. In the report, it mentioned that 42 Gang members Mike Messina, his brother Dominic Messina, Joseph LaPorte, and James DeStefano were all arrested together and questioned. After questioning, LaPorte was released when James DeStefano and the Messina brothers admitted that they robbed the Kerman Stores Company at 160 N. Michigan Avenue of $5,000 in furs, along with another hoodlum named Ambrose Russo. They said Russo was cut by glass when they broke in through the door. Mike Messina admitted dumping Russo's almost decapitated body in front of Mother Cabrini Hospital. Dominick Messina and James DeStefano plead guilty to the robbery and were sentenced to a year in Bridewell prison. As for Joseph LaPorte, it was believed that he opened his mouth too many times to police about his friend's crime waves. He was stood up against a garage wall and shot once in the mouth, once in the face, and three times in the back of the head as the Garfield Park "L" train drowned out the shots in the night air.

2) In 1947, a "police character" known as James "Jimmy the Hoop" DeStefano was arrested and questioned in the murder of Mrs. Leda Duty. Duty was killed in her dress shop on Bryn Mawr Avenue. It could not be determined if this was the brother of Sam DeStefano.

3) In 1964, it was reported that the brother of Sam DeStefano, known as Jimmy DeStefano, was working as a collector for mob boss Fifi Buccieri. The Chicago Crime Commission reported that Jimmy DeStefano, brother of Sam, was an independent juicer but under control of the mob. They list Leo Foreman as Jimmy's main collector and enforcer before Foreman was found dead in the trunk of his car.

An FBI informant told the agents in September 1971 that Jimmy DeStefano had quit the rackets and gone "legit" and had nothing to do with his brothers Sam and Mario. James DeStefano died in October 2000 and is buried at tier 2 of the Church Garden Mausoleum at Queen of Heaven Cemetery in Hillside, Illinois.

The file discussed that almost every source acquainted with Sam DeStefano advised them that he conducted most of his business from his residence on North Sayre Street. The file even spoke about how

Sam DeStefano considered himself an excellent gin rummy player and frequently engaged in games in his home with his hoodlum associates and lesser hoodlums.

One section of the file gave this account of Mad Sam, "*Chicago informants have all furnished information substantially to the effect that Sam DeStefano is a sadistic killer who takes great pleasure in torturing and beating, as well as in killing, anyone who crosses his path in any fashion. One informant who is close to DeStefano described DeStefano as a highly emotional, temperamental individual who loses his temper at the drop of a hat. He is extremely egotistic and concerned with his personal appearance. The walls of his home are lined with mirrors and as DeStefano talks to people, he continually watches his reflection in these mirrors as he walks across the room. One of our agents has noted that DeStefano is of such a temperament that he can be crying at one moment and laughing the very next. He considers himself a great person and frequently remarks 'The world lost a great man when they framed Sam DeStefano for rape at the age of 17.' He feels that if he had not been 'framed' in this regard, he might now be the president of the United States.*"

Associates

There is a section in the file of the 1964 investigation entitled "Associates of Sam DeStefano" which lists some of the members of organized crime that DeStefano was known to be in contact with at that time or the contacts that he admitted knowing. Listed below are the names and descriptions of those listed in the file.

Anthony Accardo

On August 24, 1960, FBI agents interviewed Sam DeStefano at which time he admitted that he was a very close friend of Tony Accardo, who he refers to as Joe Batters, and his wife Clarice Accardo. He stated that Accardo frequently visits his residence and the last time, prior to the interview, was on August 14, 1960. DeStefano stated that he has frequently visited Accardo at Accardo's residence at 915 Franklin Avenue in River Forest.

On May 11, 1961, the Chicago PD furnished the FBI with a list of individuals who attended the marriage of Linda Lee Accardo and Michael A. Palermo on April 27, 1961. It was noted that Sam and Anita DeStefano were present at the gathering.

Phil Alderisio

Files indicate that "Milwaukee Phil" Alderisio is a friend of Sam DeStefano and that Alderisio had visited the DeStefano residence on three occasions during the months of May thru July 1963

William "Smokes" Aliosio

Chicago files advised that "Smokes" Alioiso was a prisoner at Leavenworth Federal Penitentiary in Kansas at the same time that Sam DeStefano was there. Alioiso and DeStefano have remained good friends ever since.

Briatta Family

When DeStefano was arrested in Wisconsin in 1946, a notebook was taken from the person of Sam DeStefano. The following notations were written in the book, "M Briatta, Hay, 9757" and John B. and Son, 1074 West Polk Street (barbers)."

According to FBI files, the barbershop located at the corner of 1074 West Polk Street in 1946 was the focal point of the operations of the Briatta brothers; Louis, Joe, Mike, Tom, and John; most who were prominent Chicago bookmakers.

In 1962 a car registered to Sam DeStefano was observed at the wedding of Michael Briatta Jr. and Diane Marterie, daughter of musician big band leader Ralph Marterie, who is related to Frank "Frankie X" Esposito, syndicate labor leader in Chicago.

Joseph Colucci

Included in the above described notebook taken from DeStefano in 1946 was the following, "J.C. – 2961 Madison, Park Side Motors, 2810 West Madison." Chicago advised that Joseph Colucci is the owner of Park Side Motors and that he is an associate of organized crime in Chicago.

William "Willie Potatoes" Daddono

Intelligence Unit, Chicago PD advised that they arrested Sam DeStefano in 1963 in the company of William Daddono. Sam DeStefano advised FBI agents on June 28, 1961, that at that time he was very upset due to the writings of Sandy Smith, a reporter with the Chicago Tribune newspaper. DeStefano advised that when the Chicago PD stopped him and Willie Daddono, as set out above, he made "the coppers look like idiots" whereas the version of this occurrence as written by Smith made "the coppers look like heroes" and made DeStefano and Daddono look like idiots.

Paul DeLucia, aka Paul "The Waiter" Ricca

Sam DeStefano was associated with Paul DeLucia in 1947 while in the U.S. Penitentiary at Leavenworth, Kansas. DeStefano acted as a go-between for DeLucia and was involved in the murder of Chicago Police Lieutenant William J. Drury, who was slain in the garage of his residence in Chicago in October 1950.

John Lardino

On September 9, 1959, Oak Park PD advised that they had observed an automobile registered to Sam DeStefano at the residence of John Lardino, 1201 Bellefonte Avenue in Oak Park, during the months of 1959. John Lardino was a labor union boss and known mobster.

Sam Giancana

Among notations found in the notebook described previously, which was taken from the person of DeStefano in 1946, was "Mooney, Col.6422." Chicago advised that this is a well-known alias of Sam "Momo" Giancana, Chicago mob boss.

DeStefano advised FBI agents on August 24, 1960, that he is a good friend of Sam Giancana, having grown up with Giancana on Taylor Street in Chicago. He stated, however, that he has not been particularly close to Giancana during the past several years, although he runs into Giancana from time to time at various wakes and other gatherings.

A Chicago informant stated that he has observed Sam DeStefano making large loans ranging in the amounts of $5,000 to $100,000 to Chicago hoodlums. This informant advised that in May 1964 he had a conversation with another leading member of organized crime in Chicago and that it was the opinion of this individual that DeStefano was not under the discipline of Sam Giancana; however, on numerous occasions has made large non-profit loans to various members of organized crime that are under Giancana.

Leonard Gianola

Located in the notebook on the person of Sam DeStefano when arrested in 1946 was "Needles, Mon. 4950." Chicago advised that "Needles" is the well-known nickname of Chicago hoodlum Leonard Gianola.

Gianola was born on November 19, 1910, in Chicago and lived at 7344 N. Tripp Avenue in Lincolnwood. In 1932, he was sentenced to months in prison for malicious mischief and in 1935, he was convicted on federal charges of theft from interstate commerce.

He was also a labor leader for the mob-controlled Cleaning and Dye House Workers International Union Local 46 in Chicago with hoodlum Gus Zapas. In 1969, Gianola was listed as being involved in "juice" operations at the corners of Halsted Street and Congress Parkway, Racine Avenue and Taylor Street, and Diversey and Pine Grove Avenues in Chicago. Gianola died in July 1974.

Two Sam DeStefanos

During an investigation, it was learned that there were two Chicago hoodlums by the name of Sam DeStefano. The other Sam DeStefano lived at 1113 North 20th Street in Melrose Park, Illinois, in the 1930's and 40's. Born in Italy in 1909, he came to America around 1929 and was arrested 2 years later on December 25, 1931, for bootlegging and served 90 days in Cook County Jail. He was arrested once again on April 22, 1939, when he was hauling materials to a working still and alcohol from the still. Arrested with him was Carl Culicchia, aka John Cole, aka Karlo Papis, from Oak Park, Illinois, and Eugene Presta from Chicago. It's believed this Sam DeStefano died in February 2004.

Legitimate business for DeStefano

FBI agents wanted to find out if DeStefano had any legitimate business he was using in his "juice" operations. One Chicago informant advised that Sam DeStefano owned an apartment building at 152 West Superior and Clark Streets on the near Northside of Chicago. It was this informant's belief that the legal papers for the property indicated that one Angelo Milano was the actual owner of this building. The informant insisted that DeStefano owned the building and used Milano as a front in the operation of the building to hide his interest. Angelo Milano was a Chicago Police Officer at the time and a nephew of DeStefano.

Sam DeStefano's health as of 1964

A section in the file gave concern as to the health status of Sam DeStefano in 1964. As they searched their files, they uncovered reports from informants regarding his health. In 1960, the FBI was contacted by one of its informants concerning the health of Sam DeStefano. The informant stated that DeStefano was suffering from an arthritic sciatica nerve, a slipped disc in his back, and an enlarged prostate gland caused by an old bullet wound.

In March 1962, the FBI was contacted once again concerning DeStefano's health. This time the informant advised that he had recently met Sam DeStefano on the street and hardly recognized him. He said that Sam had had some sort of an operation on his nose and possibly on his facial skin. He had also cut his hair in a crew-cut style and dyed it black. In the past, DeStefano always wore his hair extremely long and it was a naturally steel gray in color. It was the informant's opinion that DeStefano had become more emotionally unstable than ever. He said that DeStefano was extremely surveillance conscious and felt that he was constantly under surveillance, both by the "G" and by the Chicago PD. He said that DeStefano spoke loud and obscenely concerning law enforcement officers. He said it appeared to him that DeStefano was cracking under the strain and even though he always had a persecution complex, this complex had deepened to such an extent that not only was DeStefano constantly stirred up with it, it is possible that some slight provocation might serve to push him off the deep end and to an attempt to physically avenge himself.

In November 1963, the informant contacted the FBI once again and stated that DeStefano was going into the hospital for surgery. DeStefano was seriously ill with cancer of the rectum and was "terrified" that his days were numbered. A week later, the informant said that DeStefano was discharged from the hospital and he was in bad shape. He also added that Sam looked haggard and that he had to make his bowel movements through the use of a bag attached to his side.

This illness could not have come at a worse time since it was reported that DeStefano had in excess of 200 individuals owing him "juice" money at that time. One informant stated that his weekly income or "take" from this "juice" would range between $4,000 and $8,000. It was this informant's opinion that former mob boss Tony Accardo was receiving a cut of DeStefano's "juice" money and was not happy to see his weekly pay-off disappear.

Further information attached to the file concerning DeStefano and Tony Accardo was that *"Sam DeStefano is a heartless and vicious individual who is recognized as 'outfit' being sponsored by Anthony Accardo; however, this source does not believe DeStefano is 'outfit,' but does derive his power and apparent immunity from his friendship with Anthony Accardo."*

It further stated that in 1961 a Chicago informant advised that Sam DeStefano played gin rummy on a regular basis with Tony Accardo, Jack Cerone and, others and it was at these gatherings that DeStefano would pay his tribute to Accardo for letting him run his "juice" operations.

The FBI's investigation on Sam DeStefano lasted until his death. For the rest of his life, the "G" would be watching and doing what they could to destroy Mad Sam.

Chapter Ten

Time to Vote

The FBI turned out to be the least of Mad Sam's problem. The years of 1964 and 1965 were intertwined with one arrest and court appearance after another. It got very confusing as to which day Mad Sam was in court defending himself on which charge since many had been filed against him.

On May 1, 1964, seven Chicago hoodlums could have awakened that morning and begun their daily routine, taken a shower, eaten some breakfast, went to see a guy who owed them money and broken his face; a normal day. On that day, those hoodlums awoke to Chicago detectives standing over them with guns and handcuffs. These detectives were headed by Charles Siragusa, then Executive Director of the Illinois Crime Investigating Commission. Siragusa ordered that the seven be rounded up and arrested. The charge was violating election laws for simply "voting" in a government election. Under the law, ex-convicts can only "vote" in elections after their rights have been restored by a presidential pardon or by gubernatorial action. Siragusa received information that seven hoodlums had "voted" and sent his boys out to get them. The seven hoods caught were:

Joey "Caesar" DiVarco—listed as a Northside mob boss who was convicted of unlawfully possessing, selling, and exchanging $40,000 in counterfeit $10 and $20 bills in 1937.

Anthony "Poolio" DeRosa—a convicted cartage thief who was a muscle man for Chicago Loop gambling boss Louis "Lou the Barber" Briatta. DeRosa was also listed as a labor thug for Frank "Frankie X" Esposito mob labor union boss. DeRosa was also a known "juice" man operating in the areas of Racine Avenue and Polk Street and Roosevelt Road and Narragansett Street.

Charles "Specs" DiCare—a convicted hijacker and daily acquaintance of mob boss Ralph Pierce.

Mike Dakoff—a New York hoodlum who became a Cicero, Illinois, bookmaker for the Chicago outfit. Dakoff had been convicted on November 15, 1932, for robbery in New York.

James Cordovano—a known hoodlum and convicted narcotics dealer. When arrested, Cordovano told the police, *"The next time you take me, you'll have to kill me."*

Mario DeStefano—a convicted murderer and loan shark chief for his brother Sam.

Sam DeStefano—listed as top loan shark boss in Chicago, convicted of rape, counterfeiting, and bank robbery.

When the police entered Sam DeStefano's house to arrest him, he was wearing pink striped pajamas. Once again, Sam tried to offer his "special" Italian piss coffee to the officers but they declined. The police insisted that Sam put on his street clothes before they slapped the cuffs on. After many hours of being questioned and officially booked, DeStefano was released on $2,500 bond. However, Mad Sam fought with the police for 30 minutes as he insisted on not signing a release form so his glasses could be given back to him. He also refused to sign the form to receive his $30, which was taken from him when he was booked. He finally gave in and his possessions were returned. As he walked out, 50 reporters waited and hoped for one of Sam's legendary comments, he simply told them, *"I voted 13 years in my ward and in November I will be back to vote again."*

The official charge:
"Sam DeStefano committed the offence of Illegal Voting in that he knowingly voted at Primary and Aldermanic elections held in the City of Chicago, Cook County, Illinois, and in Precinct 64 of Ward of the City of Chicago, when the said Sam DeStefano had been convicted of the offense of

*rape in Criminal Court of Cook County in the State of Illinois on December
23, 1927, and when the said Sam DeStefano thereafter had never received
a certificate restoring his rights of citizenship from the Governor or Court
entitled to grant such certificate, in violation of Chap. 46, Section 29-26, Il.
Rev. Stat. 1961."*

On May 4, 1961, Mad Sam showed up for his court case wearing pajamas
and was wheeled into the courtroom lying on a portable hospital bed. In
DeStefano's hand was a transistor-operated megaphone, which he would
use to raise his voice because he said he had been weakened by a hernia
and recent abdominal surgery. He began screaming into the megaphone
when the chief of the criminal division for the state's attorney office, John
Stamos, asked him who was representing his brother Mario. DeStefano
replied, "*I am,*" through his megaphone. When Stamos informed him
that it was not possible for him to represent his brother, DeStefano
became so enraged he started screaming without his megaphone. Then
in an attempt to irritate DeStefano further, John Stamos stared at him,
which brought DeStefano's blood to a boil. When the judge entered the
room, he gave the trial a continuance and DeStefano left the courtroom
on his stretcher.

While he was being rolled out, he pointed his megaphone at the witness
and shouted, "*Greetings, gentlemen, hello, stool pigeons.*" Then DeStefano
called Charles Siragusa, "*Snaky Siragusa, the one hundred percent imported
stool pigeon and a thief who has stolen one hundred thousand dollars from the
taxpayers of Illinois,*" through his megaphone to the crowd. The reference
was to Siragusa receiving one hundred thousand dollars as an executive
director of the Illinois Crime Commission. He even sent Siragusa a letter
saying, "*If you should come to Europe in the near future, please stop to visit
me. The welcome mat is always out for you, dear countryman, and we will
make lots of whoopee, and be merry, and sing songs together as we ride among
my vineyards with its fountains overflowing with red, red wine.*"

Two days later Sam DeStefano arrived once again at the courthouse
dressed in a bathrobe and his pajamas and was wheeled in on his
stretcher with his megaphone in hand to sign a $7,500 bond. This time
DeStefano was told by the judge, "*If you bring that megaphone anywhere*

in this building again, you'll be in contempt of court." DeStefano replied, *"Judge, this is my property, I won't use it in your courtroom, but I don't think you have the authority to stop me from using it outside your courtroom."* The judge repeated his treat to DeStefano who replied, *"Counsel for Sam DeStefano objects to the ruling and takes exception."*

While DeStefano sat in the courtroom waiting for the judge to return from a long lunch break, a reporter asked Sam if he could walk. DeStefano became angry and started to rip off his bandages to prove he had stitches from surgery. After DeStefano calmed down, the judge approved his bond. DeStefano responded with, *"An example of judicial tyranny."*

He asked the judge if he could file a petition to have the court hold publisher Marshall Field and reporter Sandy Smith in contempt of court for their news articles and editorials they had published about Mad Sam. The judge refused and told DeStefano he could not file a petition. An angered DeStefano signed his bond and left the court screaming *"Gestapo Cook County justice."*

At the end of the month DeStefano appeared once again, this time he walked into the court and noticed that Internal Revenue agents were waiting in the hallway to serve him papers. DeStefano put his hands up to his ears and shouted, *"I don't want your papers. If you want to serve me with something, you know where I live. Come out to my house,"* then hurried to the elevator making his escape.

All through the month, DeStefano tried to get every media outlet to back him in his case. He even attempted to purchase a small radio station in Chicago so he could broadcast what a bunch of bums he thought the government was, but the deal fell through. The FBI discovered that DeStefano was hired as a regular columnist for the *Chicago Daily Defender* newspaper and his column was going to be under the title of *"An AXE to Grind by Sam DeStefano."* After DeStefano turned in his first two columns, he was fired. The publisher fired him because the columns contained venom against Sandy Smith and many public officials in Chicago.

Contained below is a press release by Sam DeStefano:

Press release Issued by Sam DeStefano:

"Good morning, my fellow Citizens:
I have a few words to say to my fellow Americans.

Wake up, Fellow Americans! Wake up before it is too late! You have in this city, the city of Chicago and the county of Cook-a Gestapo City and County, a Gestapo police department and sheriff, and some Gestapo courts, run by a Gestapo Journal-the Chicago Sun-Times and the Chicago Daily News...who rules your city and county like Khrushchev rules Russia and its people.

You too, are enslaved like the people of Russia are enslaved. Do you want our children to be enslaved too? Do you want yokes around our children's necks? I beg of you, Citizens of Cook County, wake up before it is too late! Did you see and read the editorial page of the Chicago Sun-Times and the Chicago Daily News, Friday, May 8, 1964? Did you read the other articles in the same issues by reporters Frank Sullivan, and mentally ill Sandy Smith? Those editorials and articles were direct criminal contempt of Judge Daniel Ryan of the Felony Court and of Chief Justice Alexander Napoli of the Criminal Court. I ask, in all fairness and justice, to each and every citizen of this country. What are Judge Ryan and Judge Napoli going to do about it? Are they afraid of the Chicago Sun-Times and the Chicago Daily News? Are they going to let the Chicago Sun-Times and Dailey News dictate to them, coerce, and intimidate them, and all our courts, including Chief Justice John Boyle?

I, Sam DeStefano, at no time during my court appearance before Judge Napoli, was contemptuous of the Court; nor did I defy the Court. If I had been, let me assure each and every one of you-Judge Napoli would have sent me to jail for contempt! That same statement about Judge Napoli goes for Judge Ryan, not only on my appearance in his courtroom on Monday, May 4, 1964, but during my trial and persecution in 1962! I demand my equal rights and the protection of the Courts. I respectfully demand that Judge Napoli and Judge Ryan; haul these Gestapo newspaper-gangsters into Court and hold them to answer to the charges of criminal contempt, criminal intimidation, and extortion. Their bite and brazen contempt of the courts is unbelievable! I don't attempt to deny them their legal rights. Marshall Fields, the owner of those two newspapers, a great man in many respects, isn't fooled by his mentally ill reporter, Sandy Smith. Or is he?

101

Page 2

All my legal rights are being denied me, even before the eyes of the whole wide world. What are you good people waiting for? Today, it is me. . . Yesterday, it was Jimmy Hoffa. . . Tomorrow, it will be you, and you, and you, and then, last but not least, our dear children.

Soon our children will be told by our Gestapo Government, where to work. When to breathe. When to go to the lavatory! Yes, I said, when to go to the lavatory!

As you know, a pen is mightier than a sword; but a poisonous pen in more dangerous, more vicious, and much more deadlier than are weapons, bar none, swords, guns, or even atomic bombs! A poisonous pen is like an . . . candor. It spreads all over, not only to the immediate victim, but to his beloved family, his wife, his dear children, his good friends and neighbors, and to all his loved ones, to all humanity throughout the land. A law should be passed against a poisonous pen. The wielder of a poisonous pen is much more a more vicious, inhuman murderer than a murderer with a gun or any other type of weapon. Passing a law of that kind would not be infringing on the freedom of the press. An honest reporter or an honest journalist should not begrudge or deny its citizens of its protection. A poisonous pen murderer is the foulest murderer in the whole wide world, bar none.

Thank you very much for listening to me. I am just a poor victim of a poisonous pen murderer, who is mentally ill, Sandy Smith, reporter for the Chicago Sun-Times.

"/s/ Sam DeStefano
1656 N, Sayre Avenue
Chicago, Illinois 60635

On June 10, 1964, DeStefano was denied a change of venue for his up and coming trial. He attempted to get a change of venue on the grounds that newspapers, radio shows, and TV stories about him over the past 4 years depicted him as a top crime syndicate hoodlum and there was no way to get a fair trial in Cook County. For an hour, DeStefano argued that the publicity was part of a "malicious conspiracy to destroy me and my family." Sam even made Peter Cappelletti and Sam Gallo testify that the alleged adverse publicity would prevent an impartial trial. He introduced 68 newspaper clippings about him to support his motion.

Judge Richard Harewood denied his motion stating that there was no evidence that publicity about him had created prejudice towards him.

While FBI agents listened in at the old First Ward offices in Chicago on a hidden microphone, they overheard mob lawyer Michael Brodkin complain about DeStefano and his ongoing court case. Brodkin commented that, *"This guy is so nuts, he even believes he is a lawyer."* Brodkin continued to complain that DeStefano was constantly attempting to contact him so the two could meet to discuss his case. Brodkin repeatedly told him he was too busy but said, *"I won't have anything to do with him."* He then added a DeStefano story, *"I remember the time he made a loan to some fellow that was no good and then he wanted to shake him. He came to [hoodlums name blocked out] for help. We refused to help because we said he failed to go through the proper channels. When the little guy was living [referring to Jake "Greasy Thumb" Guzik] they had to come through him before coming to us, but when he died, the policy is now that either Humpy* (Murray Humphreys) *Strongy* (Frank Ferraro) *or Mooney* (Sam Giancana) *has to approve before they come to us. By this policy, we don't get involved in something that we shouldn't be in. We'll never get hurt this way."*

Because of DeStefano's wild antics during his past court hearings, Sam DeStefano was not invited to one of the biggest underworld events ever held that night. That evening was the wedding of Anthony Ross Accardo and Janet Marie Hawley at Sam Giancana's Villa Venice. Anthony Ross Accardo was the son of top mob boss Tony "Joe Batters" Accardo. Over 1,000 people attended, all carrying white envelopes stuffed with dirty money. Snubbed were Sam DeStefano and his brother Mario.

Visit to the FBI Offices

On June 29, 1964, Sam DeStefano appeared at the offices of the Chicago FBI and requested an audience for the purpose of registering a complaint. DeStefano was accompanied by his family consisting of his wife Anita, his son John, his daughters Sandra and Janice, and a family friend from Cincinnati, Ohio. DeStefano requested that his family be present while he registered his complaint, which request was granted.

Agents quickly asked DeStefano what was the nature of his complaint and after being asked this question, he proceeded in a tirade as to the damage, which the FBI investigation had done, to him and his family's reputation in their community standing. He was very emotional in this discussion and showed extreme ranges of emotion. He would go from complete clam to an irrational state and then, at the insistence of the interviewing agents, back to a complete clam.

DeStefano dealt excessively in non-specifics and could not cite any instance in which the investigation by the FBI had damaged his or his family's reputation or character. He referred to the numerous people who came to him with stories of being interviewed by the FBI about him. Mad Sam refused to identify who these people were.

He continued that he had been in the bail bond business in Chicago for a number of years until he was forced out of this business. He stated that, in fact, he was still in the bail bond business, with his wife acting as a front for him.

DeStefano repeatedly referred to newspaper articles and felt that the FBI should have the newspapers retract statements made about him. He was made aware of the fact that the FBI had no reason or obligation to interfere with the press on his behalf and was not responsible for any of the newspaper publicity, which he received. DeStefano did not know the source of the newspaper articles and stated repeatedly that Sandy Smith was a liar and an irresponsible reporter. He stated he did not sue the papers himself because he was advised that when he allowed articles to go uncontested in the past it set a precedent, which prevented him from taking action now.

The FBI had investigated and learned that DeStefano had been in contact with a Chicago defense attorney on several instances. One informant advised that he understood that Mad Sam was anxious to file a false arrest suit against Charles Siragusa in regard to the arrest of the Illegal Voting Charge. DeStefano also had consulted a Chicago attorney concerning his desire to sue the Chicago Sun-Times reporter Sandy Smith and the Chicago Sun-Times for libel based on recent articles concerning him in the Chicago Sun-Times. He also consulted this attorney concerning his desire to sue Bill Doherty regarding the mention of DeStefano by another name in the book published by Doherty about organized crime in Chicago. It was learned that this attorney encouraged DeStefano to file the suits against Siragusa and against the Chicago Sun-Times and Sandy Smith, but had discouraged him from filing against Doherty. The reason was since DeStefano was not mentioned by name, but rather by a pseudonym, DeStefano would have a poor chance of successfully prosecuting Doherty. Mad Sam left the FBI offices without incident.

Once back in front of the judge, DeStefano was denied by the court when he insisted that he be allowed to subpoena all voter registration lists dating back as far as 1927, to prove that other ex-convicts were allowed to vote. He was allowed to subpoena his records from Joliet Prison to show that he filed an application through the warden's office then to restore his voting rights. Once again, he was granted a continuance. When jury selection began, Attorney Robert McDonnell signed on as co-counsel representing DeStefano; the reason given was that DeStefano needed help because he was a "sick man."

When the three-week trial began, DeStefano was cited twice for contempt of court. When Judge Herbert R. Friedlund was questioning a witness, Mrs. Mary Austin, one of the election judges, Robert McDonnell stood up and began to shout at the judge that the woman had mistakenly identified a vote application as a ballot. The judge, angered by the outburst, told McDonnell not to shout. That provoked Mad Sam to stand in anger; the judge ordered him to sit down, but when DeStefano continued to talk, the judge called the attorneys into his chamber and dictated a contempt finding against DeStefano. When DeStefano began to argue back with the judge, a second contempt charge was given to him.

The transcripts are as follows:

Mr. Tutte:	Q. Mrs. Austin what, if anything, happened after that, after the defendant signed his name on that document?
Mr. McDonnell:	Objection. Objection. It's obvious what this witness is doing. The witness is saying what—
The Court:	Keep your voice down.
Mr. McDonnell:	I beg your pardon.
The Court:	You don't have to holler at me.
Mr. McDonnell:	I am not hollering at your Honor.
Mr. DeStefano:	Excuse me.
Mr. McDonnell:	This witness is reciting what is ordinarily done.
The Court:	Sit down and be quiet.
Mr. DeStefano:	May I address the Court?
The Court:	No.
Mr. DeStefano:	Exception. The Court won't let me address the Court.
The Court:	Sit down and be quiet.
Mr. DeStefano:	You were hollering at my co-counsel.
The Court:	Step in the chambers
The Court:	I am citing Mr. DeStefano for contempt. On the record. Your remarks have been contemptuous. You totally disregard the Court's order and instructions. You have been warned many times. At the end of this trial, we will take action on it.
Mr. DeStefano:	May I address the Court?
The Court:	You may.
Mr. DeStefano:	May I make a statement for the record? I didn't mean to, your Honor. I didn't want to. But you were shouting at Mr. McDonnell much more than he was raising his voice.
The Court:	That's contempt, also.

On November 27, 1964, Sam DeStefano was found guilty of illegally signing an application, however, the jury could not agree on the second charge of having voted illegally in the election. That forced the judge to declare a mistrial on the second count. The third contempt of court charge came when DeStefano made a personal closing argument before the jury just before they were to begin their deliberation. He said, *"I want to thank his honor for showing me and you that Sam DeStefano cannot get a fair trial. He is a man of 56 years, a mild man, an impartial and merciful man. What prompted him to become vicious and angry, I don't understand. I am very upset and very angry over the way my family was routed out of here with a cat-o-nine-tails."*

Then Judge Friedlund excused around 50 people, some of them DeStefano relatives, from the courtroom after they applauded following McDonnell's statement to the court, *"Its living proof that a jury system is the only defense against the police state."*

The next day Sam DeStefano arrived at the criminal courts building to place a mourning wreath on the courthouse steps. The horseshoe shaped wreath of flowers had a ribbon draped across it reading *"To the honorable Herbert Friedlund and Assistant State's Attorney Patrick Tutte. In sympathy for your hollow victory, Congratulations. Sam DeStefano."*

As he lay the wreath down, he gave the following speech *"I have never seen such a travesty of justice in my whole life, not only in the United States, but also in communist Russia, Hitler's Germany, and Mussolini's Fascist Italy. I believe I am as honest and upright a citizen as anyone else."*

To add to his pain, DeStefano was not pleased when he heard that one of the other hoodlums arrested on the voting charge got his case dismissed. Joseph DiVarco qualified for a general Presidential pardon because he served in the Armed Forces from April 1942 to December 1945 during a time of war.

On December 9, 1964, Sam DeStefano was sentenced to 1–3 years in county jail. He was also found guilty on all three of his contempt of court charges for his outburst and was given one year in prison for each citation.

Chapter Eleven

Let me Take Care of This for You

While DeStefano was involved in his voting troubles, he was arrested on another charge. DeStefano and one of his killers, Charles "Chuckie" Crimaldi, were arrested on charges of conspiracy to commit perjury. On October 5, 1964, three hoodlums robbed Ben's Place tavern located at 718 N. Albany Avenue in Chicago at gunpoint and escaped. DeStefano was accused of paying a $1,000 bribe to a Henrietta Burns and a Norma McCluskie, both owners of the tavern, to "forget" who they thought robbed them so the hoodlums could not be convicted. Crimaldi was involved because he had worked there as a part-time bartender and was "Sam's Man," there to collect his "juice" loans.

The hoodlums who robbed the place were Frank Santucci, Anthony DiDonato, and Robert Chessher, all thieves who had worked for Sam DeStefano from time-to-time. During the robbery, Mrs. McCluskie pulled out a revolver from behind the cash register after the robbers took $1,100 from it. She began to fire the gun at the holdup men, getting off six shots, shooting Frank Santucci in the chest, which caused him to drop his mask. The other two returned fire and tossed a bar stool at her before all three managed to escape. Santucci was arrested a few days later in the apartment of Mrs. Jean Hanson at 1701 N. 35th Street in Stone Park. Mrs. Hanson was known as the "kiss of death" woman after two of her former friends, Paul "Needle Nose" Labriola and James Barsella, were killed in mob fashion. Santucci was later identified in a police line-up by Norma McCluskie. When police asked him to take his shirt off, his left shoulder was wrapped from a gunshot wound.

Frank Santucci was born on October 13, 1926, and was known as a syndicate thief. Santucci had been arrested 31 times between 1930 and 1960 but never spent a night in jail. His only conviction came in 1952 for lewd and lascivious conduct in Milwaukee, Wisconsin. In 1953, he was arrested with his stripper girlfriend Billie Eggleston when police found $15,000 worth of jewelry and furs in his apartment. Charges were later dropped. In May 1959 he was arrested with Anthony De Paolo when the two were caught fleeing from a pawnshop on Madison Street in Chicago. The police caught Santucci screaming, *"Don't shoot,"* while hiding under a car in an alley blocks away. Five to ten feet away from Santucci was a bag full of diamond rings valued at $30,000 and his pockets were stuffed with almost $2,000 in silver dollars. Santucci managed to get an acquittal at his trial. In February 1960 Santucci screamed the words, *"Don't shoot, I surrender,"* once again as police began to shoot at him as he was running down a fire escape outside a store on Belmont Avenue. Police found the outside door of the business pried open and the inside doors burned with an acetylene torch. Inside the room was a safe containing $10,000 but Santucci and his crew of two were unable to open it before police arrived. His luck finally ran out when he was sentenced to serve 5 to 30 years in prison for that attempted burglary.

Santucci appealed and managed to win a new trial when he was arrested once again in April 1962. This time he was arrested with Vito Lombardi, Constantino di Stasio, then owner of the Guest Lounge on Mannheim Road, and Martin Accardo, brother of top mob boss Tony Accardo. State's attorney police received word that perfume from a $25,000 burglary was being sold at the rear of the Guest Lounge. When the police arrived, Santucci was standing outside the lounge acting as a look out. When his car was searched, found in his trunk were 500 coins from a robbery days earlier. Moments later two cars pulled up to the lounge, in one car was Martin Accardo, and in the other was Vito Lombardi. When police searched Lombardi's car, they found burglary tools, one matching a screwdriver left at the home where the burglary of the coins occurred. Accardo and di Stasio were arrested and charged with disorderly conduct.

Frank Santucci, Anthony DiDonato, and Robert Chessher were arrested and charged with the robbery of Ben's Place tavern. At the trial, Henrietta Burns and Norma McCluskie changed their statements and became reluctant witnesses. Henrietta Burns did tell the jury that Robert Chessher was in the tavern for a drink shortly before the robbery but could not positively identify him as one of the robbers. After inadequate evidence and the changed testimony, Santucci, Chessher, and DiDonato were acquitted in July 1963. Frank Santucci died on October 9, 1995, in Mesa, Arizona.

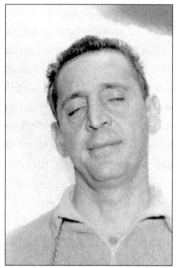

Frank Santucci

The information that dragged Mad Sam and Crimaldi into the picture came from one of DeStefano's goons named Vito Zaccanini. Zaccanini, who had been recently convicted of Interstate Transportation of Stolen Property, agreed to help the FBI because he found out he had been marked for death by DeStefano. With that information, DeStefano and Crimaldi were arrested and charged with perjury. Zaccanini told them that the witnesses had been terrorized and scared by DeStefano and forced to accept his bribe.

Soon after Crimaldi and DeStefano were arrested, tragedy struck the McCluskie's on October 24, 1964. Norma McCluskie's 5-year-old son and another bartender working at the tavern named James Pugh died when the upstairs apartment in which the McCluskie's lived in caught fire. At the time, the house was under police protection against gangland vengeance because Mrs. McCluskie was called as a witness against DeStefano and Crimaldi. It was believed that the fire had nothing to do with organized crime or Mad Sam.

Separate from the bribe case on October 27, 1964, DeStefano was found guilty of contempt and sentenced to 30 days in county jail. DeStefano was shocked at the ruling and immediately filed a motion for a new trial, which was denied. He was found guilty of illegally communicating with a special grand jury investigating arsons and bombings in the Chicago area. DeStefano admitted writing a letter to the grand jurors on October 2, in which he suggested that the jurors call him on the phone before they make a decision in order that they *"might get the dope from the horse's mouth."*

DeStefano was called before the grand jury to testify but he refused to take an oath unless they would promise to restrict the questions to matters concerning restaurant bombings. Judge Alexander Napoli ruled that when DeStefano refused to take the oath after being called before the jury, he delayed the jury's deliberations.

After being convicted on illegal voting charges, DeStefano was brought back to court on December 14 and was held in contempt once again. This time he turned his back to the judge and shouted, "*Would you kindly take that knife away from my back. It hurts. I believe I'm in enough trouble without this.*"

After the outburst, the judge denied his motion and he could not question prospective jurors in his up-and-coming-trial for perjury. DeStefano then argued he could not have a fair trial in Chicago because of his unfavorable publicity. When that motion was denied DeStefano yelled, "*Why don't you just go ahead and sentence us?*"

DeStefano was quickly taken back to his cell at county jail. Days later, he received word that he was being fined $300 for his contempt of court charge for the "knife" comment he had made to the judge. In anger, Mad Sam insisted the court reporter had made an error in recording his remarks and demanded that she stand trial for framing him. The court didn't buy it. Stemming from the incident, the Chicago Police Department received a phone call days later stating that an attempt on the life of Judge Herbert Friedlund was going to be made. He was placed under police protection.

Mad Sam knew he wasn't going to win this fight, so he decided to turn to the Outfit for help. The FBI had installed a hidden microphone in the offices of the Chicago Democratic Party located in the old First Ward in Chicago. As the FBI listened in on December 15, 1964, Mario DeStefano stopped in to see mobster Pat Marcy. Mario was there to ask Marcy to help him obtain a change of venue for his brother Sam who was scheduled to appear before Judge Alexander Napoli. DeStefano desired that the change be made so that this case would appear before Judge George Leighton. Marcy spent a great deal of time telling DeStefano how much he thought of him and his brother and how he would like to help him in this matter but how his hands were tied. The moment

Mario left the office, John D'Arco walked in, and Marcy said to him in a disgusted voice, "*I would never do anything for that fuck. I don't care who he is.*"

Two days later Marcy, D'Arco, and Anthony Tisci held a meeting at which time Marcy brought up the DeStefano situation concerning the fact that the morning newspaper indicated that the case had been transferred to Judge George Leighton even after Marcy told Mario he would be unable to have the case transferred. Marcy asked Tisci if DeStefano had gone to him or possibly Dom "Butch" Blasi to have this case changed. Tisci said he knew nothing of this and felt certain that Blasi had not been contacted. Both were extremely surprised at Judge Napoli's assigning the case to Leighton, feeling there was too much publicity on it and that it would be a bad case to start his career on the bench. Marcy said he was going to contact Frank Fiore, his contact at the Criminal Courts building, and learn from him why Napoli changed the case. The FBI was unable to discover why the change was made.

A month later at the perjury trial in January 1965, the focus turned to the information that Chuckie Crimaldi was alleged to have been the go-between in the bribe between DeStefano and McCluskie. Crimaldi was said to have taken the two women to DeStefano's house to give them the bribe money. However, Mrs. McCluskie testified that Sam DeStefano came to the tavern after the indictments were returned against the trio and, "*offered to help us to get our money back.*" The only condition on getting back $1,000 of the $1,100 loot was that there would be no positive identifications made against the robbers. Mrs. Burns told the court, "*Sam DeStefano told us that he had been contacted by Frank Santucci and that he did not want to go back to the penitentiary and that he offered to give us $1,000 not to positively identify any of the robbers.*"

The case continued and began to take its toll on Mad Sam. His blood was at a boil after the last 9 months of courtrooms and jails and it was time to do something about it. On January 9, 1965, Mad Sam stayed true to his nickname and went berserk. As he was being returned to county jail, he was being led into the hospital ward of the jail where his cell was. The guards began to search his clothes before letting him into his cell when DeStefano suddenly attacked another inmate. Guards quickly swarmed DeStefano, dragging him into a shower room, until the warden, Jack Johnson, and the captain of the guards could be summoned. As DeStefano was dragged to the isolation cell, he screamed at the top of his voice that he was going to have his "boys" take care of the captain, the rest of the brass and all the people in the prison, and that he would give the order to the syndicate to have the jail officials killed. He promised that warden Jackson would be dead in 24 hours. Once inside the isolation cell he shattered a toilet, and then broke a steam pipe leading to a radiator, which caused hot water to flood the entire basement of the prison. Eleven men ranging from plumbers, electricians, and steamfitters were called in to repair the damage caused by Mad Sam. Forty inmates brushed the hot water into the sewer and mopped up as much water as possible. Because of this, officials wanted to delay DeStefano's on-going trial and have him undergo a psychiatric examination. However, Judge Leighton denied the motion saying, *"I'm not responsible for what happened there in jail, I want to get along with this trial."*

On January 12, 1965, Mad Sam was found guilty of conspiracy to commit perjury. DeStefano stood in the courtroom calmly while his wife Anita and their three children, who were sitting among the spectators, and broke into tears. Six days later an attorney for DeStefano named Julius Lucius Echeles filed a petition for a writ of habeas corpus in the state Supreme Court. On January 29, DeStefano was granted a new trial on the grounds that there was prejudicial conduct in the form of remarks by prosecutors during the trial. For some reason, Mad Sam then fired his attorney, Julius Echeles, just before a second trial was underway in February 1965. This time according to reports, Mrs. Burns once again took the stand and said she and Mrs. McCluskie had received phone calls warning them not to testify. She added that she asked Charles Crimaldi to see what Sam DeStefano could do about halting the threats. She also testified this time that she and Mrs. McCluskie met with Sam DeStefano in his home and that subsequently DeStefano gave her husband, Pat, $1,000 of the now $1,500 taken in the robbery. That trial was declared a mistrial when the jury reached a deadlock. Finally, DeStefano was allowed to make his $5,000 bond while he awaited a third trial and was set free.

Information was overheard by the FBI concerning this trial through one of their hidden microphones. On February 5, 1965, mobster Felix "Milwaukee Phil" Alderisio was having a conversation with mob lawyer George Bieber when they began to discus the fact that *"Leighton is all right"* after Judge George Leighton helped Mad Sam by using the excuse of inflammatory remarks excuse to get him a new trial. The FBI wrote in a report, "It should be noted that the Chicago Office feels that this situation is a real miscarriage of justice. Leighton, the attorney for Sam Giancana in the case against the FBI surveillance in the summer of 1963, was recently elected a Cook County judge. The Chicago Office is aware that Leighton is a close friend of Sam DeStefano and that although he never formally represented DeStefano; DeStefano frequently consulted him concerning preparation of cases in which DeStefano was involved. DeStefano, when convicted by a jury, then granted a new trial by Judge Leighton on the basis that he, Leighton, made inflammatory statements in the presence of the jury concerning DeStefano. This case has been reassigned to Judge Finnegan, a former Congressman."

With Sam out, another attempt was made by law enforcement agents to drive Sam nuts. On February 18, 1965, Sam's brother Mario was arrested by the Cicero Police Department. The FBI contacted the Cicero PD and asked why Mario DeStefano was allowed to continue to run his "juice" activity out of Mario's Restaurant at 1304 Cicero Avenue. Agents informed them that because of another investigation it was discovered that Mario's Restaurant was not in possession of a city food license. When this information was given to the Cicero PD, they immediately arrested Mario for failure to possess a necessary license. The FBI report on the arrest had the closing notation, *"Noted Cicero PD long under the influence of Chicago hoodlums, however, apparently felt compelled to take appropriate action in view of obvious violations of city ordinance."*

In March 1965, Mad Sam was allowed to leave the state to go to the Mayo Clinic in Minnesota for a medical reason and to visit his son in Denver, Colorado. When DeStefano returned to Chicago, Judge Nathan Cohen of the Criminal Courts ordered him, undergo a psychiatric examination. At his sanity hearing on April 26, they found him to be sane and declared he was competent to stand trial. Dr. William Haines, director of the behavior clinic of the courts, testified that DeStefano suffered from a personality disturbance.

On May 11, 1965, Sam DeStefano appeared back in court, but something was not right. After the court hearing, he walked to his black sports car in the parking lot and noticed two detectives following him on foot. DeStefano paused and started at them for a moment, then got into his car and sped off. What he did not know was that Judge Cohen had received a letter in the mail that a hoodlum from New York was on his way to Chicago to assassinate Sam DeStefano either in the courtroom or the parking lot outside the courthouse. The hit man was to use a shotgun and blast Mad Sam in the face. DeStefano, unaware of the threat, stood in court with a dozen sheriff's bailiffs and detectives secretly guarding him. They even had one deputy sheriff standing behind the judge's chamber door with a shotgun ready to take the assassin out.

While DeStefano was waiting for his next court appearance, a story broke on July 21, 1965, that a car with the license plate number registered to Anita DeStefano struck a parked car belonging to a federal employee and sped away. When the police went to DeStefano's house to question her about the hit-and-run, she told the police her husband usually used the car and had not known of any accidents. Sam DeStefano addressed this allegation in court saying the story was a complete fabrication and none of his cars were involved in any hit-and-run accidents. He said that the story was just further evidence that the Chicago newspapers were harassing him, printing un-true garbage to disrupt the lives of his family.

In September 1965, the third trial was under way and Mrs. Burns testified once again. She told the court that she, Mrs. McCluskie, and their husbands were told by Sam DeStefano that they could make up their own mind on what they wanted to do, but warned them that Santucci was a desperate man and he could not guarantee Santucci would not harm them. She said she told Sam, *"I only recognized Chessher,"* with Sam replying, *"That's all right, but don't identify him positively."* She also changed her story a little and said that Sam had come to the tavern the night after the robbery and said he could *"reach out and get their money back, but there must be no positive identification of the gunmen."*

On September 10, 1965, Mad Sam was found guilty for the third time on the same charge. The line used by the prosecutor to win over the jury was, *"DeStefano was putting his arm of protection around his robber friends; in the vernacular of the street, he put the fix in."*

Seven days later, DeStefano walked into court wearing his blue suit with a white shirt and blue tie, ready for his sentencing. As he sat, he made sure everyone in the courtroom could see him yawn while the prosecutors read his record of past offenses, waiting for his sentence to be announced. His lawyer then admitted that his client had telephoned one of the jurors and had attempted to make contact with two others. Two of the jurors contacted the judge and told him that they had received phone calls from a man who identified himself as Sam DeStefano and asked them if the jurors had been sent notes from the state's attorney office while deliberating or had been pressured into their verdict.

Mad Sam DeStefano

DeStefano remained unusually quiet as the judge announced that he was sentenced to 3 to 5 years in prison. He was hauled out of county jail and sent back to Joliet State Prison. It had been 34 years since he walked out of Statesville and DeStefano was shocked at the change that had occurred in his old home. He didn't have to stay long; he was released six days later when Justice Harry B. Hershey of the Illinois Supreme Court allowed his release on $10,000 bail while his appeal was filed. Reporters gathered at the front steel gates of Joliet Prison and waited for Mad Sam to be let out. As Warden Frank Pate walked him to the front gate, DeStefano screamed to the reporters, *"Don't take my picture thru those bars. I'm not a hoodlum, and I'm being persecuted."*

Trouble with the outfit

Up until 1964, Mad Sam had made some enemies in the Outfit but he was still in good graces. In the FBI files on Chicago mobster Jack Cerone a section titled July of 1964 indicated that Jack Cerone, Americo DiPietto, and Phil Alderisio were in conference with an unknown attorney concerning the appeal of DiPietto, which was filed before the United States Appellate Court for a narcotics conviction. Regarding this conference, Jack Cerone and Charles Nicoletti still turned to their old friend Mad Sam in order to determine from DeStefano if this attorney was a standup guy.

However, DeStefano was in trouble with his old friend Sam "Momo" Giancana. During an undercover investigation, it was learned that Giancana and DeStefano had a sit-down where Giancana lashed out at DeStefano for his crazy outburst in court and in the press, and the attention it had drawn to his "juice" operations. The conversation changed as DeStefano summoned his anger at Giancana for when he ordered DeStefano to stay away from the wedding of Tony Accardo's son. That anger caused DeStefano to lash back at Giancana--telling him off. Because of the lashing, the two clashed, making DeStefano respond with strong language and heap verbal abuse on Giancana; he was not happy and it was believed that DeStefano was heading "for the trunk." Because of this incident, it was learned through an informant that DeStefano's loan shark operations were being curtailed and DeStefano was on his way out. Another informant said that Giancana made the decision that DeStefano was too wild to be controlled by other hoodlums and should be done away with. Evidence of this began to show on the streets as many of DeStefano's "juice" collectors were seen working for other loan sharks on the near Northside of Chicago.

However, on October 16, 1964, an urgent teletype from the FBI was issued stating the possible thefts of truckloads from the GE Appliances Company in Chicago were connected to DeStefano. Agents were to follow the situation closely and watch people handling the GE load because it was believed they were active members of the Sam DeStefano group. That led the police to believe that DeStefano was still in control of his gang.

It appeared that Sam DeStefano got back in the good graces of Sam Giancana by July of 1965 when it was reported that one of the guards in the county jail was supplying Giancana, who was in jail on a contempt of court charge for refusing to answer mob related questions in a Federal Grand Jury hearing, with whisky, cigars, fine dining food, and arranged to have Giancana's laundry done. It was also reported that Giancana was allowed to roam the corridors of the prison. One of the guards doing these favors for Giancana was named Frank Rinella. Rinella had been seen at the home of Sam DeStefano who was credited with masterminding the care of Giancana. It was believed to be a peace offering to Giancana from DeStefano for the harsh words they exchanged. Rinella was also found guilty of taking care of DeStefano when he spent time in county jail in January and February of 1965. He did DeStefano's laundry and arranged for Sam to have special meals. Rinella did admit that he was very close to Sam DeStefano and that he and his wife Violet usually spent Friday and Saturday nights at DeStefano's home. He said that his wife was a nurse and when Sam needed homecare after many of his illnesses, his wife was DeStefano's homecare nurse. He added he was paid $75 a week to take care of Sam Giancana by DeStefano because *"I wanted to help the big guy out."*

Chapter Twelve

Dear Mr. President

On September 21, 1965, Sam DeStefano was released from Joliet Prison and headed straight home to write, then president of the United States, Lyndon B. Johnson, a private letter. In DeStefano's mind, Sam figured out and offered a solution to all crime problems plaguing America by making free narcotics available to addicts.

On the following page is the letter explaining his plan and service to the President Johnson:

36th President of the United States, Lyndon B. Johnson

L. B. Johnson, President
U. S. A.
White House
Washington, D. C.

Sept. 22, 1965

My Dear Mr. President:

After observing you and your family's actions since you became President, I am convinced you are sincere in your desire to do great things for our Country and our people.

If you get the desired help from Congress, the Senate, and the people, I predict you will go down in history as the greatest President to date and possibly ever after...

You have many serious domestic problems as well as foreign. I can help you in some of your important domestic problems. I am not seeking anything for myself, not even glory...just anonymity, and no publicity on behalf of myself under no circumstances.

The following will solve your crime problem. Seventy percent (or more) of crime is committed by drug addicts. Simply sell narcotics at cost or give it away free to addicts. Dispense it from our T.B. stations or health stations which are already set-up throughout each county in the U.S.A. The cost will be nil. The savings will be billions of dollars in cold cash...in lives, in heartaches and blood...

Let me point out to you, Mr. President, when an addict can get a supply of narcotics at cost or free...that addict can hold a job down, and if necessary, support his or her habit without resorting to crime, and become a credit to his family and to his community and not a great, big, red, liability! A user of narcotics resorts to crime because of the high cost of narcotics!

L. B. Johnson, President
Sept. 22, 1965
Page Two

To prove my theory (I have living proof right here)--
England has a population of approximately 90,000,000 people,
half of the population of our Country. Do you know how many
drug addicts England has? Five hundred. Astounding!

My Dear Mr. President, that is something I advocated
thirty years ago and nobody would listen to me because I was
just a little guy, a nobody. Please heed my plea. I know
what I am talking about. Just let me speak to the crime board
you just created and appointed just recently. I am at your
service, free of charge.

Mr. President, I also will be able to help you
greatly in your poverty program, and Mrs. President, in her
campaign to beautify our Country. These are things I've
dreamed about for many years, for our Country and our people.

And in the field of Penology --- I am an expert, although unknown publicly. Let me help you, Sir, at my own
expense and without salary.

Mr. President, you also have a great serious and
dangerous domestic problem that is destroying our Nation...
That problem is the Gestapo tactics of our former beloved
F.B.I., I.R.S., Judges, etc., are using these days. It became serious (with all due respect for our late beloved
President) during Bobby "Boy" Kennedy's Administration and
now is a nightmare to each and every citizen, young or old,
throughout our land.

There is no more Justice and Constitutional law
meted out in our Courtrooms, Federal or State. Judges,
Prosecutors, F.B.I., I.R.S., etc. are tyrants. The newspapers rule them in my City and State, and I believe in most
States.

It is lynch law, the kind Bobby "Boy" Kennedy
taught them...personal vengeance with Gestapo tactics and
with taxpayers' money. Arrest, frame, and buy evidence,
is the order of today. Fill the penitentiaries up, clog the
Courtrooms with framed testimony and railroad people to
prison!

L. B. Johnson, President
Sept. 22, 1965
Page Three

Sir, I now have a little sad news to relate to you.
I am the infamous Sam DeStefano of Chicago, Illinois. The
newspapers call me a "gangster" and "mobster," "Costa
Nostra," etc. I am none of those things! I am and have been
terribly maligned for six (6) long years by the press of the
City of Chicago because of a personal feud with a reporter by
the name of Sandy Smith which started over my job as
"Foreman" with the City and because I was an ex-convict.
But that's not "here or there." I seek nothing from you, Sir.
I just want to help you, our Country, our people, and last
but not least...my children (3 in College), all children, to
have a better life!

With kindest wishes to you and yours...I am,

Respectfully & Obediently Yours,

Sam De Stefano
Sam DeStefano

1656 North Sayre Avenue
Chicago, Illinois 60635

P.S. Please do not divulge this letter to the press. Thank
you.
S.D.

When the letter was turned over to the FBI, it was determined no
further action would be taken concerning the matter. It was just Sam
being Sam.

Chapter Thirteen

Back to Court

On November 10, 1965, the Illinois Appellate Court ordered that Sam DeStefano be given a new trial on his illegal voting charge for which he had been found guilty. The decision made by Judge Herbert Friedlund was reversed when it was decided that he made an error in declaring a mistrial and dismissing the jury, then calling the jury back, which found DeStefano guilty. The appellate panel also ruled that the judge was wrong in refusing DeStefano's request that the jury be polled on its guilty finding.

To celebrate his victory for a new trial, Mad Sam applied for a private pilot license with the Federal Aviation Agency in Washington D.C. The possibility that DeStefano would fly himself out of the state, escaping his sentencing, was discussed and became a concern.

The year 1966 started with DeStefano still in hot water. On January 20, he was notified that he had until February to show why his voter registration should not be canceled. DeStefano went in front of the Chicago Board of Election Commissioners protesting this action. Sidney Holzman, then the election board chairman, assured DeStefano that he would review the case. An angry DeStefano shouted at the three board members present, *"I've had a registration card for 30 years. There is no use of me being here, after 30 years of precinct captains dragging me out to vote. I charge them with being Gestapo's. You two 'Holzman and Judge Nathan Cohen' are a little Hitler and Gestapo dictator."*

In February, Mad Sam had to appear in court on a speeding ticket. On February 7, 1966, DeStefano was arrested in Northfield Township for doing 62 miles an hour in a 45-mile-per-hour zone. DeStefano asked the sheriff during the arrest, *"Can't you give me a break? I'm a sick man. I'm in enough trouble already, I obey all the laws."* He was found guilty and fined $70.

On February 9, 1966, the FBI paid Mario DeStefano a visit and interviewed him with little cooperation. Weeks later on March 8, Mario was in court without his brother. He pled guilty to his charge of illegal voting and was fined $1,000. He was released and placed on probation.

Weeks later Sam DeStefano was reported to be in the hospital where surgery was performed. Weeks after the hospital stay a letter arrived at the Illinois Crime Investigating Commission stating that Sam DeStefano would spill all the mob secrets he knew if they would grant him immunity from any and all prosecutions. They refused and DeStefano was never offered a deal.

On December 12, 1966, the Supreme Court denied DeStefano certiorari. Two days later, his surrender was ordered and he was being sent back to prison to serve a one-year sentence for contempt. Five months later, a hearing was held to see if DeStefano was receiving special treatment. It was alleged that DeStefano was taken from the jail a few times a month and brought to the Cook County hospital for medical reasons. There he would be given Italian foods, wines, cigars, and a private room so he could spend time with a female companion. It was also learned that the person who drove DeStefano to and from the hospital and the jail had lied about his criminal past. The deputy sheriff, named Vincent "Jimmy" Truppa, lied about his criminal record so he could be hired as a sheriff's deputy. Truppa had been arrested 11 times since 1928 with three convictions. Other reports state that DeStefano had the run of the jail and the places used by the clerical staff. He would annoy the girls at their typewriter desks and was told to stay away from them by the warden. It was even reported that the jail priest, Father Merald McCormick, made phone calls for DeStefano from his office. McCormick denied the report stating that, *"I never would allow that to happen."*

On April 11, 1967, Sam DeStefano finally pled guilty and was sentenced to six months in prison and fined $1,000 on his 1963 illegal voting charge. Judge Richard Fitzgerald waived his previous jails terms because DeStefano had already been serving time. On April 18, he was released from prison on an appeal bond of $5,000. Also cleared was Vincent Truppa who passed a lie detector test that he was not involved in favoritism given to DeStefano, and was restored to the transportation division of the sheriff's office. When asked about his arrest record, Sheriff

Joseph Woods replied, *"I'm not going to hold a disorderly conduct arrest of years ago against him in light of the fact that he was raised on Taylor and Halsted Streets and knows many crime syndicate figures by sight."*

The FBI speculated that in March of 1967 Mario DeStefano was handling most of his brother's affairs concerning organized crime. Mario was spotted at an Albano Bakery, which had a back room used by Tony Accardo, Paul Ricca (DeLucia), Sam "Teeze" Battaglia, Jackie Cerone, and Joe Esposito. On many occasions, Mario was summoned to the back room concerning his brother.

On August 1, 1967, Sam DeStefano applied for a passport with the intent to leave the country. Once the FBI found out about this application, they informed the passport office about DeStefano and his passport application was denied.

Once again, the tide turned for DeStefano when the Illinois Appellate Court upheld his conviction forcing Sam DeStefano back to Joliet Prison. On January 3, 1968, DeStefano was arrested at his house and was transported to the prison to begin a 3-to-5 year sentence of conspiracy to commit perjury. In March of that year, DeStefano was denied a United States Supreme Court review of his 1963 conviction.

In August 1968, Sam DeStefano was transferred back to Cook County jail so a team of Chicago physicians could examine him. He had become ill while in Statesville and his private doctors, Dr. Frank Caporale and Dr. Otto Trippel, said that DeStefano was in urgent need of immediate vascular surgery and surgical correction of an obstruction in the urinary tract caused by bladder surgery during his youth. He was also suffering epididimytus and had partial paralysis of the right arm with only 60 percent use. This occurred during an injury to the radial nerve from a penicillin injection.

Dubbed "Sick Sam" DeStefano, he was brought to Augustana Hospital, a private hospital in Chicago, and placed in a private $50-a-day air-conditioned room. What amazed everyone in law enforcement was that no one had ever remembered if a prisoner had been removed from the prison's jurisdiction for private medical services in Chicago's history. And if a prisoner in Statesville had ever needed surgery in the past, he was taken to a hospital in Joliet, not Chicago. For eighteen straight days,

Sam DeStefano had a party and ran his criminal organization from his private room. What did Sam get to do?

1. While all prisoners were required to be handcuffed to the bed while in the hospital, "Sick Sam" was allowed to roam freely throughout the hospital when he felt like it.
2. Prison guards were assigned to guard him but they let Sam's "juice" loan operators and women visit him, and he was allowed to have his room door closed 90 percent of the time.
3. He had wine, Italian food, and liquor deliveries made to his room and accepted by the guards.
4. Hoodlums Charles Crimaldi, Sam Gallo, and his brother Mario DeStefano would come and go from the hospital as they pleased. On a few nights, they held card games in DeStefano's room.
5. On one occasion, the nurse went to DeStefano's room for a checkup and he was not there. She searched the hospital but he could not be found anywhere. She later said that on another day, DeStefano had threatened to *throw her out the window.*

When hospital records were reviewed, they indicated that DeStefano had not received any surgery and was never scheduled for any surgery. After an investigation, it was learned that DeStefano spent much of his time in room 814 of the hospital with another patient. That patient was named Louis Mustari, the owner of a tavern located at Wabash Street near Van Buren.

One of the security guards gave a statement in the investigation about what he saw. He reported, *"It was quite difficult to tell what goes on in DeStefano's room because the door is closed most of the time. It seems that in addition to his family, there are three or four regular, rather large, middle-aged men who are there quite late. Last night, these two men were there at 11:15 PM, playing cards past the regular visiting hours of 9 to 9 p.m. The nurses tell me that they frequently smell liquor in the room. The visitors seem to be the same men constantly. When some of them leave, others come by two or three. Thursday night, he was again in room 814, with six visitors, all female and one male. The patient in 814 seems to know him very well. They see each other nightly and shake hands. DeStefano complained about some of the deputies--that he had trouble 'breaking them in.' He didn't want the guards interfering with his affairs. DeStefano spoke of Mandel "Manny" Skar, a Chicago mob associate who was murdered after he built the Sahara North Inn near O'Hare Airport with money borrowed from Marshall Savings & Loans Company. DeStefano expressed displeasure with Marshall Savings & Loans in the matter. While he was in room 814, the guard was not present and I haven't the foggiest notion where he may have been. From that night on, I noticed that he had the run of the floor. He would enter and leave his room at will and no one on the floor showed any concern. I have had one discussion with him and I have walked by and greeted him on subsequent nights."*

After a patient complained about Sam DeStefano's profanity, noisy conduct, and abusive language to the *Chicago Sun-Times* newspaper, a reporter showed up to investigate. The reporter walked into DeStefano's room 810 and saw Mario DeStefano and Dr. Caporale talking to Sam as he lay on his hospital bed in his white blue-striped pajamas, smoking a cigarette through a long ivory holder. Once DeStefano noticed a cameraman enter his room, he jumped out of bed and chased the photographer down the corridor, and screaming to everyone around *"Arrest that man, Arrest him!"*

After the reports came in, Judge Powers ordered DeStefano confined to his room, no visitors, and his telephone disconnected. The county jail guard assigned to guard DeStefano was named Joseph Soil; he defended his actions, *"I never sought, nor did Mr. DeStefano ever offer a bribe. I always looked thru the room at the beginning of my duty tour and never found any signs of cigarettes, liquor, or of women having spent the night. He got a lot of calls, too, and when he made calls, he put me on the telephone; it was his idea, not mine. He got calls from an attorney, his sister, and many calls from his wife. He called his home many times. When he did ask to leave the room, he would always tell me where he was going. He told me, 'if anyone comes to see me, or if you need me, just call.' He was visiting people across the hall. I could hear the conversation or see him whenever he left."*

It was later learned that one night DeStefano summoned Charles Crimaldi to his hospital suit to conduct some business. DeStefano informed Crimaldi that four people that angered him were to be killed.

The four were Circuit Court Judge Nathan M. Cohen; Patrick Tuite, then the assistant state's attorney who prosecuted DeStefano; Julius Lucius Echeles, DeStefano's lawyer that failed to get him off the hook; and an un-known County Hospital doctor who refused to do DeStefano a favor while he was in county lock-up. DeStefano informed Crimaldi that he would call his wife Anita and give her a number to give to him. Number 1 would be Judge Cohen, number 2 Echeles, number 3 Tuite, and number 4 the doctor. When the number was given, that man was to die. In weeks to follow, only one number was given to Anita and relayed to Crimaldi, number 2, Echeles. Therefore, Crimaldi made his plans to meet Echeles in his office on a Saturday and kill him. When Crimaldi arrived, he noticed that Echeles secretary was there working, which she never did on a Saturday. Crimaldi knew there was no way to kill Echeles without her knowing what happened. The only other option was to kill both, but Crimaldi decided to wait for another occasion to carry out his contract. Luckily, for Echeles, Crimaldi had a fallout with DeStefano's wife and he quit Sam's employment.

Crimaldi then claimed that there was an attempt to organize a killer for Judge Cohen before Sam went into the hospital. Sam demanded that Cohen and any living thing in his home be killed, including the pets, bed bugs, and goldfish. Yes, Sam ordered the death of Cohen's goldfish. When Crimaldi backed out of the hit on a judge, Sam said he would take care of it. Sam had met a man by the name of "Leo" while in jail and this "Leo" was supposed to be a good hit man. So, Sam arranged to get him out of prison and gave him $2,500 to pull off the hit. This "Leo" tried 4 or 5 times to get a partner to go with him on this hit but failed. As time went on, "Leo" was not doing anything to further his murder plans on Cohen so DeStefano had Crimaldi bring this "Leo" to the hospital for a talk. Once Leo arrived, Sam told the police guard to "scram" while DeStefano and Crimaldi beat and slapped "Leo" around the room, demanding the "hit" money be returned with interest.

Crimaldi added that Sam DeStefano had given out about 20 beatings while in his hospital room to people who were late in paying up. Crimaldi even told about how Sam sent him to the old Polk Brothers store in Melrose Park to get a refrigerator for him so he could use it in Jail.

On September 12, DeStefano underwent minor internal surgery and walked out of the hospital doors refusing a stretcher for his ride back to Cook County jail. When DeStefano was being transferred back to jail he screamed, *"I'm being held incommunicado! Even my lawyers can't see me."* When he arrived there and was wheeled into the hospital ward, word spread to the 1,900 inmates that he was back. They all began to chant, *"Crying Sam is back."*

When Judge Joseph Power agreed to have DeStefano transferred from Statesville to a private hospital he would only say, *"I was informed that DeStefano was desperately ill and in need of immediate surgery."*

The warden at County jail was asked how DeStefano could get away with the things he had done with security guards on him 24 hours a day. Warden Winston Moore said, *"Sam DeStefano has so damn much money that he can bribe any guard I assign to him. Powers gave me orders that were impossible for me to follow. There is no sense in DeStefano being allowed out of Statesville in the first place. I don't think it ever was done before in the history of Chicago. Statesville has a hospital, and DeStefano could have had surgery there, if he needed it. The prison hospital is good enough for other inmates. Why not DeStefano, with all his money."*

Charles Siragusa was quoted as saying, *"I know that DeStefano had booze in his room, and when you have a jail guard sitting in DeStefano's room reading the newspaper and watching television that's a hell of a way to guard a prisoner."*

Sheriff Joseph Woods said his office was not informed of his responsibility to guard DeStefano until he was in Chicago. Woods challenged Siragusa to find the evidence that his jail guards did something wrong and added that Siragusa was waging a "personal vendetta against Italian-Americans." He said, *"I never heard him 'Siragusa' as being against anyone other than Italian-Americans. He seems to hate Italians. I'm not going to go on the evidence of his statements. I want testimony in open court. I am investigating, but not because of Siragusa's reports. He has hurt the image of Cook County. How did we get stuck with this job? DeStefano's the responsibility of state prison officials. Let him bring his witnesses, if Siragusa or anyone else has any proof of wrongdoing on the part of my men, deputies or jail guards, I will fire them."*

Siragusa responded to Woods comments, *"My capability as an investigator speaks for itself. I won't dignify that with an answer. As to the slur on Italians, I want it known I am a Sicilian Italian. I have been knighted by the Italian government, cited by the Italian Treasury Department. I am sure my accomplishments have been recognized much more widely than those of Mr. Woods."*

After further attempts to get himself out of jail, DeStefano went back to Joliet to serve his time. A report was issued in February 1969 that "Sick Sam" looked healthier and had put on 16 pounds.

It was around this time that Sam DeStefano made his final decision to enter the narcotics racket. He had been planning to enter the racket years earlier because his clientele had declined in the "juice" racket and his profits were shrinking. He had decided that the future was drugs; not because he had the connections, but because white boys and girls in the suburbs of Chicago were buying drugs and getting hooked with their mommy and daddy's money. Sam saw a gold mine in drugs and had gone to get permission to sell it. DeStefano had received word from Sam Giancana that he had given his permission to sell drugs as long as he received a cut. The Outfit in general did not usually get involved in narcotics as a main source of money; however, most of the top mobsters had their own deals on the side, receiving money from narcotics.

According to Chuckie Crimaldi, Sam had set up his drug connections through the Cotroni brothers. Giuseppe "Pepe" Cotroni and his brothers Frank, Mike, and Vince "The Egg" were the top mobsters in Canada controlling the Canadian Italian mob from Montreal. The Cotroni family had connections with a supplier in France and was going to handle all the arrangements to get the drugs to Canada. DeStefano had to make arrangements on how to get the drugs from Canada to Chicago. The Cotroni's refused to handle the drugs; they would only handle money.

The Cotroni family, headed by Giuseppe Sr. and Maria-Rosa Michelotti, came from the town of Reggio, in Calabria, Italy. Joe Cotroni lived at 3615 Ridgewood Street in Montreal, Canada. His arrest record list arrest from 1937 for possession of stolen bonds, theft, violence, narcotics and receiving stolen property. Vincent Cotroni lived at 4800 Pie Neux Blvd, in Montreal, Canada. He was married to Martia Brisciani and had a daughter named Rosina. His arrest record showed arrest for narcotics, counterfeiting, felonious assault, rape, false pretenses, theft and receiving stolen property. Other Canadian mobsters listed as being with the Cotroni brother were Carime Galante, Sal Giglio, Angelo Turminaro, Dante Gasbarrini, Frank Moccardi, Frank Mari, Antonio Sylvestro, Saverio Monachino, Patsy Sciortino, Emanuel Zicari, Nicolo Gentile, Joe Falcone, Daniel Gasbarrini, Sal Falcone and Pat Monachino.

In July 1959, the Cotroni family had a connection with Chicago when Giuseppe "Joe" Cotroni was arrested with five other alleged organized crime figures in what was dubbed as "The world's largest burglary." Along with Cotroni, William Rabin, Sam Mannarino, Norman Roth, and Rene Martin were arrested for attempting to dispose of 14 million dollars worth of stolen Canadian bonds. The burglary occurred in Brockville, Ontario, on May 3, 1958. The men sliced through the bank's roof with torches and stole the Canadian bonds, $15,000 in cash, and $40,000 worth of jewelry. The investigation led law enforcement officials to Montreal, Chicago, Miami, Pittsburg, New York, Milan, Rome, Bern, Basel, and Lichtenberg.

When the Royal Canadian Mounted Police raided a motel room to arrest Joe Cotroni and his chauffeur, Rene Robert, they found 16 pounds of heroin worth an estimated 8 million dollars at that time. The Cotroni family ruled the Canadian syndicate until 2004 when the last of the brothers, Frank Cotroni, died of cancer.

According to Crimaldi, DeStefano began his drug racket around 1969, but it was not known to what extent.

Joseph Cotroni	Vincenzo Cotroni
Aka Pepe, Joe Catrone	Aka Vic, The Egg
Born 2-22-1920 (Reggio, Italy)	Born 11-10-10 (Calabria, Italy)
Died September 1979	Died September 18, 1984

Chapter Fourteen

Take Him to the Basement

One of the many outrageous activities associated with the myth of Sam DeStefano is the infamous torture chamber located in the basement of his house on Sayre Avenue. When DeStefano said, *"Take him to the basement"* it struck fear in the eyes of his victims as they knew they were about to be beaten, tortured, humiliated, and possibly the long walk down the steps would be the last they would take.

The Interview

On August 24, 1960, while FBI agents interviewed DeStefano at his house the agents asked him whether he ever took anyone down to his basement or physically beat them or threatened them. In answer to this question, DeStefano related the following occurrence:

"He stated that some years ago an individual whom he was very friendly with came to his home with another individual whom he did not introduce. His friend told him, DeStefano said, that he and the other individual had just been convicted of burglary, and that they wanted DeStefano to fix the judge so that they would receive a light sentence. After several minutes of dickering concerning this, DeStefano finally agreed to approach the judge telephonically and as he picked up the phone to talk to the judge, he asked the second individual for his name. The second individual refused to give DeStefano his name but when DeStefano pointed out to him that it was impossible to fix his case without knowing his name, the second individual finally furnished DeStefano with his identity. DeStefano stated that he very calmly telephoned the judge and arranged for a future contact. He stated that he then hung up the phone and asked to be excused. He stated that he went into another room and got his gun, and when he returned he placed the gun to the head of the second individual and told him to proceed to the basement.

He stated that he then tied this individual to a chair in the basement and then went to the telephone and summoned a member of his family to his residence. He then advised that this member of his family had been chasing this individual for a year and a half as a result of a misdeed committed by this individual against a member of the family, the nature of which he did not care to disclose. DeStefano then told the member of his family who it was that he had tied in the basement and the member of DeStefano's family, who DeStefano would not disclose, immediately decided to kill the individual in the basement. DeStefano stated that he told the member of his family, "We'll whack this guy while he is down in the basement, but don't forget we gotta whack the guy upstairs, too." He stated that the member of his family was not anxious to kill both individuals, but DeStefano stated that he told this individual, "If you're with me you gotta do it my way and my way is to whack them both. If the blood is gonna flow, it's gonna flow deep." DeStefano stated that the member of his family finally decided that there was no sense in killing both individuals and inasmuch as DeStefano would not agree to the killing of the man in the basement without killing the prospective witness upstairs, there was no killing at all.

Another story furnished by a Chicago informant advised that he happened to be present at the home of Sam DeStefano in the spring of 1961 when a runner for Sam, who was large and burly, brought a man whom DeStefano said owed him money. DeStefano and his goon took this individual into the basement of DeStefano's house where they handcuffed the man to a pipe and then beat him about the body. DeStefano them came upstairs and took another individual who was on "juice" to DeStefano into the basement to show this individual what could happen to him if he failed to be prompt in payments of his "juice" loan. On this occasion, DeStefano showed this individual a briefcase full of guns and told the individual that he would use these guns if 'a guy ever welched' on DeStefano."

Among the countless victims who faced the wrath of DeStefano, many are no longer around to tell their stories. However, some of the stories survived showing the many ways DeStefano took his pleasure in inflicting pain on others. The FBI files list several victims and their stories of torture and circumstances. Due to the privacy act, some of the names have been withheld.

Listed below are some of the stories:

1) In April 1960, it was alleged that Chicago defense Attorney Robert McDonnell borrowed money from Sam DeStefano in the form of a juice loan. McDonnell fell behind on his payments and DeStefano sent one of his best collectors, Tony Spilotro, to collect. Spilotro hounded the victim for payments. When McDonnell could not settle his debts, DeStefano send word to Spilotro that he wanted him to contact McDonnell on a particular night in April 1960, and if he did not settle up on that night drastic action would be taken. As a result, McDonnell went into hiding and did not make contact with DeStefano. On the night of March 9, 1960, at 2:00a.m., DeStefano threw a naphtha bomb into the bedroom window of the luxurious home of McDonnell's mother's house in River Forest, Illinois. The next day McDonnell contacted Spilotro who took him to see DeStefano. DeStefano told him that he, himself, had thrown the bomb into his mother's house and that he would resort to even more violent action if McDonnell did not immediately make proper arrangements to settle his loan. It was on this occasion DeStefano informed McDonnell that he had committed many murders.

According to information provided by an informant, McDonnell was able to make arrangements through his uncle, a wealthy contractor, to obtain money with which to repay DeStefano. However, DeStefano's collector, Charles Crimaldi, wrote in his book "Crimaldi, Contract Killer" that he, William "Action" Jackson, and Sam drove to McDonnell's house, soaked the walls with gasoline, and set it on fire. To Sam's dislike, the fire department arrived too soon and put out the flames, Mad Sam was so upset that he wanted to burn down the fire station. Crimaldi wrote that the reason for setting McDonnell's River Forest home on fire was Chuckie Crimaldi's brother, Tony Crimaldi, had been arrested and had to appear before the judge. Crimaldi had gone to DeStefano to have the case fixed and told Bob McDonnell to appear at the court date to represent Tony. McDonnell never showed up and Sam DeStefano had to act as Crimaldi's lawyer. That made DeStefano so mad that he went to burn down McDonnell's house.

2) A Chicago informant advised that in approximately 1956, a "juice" victim obtained a $200 loan from Sam DeStefano. The victim thereafter paid the loan back for a period at the rate of $22 per week. This amount of repayment was merely the interest for the loan and did not reduce the principal at all. The victim repaid the loan to DeStefano until about June of 1962, when he made additional loans bringing the amount to about $700. After not making payments for about five weeks in June and July of 1962, DeStefano tripled the amount owed to $2100 and raised the weekly payments to $40 per week.

According to the informant, when the victim originally took out the $200 loan, he had to sign a blank check with DeStefano, which could be used by DeStefano if the victim failed to pay back the loan. The informant said that this was a common practice with DeStefano so that if the person declined to pay off the loan, the check is filled in and cashed and the person is then reported to the authorities for cashing a bad check.

The informant advised that on September 1, 1962, the victim went to see DeStefano at his home. During the discussion, he was told by DeStefano, "I want your money or your blood. I think I'll kill you." The informant said that the victim was threatened with a chair during the conversation and at another time was struck in the temple by DeStefano.

3) The Cook County State's Attorney Office contacted the FBI on June 1, 1962, informing them that they had been in contact with an Alvin Schultz concerning a juice loan. Schultz informed them that he had borrowed about $6,950 from a Nicky Visco in approximately 1960. Visco was the owner of the Mist Lounge, a syndicate hangout located at 6412 W. Montrose. He was alleged to be involved in "juice" loans and was under indictment for keeping a gambling house. According to Schultz, he paid Visco approximately $2,000 of the amount owed by January.

In January 1962, Alvin Schultz was contacted by an attorney who was acting on behalf of Sam DeStefano and a meeting with Schultz and DeStefano was arranged at the Guest House, a place operated by mobster Americo "Pete" DiPietto. DeStefano told Schultz that Visco had asked him to collect the money owed to him. The balance was then about $4,900. Schultz told the State's Attorney investigator that he had made several payments to DeStefano, always in cash. He paid $1,000 in February but was told about a week or so later that he still owed $4,400 and that his interest would be $440 a week, and if he was late in paying, the interest, he would then owe $880. Schultz paid this interest for several weeks. He was late in paying several times and made payments of $880 and even one payment of $1,320.

On May 29, 1962, DeStefano called him on the telephone and told him to come to his residence. It appears that Schultz had first called DeStefano that morning asking if he could talk to him. On this occasion, Schultz complained that he had paid some $13,000 on the note already and he felt his debt was paid. Once Schultz arrived at Sam's house, he said that DeStefano beat him up, striking him some 8 or 9 times. Schultz claimed that DeStefano had threatened him on numerous occasions when he was late in making a payment. The threats were usually obscene and Schultz was unable to give the State's Attorney men exact wording except that DeStefano would "have his blood" and that of his family.

Schultz recalled that some of the threats made to him on May 29 were that if he did not pay $2,950 that day, he (DeStefano) would cause the worst holocaust in River Forest that that city had ever seen and that neither Schultz nor his family would continue to live. Schultz reported the threats and beatings to the River Forest PD after the beating on May 29. The River Forest PD notified the State's Attorney office and the FBI, which provided protection for Schultz. Schultz was placed under guard by 4 policemen and a warrant for DeStefano's arrest was issued.

At the time, Schultz was appealing a 2-to-5-years sentence in prison for his part in a confidence game in which $1,600,000 was embezzled when he was an executive of a steel company. On June 2, Sam DeStefano surrendered to police, and within hours was out on a $3,000 bond. DeStefano refused to give a statement to investigators concerning the case but claimed he was "a legitimate business man." His first hearing was held on June 27 when DeStefano called the assistant state's attorney a liar because he said two witnesses were unavailable. Schultz said at the hearing that DeStefano had contacted him a few days before the hearing and told him if he didn't drop the charges he would be sorry. A continuance was granted.

During the trial in October 1962, Sam DeStefano acted as his own lawyer. When Schultz took the stand, he testified that Sam DeStefano politely asked Schultz for his glasses; when Schultz removed them and handed them to DeStefano, DeStefano poked Schultz in the eye. During cross-examination, DeStefano asked James Paulus to the stand. Paulus, an associate professor at the Art Institute of Chicago testified he was in the home of DeStefano the morning of May 29 and heard no commotion.

The case was dismissed because in May 1963 Alvin Schultz died at Oak Park hospital, reason unknown.

4) In 1958, a disturbing story concerning Sam DeStefano and his wife Anita was told to the Chicago Police Department. An African-American man told the police that he was standing on a street corner on the south side of Chicago when a Cadillac pulled up and Sam DeStefano jumped out, pointed a gun at the man, told him to get in the car, and shut up or he would kill him. The man did as he was told and entered the car; he noticed that DeStefano's wife was in the car. DeStefano drove to his garage behind his home on North Sayre and forced the man to have sexual relations with Anita both in a natural and unnatural manner under gunpoint. The reason for this was Sam DeStefano and his wife Anita had a quarrel and because Anita upset Sam so much, this was his method of reprimanding her. When it was finished, DeStefano drove the man back to his street corner and told him to get lost.

The man then went to the police and told them how he was kidnapped and was forced to have sex with Sam DeStefano's wife. The police did not place too much credence in the information provided by the victim until he mentioned that he left his lunch bucket, which he was carrying when he was accosted by DeStefano, in the back seat of Sam's Cadillac and asked the police officers if he could at least get it back. So the police went to DeStefano's and asked Mad Sam if this was true, DeStefano laughed and told the officers "no." The officers then asked to look inside

DeStefano's Cadillac, which he agreed to, and lying in the back seat was the man's lunch bucket with his lunch still in it. DeStefano denied he ever kidnapped anyone and could not explain how the lunch bucket could have gotten in his car. The man was given his lunch bucket and no charges were filed.

5) In early May 1964, a Chicago informant stated that an associate under the control of DeStefano was arrested by the FBI in a counterfeit traveler's check violation. The arrest of this individual immediately caused great concern on the part of Sam DeStefano. The informant stated he was immediately summoned to the "House of Horrors," the name of DeStefano's residence as widely used by members of the hoodlum element in Chicago. On this occasion, DeStefano acted like a wild man and ranted and raved about all the trouble this individual would cause him if he was so inclined. This informant also advised that DeStefano was very concerned with this arrest, due to the fact that it placed the bail bond business of this individual actually owned by DeStefano, in jeopardy.

6) A local hoodlum was in Miami, Florida, with his girlfriend and ran out of money. In the presence of the girlfriend, this hoodlum made a long distance telephone call to one of DeStefano's goons and requested a "juice" loan of $500 through DeStefano. The money was sent to him via Western Union and his girlfriend accompanied him to pick up the money. In addition, this girlfriend had to sell two lots, furniture, and her beauty shop to satisfy the "juice" payments of DeStefano.

7) In 1962, a man believed to be named Charley "The Janitor" Grundellio took out a $1,500 "juice" loan from Sam DeStefano. Grundellio was a small-time gambler in Cicero and boasted that he was "friends" with mob boss Joey Aiuppa. He gained the name "The Janitor" since he was a janitor during the day and a mob gambler at night. After the third time being late on his payments, DeStefano received word that "The Janitor" had told Sam to *go fuck himself.* This wasn't the first time Grundellio angered DeStefano; years past, Sam gave him a beating

that permanently disfigured one of his fingers. DeStefano sent Chuckie Crimaldi to rough up Grundellio to remind him that it wasn't a good idea to ever tell Sam DeStefano to *"go fuck himself."* According to Crimaldi, he beat Grundellio so bad that he spent 20 days in the hospital. Grundellio paid off the "juice" loan when his mother took out a second mortgage on her house to save her son.

8) In November 1961, *Chicago Tribune* newspaper reporter William Doherty heard rumors that Sam DeStefano had been missing for a week. Because of recent gangland murders at the time involving the "juice" rackets, Doherty thought he might have a good story to report. On November 12, Doherty went to DeStefano's house to get to the bottom of these rumors. Sam DeStefano made sure Doherty got his story and then some. According to Doherty, he parked his car in front of DeStefano's house and went to the front door and rang the bell. DeStefano's wife Anita answered the door and recognized Doherty, inviting him in.

Doherty had been to the DeStefano house before on August 21, when he interviewed Sam DeStefano about the loan shark rackets. The two had spent over two hours in the interview that day so the sight of Doherty by Anita was not one of surprise. During that interview, Doherty claimed DeStefano informed him that he made $28,000 as a consultant to hoodlums, proving it to him by showing Doherty his old tax return forms. He informed him of how he, DeStefano, would make high interest loans in which he collected 20 percent interest by lending money to criminals, bondsmen, and paying for lawyers for criminals. DeStefano even expressed a fear that he could be killed in his line of work and showed Doherty that he kept a loaded revolver in the kitchen for easy access.

During that November 12, visit, Sam came walking into the room dressed in white silk pajamas and held his hand out to Doherty, in friendship. As Doherty extended his hand to shake DeStefano's, Doherty claims DeStefano smacked Doherty in the face with a closed fist. Shocked and stunned, Doherty claimed he, in retaliation, then punched DeStefano in the face, knocking him across the room onto the floor. A stumbling DeStefano hurried to his feet and headed into the kitchen where Doherty knew DeStefano kept a loaded gun under a telephone table. Knowing this, Doherty ran as fast as he could out of the house accidentally dropping his car keys in a panic. In fear for his life, he continued to run to his car and then towards North Avenue which was only a block or two away from Sam's house. Once there, he found a drug store and rushed into it to place a call to the *Tribune's* city front desk informing them where he was and that he needed immediate help from the police as DeStefano just assaulted him.

Doherty then walked outside onto the street and awaited the police. Doherty stated that DeStefano frantically pulled up to him in his car, rolling down the window screaming, *"I'm going to kill you and I'm going to kill every member of your family. I'll kill you if it's the last thing I do."* Doherty claimed that DeStefano, while screaming, held up a gun and pointed it at him through his window.

Doherty, once again fearing for his life, took off running down North Avenue while DeStefano was caught in a traffic jam. Doherty stated that he turned into an alley to escape and noticed that DeStefano had driven too far and missed the turn into the alley. Running two more blocks, Doherty found another telephone and phoned the police himself. Once the police arrived, three officers escorted Doherty back to DeStefano's house to retrieve his car and keys. Upon arrival, Doherty noticed that every widow in his car had been smashed and an irate DeStefano was standing in his driveway continuing his threats against Doherty and his family. It should be noted that during all of this, DeStefano was still dressed only in his white silk pajamas.

While the police guarded Doherty and assisted him in finding his keys, DeStefano placed a phone call to his lawyer, Robert McDonnell. McDonnell quickly called the police captain of the Shakespeare police station and offered to surrender his client to police Captain McLaughlin. The captain refused and ordered DeStefano arrested. DeStefano refused to cooperate, demanding a warrant be issued for his arrest. Once the warrant arrived, DeStefano requested that he be arrested and transported in a squad car. To humiliate DeStefano, a patrol wagon was called in, and as DeStefano walked out of his house in handcuffs, he demanded that his tan topcoat be pulled over his head so the reporters could not get a good photo of him.

DeStefano was taken to the police station, then the Bureau of Identification, where he was fingerprinted and a mug shot taken. He was charged with assault with intent to kill, battery, and malicious mischief. DeStefano was released on $7,500 cash bond that was supplied by bondsman Harry Schorr. Doherty, being the son of a Chicago police officer, had no expense spared and was placed under around the clock police protection in and around his house.

An FBI report contained in the file of Sam Giancana stated that FBI agents confidentially learned that the *Chicago Tribune* intended to press this matter vigorously and in doing so had assigned three full time reporters to cover DeStefano and his associates. The *Tribune* intended to exert full pressure, including all the heat it could manifest against any "syndicate" activity, including DeStefano's good friends, Sam Giancana and Joey Glimco.

The next day DeStefano appeared in court with his wife and brother Mario by his side. Still mad, he made a scene in the courtroom, yelling and cursing at all the reporters he could find. He was given a continuance until December of that year.

The incident made its way through hoodlum circles, all the way to the hidden microphone located at Sam Giancana's headquarters at the Armory Lounge in River Forest. The FBI report reads as follows:

11-18-61
Sam Giancana
File 92-3171-492

"Daily Summary, CG 6486-C* advised last night that two unknowns held a conference; a large portion of which was unintelligible due to background noise and whispers. However, certain significant portions were ascertained to pertain to Sam DeStefano, on whom considerable information has been reported during this week. Informant relates that the unknowns stated as follows, *'He should be here any day. Anything important, go see Moe* (referring to fact that Sam Giancana is expected back shortly). *He's* (DeStefano) *crazy! He's a danger to Giancana, fighting* *the Tribune. In the event I run into him, get him in the car and I'll finish him myself* (whispers) *knock off* (whispers) *in the car.'*

The name DeStefano was mentioned in conversation along with enough events to identify the subject of conversation as DeStefano's. This conversation reflects that the Giancana group is concerned about DeStefano's erratic nature enough to seriously consider killing him, and they are apparently discussing the correct method to perform this killing, however; the final word awaits the return of Giancana from Europe."

In an FBI report from the files of Murray Humphreys it states:

"Chicago informant advised that all leaders of organized crime in Chicago have become greatly concerned over the situation involved in the alleged assault by minor hoodlum Sam DeStefano on 'Chicago Tribune' reporter William Doherty, during the middle of November 1961. The hoodlums are concerned with this situation due to the fact that as a result of it they have obtained unfavorable publicity in the Chicago newspapers, and that as a result of this publicity, law enforcement agencies in Chicago have stepped up their investigations of the hoodlums. These hoodlums are also upset due to the fact that DeStefano is not a member of organized crime in Chicago, but instead operates independently from the organized criminals.

This informant advised that the hoodlums have been giving Murray Humphreys credit recently due to the fact that some time ago he issued a warning to them that DeStefano was going to cause them trouble due to the fact that he was neurotic and had a 'big mouth.' The informant advised that apparently sometime ago, Humphreys counseled his associates that they should have it out with DeStefano.

DeStefano has been interviewed on several occasions during the past two years by FBI agents. He has refused to discuss any relationship he might have with Humphreys except to say that he is acquainted with him and has advised that he is in no way connected with the 'outfit' in Chicago.

On November 21, 1961, DeStefano was interviewed by FBI agent Marshall Rutland. He advised that following threats which were made by DeStefano on the life of 'Chicago Tribune' reporter Sandy Smith in

December 1959, Smith decided to 'dirty him up' and make it appear that he was a 'stool pigeon' for Smith. This, DeStefano claimed, was intended by Smith to cause DeStefano's 'own people' to kill DeStefano."

Are you wondering why Sam DeStefano went crazy and attacked William Doherty? FBI agents only had to look in their files for the answer. When FBI agents interviewed DeStefano back on September 13, 1961, concerning the whereabouts or murder of Jack Silva, DeStefano informed them that he considered the "*Chicago Tribune*" reporter Bill Doherty as having double-crossed him in obtaining from him an interview, which served as the basis of 3 articles in the *Tribune*. DeStefano made threats on several occasions during the interview against the life of Doherty and indicated that he had "*not yet decided whether to blow my top and go down to the Tribune with my heater and blow Doherty's head off.*" DeStefano indicated that in the event he did kill Doherty in the above fashion, he could probably get away with only a minimum sentence because he could pretend that he was insane at the time of the killing.

DeStefano also said that he telephonically contacted Doherty at the *Tribune* on the evening after the printing of the first article and called Doherty several obscene names. He then contacted Sandy Smith, another reporter for the *Tribune* at the time, and apologized to Smith whom he previously threatened to kill by indicating to Smith that at least Smith had the courage not to pretend he was going to write a sympathetic article concerning him.

In another interview with agents, DeStefano indicated that he had obtained considerable information concerning the involvement of Doherty with different burglars and minor hoodlums and that he intended to bring that information out when he went on trial for the assault of Doherty. He indicated that he would desire that the agent make it known to appropriate officials of the *Chicago Tribune* that he had this information. He also made it known to them that if they persuaded the State's Attorney office either to dismiss the assault charges against him or to provide leniency for him; he would bring his information to court and make it available to the public. The FBI agent indicated that he had no interest in this regard.

At DeStefano's court date in December of that year, all the felony charges were dropped which allowed DeStefano to plead guilty to assault with a deadly weapon. That charge was a misdemeanor for which he was fined $200 and released.

It was not until January 7, 1963, when FBI agents were interviewing a past "juice" collector for Sam and Mario DeStefano in a room at the Webster Hotel that he brought up the case with Doherty. This person informed them that the truth of what happened was that Doherty and DeStefano got into an argument and DeStefano chased Doherty out of his house. Shortly after the charges were filed, DeStefano contacted an official of the *Chicago Tribune* informing him that he had in his possession damaging tape recordings, which involved someone at the company, as well as over-incriminating evidence against others. DeStefano threatened to expose this person and the *Chicago Tribune* unless the charges against him were dropped. This official went to Doherty and was responsible for getting him to drop the charges against DeStefano.

9) One victim who may have escaped DeStefano's torture was Joseph Weisphal. Around 1964 "juice" loan hoodlum William "Wee Willie" Messino, listed at the time as the number two man in the Joseph "Gags" Gagliano's gang specializing in gambling and "juice" loans, took Weisphal to DeStefano's house in an effort to sell the victim's account. Weisphal was in default with Messino on a $2,000 debt and Messino tried his best to unload him on DeStefano. In his sales pitch, Messino made no mention of Weisphal's bad record of not meeting his payments on time. Messino told DeStefano that his working capital was becoming overextended and he needed to cut back on his clients. DeStefano passed on Weisphal telling Messino, *"A guy that owes me $10,000 just skipped. I'm hunting for him."* This story became known because Weisphal feared he was going to be killed by Messino and went to the police for protection. (See more of this story under the "Outfit" section.)

10) A disbarred attorney named Stanley Piotrowski was arrested in March 1962 and was found guilty of theft by deception. Piotrowski was an ex-convict who was sent to prison for 4 years in 1948 on charges of operating a confidence game. In 1962, he tried to cash a check for $3,750 made out to him but signed by a Dan Mundo. The reason he attempted to cash that check was because he fell behind in his payments and owed Sam DeStefano allot of money. At Piotrowski's trial, DeStefano sat as a spectator staring at Piotrowski every second he could to remind him that he would always be there until he was paid off.

11) During Mad Sam's voting problems, DeStefano was investigated for his role in the bombing and arson of restaurants and taverns in the Chicago area. An FBI informant advised that Sam DeStefano owned real estate at 4100 West Roosevelt Road in Hillside, Illinois. This property, located just west of Mannheim Road on Roosevelt Road, was the location of the Slo-Dawn Restaurant, which was allegedly operated for DeStefano by a Mr. and Mrs. Bruno Miller. Mrs. Miller was believed to be the niece of DeStefano, according to this informant. He also advised that in the spring of 1964, DeStefano took this property from the Miller's and Mario DeStefano stepped in and turned it into a restaurant.

On May 7, 1964, then Chief Robert Huffman of the Hillside police department advised the Village of Hillside that he had received an application for a food dispenser's license from Mario DeStefano for business at the Slo-Dawn Restaurant. This informant had personally seen Mario and Sam around the restaurant. The Village of Hillside attempted to deny the license. The records of the City Clerk's office in Hillside listed the taxes of the place being paid by a Sam DeStefano.

In September 1964, the story broke in the press. Sheriff Richard Ogilvie wanted to use the recent wave of bombings of restaurants and taverns at that time to look into the trust records concerning the Hillside restaurant owned by DeStefano. Put in charge of this task was Richard Cain, the chief investigator working on the bombings at that time. Cain, who was on the payroll of the Chicago Outfit and a personal friend of mob boss Sam Giancana's, investigated to see if syndicate figures were the ones setting fires and planting the bombs in other restaurants who were in direct competition with mob owned restaurants.

Cain interviewed Mr. and Mrs. Anthony Colosky, former owners of the Slo-Dawn Restaurant. Colosky stated that in October 1961, DeStefano approached Colosky and offered to buy the restaurant for $40,000, with an additional $5,000 in cash as "earnest money." Colosky refused the cash until his attorney was present. Days later, the two met at the Chicago Title and Trust company offices in the Loop when the money was exchanged.

In October a special Cook County grand jury investigating arson and bombings had decided to look into the business affairs of Sam DeStefano. The first witness called was Anthony Colosky. He stated that DeStefano bought the restaurant for Bruno and Frances Miller to run it. He said that Mrs. Miller informed him that DeStefano was her uncle.

Issues brought up were the burning of Richard's Lilac Lodge in Hillside on May 26 of that year. Another restaurant in Hillside, the Lulu Belle's, which was right across the street from the Slo-Dawn, had been the target of two arson attempts in August and September of that year. In response to those incidents, they said the Slo-Dawn was a glorified hamburger stand and that it was ridiculous to think it could have competed with the Lilac Lodge or Lulu Belle's.

When Mrs. Miller took the stand, she refused to answer any questions on the grounds she may incriminate herself. Three days later she was brought back and informed that she was being granted immunity from prosecution and if she did not testify, she could be sent to jail. She then told the jury that she bought the restaurant from Anthony Colosky for $49,000 in 1961. Mrs. Miller borrowed the money from Sam DeStefano on a juice loan and was supposed to make "juice" payments of $359.93 or more a month with 7 percent interest. When Mrs. Miller fell behind on her payments, DeStefano took over the restaurant but had her continue to operate it for a while. Then DeStefano sent his brother Mario in to take over running the place. Eventually the place closed.

On October 7, Sam DeStefano was called before the grand jury but refused to say a word. He even refused to take the oath or tell the truth before the judge and jury. DeStefano did admit that he wrote and sent a letter to the jury a week earlier telling them that if they wanted to learn the truth about the bombings and arson cases, they should contact him and "get it straight from the horse's mouth." Because it was against the law to try to communicate with the grand jury, attempts to lock DeStefano up in jail for contempt became the focus. It was this letter that got DeStefano called as a witness to testify in the hearings.

On his way out of the courtroom, a swarm of reporters emerged and began to bombard DeStefano with questions. One reporter asked whether he had recruited juice loan victims to bomb and burn Chicago area restaurants. DeStefano cupped his hands to his ears and screamed, *"I can't hear you! I resent being subpoenaed by the grand jury. I volunteered to appear willingly, but they went ahead and subpoenaed me anyway. The assistant State's Attorney would not permit me to address the jury. I was ushered Gestapo style out of the jury room. I refused to testify because the state's attorney's office declined to agree to limit the questioning to my ownership of the Slo-Dawn restaurant and what I know about the bombings and arson fires."*

In 1967, the restaurant was known as "Snack Time" and was listed as being owned by a Damian Constantine. It was not known if Mad Sam was still connected to it or not.

12) This incident is not so much about Sam as a victim but more of a work hazard. In February 1962, an informant came forward and said that mobster Ernest "Rocky" Infelice was in trouble with the "Outfit" over money he owed to them. As a result, the "Outfit" burned down Infelice's steak house located on North Avenue in Melrose Park. The informant then stated that Infelice owed a large portion of his outstanding "juice" loan to Sam DeStefano.

13) In June 1961, information was reported that a Connie Pitt of Pitt Realty Agency in Chicago attempted to collect a debt owed to Pitt by two individuals connected with Chicago art galleries. The two individuals gave a check in the amount of $5,000 stating that they could not come up with any more at that time because they had recently been given $50,000 by Sam DeStefano on a "juice" loan. This informant then heard that the "juice" loan was actually Sam Giancana's money and Sam DeStefano was acting as a personal representative in the "juice" field for Giancana.

14) On December 18, 1961, an individual borrowed money from John "Johnny the Bug" Varelli, true name John Schiverelli who was listed as a muscle man for William Messino and George Bravos. Varelli introduced an individual to a gambling operation where this man lost a large sum of money. He was then introduced to Mario DeStefano. With Sam DeStefano's approval, a five-figure loan was obtained with interest set

at 10 percent a month. When the man defaulted on his loan, DeStefano came to his house and threatened him by saying he would kill him and his wife and child if he didn't make a payment that moment. He did come up with the money and the next day the victim went to Leo Rugendorf and Felix Alderisio to obtain a loan to pay off DeStefano. His new loan was awarded at a rate of 3 percent interest per month. Unfortunately, this man was unable to pay the loan to Alderisio and Rugendorf on time so Varelli sent him to Messino and Bravos for another "juice" loan. This man took the money from his new "juice" loan and attempted to recoup and double his money by gambling. Once again, he lost all his money and could not make his payments. He was forced to go borrow more money from a Cicero "juice" man by the name of Rocky Joyce and money from mobster Fifi Buccieri. His indebtedness rose to staggering amounts and interest on the loans amounted to well over $300 a week. The man's salary was such that he could make only a nominal payment on this amount and was forced to gather as much money as he could in an attempt to regain his losses in a Las Vegas casino, which proved to be unsuccessful. It was not known for sure what happened to this individual but rumors are that he is swimming with the fishes in a lake somewhere.

15) A Max Missry, also known as Murad Mussara, was a partner in the business at 600 South Michigan Avenue in Chicago with a man by the name of Albert George. This company was under the name of Michigan Avenue Art Galleries. Albert George started this business in October 1960 and Max Missry joined him about six months after the business was initiated. In the spring of 1961, Missry bought out George and assumed all debts of the business. George at the time was a big spender and was on "juice" to Sam DeStefano.

In order to maintain the business, Missry borrowed $2,500 a month from DeStefano to pay the store's rent. As time went on, he became deeper and deeper in debt to DeStefano. In order to make "juice" payments to DeStefano, Missry bought silverware from Birmingham Silver Company in Yalestown, Connecticut, on consignment, which he sold to Bracca's Store on State Street in Chicago at about cost in order to keep up these "juice" payments.

By June of 1961, Missry had borrowed nearly $30,000 at 10 percent a week interest from DeStefano and was also borrowing "juice" from a mobster named Leo Manfredi. Manfredi at the time was associated with the Towns Currency Exchange on Cicero and Laramie Avenue at 26th Street in Cicero.

DeStefano began to demand his payments. In order to keep him out of Missry's store and not make a scene in front of his customers, Missry had someone from his store go to DeStefano's house and make the payment. In addition to DeStefano demanding his money, Leo Manfredi also began to show up at Missry's store to collect his payment. To pay DeStefano and Manfredi, Missry went to another "juice" man by the name of "The Ghee's Brother."

Between April 1961 and January 1962, an employee of the store made over twenty trips to DeStefano's home carrying between $200 and $700 to cover interest on Missry's "juice" loan. Manfredi made it possible for Missry to cash checks at the Towns Currency exchange to avoid having the United States government find out how much money was passing through the Michigan Avenue Art Galleries.

During this time, a warrant for Max Missry was issued alleging that he and Albert George were charged with conspiracy to commit a confidence game by a Miss Harriet Short. Short filed a complaint that Missry and George did not pay her $33,500. The case was later dropped.

A woman by the name of Edith Clark was working as a sales girl at the store when Missry bought the business and stayed on to work for him. In 1961, Missry and Clark began to become close to each other and both were invited to Sam DeStefano's house for dinner one night. Joining them at the dinner was Joey Glimco, then the mob's man in labor in Chicago and president of the Taxi Cab workers Union Local 777. According to an informant, Glimco told DeStefano that Edith Clark was not to be held responsible for any debts of Missry's or the Michigan Avenue Art Galleries.

After Glimco left the DeStefano's house, a man who worked for DeStefano named "Sam," possibly Sam Gallo, brought another man who owed DeStefano money into the house. This other man was taken into the basement and handcuffed to a pipe. The man was then punched and kicked in the body until he was covered in blood. DeStefano then invited Missry into the basement in order to show Missry what would happen if he failed to be prompt with his "juice" loan payments. Then DeStefano showed Missry a briefcase full of guns and told him that he would use them if anyone ever welched on a loan to him.

In mid-summer 1961, Edith Clark sold her jewelry and secured $1,000 in cash from her savings account to give to Missry to pay DeStefano and Manfredi for "juice" interest. She also borrowed between $4,000 and $7,000 from her mother, Mrs. Mary Johnson, who lived in Miami, Florida, to pay DeStefano, Manfredi, and The Ghee's Brother.

By fall of 1961 Missry was about $60,000 behind in "juice" payments to all three individuals. Around this time, Manfredi and the "juice" man known as "The Ghee's Brother" went to Missry and told him how to get the money to pay off DeStefano. The money was to come from Felix "Milwaukee Phil" Alderisio. Manfredi and "The Ghee's Brother" were willing to make this arrangement because DeStefano had threatened to take over the Michigan Avenue Art Galleries and had made threats on the life of Missry and his three children. The purpose of this deal was to get DeStefano paid off before he did something which would cut off the "juice" payments to Manfredi and "The Ghee's Brother." In connection with the payoff to DeStefano, Missry agreed not to borrow additional money from DeStefano. Subsequently Missry, Manfredi, and "The Ghee's Brother" met an unknown person, picked up $15,000 to $18,000 and returned to the art gallery before Missry took the money and went to DeStefano's house to pay off his loan.

Missry lived up to his bargain with Manfredi and "The Ghee's Brother" until around November 1961. In a bind once again, Missry went to Manfredi and "The Ghee's Brother" for another loan; neither one would allow him another loan because the interest owed to both totaled over $8,000 a week. In addition, both agreed to stop interest payments on their loans and held the amount owed to them at the principal. So what did Missry do? He once again approached Sam DeStefano and borrowed several thousand dollars from him.

In January 1962, Missry paid his federal excise tax, Social Security debts, and his income tax with bad checks. This tended to accelerate the closing of the Michigan Avenue Art Galleries, which then had an involuntary bankruptcy suit filed against it. In November 1961, Missry wanted to close the store under bankruptcy proceedings. However, Manfredi and "The Ghee's Brother" wanted him to continue to "bleed" the store as long as possible. During bankruptcy proceedings, Missry was selling merchandise from the store and "The Ghee's Brother" and Manfredi were also helping themselves to merchandise from the store. This merchandise included chairs, linens, Dresden China, picture frames, marble top tables, and antique furniture. Also during this period, Sam DeStefano went to the store every other day and took money from the cash drawer. He would also demand money from store employees and he usually left with a considerable amount of money. Missry's attorney, Dino Di Angelo, notified the store that the courts would close it in mid-January.

Shortly after January 1, 1962, Missry and Edith Clark left for Seattle, Washington, because they were afraid of being killed by DeStefano, Manfredi, and "The Ghee's Brother." Upon returning from Seattle, they filled their car with merchandise, including handkerchiefs, Dresden figurines, and other merchandise, which had been delivered to them at a motel on the Southside of Chicago. They were afraid to visit the store for fear that Sam DeStefano or Manfredi had their men watching it.

With the car packed, Missry and Clark immediately left for Florida. They were in such a hurry to get out of town that they left all their records, invoices, and shipping orders from the gallery at their apartment at 2300 North Commonwealth Avenue in Chicago. Within a week after they left, all their possessions were picked up by a storage company because they had left without paying the back rent. They stopped in Clearwater to sell some of the items to an art store at the Clearwater Beach Hotel, Traveled through Siebring, Miami, and wound up in Daytona Beach, selling various items.

While Missry and Clark were in Daytona Beach, Missry picked up part of his stock from the Michigan Avenue Art Galleries which had been sent to a friend living there named Buddie Jabara. During this time, Missry and Clark were buying merchandise to sell and opening various checking accounts in Edith Clark's name. Missry wrote bad checks on these accounts and used the money to take over a cigar stand, gift shop, and a beachfront snack bar at the Dayton Plaza Hotel.

During this period, an angry Sam DeStefano was looking for them. One Day a white Cadillac was seen in front of Edith Clark's mother's house in Miami. Two men got out of the car and walked around Mrs. Johnson's home while another waited in the car. They returned to the car and drove off. From the description of the car and the men walking around the house, it was believed that one of the men was Sam DeStefano.

One day the phone rang in June 1962 and Missry answered; on the line was Sam DeStefano. Mad Sam threatened his life and the lives of his kids unless he paid the money he owed him. Before DeStefano hung up the phone, he told Missry, *"I hope you get enough sun because where you're going there isn't any, six feet under the earth."*

During the summer of 1962, Missry and Clark went to Maine to continue selling merchandise. During December of that year, the two returned to Chicago in an attempt to obtain their personal effects from the storage company. During that attempt, the FBI found Missry and brought him in for questioning. He admitted he knew DeStefano, Manfredi, and a "juice" man by the name of "Tony" but said he was not on "juice" to anyone. After his release, future attempts to locate Missry and Clark came up empty. It is not known what happened to them. Did Sam get them? Or did they get away to live out their lives?

16) Charles Crimaldi told a story about a forest preserve police officer who was on juice to Sam DeStefano in 1966. This policeman would shake down lovers who parked in the forest preserve at night to have sex. He would sneak up and wait for the couple to engage in sexual relations, then bang on the window shining a flashlight into the car asking them to step out. Then he would demand money or they would be arrested. This policeman fell behind on his payments to Mad Sam so Charles Crimaldi kidnapped him and brought him to the "chamber" for a beating. After a good scare and talking to, he was released.

As time went by, this policeman still didn't make his payments so DeStefano sent his goon out to shoot him. The policeman was shot in the leg as a final warning to pay up. The incident was never reported as the police officer went to a syndicate doctor for the gunshot wound.

DeStefano called the policeman two days later telling him he had heard that he was shot and he was sorry to hear that and hoped he had a full recovery. The policeman was never late in paying his "juice" loan again.

17) An unknown bondsman was in debt to Sam DeStefano for $3,000 and was a few weeks past due. Sam sent Chuckie Crimaldi to pick up him and his wife so he could have a talk with them. In the DeStefano home, Sam was dressed in his trademark pajamas while he sat the bondsman and his wife on the coach. Like Doctor Jekyll and Mr. Hyde, Sam went from a calm person to an irate mad man, then would stop and in the kindest voice ask if they would like some fresh coffee. After serving them coffee, he resumed telling the bondsman that he was going to die and would be fed to the pigs on a pig farm. Then he would stop once again and return to the pleasant voice asking if they were hungry and wanted some fresh pie that his wife had just baked. After they ate the pie, Sam resumed berating the couple. He demanded Crimaldi go and get the shotgun so he could blow them away in his living room. He even put them in a car and drove them to a place where he was going to kill them, but decided to let them live.

18) An unnamed Cicero collector for the outfit did odd jobs for Mad Sam in the "juice" field. When Sam found out that this collector had been skimming money from the collections he was making for Sam, his death was ordered and the job given to Chuckie Crimaldi. According to Crimaldi, he waited in the bushes at the collector's house and as this man walked from his garage to his home, Crimaldi jumped out with a shotgun and blew off the man's arm and face, killing him. This story came from Crimaldi himself.

19) Mad Sam sent Chuckie Crimaldi to rough up a runner who was working for DeStefano and was late in his "juice" payments totaling over $5,000. According to Crimaldi, this runner, named "Smitty," showed up at Crimaldi's house and was beaten by Crimaldi with a blackjack club. Crimaldi told the man he had 3 days to pay up or he was dead, then told the man to go down the hall to his bathroom and clean up. The runner knew he could not come up with the money and he was a dead man so he cut his wrist in a suicide attempt. When blood flowed out from under the door, Crimaldi called an ambulance and the man lived.

20) A Chicago informant advised that DeStefano had brothers who owned and operated a restaurant on Cicero Avenue just south of Roosevelt Road in Cicero, and that these brothers were also active in the "juice" business. This informant advised that he had lost a great deal of money in gambling operations in Cicero prior to 1961 and that he was forced to contact DeStefano. Introduction to DeStefano was made through Mario DeStefano. A loan of $10,000 was made by DeStefano to the informant with interest at 10 percent a month. This informant advised them that after the first month or so he encountered difficulty in making the payments on the loan. He received a threat from DeStefano concerning the safety of his wife and children if payment was not immediately made. The informant said that he realized that he had a tremendous problem with DeStefano. He went to another Chicago hoodlum and borrowed enough money so that he could make a payment to DeStefano. He also said that it was the practice of DeStefano to warn his customers prior to loaning money to them. He added that when a man contacts DeStefano to obtain money, this man will usually be invited to DeStefano's home for coffee. After some casual conversation, DeStefano will point to the clock and advise the man that if he takes the money it will be due and returnable with interest exactly one week from that time. DeStefano indicates that if the payment is as much as an hour late he will become unhappy. If the payment is as much as a day late, he will become very unhappy. If the payment is more than a day late, it will not be accepted and it will be taken out in the man's blood. On this basis, the money is lent if the customer still feels that he can do business with DeStefano.

Chapter Fifteen

The Murder of Arthur Adler

In January 1960 Arthur Adler, the owner of the old Trade Winds Restaurant and night club at Chestnut and Rush Street, the Latex Distributing Company at 809 Roosevelt Road that was Chicago's largest distributor of prophylactics in Chicago, and of the mob's old Black Onyx night club, disappeared from his office on the near south side of Chicago. Adler left around 6:40 p.m. when he told his employees at the Latex Company, *"I'll go out and get my car,"* promising to take an employee to the Illinois Central railroad station at Michigan Avenue and Roosevelt Road. He was supposed to meet his wife at the old Whitehall Club for dinner but he never showed up. The next day Adler's wife Marie, also known as Mary, reported her husband missing and told police, *"I know he's dead."* That same day his car was found at the southwest corner of Roosevelt Road and Peoria Street but no sign of Adler could be found.

A couple of weeks later his wife thought he might have amnesia saying, *"I know he's alive, but he just doesn't remember who he is."* Days before their son Michael's Bar Mitzvah ceremony, Adler's wife placed a long story in the *Chicago Sun-Times* newspaper hoping that Adler might see it and snap out of his amnesia. She also said that other hoodlums in the area were coming up to her concerned over Adler's disappearance staying that it was, *"putting heat on all of us. If we knew what happened, we'd tell you."*

Arthur Adler

On March 28, 1960, sewer inspectors Hy Fligelman and Edward Goggins were on a routine investigation checking manhole covers in the residential street of 1625 N. Neva Avenue in Chicago. It was there that they found the naked body of Arthur Adler stuffed into the sewer. The body was on its back with his legs straight up in the air and his knees pushed up to his chest, his arms were crossed and his head was facing south lying in the 9-inch tile through which pollution is normally carried from Neva Avenue homes into the North Avenue Main, about 12 feet below the street surface.

Investigators had determined that he had been dumped into the sewer headfirst. Edward Goggin's statement was, "*At about 1700 North Neva, my partner and I lifted a manhole and noticed the water was higher than usual, and flowing sluggish, so we checked the next manhole south of it. There the water was even higher and we thought we had trouble, maybe a cave in or a clogged through. We moved to the next sewer and lifted the manhole cover and found Adler's body. At first I thought it was a manikin because the legs were so white, but when we got a closer look, it was a body alright, and we called police.*"

Once the police arrived, a pathologist went down into the sewer and examined the naked body for a while before tying a rope around Adler's ankles and lifting him to the surface. At the Cook County morgue, they removed his fingers for printing and informed his wife, Mary that the fingerprints matched and it was her husband. The news caused Mrs. Adler to collapse as she cried, "*Why can't I die of a heart attack and be with him? How can I phone our son at Harvard (University) and tell him his father was found in a sewer? Poor guy, he never hurt anybody. He loved everybody.*"

His wake was held at Piser Memorial Chapel at 6935 Stony Island Avenue and he was buried at Waldheim Cemetery. Arthur Adler once said about the hoodlums coming to his establishment, "*I can't keep them out, I operate a restaurant. I got an open door.*"

Arthur Adler was born on August 20, 1917, in Chicago to Jewish parents named Morris and Anna Adler. The family lived their entire life at 4623 North Spaulding in Chicago and Morris made his living as a street peddler. The young Alder started working at the age of 13 before attending Marshall High School in Chicago. He would go on to complete one year at the University of Illinois. At age 18, he was working as a sales manager for a wholesale distributing firm before he started a latex business with his father, which gave Adler a wealthy living. It was around the time he started his business that he met his wife Mary on a blind date. Mary Adler was a Northwestern University graduate and was working as a humanities instructor at Herzl Junior College. The two would go on to have five children: Norman, Stewart, Michael, Jimmy, and Sheryl. In 1940, Adler was listed as working as a vice president of the United Razor Blade Corporation in Chicago. From 1941 to 1949, he was the owner of Keystone Sales, which was located at Madison and Halsted Streets in Chicago.

It was when Adler and his wife started going to the Rush Street area in Chicago that their lives would change. Arthur was amazed at the bright lights and social setting the clubs provided and fell in love with the idea of opening his own club. When a man by the name of Hy Ginnis died, Adler found his opportunity to become a player in the nightclub circuit. Ginnis owned the Supper Club at 867 N. Rush Street known as the Trade Winds. It was known for employing Ralph Capone Jr., son of Ralph "Bottles" Capone and nephew of Al Capone. When Ralph Jr. died of alcoholism at the age of 33 in 1950, Hy Ginnis said about his employee, *"He was a hard worker and a fine person to employ."* In July 1954, Hy Ginnis was questioned about the murder of Donald Pontone. Ginnis was accused of being involved in a quarrel outside his restaurant just a few hours before Pontone's body was found beaten and strangled to death. Pontone was at the Trade Winds that night with mobster Johnny Carr and Daniel Covelli, Jr., son of then Criminal Courts Judge Daniel Covelli. Hy Ginnis died in September 1955 and Arthur Adler negotiated with another owner named Michael Fritzel, and Ginnis' widow, Ruth, about purchasing the club.

During the Adler murder investigation, it was learned that Hollywood entertainer and comedian Joe E. Lewis had a piece of the Trade Winds. Superior Court Justice Abraham Marovitz had been executor of the Fritzel estate who represented Joe Lewis, told the FBI that he had been very close to Lewis for many years and that Lewis was a gambler and was very generous with his money. Fritzel had tried to get Lewis to invest his money and talked him into becoming a partner in the Trade Winds. Marovitz told the FBI that Adler gave Lewis $30,000 for his interest in the Trade Winds.

Practically every law enforcement agency, which had anything to do with the investigation of Adler's murder, felt that Sam DeStefano was the person responsible for the murder. During the approximate period of time when Adler was killed, a Chicago informant was in contact with DeStefano and this informant felt that Sam DeStefano undoubtedly had something to with the death of Adler. He stated that he understood that Adler was in serious financial difficulty and that after Adler had attempted to obtain financing through legitimate sources of money and was unable to do so, he understood that Adler turned to the moneylenders of the Chicago underworld in an attempt to obtain some. The informant believed that Adler contacted DeStefano in this regard and felt that Adler became delinquent in making payments on his "juice" loan to DeStefano; he very possibly may have gone to the residence of DeStefano and then was taken into "the torture chamber" located in the basement of DeStefano's house. This informant's theory was that Adler, who was not known for courage, might have been stricken with a heart attack when undergoing grilling and threats by DeStefano. Adler's body was found approximately a block and a half from the residence of Sam DeStefano at 1656 N. Sayre.

The informant stated the fact that since DeStefano was once on the payroll of the Streets and Sanitation Department of the City of Chicago, he was very familiar with streets and sewers, particularly in his district. If Adler died of a heart attack in the basement of his residence, he quite naturally disposed of the body of Adler in the sewer in the 1600 block of North Neva where it was found after the winter thaw.

FBI agents went to the home of Sam DeStefano on August 24, 1960, and questioned him about his involvement in the murder of Adler. The interview lasted just over 6 hours. DeStefano steadfastly and adamantly denied any knowledge concerning the murder of Adler. He said that he first heard of the murder of Adler when he was driving down Neva Avenue and saw a large crowd congregating where the body of Adler had been discovered in the sewer approximately a block and a half from his residence. DeStefano became very emotional and excited on several occasions during his questioning about this matter. He finally called his wife, son, daughters, and two or three girlfriends of his daughters who were in the house during the questioning, into the den in his residence where the questioning was taking place. In a very heated and emotional manner he called upon *"the good Lord above, if there is such a person"* to come down and put cancer in the eyeballs of his wife, son, daughters, and their friends if he had anything to do with the murder of Arthur Adler. He told the agents that to the best for his recollection, he never had any social or business dealings with Adler and stated that he could not recall ever meeting him.

In 1961, DeStefano gave a tour of his house, especially the "torture chamber" in his basement to a newspaper reporter, pointing out the bar and billiard table with his racks of pool cues. He told the reporter, *"Now I'll show you where I'm supposed to have killed people. The government told me that I took Adler down here, beat him to death, stripped off his clothes, and carried him down to the sewer. Does this look like that kind of place?"*

During the investigation, information filtered out about Adler and his association with Chicago gangsters. It was learned that when Adler took over the Trade Winds café on Rush Street in 1956 mobsters John Marshall Manitti Caifano, otherwise known as Marshall Caifano and Phil "Milwaukee Phil" Alderisio, used the place as their headquarters. Other mobsters seen there from day-to-day were Albert "Obbie" Frabotta and Lennie "Needles" Gianola. Also spotted there from time to time were Gus Alex, Lennie Patrick, Joe DiVarco, Jackie Cerone, Ross Prio, Murray Humphreys, Chuckie English, Harry Nassan, and one time Sam Giancana showed up with Frank Sinatra. On February 12, 1958, a meeting was held at the Trade Winds, attending were mobsters Gus Zapas, Marshall Caifano, Lennie Patrick, "Chick" Ross, James Allegretti, Phil Alderisio, Irwin Wiener, Walter Spritz, Tony DeRosa, and two gentlemen known as "Ramey" and the "Sheriff."

Phone records show that mobster David Yaras called Adler on the phone from Florida for some reason in 1959. Adler was seen by law enforcement officials many times at the house of Caifano; however, they were never able to find out why. Adler was even linked to doing some unknown business with mob hit man Vincent Inserro and was a "friend" of mobster Gus Zapas, then president of the mob-controlled Laundry Workers Union of Chicago Local 46. Adler was also known to be good friends with Vincent Morretti, then a Chicago Police officer, mobster, and self-proclaimed "ladies man" who dated one of the prostitutes from the Trade Winds and forced all the other girls to "be nice to him" or he would arrest them for prostitution. On one occasion at the Trade Winds, Morretti was sitting with Obbie Frabotta at a table when Morretti became loud and abusive and was ordered out of the restaurant by Frabotta because he was embarrassing the then chief of the Chicago Police Department. On another occasion Morretti, who had a violent temper, went on a date with one of the girl singers at the Trade Winds in 1959. After the date, the two returned to the Trade Winds and Morretti began to beat this woman up. On another occasion, a mobster by the name of "Frank" who seemed to have all or part of one ear missing, came walking into the Trade Winds and sat down. This Frank immediately called the violin player to his table and told him, *"Play that damn squeak box at this table until I say stop, and play it loud."* Then this Frank yelled across the restaurant and instructed Morretti to come over to his table. For a 5 to 10 minute period, Frank "read the riot act" to Morretti and told him, *"Keep away from that girl because if you ever mess around again, you will wind up in a ditch!"* One of the people who witnessed this said that Morretti was visibly afraid of this Frank, and during the time, this Frank was cursing and swearing at him, Morretti apologized to Frank and left the table when Frank told him to, "beat it." This "Frank" turned out to be mobster Frank "One Ear" Fratto.

Adler's name even surfaced when mobster Ju Ju Grieco was convicted of raising the amounts of customer's checks at nightclubs without them knowing about it. Grieco used some checks from the Black Onyx to steal money while Adler was the owner.

Just before Adler sold the Trade Winds in 1959, Marshall Caifano, Phil Alderisio, and Obbie Frabotta met with Adler for several nights in the office at the Trade Winds for around 5 hours. Right before Adler's disappearance, Adler had made two trips to Las Vegas and one trip Miami, Florida, where he met with known hoodlums connected to the Chicago Outfit.

Adler was also known to have a piece of the prostitution racket running out of his Trade Winds restaurant. Adler had full approval of the women working in the Trade Winds, and before any girl could work the room, they were told by the Outfit that they had to "lay up" with Adler. The girls were called "26 Girls" and one of them, who was known as a nymphomaniac, was known as "Frabotta's girl" and every time Frabotta would come to the Trade Winds this "26 Girl" had to sit with him all night.

The day after Adler's body was found, the police set out to arrest Obbie Frabotta and his brother Joe Frabotta. The reason given at the time was that the way Adler's body was disposed of fit the gangland pattern in the manner in which the body of Anthony Ragucci was disposed of in 1953. Ragucci was known as a narcotics racketeer whose body was found on August 9, 1953, in a sewer at 35th Street and Winchester Avenue. Joe Frabotta was arrested as a prime suspect but was released due to lack of evidence.

The new owners of the Trade Winds were interviewed by the FBI and said that Adler had approached them in November 1959 and offered them the Trade Winds if they would assume all of the financial obligations, which amounted to approximately $63,000. They added that no cash changed hands and they knew of no hoodlums connected with the Trade Winds. The FBI also discovered that after the new owners had taken over the Trade Winds, Jimmy Allegretti and Marshall Caifano were the new secret owners; and during the time Adler had owned it, one of the silent owners was Sebastian Vermiglio, a Milwaukee, Wisconsin hoodlum close to Caifano and Phil Alderisio. Vermiglio was an associate of New York mob boss Joseph Bonnano and Detroit top hoodlum Pete Licavoli.

When Adler owned the Black Onyx, an informant told the FBI that Jimmy and Benny Allegretti would come into the nightclub and never paid for any drinks or food that he or his guests would order. When this informant asked Allegretti why he did not pay, Allegretti replied, "*Why should I pay when it's my place!*" Two days after Adler's body was found in the sewer, the informant was told from "Jimmy A" that the, "*boys were to stay away from the club because there was too much heat on the place.*"

One interview with an FBI informant told the agents that Obbie Frabotta was at the Trade Winds almost every night and generally stayed until six in the morning when the restaurant closed. He said Frabotta usually occupied a table to the rear of the restaurant and that at least twenty different people regularly came in to talk to Frabotta. He also added that Adler was well acquainted with all of these individuals and he believed that the relationship between them was much more than a customer-owner relationship. He told police that one of the men who often met with Adler and Frabotta in the past was Leon Marcus who was killed in 1957. One of the waitresses told the FBI that sometimes when Frabotta walked into the Trade Winds he would ask her sarcastically, *"Where is the so-called boss?"* or *"Who is watching the store?"* Because of these sayings, the waitress believed that Frabotta either owned the place or was a partner.

Arther Adler

Arthur Adler was described as a soft-spoken man who always had a smile on his face and dressed in flashy cloths but was devoted to his wife and five children. However, many of the employees painted a different story. One told the FBI that Adler wanted to act like a "hood" but just didn't fit the part. This employee had heard that Adler often "played" around with other women but could not furnish the names of his other girlfriends. He was known to have affairs with female employees of his restaurant and had many well-known prostitutes from the Northside of Chicago. As the FBI interviewed known prostitutes, more and more information about Adler and his thirst for women and booze came to light. One girl interviewed said that Adler loved to frequent an African-American house of prostitution at 47th Street just west of Lake Park. This house of prostitution was known to be a high-class house of whores with the theme of the old New Orleans house of prostitution. The madam of this house wore excess jewelry and gaudy costumes and the bartenders wore white coats with a red tie. He added that many sexual acts, natural and unnatural, were performed for or by the customers in this house. She added that Adler would pay money just to be entertained by others performing the sexual acts. One of Adler's girlfriends said that Adler needed to watch because he was sexually bored and needed unnatural sex acts to get him excited.

She also added that Adler often visited African-American nightclubs such as the old Benny Strum's Tropics on 51st Street and the old Sutherland Hotel on the south side of Chicago. This girl also added that Adler really enjoyed the company of African-American prostitutes and boasted many times how he could get furs and jewelry cheap. She added one time that while on a date with Adler, he had to stop and visit with mobster Jimmy "Monk" Allegretti at the old Devonshire Hotel in Chicago for a meeting. Another girlfriend said that Adler was emotionally troubled and liked to receive sympathy. After he started drink heavily and couldn't drive, Adler would ask this girlfriend to drive him around to various after-hour clubs and would sometimes drink until noon the next day. Another African-American prostitute Adler used to frequent was known to be bisexual and told the FBI that she knew how to please Adler.

Other information was uncovered showing that Arthur and his wife Mary were both having extra marital affairs. Employees told the FBI how Adler and his wife would have violent arguments in the Trade Winds in front of their employees and customers over each other's affairs. One person who knew Adler said that on three occasions Arthur had to send his wife home because she had too much to drink and would begin to fight about the woman he slept with. On at least two different occasions, Mary Adler hit her husband in front of customers and employees screaming and crying, "*You're no dam good.*" This man stated that Arthur had, "*over a hundred on the string*" and that Mrs. Adler was, "*not too fussy herself.*" One of the arguments was when Adler found out that his wife Mary was having an affair with Vincent Morretti. After the fight, Mary took the children and went to Florida without telling her husband. Arthur Adler went to Florida and the two decided to work on their marriage.

Arthur Adler was known as a famous host at his Trade Winds club. Top movie stars of the time like Milton Berle, Elizabeth Taylor, Mike Todd, Betty Hutton, and once the lord mayor of Dublin, would head to his club for entertainment. Adler was also close with Chicago columnist Irv Kupcinet who, when interviewed about his relationship, admitted being a close friend of Adler's. But at the time of Adler's death, many close to Adler said he was having trouble booking top entertainment at his clubs because he was under increased pressure by tax agents investigating the financial affairs of Marshall Caifano. Chicago Police had always suspected Adler was merely a front man for Caifano and Frabotta. Irv Kupcinet even asked Adler if he was fronting for hoodlums and Adler denied any such association and offered to show his books to Kupcinet in order to prove no such affiliations. Kupcinet declined to view the records.

The FBI had encountered Adler in the past. In 1957, a survey was taken by the Chicago FBI office regarding obscene matters in the Chicago area. Arthur Adler was questioned as to his knowledge of the obscene matters in Chicago since he owned a latex company. Adler told the FBI that he would sell nothing illegal like obscene novelties, photographs, or playing cards since he would never put his investment in the business in jeopardy.

Friends of Adler told police that Adler had complained in November 1959, telling his friends he was "pushed out" of the Trade Winds by hoodlums. It was also learned that Adler might have been forced to sell his other club, the Black Onyx, which he owned for 8 months during 1958, when it was learned that the buyer was Charles Leonardi, a bartender and distant relative of mob boss Sam Giancana. In a later report, it stated that Adler had no "silent partner" in the Black Onyx lounge and that Leonardi told the police that he made a deal with Adler to buy the lounge but the deal fell thru when he could not raise enough money.

Then on April 4, 1960, a mob informant told FBI Agents that Arthur Adler had obtained money to run his enterprises through the Hacking Brothers Company. The investigation disclosed that a Joseph J. Panucci, listed as the President and Manager of the company, ran Hacking Brothers. Agents went to the company located at 185 North Wabash Avenue in Chicago and interviewed Panucci. Panucci informed the agents that on August 21, 1959, his company had loaned $10,000 to Black Onyx Inc, to operate the Black Onyx Night Club at Walton and Rush Street. Panucci advised that Charles Leonardi, who was listed as president of the Black Onyx, Inc, negotiated the loan. He also added that, subsequently, the former officers of the Black Onyx, Inc. had resigned; Charles Leonardi was elected president and his wife, Jean, as the secretary. The agents learned that Hacking Brothers Company was a "juice" loan operation and it was under the control of the "Outfit." Mob associate Leo Rugendorf was listed as a "juice" collector for the Hacking Brothers Company.

Immediately the conclusion of why Adler was killed was believed to be from his appearance as a cooperating witness in front of a federal grand jury in March 1959 investigating organized crime in the Rush Street area. Adler did tell someone close to him that the day following his appearance before the private committee he received a phone call from a well-known Chicago hoodlum not named. This hood repeated to Adler, over the phone word-for-word, the testimony of Adler to the jury. Adler asked this hood; how did he know what was said during the "closing hearings" and was informed that one of the jury members was "our man." Another person called in those hearings was Joseph Bronge. Bronge was shot many times as he tried to escape his killers running down Division Street in Melrose Park in 1959. He would die months later from his wounds. Just before Adler disappeared in January 1960, it was thought that he was going to be called upon once again to testify against organized crime.

One witness, a Miss Hope Vela, a waitress in a tavern on Roosevelt Road, came forward and told police that Adler bought three packages of cigarettes in the tavern at about 6:30 p.m. the night of his disappearance and left the bar, walking down toward Halsted Street. She said he walked past his car and out of view. Days later, Marshall Caifano, Ralph Pierce, Joseph "Caesar" DiVarco, and Vincent Inserro were picked up and brought in for questioning concerning the Adler murder. All denied having anything to do with Adler and all said they had not seen him in months. DiVarco was questioned because he had forced nightclub owners on Rush Street, including Adler, to buy his expensive glass washing machines from the company he owned. Ralph Pierce was so mad at being arrested and questioned in the Adler murder case that he filed a false arrest suit against the Chicago Police Department. The FBI discovered during the investigation the following information concerning this arrest, *"It is noted that Pierce was arrested in April 1960 by the Intelligence Unit of the Chicago Police Department and that the Intelligence Unit arrested Pierce more as a matter of harassment rather than for purpose of interview in the Adler investigation inasmuch as the Chicago Police Department had developed no information showing any concrete connection between Pierce and Adler except for the fact that the residences of Pierce and Adler are relatively close."*

One report stated that Adler caused top mob bosses to lose $100,000 in a business venture. One informant even told the FBI that she heard Adler was kicked in the groin and dumped in the sewer alive.

In May 1960, the official report from the deputy coroner said that Arthur Adler might have been scared to death. Medical authorities were unable to determine what caused his death and added, *"It's quite possible he died of fright, we've had other such cases."* The autopsy showed no gunshot wounds, broken bones or other indications of cause of death.

Mary Alder's theory as to why her husband was killed was, *"it was a horrible mistake."* She believed that many major jewel and fur thieves rolled into the Trade Winds late at night and would have too much to drink; talking too much about jobs, they pulled. Her theory was that Art Adler overheard some of the conversations and one of the thieves killed him. She also said that she believed that her husband was "ordered" to "get lost" by certain parties that she refused to elaborate on. She did show the FBI a letter she received in the mail dated April 1, 1960. The letter read:

Dear Mrs. Adler,

You are smart in stating that you do not think hoodlums murdered your husband, as you have your children to consider and they need a mother. Hoodlums would not stop in murdering you, too, if you tried to make charges against them, and this wouldn't bring your husband back. It is indeed too bad these hoodlums have such a stronghold, but as stated above, your children need a mother and it's best to retract your former statements, as you have done. May god ease your sorrow and in time, it will.

The Feds went to interview an informant who had been around the Chicago mob since the days of Al Capone to ask for information about Adler's death. This informant said that information he received was that Adler was killed due to the fact that he *"married the outfit and then tried to leave the family"* by disengaging himself from the nightclub enterprises which he operated for the hoodlums. This informant added that when a legitimate businessman throws in with Chicago hoodlums it is only under special circumstances that he is later allowed to divorce himself from them. This informant added, *"Adler bucked hoodlums by refusing to front for them any further and that as a result he was disciplined in order to warn others who might feel similarly."*

However, the feds had been listening in on many of Chicago's top mobsters over hidden microphones and were surprised that many didn't know who killed Adler. Two of the top hoodlums discussed that clearance must have been received from the leaders before they could kill someone connected with hoodlums or whose killing would bring heat on the Outfit. This puzzled the FBI because even if top hoodlums did not kill Adler they should have been aware of Adler's killer unless it was Sam DeStefano, who was crazy and unpredictable.

One informant close to mobsters from the old Tam-O'Shanter Golf Club told the Feds that he heard that Adler was killed by Marshall Caifano and Jackie Cerone. He also added that the two had also recently killed mobster Roger Touhy in December 1959. When the FBI pressed the informant as to how he knew this, he finally admitted that it was not first-hand information and that if he gave the name of the source, he would be killed if the FBI approached this man.

Sam DeStefano even told FBI agents during an interview that if Adler was a front man for Caifano and Frabotta that he would never go to anyone else for a loan but would instead receive his financing directly through Caifano and Frabotta. For that reason, Mad Sam told the Feds that he could not understand why anyone investigating the death of Adler would suspect him.

One of Adler's girlfriends told the FBI that Adler had told her just a few weeks before his disappearance that if anything happened to him, his wife and children would be taken care of and that he loved his wife but she spent too much money and drank too much. This woman said that she didn't think Adler was the kind of man who would take his own life but added that she felt it was not beyond the realm of possibility that he may have paid someone to kill him so he didn't have to.

While the FBI went around interviewing many hoodlums, one report talks about the interview with old First Ward Alderman John D'Arco Sr. on April 28, 1960. Agent William Roemer went into the First Ward offices at 100 North La Salle Street in Chicago's Loop and asked D'Arco if he had any knowledge of the death of Arthur Adler. D'Arco stated that he could not understand why he would be contacted in the Adler case. Roemer pointed out that D'Arco was known to be an associate of Adler, and that he frequently patronized the Trade Winds. He also was an associate of many of Adler's associates, who were somewhat questionable as to reputation. D'Arco denied that he was in any way associated with hoodlums, except that he knew some of them through his associations with the First Ward. He admitted that he was a good friend of Adler's and handled some business for the West Side Latex Company. He had nothing to say about the Adler murder. Then Roemer interviewed mobster Pat Marcy, who was then the mob's First Ward fixer, about his association with Adler. Marcy said that he felt badly over the death of Adler but knew nothing concerning his death.

As it turned out, the reason D'Arco and Marcy were interviewed was because the FBI discovered that Adler had several insurance policies with Anco Insurance Agency in which D'Arco was a partner with Pat Marcy, Frank Annunzio, and old time gangster Buddy Jacobson. Another reason was the fact that D'Arco and Marcy were close to Anthony "Tony X" Esposito Sr. It was learned that Tony X's son, Anthony "Sonny" Esposito Jr., met regularly at the Trade Winds Club with his gang of burglars. Esposito, Charles Vaughn, William Carroll, Manny Stasin, and Robert "Chimes" Owca would plan their robberies in the club and Adler was seen many times as being involved in these conversations. One informant said that Esposito was very close to Adler and that Adler was involved in smuggling watch parts from Switzerland through vessels traveling the St. Lawrence Seaway. The informant stated that at the time this operation was a very lucrative situation for the racket elements in the Chicago area.

The FBI showed up at the residence of Marshall Caifano located at The Delaware Towers at 25 East Delaware in Chicago on July 25, 1960. Caifano refused to open the door and held the conversation with the agents in the hallway. Caifano told the agents that he knew nothing about the Adler murder, and if they wanted to continue the interview, it had to be in the presence of his attorney. When the agents asked who was his attorney he replied, "*You guys know*" and ended the conversation. Next, the agents went to Obbie Frabotta's apartment at 2950 Lake Shore Drive for an interview. This time his wife answered the door and told the agents that, she had no idea where Obbie was and that she couldn't help them. Then the agents headed over to Sam DeStefano's house to catch him by surprise but he was not home. The agents tried to surprise DeStefano on July 28 and 29 but both times DeStefano was not home.

There was even a mention of a hoodlum from Adler's past living in Baltimore, Maryland, who was interviewed. This unnamed hoodlum stated that he would steal watches from the company he worked for. He mentioned that an incident occurred where he was caught withholding money from Adler and another unnamed man who was Adler's partner in the fencing of these watches. This hoodlum was severely beaten before he agreed to pay $10,000 to Adler and his partner as restitution.

By June of 1960, the Chicago Police had placed their investigation into inactive status after they concluded that Adler's death was caused by a heart attack, possibly during sex with a prostitute. This conclusion was based on the fact that Adler was found in the sewer naked. The FBI closed their investigation into the murder in March 1961.

On August 10, 1960, the Coroner's office returned a verdict as to the cause of death. They believed Adler was killed by strangulation due to marks on the neck that could have been from human hands. The official report reads as follows, "On the basis of a review of the records of the necropsy performed by Dr. Joseph E. Campbell on the body of Arthur Adler, March 28, 1960; the results of the toxicological analysis of the tissues submitted and as reported; and further with the significant changes disclosed by the microscopic examination of many tissues of the body, death in our opinion in all probability resulted from pulmonary asphyxia associated with extensive recent traumatic lacerations, recent hemorrhages, and initial phases of an acute cellulites of the superficial and deep tissues of the anterior portion of the neck."

Both the Chicago PD and the FBI would add information as time went on when Adler's name was mentioned in other investigations. One time Arthur Adler's name appeared in a report when the FBI interviewed Jane Epsteen, the one-time wife of mob associate Peter Epsteen. Jane told the agents that one night in 1961 she overheard her husband and Irving Gordon, a one-time political power house in the old First Ward of Chicago, talking about how, in their opinion, the Outfit had Adler killed and that they wanted to ask about the death but were too afraid to discuss it with Rocco and Joe Fischetti.

In 1964, an informant came forward and told FBI agents that he was told personally by mobster Albert "Obbie" Frabotta that Sam DeStefano killed Arthur Adler. FBI Agent William F. Roemer Jr. wrote in his book "The Enforcer" that Adler was brought into DeStefano's basement, stripped naked and tortured with an ice pick. Roemer went to DeStefano's house to ask him straight out if he killed Adler. As mentioned before Roemer wrote that DeStefano called his wife and kids into the room where they all witnessed DeStefano exploding in anger, proclaiming to have God put cancer in his family's eyes if he killed Adler.

The FBI also interviewed a prostitute who frequented the old mob hangout, the Le Bistro, and she told the FBI that she heard rumors that Marshall Caifano personally did away with Adler.

Whoever killed Adler, whether it was Sam DeStefano, Marshall Caifano, Obbie Frabotta or the robbery gang he got involved with, no one has ever been arrested for the murder of Arthur Adler and it's still technically an open murder investigation. However, the Chicago PD cannot find the Adler murder case files, they seemed to have disappeared.

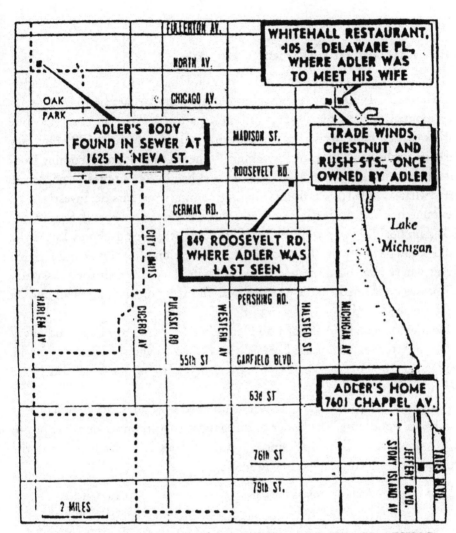

WHITEHALL RESTAURANT, 105 E. DELAWARE PL., WHERE ADLER WAS TO MEET HIS WIFE

ADLER'S BODY FOUND IN SEWER AT 1625 N. NEVA ST.

TRADE WINDS, CHESTNUT AND RUSH STS., ONCE OWNED BY ADLER

849 ROOSEVELT RD. WHERE ADLER WAS LAST SEEN

ADLER'S HOME 7601 CHAPPEL AV.

SITES INVOLVED IN ARTHUR ADLER SLAYING

Chapter Sixteen

The Murder of Charles Vaughn

The 942nd gangland killing since 1919 in Chicago was Charles Vaughn. On March 31, 1960, Charles Vaughn told his wife Barbara he was going out for a moment to walk his dog and get a newspaper down by the corner. While Barbara sat at home in their four room basement apartment at 1705 Diversey Parkway with their 2-year-old daughter, she heard a loud "bang" coming from outside but quickly wrote it off as a car backfiring. As minutes went by, she heard what sounded like a whimpering dog coming from outside. Investigating, she found her fox terrier had returned home without her husband. Scared, she picked up her child and walked outside to see where her husband was. As she walked down the street, she reached the intersection of Diversey and Paulina Street where she could see her husband laying face down in the crosswalk. Witnesses confirmed that it was her husband lying on the pavement and he had been shot dead.

Charles B. Vaughn was born on December 13, 1930, to Henry and Mary Vaughn. After serving in the U.S. Marines Corp during the Korean War, he headed back to Chicago where he became involved in burglaries and narcotics rackets.

Vaughn was part of a gang of mob-connected wise guys, drug addicts, and small-time hoodlums. The leader of this gang was Anthony "Sonny" Esposito Jr., also known as "Tony Boy" since his father "Tony X" was a member of the Outfit. The gang consisted of the following:

Anthony "Sonny" Esposito Jr.	William Carroll
Emanuel "Manny" Stasin	Robin Dragin
Robert "Chimes" Owca	Albert Spagnola
Salvatore "Sal" Romano	Robert Luther
Edward Speice	Vincent Deora
Elvin "Corky" Groenemeyer	Rob Regan
Frank "Butch" Esposito	Sam Taglia
Arlene Romano "Collins"	Charles Vaughan

Through his friendship with Anthony "Sonny" Esposito Jr., Charles Vaughn was placed on the city of Chicago payroll in 1956 as an asphalt helper being sponsored by Sonny's uncle Frank "Frankie X" Esposito. At the time of his death, he had recently been given a temporary appointment as a section foreman in charge of a labor crew that hauled garbage.

Witnesses said a car with 2 to 3 people riding in it pulled up to Vaughn. One who looked like a woman got out and shot Vaughn in the abdomen, chest, and right arm. The killer jumped back into the car and it sped off down the street.

Police learned that Vaughn, Sonny Esposito, William Carroll and Manny Stasin had been involved in a robbery when the gang broke into a card game held by the wives of syndicate bosses and robbed them of all their money and jewelry. During the robbery, one of the wives was pistol-whipped and thrown to the ground. It was mentioned that the robbery might have netted around $30,000 worth of furs and jewels. The husbands of the wives that were robbed discovered the members of this gang and made a demand for the stolen loot to be returned. The gang refused.

On November 7, 1959, Sonny Esposito and William Carroll were kidnapped, handcuffed, dumped in sewers in Melrose Park and Broadview, and Esposito was shot. Both survived and managed to crawl out of the sewers to get help. Esposito was taken to Florida to hide out while Carroll would disappear never to be heard of again.

Weeks later in December 1959, Manny Stasin agreed to return the stolen goods to one of the mobsters and sent a key to a locker where the loot was stored. But this mobster decided that Manny was already a dead man. He was kidnapped by syndicate gunmen and shot four times in the head and chest but somehow managed to live. Vaughn was arrested and questioned in the shooting since Manny was known to have lived with Vaughn for a year and Manny had mentioned to others in the gang that he was scared of Vaughn. Vaughn was released, while Stasin was found guilty on a burglary charge and sent to prison.

The Chicago Police couldn't determine if Charles Vaughn participated in this robbery or merely fenced some of the merchandise. In either case,

Vaughn was badly in need of money for a period; he was not even able to buy heating oil for his residence. The police theorized that Vaughn would have found it impossible or extremely difficult to repay this mobster for any of the loot he had disposed of and this may have lead to Vaughn's death.

However, the Chicago Police Department told the FBI that they believed that Sam DeStefano was the primary suspect in this murder. One of the reasons was that a piece of paper bearing the name of DeStefano and his address was found on the body of Vaughn. DeStefano did admit that he knew Vaughn and at one time rented Vaughn a room at his house.

When FBI agents went to DeStefano's house on August 24, 1960, the possibility of his involvement in the murder of Vaughn was brought to his attention. DeStefano denied any connection with the killing and told the agents the following story:

"Four or five Chicago detectives went to DeStefano's house on the evening of the Vaughn murder and vigorously interviewed him there until approximately 3 a.m. the next morning. DeStefano stated that two of these detectives were close personal friends of his and that he was able to convince these two detectives and the others present, with the exception of one that he was in no way involved in the killing of Vaughn. He added that the remaining detective refused to change his belief in this regard. DeStefano said that shortly after the detective left, he received a phone call saying, *"Don't answer me, but you recognize my voice. Don't say nothing, your phone is tapped. Meet me right away in the usual place. It's important."* DeStefano said he recognized the voice as being that of one of the detectives who interviewed him and who was a close personal friend of his. He stated that he then put his gun in his pocket and went to the pre-arranged place where he found the detective excitedly waiting for him. He stated that the detective told him that the other detective who refused to change his belief regarding DeStefano's guilt was convinced of such guilt and was equally convinced that the Chicago Police Department would never be able to prove DeStefano's guilt. This detective told DeStefano that it was the other detective's intention to kill DeStefano in order to put an end to the killings, which he, DeStefano, was allegedly involved in. The purpose of the meeting then was to alert DeStefano concerning this other detective's intentions.

DeStefano became so angry that this detective was going to kill him that, he went to the 11th and State Street Police Department and to City Hall and in a loud and boisterous manner informed anyone who would listen to him that if this detective should never come near him again, or even if he should pass in his car on DeStefano's street, that DeStefano would, "shoot him in the head."

With Vaughn dead, Stasin in prison for 5 to 10 years, Carroll missing, and most of the other gang members in jail, the incident faded away. Sonny Esposito's father, Anthony "Tony X" Esposito Sr., went to Sam DeStefano and Gus Alex to have the contract on his son's life called off. Sonny was allowed to return to Chicago and resume his activities in the mob's rackets. It was later learned that mobsters George and Nick Bravos were behind the kidnapping and shooting of Esposito and Carroll, but DeStefano and his right-hand man, Charles Crimaldi had a hand in the incident involving the 4-gang members.

The coroner's jury returned a verdict of murder by persons unknown for Vaughn. The Chicago PD testified at the inquiry that they believed that the motive for the murder was vengeance since slugs from three different calibers were found in the body of Vaughn. The murder investigation into Vaughn's death is listed as a cold case and is still active today.

Chapter Seventeen

The Discovery of a Decomposed Body in Broadview, IL

When William Carroll and Sonny Esposito were kidnapped on the night of November 7, 1959 by syndicate gunmen, all that was supposed to happen was two more names would be added to the list of mob murder victims. Instead, a mysterious third victim came to the attention of the police.

Esposito, kidnapped by mob killers, was taken to Rice Street between 10th and 11th Avenues in Melrose Park, handcuffed, beaten, dumped into a sewer and after he landed at the bottom, the hit men fired down into the sewer. Esposito was hit with one .38 caliber slug in the right thigh. Once the gunmen were gone, Esposito managed to crawl out of the sewer and make his way to one of the nearby houses where he knocked on the door and collapsed. The startled homeowner called the police and arriving officers took Esposito to a nearby hospital.

After leaving Esposito for dead, the mob killers then drove a few miles south to the town of Broadview, Illinois. Stopping at the secluded intersection of Beach and Lexington Streets, they would repeat the same act on William Carroll. This time the mob killers may not have had as much time to beat up and shoot Carroll. A car may have spooked them, causing them to rush the job. Handcuffed, he was pushed into the sewer headfirst and left to rot. However, as Carroll hit the bottom of his intended tomb, he discovered the spot had already been taken. Staring Carroll in the face was the decomposing body of the last person to anger the mob. Carroll was able to climb eleven feet from the bottom of the sewer to street level by using the rungs built into the sewer wall while still handcuffed. Once out of the sewer, he walked to a gas station on 1st Avenue in the neighboring town of Maywood. Seeing a disheveled, handcuffed man enter, the attendant quickly called the authorities.

When Carroll explained the story of his kidnapping to the police, the police went back to the sewer where he had been dumped. There they made the gruesome discovery of the decaying corpse. The body was recovered from the sewer whereupon the police and coroner noted that the victim was a male who had been shot in the head. Both of the victim's hands had been cut off. The initial police investigation never solved the case and the man's identity remains a mystery to this day.

In 2005, the Broadview Police re-opened this case. According to Lieutenant James Kosik, several new leads were investigated, but as of 2008, the case remains unsolved. The victim has never been positively identified and the reason for his murder remains shrouded in mystery. Should anyone have any information about the 1959 mystery man or information regarding Esposito or Carroll, the Broadview Police are interested in solving this cold case.

The use of the sewers for disposing of bodies was one of Mad Sam DeStefano's favorite past times and it is speculated that this man was or had something to do with Sam DeStefano.

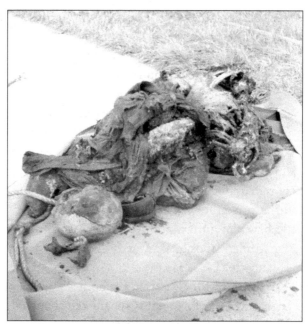

Unknown murder victim from sewer (author's collection)

Body & sewer in Broadway, Illinois (author's collection)

Chapter Eighteen

The Murder of William "Action" Jackson

On April 11, 1961, Chicago patrolman George Petyo was driving his squad car on the lower level of Wacker Drive when he noticed a green two-door 1957 Cadillac parked on the side of the street between Franklin and Wells streets with a flat tire. When he went to investigate, he noticed an odor coming from the car and called for Sergeant John Costas to come and investigate. The two found the car doors unlocked and the keys in the ignition. When they opened the trunk, there lay the decomposing body of 40-year-old William Patrick Jackson, known as "Action" Jackson.

William "Action" Jackson

William "Action" Jackson was married to Marian Jackson and they had 2 daughters, Patricia Ann and Margaret Alice Jackson. Action was known in syndicate circles as a mob "juice" collector who specialized in pain for delinquent customers. Chicago Police described him as a man with the body of a giant and the brain of a child. Action Jackson was living at 1215 S. 49th Court in Cicero where his reputation as a goon was feared by many men and woman. Weighing around 300 pounds, he used his position and weight to get the job done when ordered to. However, one informant told investigators that Jackson was a coward at heart. If anyone stood up to him, he would cringe; and whenever he was around someone with power, he would tremble in fear. Reports date back to 1941 when William Jackson was arrested in Green Bay, Wisconsin, for assault and robbery, which landed him in prison. In 1947, he was arrested and charged with rape; he would go on to beat those charges, but gained the reputation of being extremely brutal towards women. At the time of his arrest, he was listed as William "Fat Boy" Jackson. In 1949, he was arrested and sentenced to 4 to 8 years in Joliet Prison for robbery. In 1953, he was paroled and became known as a "sadist with an apologetic tone" muscle man for gangsters in Chicago. In February 1960, Jackson broke into the apartment of a fellow burglar who was in prison for raping and committing brutalities.

On April 14, 1961, Action Jackson, Joseph Airdo, Dominick Rossi, aka Frank Martin, and William Mazzuca of 1406 22nd Street in Melrose Park, a Cook County highway department employee, were arrested at a warehouse at 1731 Pershing Road as they were unloading $70,000 worth of electrical appliances from a stolen truck. The loot was from the robbery of the Chicago Burlington & Quincy railroad yards at 31st Street and Ogden Avenue in Cicero. When police arrived, Airdo tried to escape by jumping through a window but was captured. Rossi tried to hide under a truck but was caught. Jackson stood still because he was just too fat to move. Agents arrested Jackson who used the name William Murphy to try to conceal his identity and his connections with Sam DeStefano and William Daddono, but FBI agents soon uncovered who he really was.

Agents learned that Jackson was a "juice" collector for DeStefano and when not in use, he worked for Daddono as a "muscle" man in his gambling operations. He earned his nickname of "Action" because "Action" was slang for "Juice Man" which meant debt-collector. While on bond for the arrest, Joseph Airdo was arrested for the armed robbery of two National Tea Company stores and sent to Statesville prison. At the trial, Rossi and Mazzuca testified that Action Jackson had called them and demanded that they help him unload the truck. Both said that they were so frightened of Jackson's terrorist reputation that they had to do as they were ordered. They also added that they both turned to crime because of the fees mob loan sharks were charging them. Joe Airdo was sentenced to 5 years in prison after he completed his other prison term; Mazzuca and Rossi were sentenced to 4 years in prison. It was believed that Mazzuca was somehow related to William Daddono but no further information was revealed.

When police found the almost nude body of Action Jackson in the trunk of a car parked in Chicago, his body was face forward with rope marks on his wrists and feet. He had many cuts and burns all over his body and it was apparent to police that he had been tortured. The car was registered to a William Kearney, which had been an alias of Jackson's in the past. It was believed that the body had been there for a few days. They found that his chest had been crushed, he had a hole in his right ear from some kind of sharp object, and they confirmed that he had been beaten to death. One policeman who had arrested Jackson in the past told a reporter that, *"Jackson was kinda goofy. Maybe there were some people who were afraid he wouldn't stand up under pressure. He might have been killed to keep him from talking."*

The coroner's report on Jackson's death listed the following:

1. Impaled on meat hook, doused with water. Cattle prod (electrical) used in rectum and pubic area.
2. Limbs cut (apparently with an ice pick).
3. Beaten about most of the body (apparently with baseball bat).
4. Severe body burns, inflicted with a blowtorch.
5. Incineration of the penis.

Two days after the discovery, his body still lay in the Cook County Morgue, unclaimed. The attendant told reporters, *"I know who he is from the newspapers but nobody bothered to stop by here and tell us for the record. Nobody wanted to claim the body."* Eventually his body was claimed and his wake was held at Raleigh Funeral Home located at 2307 S. Laramie in Chicago.

Days after the discovery of Jackson's body, police sent word out that they were searching for Sam DeStefano, William Daddono, Larry "The Hood" Buonoguldi, Sam Lewis, John Matassa, Frank "The Calico Kid" Teutonica, and Nick Vallo for questioning. They also arrested a taxi cab driver named Henry "Ace" Sammarco. Sammarco left a note at Jackson's apartment a day or two before his body was found telling Jackson, *"I have $100 for you. Meet me at the airport."* Jackson's wife told police that "Ace" Sammarco called the apartment and said, *"I want to get off the books. Tell Action I have the $100."* He did tell police that he saw Jackson alive as late as 2 p.m. on Tuesday, August 8, when he saw Jackson sitting in his car in the O'Hare Airport parking lot eating a sandwich. After 20 hours of questioning, "Ace" was released from custody. Police were also seeking an unnamed woman seen sitting in Jackson's car with Jackson on the last night he was seen alive. It did not help the investigation that the Chicago Police Detective Department had demoted 21 of their officers for not solving or coming close to solving 11 of the last gang-related murders as of 1961.

A Chicago informant to the FBI who was questioned about the Action Jackson murder said that Jackson was one of the leading enforcers for Sam DeStefano and that Jackson rivaled DeStefano as being sadistic and enjoyed torturing individuals. This informant claimed that Jackson was killed because he was giving information about Sam DeStefano and his associates to a reporter working at that time for the *Chicago Tribune* and because Jackson was receiving money for information. He said it was a common belief in the Chicago underground that Jackson was an informant of some kind. He stated that on one occasion about a month before Jackson was killed, Jackson drove out to Woodstock, Illinois, with a companion and while there, left the car and contacted someone for about an hour-and-a-half while his companion remained in the car. Later, this companion discussed the situation with Sam DeStefano, who resolved from the description that Jackson was visiting a *"Tribune"* reporter who resided in Woodstock, Illinois. FBI Agents believed the informant about Jackson's association with DeStefano when they checked with the Chicago PD who had observed a series of meetings between DeStefano and Jackson on DeStefano's front porch a month before Jackson was killed.

Once again, Sam DeStefano was questioned at the Austin Police Station by the Chicago PD about this and his association with Jackson. DeStefano stated he knew Jackson only socially and that he knew nothing of Jackson's business activities. Agents again went to DeStefano's house in the fall of 1962 to question him; again, DeStefano said he had nothing to do with the killing of Action Jackson but that he understood that Jackson was killed because he was an informant for a Chicago newspaper reporter.

In August 1961, DeStefano told a newspaper reporter that, "*I helped Jackson with his problems with the government* (referring to a hijacking case in which Jackson was involved with), *and I helped him get a lawyer and a bondsman. I help people in trouble like Jackson, and then collect a consultation fee from them, I'm not a "juice" man, I'm a broker.*" DeStefano told the reporter that he was worried that he, too, might suffer the same fate as Action Jackson as he showed the reporter a loaded pistol in one of his desk drawers in his living room saying, "*That's not normally there, but since this thing happened with Jackson, I keep the pistol there so it's handy. The police have questioned me in all the recent murders except that of Jackson. They came into my house and told me just how I did it. I don't know a thing about Jackson. Sure, I knew the guy. I knew he treated people rough and I warned him about that. But I don't know who hit him. It wasn't me.*"

An FBI report dated August 25, 1961, mentioned that a mob informant came forward saying that Action Jackson was associated with mobster Sam Lewis in the operation of Parr Loan Company in Oak Park, Illinois. He added that Sam Lewis was a partner of Sam Giancana. He also stated that the building in which this loan company was located was owned by Chicago PD Captain Louis Capparelli, who was described as an associate of Chicago hoodlums.

Banker Donald Parrillo, who was a known associate of alleged mob figures, owned the Parr Loan Company located at 747 Madison Street in Oak Park. Running the company under the title of "office manager" was Sam Lewis, a Capone-era gangster who served 18 months in prison for bootlegging and a known close friend of Murray Humphreys. Sam Lewis was also one of the top leading syndicate "juice" loan bosses at the time in Chicago. When Sam Lewis was interviewed about the Jackson murder, he admitted that Jackson was paid $125 a week, plus commissions, to "round up bad debts" for the Parr Finance Company. Lewis's statement was, "*I know nothing about the Jackson murder. The coppers are barking up the wrong tree when they start looking for me. How do I know what happened to Jackson? He was in a million things. He could have been killed for just as many reasons. The police have been on me all my life. I just go about my business and don't pay attention to what they say. I don't deal in 'juice,' I wouldn't take it. There are no juice loans in our company. Why, we're even licensed by the state. We couldn't do anything wrong. Jackson said he could bring in a lot of loans from cab drivers at O'Hare Field. He said he could make the collections out there. But that was a lot of baloney. All he brought in was a lot of bums. We never could catch those guys to get their payments. We wouldn't take Sam DeStefano's customers, they're all bums. Occasionally we did loan money to a guy so he could get out of the hook with a 'juice' man, but we stopped doing that because it was too risky."* After the interview Lewis agreed to a lie detector test, but later his lawyer informed the police his client would not take one.

Another informant told the FBI on May 11, 1961, that Sam Lewis and Action Jackson appeared at the informant's house and informed him that it was mandatory that he meet with them the following day to discuss the loan of approximately $10,000 which he owed to Parr Loan Company. The informant met Sam Lewis on the street near Eddie Foy's strip joint, then owned by mobster Tony Tornabene, and the result of the meeting was that he was to pay at least $1,000 within the next two weeks to Parr Loan Company. Lewis told him that he had received instructions from mobster Lester Kruse to the effect that under no circumstances was he to harm him but could insist upon payment of the debt. He added that Jackson admitted to him that he had recently been arrested by the FBI for the truck theft. Jackson told the informant that he was not directly involved in the theft, however, he had gone to the drop to pick up some merchandise, and that he was arrested for stealing the truck and trailer by the FBI.

Police found it interesting that three other gang-related murders were connected to Parr Loan Company. Ralph DelGenio, Edward McNally, and Salvatore Morretti were all borrowers from Parr Loan and all three were killed. Two years after the murder of Action Jackson, Donald Parrillo was chosen to be the new First Ward Alderman in Chicago by Sam Giancana, Pat Marcy, and John D'Arco.

Another informant speculated that Action Jackson was in trouble in the juice racket and was killed by Sam DeStefano. Police reported that Action Jackson had set up his own "juice" loan racket on the side at the same time he was working for everyone else. A Mrs. June Boniakowski was questioned and admitted that she and Jackson had their own racket.

Her husband was Casey Boniakowski, the leader of a gang of thieves and burglars. Between 1956 and 1958, Sam DeStefano financed some members of the Boniakowski gang to rob Gold Coast apartments for him. One report stated that Casey Boniakowski stole over one million dollars worth of jewels and furs and used Action Jackson to fence some of the loot. Mrs. Boniakowski told police that when her husband Casey went away to prison for burglary she gave "the beast," which Action Jackson was called on the streets, $1,300 to put out on the street as juice loans and in return, she received $50 a week. She told the police that just before Jackson was killed, he re-paid her the $1,300 and was building a clientele of victims.

Also interviewed was attorney Fred Ackerman who said that, *"DeStefano and I were talking in a breezeway at his home, he was laughing and talking about the Jackson murder. He offered to show me pictures of his mutilated body, but I didn't want to look."* Ackerman also added that just before Jackson's murder, he and Jackson spoke and was told, *"Dyno (DeStefano) is crazy. He even killed his own brother, so you know how far he will go."*

Another possibility was that Jackson was running a poker game in Cicero for the Outfit and was killed when he refused to shut it down on orders from top mob bosses when state's attorney Roswell Spencer targeted Cicero operations.

The real break in the murder of William "Action" Jackson came in February 1962 when FBI agents bugged the house that mobster Jackie Cerone rented in Miami, Florida. Cerone was sent there to kill Chicago mob labor leader Frank "Frankie X" Esposito. Cerone's murder crew consisted of Fiore "Fifi" Buccieri, Dave Yaras, Frank "Skippy" Cerone, James "Turk" Torello, Lou "The Tailor" Rosanova, Frank "The Horse" Buccieri, and Vince "The Saint" Inserro. While the group sat in the rented house and discussed some old mob murders, they brought up the Action Jackson murder. The file states:

"The individuals present also discussed the gangland murder of William "Action" Jackson of Chicago, a well known thief, burglar, and juice man, who was found in the trunk of an automobile on a Chicago street in 1961. It would

appear from the conversation that the reason for the slaying of Jackson was that he was suspected of being an informant. The men discussed and laughed about the way that Jackson, who apparently weighed between 350 and 400 pounds, was suspended on a meat hook, and tortured for a period of some 3 days before he died. The conversation heard over the hidden microphone went as follows:

Fifi Buccieri:	We had this big chair right in the plant and we had a screw here and a screw there and eyehooks, and then we had handcuffs on here. You would have laughed your (obscenity) off to see this guy in this little cubbyhole. You'd look at him and you'd walk out laughing. (Everyone laughs) That (obscenity) Jimmy, he shot that thing (obscenity). I used to put it on him real light. You know those prodders they use on cattle, they call them hotshots. Oh, this thing, you press a button and its like a spark and two nails shoot out.
Torello:	And this guy was crying and everything. (More laughter) Now, a little water makes it stronger, so we threw water on it and put it on him, and he goes OHHHHHH!
Buccieri:	Well, the coppers use them too.
Torello:	Yeah, the coppers use them.
Buccieri:	That thing has about 8 batteries in it.
Torello:	We bought this at the stockyards....but the best thing to use is the stretch thing.
Buccieri:	Oh, I wouldn't use that thing. That's a pain (obscenity).
Cerone:	Yeah, you got to put chains on it.
Torello:	We use to stretch these guys and it used to look like some pictures I used to see when I was a kid on those stretching machines, and we would pull out all their joints. I guarantee, we stretched them a foot.

Buccieri:	Yeah, I remember one time I was telling this guy, "you mean you go through all this and you won't tell us, you silly (obscenity)." And then he stated (obscenity) so I walked out, he stunk.
Torello:	And the guy was dehydrated and he kept asking for water so I gave him a little bit and I'd throw the rest of it on him (laughter). I think that's what he died from.
Buccieri:	Yeah, he sweat like a pig, and we had him in the clothes closet and we finally got him out there and we washed that out to get that stink out from that body. That was a good plant, (meat rendering plant facility), that place was. There was this guy in Melrose Park, he used to make a good plant, he'd put those guys in there and seal up those walls and you'd never know a door had been there.

FBI Agent William F. Roemer said in his book that Jackson was killed because the mob thought he was talking to the feds about their operations. Even though Jackson was observed talking to FBI agents at the corner of Laramie Avenue and Jackson Street in Chicago, Roemer said Jackson was no stool pigeon; they tried to get him to flip but he would not. So the mob kidnapped him, took him to the meat plant, put him on a meat hook a foot in the air, the hook in his rectum, and made sure he could not fall off the hook, and began to question him. Jackson insisted he was not a rat, but the mob enforcers didn't buy it. They stripped him naked, smashed his knee caps with a bat, they shot one of them with a gun, broke his ribs, stuck him with sharp objects, used a cattle prod on his penis and anus making him loose his bowels, burned parts of his body with a blow torch, and told him how they were going to kill his wife and kids if he didn't confess. He never did, so they left him to rot on the meat hook. Three days later, he was dead and tossed in the trunk of his car. It appeared that Fifi Buccieri, Jack Cerone, and James "Turk" Torello were involved in the torture but neither were ever arrested or charged.

Also recorded was Turk Torello saying, *"I still don't understand why he didn't admit he was a pigeon."* Buccieri, *"I'm only sorry the big slob died so soon. Believe me, I'll never forget how the big slob looked hanging on that hook in the cubbyhole. Boy did he stink."*

In January 1966, DeStefano was called to answer questions under oath. Among the questions was the murder of Action Jackson. As DeStefano sat on the hot seat, Charles Siragusa put the question to him, *"Did you hang Jackson on a meat hook before torturing and murdering him?"* DeStefano replied, *"What kind of hook did you say? What else did you mention? Did you say an ice pick or a knife?"* Siragusa asked, *"Did Mario DeStefano kidnap Jackson and take him to the basement of his pizza parlor? Did you order Jackson to undress and have his arms and legs trussed with a rope? Then was he hung from a meat hook by a rope around his waist? Did you stab him in the abdomen, thighs, and legs? Did you beat him with a baseball bat and apply a blow torch to his face, and shoot him in the knee?"* After each question DeStefano just giggled and took the Fifth Amendment.

In 1972, it was learned that a close friend of Sam DeStefano's named Louis Fazio was the one who told Sam DeStefano that Action Jackson was a rat giving information to the government on DeStefano. The murder remains unsolved as its files turned to dust over time.

Chapter Nineteen

The Murder of William Skally

On January 7, 1960, the murdered body of William "The Saint" Skally was found in his car in the parking lot of Grace Lutheran School and Church in the 1100 block of Bonnie Brae Avenue in River Forest, Illinois.

Skally had been shot in the head as he struggled with his killer while both sat in Skally's parked car. A Ralph Reinke went for a walk on that day around noon and noticed the blood soaked body of Skally slumped in the front seat of the car and called police. Found next to the body was Skally's hat, with powder burns and a hole in the top of the crown made from the bullet.

His wife Jane and his brother-in-law James Citta said Skally had just returned from Las Vegas and had left home the night before at 7:30, pm to get a newspaper and to meet with mob burglar Carl Fio Rito but he never returned. A Helen Stepp, who lived across the street from the where the body was found, said she noticed Skally's car in the parking lot that night at 11:55 pm. The next morning Mrs. Skally went to the police to report her husband missing.

Skally's body was found blocks from the homes of Paul DeLucia, Tony Accardo, Dominick "Butch" Blasi, and Sam DeStefano. The first person to become a suspect was DeStefano. FBI Agents went to DeStefano's house to interview him about William Skally's murder. Mad Sam did admit that he knew Skally well and that in his younger days he, "used to steal with Skally." He denied that he had anything to do with the death of Skally.

William "The Saint" Skally was born around 1910 in Chicago and used the alias of Victor Guadagno and Fred Scallio. Addresses listed as Skally's were 1006 North Kedzie Avenue Chicago (1941), 951 N. Oakley Blvd, Chicago (1952), and 1300 N. Laramie Avenue, River Forest (1960).

Skally's file contains many arrests dating back to 1927. He was listed as being paroled in 1934 after serving 4 years of a one-to-life sentence for armed robbery in Joliet Prison. In September 1941, Skally was charged with possessing, manufacturing, and selling bootleg alcohol from a 1,000-gallon container discovered in the building at 1844 Damen Avenue in Chicago. Also charged in this operation were Sam De Rosa, Nick Valente, Joe Aston, and Michael Morelli.

In 1942, twenty-nine members of the two biggest bootlegging gangs since prohibition were charged with conspiracy to manufacture and transport alcohol. One gang controlled by Joe Tarallo contained 29 men and operated out of a building at 2540 Canal Street. The Tarallo gang was charged with defrauding the government of an estimated $150,000 in taxes. This gang was also known to defraud their customers by making false bottom cans containing one quart of alcohol and 19 quarts of water. The other gang, known as the Frank Rocco and William Skally gang, consisted of seven men operating three stills in Chicago at 2223-25 S. Millard Avenue, 1844 N. Damen Avenue, and 2517 Belmont Avenue. This gang was charged with tax evasion of over $50,000 and a charge of over 30,000 gallons of mash to produce alcohol. Skally was found guilty and served 2 years in Terre Haute Prison.

In 1947, a man by the name of Fred Scallio was arrested and accused of having in his possession and transferring 600,000 counterfeit sugar stamps that were good for three million pounds of sugar. It was later learned that Fred Scallio was William Skally.

In February 1952, U.S. Secret Service agents broke up one of the biggest counterfeiting rings they had yet to discover. Arrested were William Skally, James Drake, Samuel Sferas, and his brother James Sferas. Agents charged that the men printed phony $10 and $20 dollar bills at a printing plant located at 2327 Harrison Street that was owned by the Sferas brothers. Recovered was more than $2,200,000 in bogus money and they may have made over one million dollars in counterfeit Cities Service Company bonds. Skally was listed as the top plotter and sales manager of the gang. He was arrested after he accepted $3,500 in marked money from undercover agents in return for $50,000 in phony 10's and 20's.

Other members listed in the gang were William J. Russo, a convicted robber; his brother-in-law Emil Cozzi, an ex-convict arrested for counterfeiting who headed a gang of nine men and two woman; and Michael Détente, Stanley Conforti, and Armando Piemont. Also arrested was John Drake, a taxicab driver, who was arrested for selling $3,500 in phony bills. It turned out Drake was the one who set Skally up with the U.S. agents, acting as an undercover informant. He testified against the gang at the trial. Also connected to the gang was the 1948 killing of two hoodlums named George Stathatos and Leo "Little Sneeze" Friedman. Stathatos, known as a tavern owner and gambler, was listed as one of the ringleaders when he was shot to death on May 22, 1948. Friedman, an ex-convict, was killed the next day when it was suspected that the two were holding up gambling joints. It was learned that Friedman was a distributor of the phony bills.

In December 1952 Skally, Russo, and the Sferas brothers were all found guilty on 14 counts and faced 95 years in prison. Some of the phony money printed in Chicago was recovered in Rome, Italy, Paris, France, and Germany.

Four months later in April 1953 while out on liberty bonds William Skally was once again arrested in connection with the robbery of nine valuable paintings stolen from St. Joseph's Pro-Cathedral Church in Bardstown, Kentucky. Thieves used a 25-foot ladder to climb up to three of the most valuable paintings, cutting them from their frames. King Louis Philippe of France had given the paintings to the church between 1830 and 1848. The thieves were going to ship the paintings to Europe to sell on the black market. On April 3, 1953, FBI agents searched the car of former assistant United States Attorney Norton L. Kretske and found four of the paintings in the trunk. The paintings were the "Crowning of the Blessed Virgin" by Murillo (1617-1682), "Faying of St. Bartholomew" by Rubens (1577-1640), "Immaculate Conception" By Jacob Hast (1852), and "Descent of the Holy Ghost" by Van Etck (1385-1441).

Others arrested in the plot were Joseph S. Accardi, Joseph DePietro, a deputy bailiff in narcotics court; Joseph Russo, who was listed as the man also out on bond with Skally; Gus Manotelli, a New York trans-

Atlantic ship steward, and Charles LaCamerta. A government motion dismissed charges against all the men arrested. All the paintings were recovered.

Skally fought his conviction in the counterfeiting case, taking it to the U.S. Supreme Court. He was found guilty and sentenced to 3 years at Leavenworth Prison. He was released in 1956 and was listed as operating a fishing tackle manufacturing plant at Grand and Western Avenues.

Ten months before Skally was murdered, he was involved in the breakup of an international counterfeiting ring. Reports state that Skally became a stool pigeon, which lead to 27 arrests. Two Chicagoans arrested in connection with the counterfeiting ring were William Rabiolo and Alphonso Amabile.

As the detectives began the murder investigation into Skally, they believed Sam DeStefano had a hand in the killing. First, they asked the family why someone would want to kill him. His brother-in-law said that Skally was a walking bookie and used his sporting goods company as a front.

Then detectives looked into the killing of Roger Touhy, which had occurred a month earlier. There was a report that one of the killers resembled Skally and it was thought the killing was in retaliation. Further, it was learned that William Skally had been sent to Mexico and Las Vegas to represent Sam Giancana in opening a dog-racing track in Mexico City with one million dollars of mob money. Skally was to take the million in cash, get the track running, and sell it for a profit. He failed, and Giancana demanded the money back.

Agents said that Skally was Sam Giancana's link to the narcotics racket. He used hoodlums Anthony "Tony D" DiChiarinte, Spartico Mastro, Salvatore Pisano, Carl Fio Rito, and Theodore DeRose.

It turned out that FBI agent William F. Roemer Jr. discovered that First Ward mob lawyer Mike Brodkin uncovered that William Skally was a "Rat" for the Bureau of Narcotics. Once Giancana was told, he sent word to mob burglar Carl Fio Rito to kill Skally.

Another mobster who turned government "rat" in 1963 whose identity was not released told the FBI that the mob knew Skally was a "double agent" and they knew Skally was supplying information to the government about the outfit, especially about narcotics. What they did not know was how much information he was supplying or on whom. Mob boss Tony Accardo ruled that the mob was willing to allow Skally to perform this function as long as he did not involve any of the top mob guys and reported to the "top mob guys" what the Federal Bureau of Narcotics was working on. The informant said that once Skally was killed, he was told by mobster Joe "Crackers" Mendino that Tony Accardo wanted to see him to question him about the murder. The informant appeared before Accardo and other top mobsters and was questioned as to who killed Skally. The informant didn't know, but did say that it was NOT a contract killing issued by the mob but that Skally was killed by one of the mob's members. A number of mobsters were "called in" and questioned by Accardo. The informant heard that Sam DeStefano might have had a hand in the killing. The murder still remains "unsolved" with DeStefano a subject.

Chapter Twenty

The Murder of Jack "Jelly Bean" Silva

Joachim "Jack" Silva, known as "Jelly Bean," was listed as a Chicago minor hoodlum and burglar when he disappeared sometime after October 26, 1960. His body has never been found. Silva was the leader of a gang that robbed North Shore homes in Chicago of jewels valued over $230,000. It was mentioned that he even robbed the home of a top mob figure in Chicago, netting over $25,000. The robbery was never reported to police but was known in underground circles.

Chicago informants told FBI agents that Silva was out on bond at the time he disappeared from trials in both the federal and local courts in Chicago. In May 1960, FBI agents investigating a 1957 California theft got a lucky break when they were led to Dominick Motto and Jack Silva. A tip that Silva was involved in the 1957 theft of a $6,700 diamond brooch in Beverly Hills, California, led agents to Silva's three-deck trailer home at the Buck Horn Trailer Camp on Curtis Avenue in Des Plaines, Illinois. Silva and Motto were arrested. Between $100,000 and $200,000 in stolen goods was found. Both had just robbed homes of $20,000 in furs, jewels, and cash. While FBI officers were arresting the two, Motto attempted to bribe the agents, offering them $2,000 to let him go, but failed. Silva was charged with interstate transportation of stolen jewelry.

This informant stated that the total amount of bond was roughly in the amount of $20,000 and that Sam DeStefano paid this bond for Silva. However, a bondsman under DeStefano's control actually made the payment. The $20,000 bond was lost when Silva failed to appear in either court. This informant felt DeStefano probably had something to do with Silva's disappearance. On October 28, Silva's wife, Marian, reported her husband missing, saying he had called her on the telephone telling her that he was on his way home. Another report states that attorney Robert McDonnell last saw

Silva at the North Avenue Steak House in Melrose Park. McDonnell said he was talking to "some rough characters."

FBI agents interviewed DeStefano at his home about his knowledge concerning the whereabouts of Silva. During the first hour or so of the interview, DeStefano exhibited a comparatively pleasant attitude; however, when a question was put to him implying that he possessed knowledge concerning the whereabouts and fate of Silva, DeStefano went into a rage and accused the agents of trying to develop him as a "stool pigeon." At that point, DeStefano became verbally abusive regarding law enforcement officers in general and resorted to a long string of obscenities. After DeStefano had been pursued at some length, he said that he had decided never to allow the agents into his residence again. He stated that if they or any other FBI agents should ever appear at his door again he would not admit them and if they refused to leave, *"I'll get my heater and blow their heads off."* DeStefano's statement in this regard was taken up with him vigorously and at great length. He was asked in no uncertain terms whether he meant this as a threat against the agents present or all FBI agents in general. He assured the agents that he did not intend this or any other statements as threats but meant only to indicate that he did not intend to submit to any further interviews with the agents and that it was his legal right not to allow FBI agents into his home. He stated that he realized that it is his legal right to refuse even law enforcement officers entry to his home and that he intended to exercise this right in the future. He explained that he did not intend to attempt any harm to officers unless they violated his right of privacy in his residence by attempting to enter without his permission. He assured the agents that he did not mean to indicate that he intended to attempt physical violence unless they should violate his constitutional privileges and then he would have the same right to self-help as any other citizen.

When Sam DeStefano was asked by a newspaper reporter about Silva, he replied, *"It's a shame about that Silva, he was killed by mistake."*

In September 1961, the police received a tip that Silva's body was dumped in a lake or quarry. So the police headed to Libertyville, Illinois, and searched Liberty Lake and quarry with divers, but no body was found. Years later in 1965, divers using electronic gear searched the two lakes once again on the information from a government rat that Silva was killed because he was an informant. They claimed his body was placed inside his white Thunderbird convertible and sent down to the bottom of a lake in Lake County.

Another theory for Silva's disappearance was his association with Peggy DiVarco, wife of mob boss Joe "Caesar" DiVarco. Mrs. DiVarco was subpoenaed as a state witness in a robbery case against Silva. She was seen frequently with Silva and his wife when Silva's gang was out and about in the Northwest suburbs.

Silva's body has never been found. Sam DeStefano apparently took that information to his grave.

Chapter Twenty-One

The Murder of Leo Foreman

On November 19, 1963, after a long day of work, Thomas Orsi, a garbage truck driver for the bureau of sanitation, entered the tavern at 334 S. Laramie Avenue to have a drink. As he sat and talked to the owner, Frank Morawski, he learned about a car that had been sitting outside the tavern for a few days that Frank wanted moved. Orsi then decided to go outside and take a look at the car. He walked over to 5204 Gladys Street where the car was parked and took a close look at it. He walked around the car and noticed that the doors were unlocked; he opened the door and checked inside. Finding nothing of interest, he decided to push the trunk release button in the glove compartment. In the trunk, Orsi discovered a half-naked man, stabbed and shot to death, with his undershirt pulled up and over his head. On the body were hundreds of prick marks that looked like measles, which would turn out to be torture marks from an ice pick.

The body was that of Leo Foreman, an ex-convict working for Sam and Jimmy DeStefano. He was also president of the LeFore Insurance Company located at 7050 Belmont Avenue.

The Homicide report read as follows:
"Upon receipt of a call from the communication center the reporting officer and Sgt. Fitzgerald went immediately to 5208 West Gladys Avenue and arrived on the scene at 2150 hours, 18 November, 1963. Our attention was directed to a roped off area which contained a 1963 Red Oldsmobile Starfire Sedan. This 2-door coupe had the trunk lid up. In the interior of the trunk was the body of a white male, lying on its back; the head was situated in the front right hand corner of the trunk. The victim's shirt was partially pulled up to the middle of the chest; the trousers were pulled down partway over the buttocks. (Upon examination it was discovered that the victim's belt had been cut in half

and that, the front right hand pocket had been cut or torn out.) At this time, a wound was noted in the center of the chest region. In the fleshy under portion of the victim's right forearm was noted a deep 3-inch slash wound. On the upper portion of the arm was noted a circular black mark of undetermined origin. Sgt. Fitzgerald at the scene mentioned to the reporting officer that the victim resembled a bail bondsman named Foreman who occasionally made bond at the Fillmore Station. Detective Zalski was instructed to notify the 5th area Homicides Office and have a record check made on Foreman's name. Detective Roos contacted the enquiry section and the identification section and discovered the missing persons report and gathered other background information. Meanwhile, crime lab personal were examining the body and the trunk.

Coroner Toman arrived at the scene and made an examination of the victim in the presence of Lt. Byrne and Sgt. Fitzgerald. He noted the aforementioned injuries and indicated that they were inflicted by means of knives or firearms. Dr. Toman pronounced the body dead at 2240 hours and gave permission to move the body to the Cook County Morgue.

The lack of any quantity of blood in the interior of the trunk indicates that the victim met his death elsewhere and that the vehicle was merely the means of removing the victim to the scene at which it was found.

The victim's topcoat, hat, and sports jacket found in the trunk with the victim were gathered by crime lab personnel, placed in a plastic bag, and handled as evidence. Interior of the automobile was dusted for prints and car removed to pound #1.

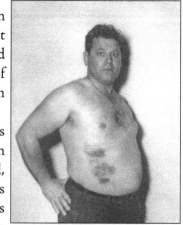

Leo Foreman shortly before his death
(Author's Collection)

The personal effects and paper belonging to the victim were inspected and dusted for fingerprints. Some latent fingerprints were brought out on papers found in the automobile.

These were photographed and sent to the crime lab for evaluation. Upon inspecting the clothing of the victim, it was noted that on Foreman's overcoat were found discolorations that in the judgment of the crime lab personnel were powder burns. These discolorations were found around two holes in the fabric. One hole was located at the rear center of the left shoulder, the second was on the inside portion of the topcoat's left collar. These marks would match up with the wounds that were described as gunshot wounds in the head. The victim's shirt was cut in places that would coincide with most of the wounds found on the body of Leo Foreman. This was also the case with the sport jacket found. On the left knee of the victim's trouser, an unidentified gritty substance resembling sand was clinging to the fabric. The crime lab was asked to evaluate this matter. On the bottom of the victim's left shoe was found straw imbedded in some unknown substance. Crime lab was asked to compare this material with any substance found on the automobile the victim was found in. Particular attention was to be paid to the wheels to try to ascertain if material found in the wheel is similar to that found on the shoe. All material was inventoried and sent to the crime lab.

The official Chicago Police Department homicide report dated November 18, 1963, listed the following injuries found on the body of Leo Foreman:
1) Two gunshot wounds lower left side of head; entrances left side of neck about one inch apart, no apparent exit noted.
2) Graze wound from gunshot, upper portion of left shoulder, no entrance noted.
3) Gunshot wound, outer portion of left buttocks, no exit wound found.
4) Possible gunshot wound, right forearm, upper portion, exit wound.
5) Narrow stab wound, center of chest.
6) Wide slash or stab wound under left pectoral muscles with shell puncture wounds directly above.
7) Three inch slash wound under portion of right forearm.
8) Six stab wounds along left side of back.
    A) Outer portion of lower back just above hips.

B) About four inches higher and to the right.

C) About three inches higher and slightly to the left of "B"

D) About two inches about wound C.

E & F) About three inches above wound D, side by side about one inch apart.

9) Lacerations to back of head.

10) Bruises to face around nose.

Evidence found at the scene:

1) One spent pellet, caliber to be determined by crime lab found under body of victim by Patrolman McGuinnis. Inventoried at area #5.

2) A bloodstained mat taken from trunk of auto.

3) Brown brief case, miscellaneous papers and receipt book.

4) Sun glasses and case and keys found in trunk of auto.

5) Miscellaneous Chrome work taken from interior of car.

6) Victim's clothing.

7) One white metal ring with three white stones.

Leo Foreman's body was found in the pictured car (Author's Collection)

FBI reports obtained on the murder of Foreman indicate the following:

11-19-1963
    File 62-9-9-1395
"Leo Foreman, FBI number 1818869, has been utilized by the Chicago PD as an informant for the past year according to Lieutenant Joseph Mueller. Chicago informant reports that associates of Sam DeStefano had been warning DeStefano about Foreman being an informant for some time.

Black book belonging to Foreman mentioned in retell is presently being utilized by PD homicide in connection with their murder investigation. Book will be made available to Chicago Division in near future and a quick review conducted on this date reflects book contains names and phone numbers of several minor Chicago criminals and a few Chicago police officers. Chicago PD is convinced Foreman murdered by DeStefano or at his direction.

Leo Foreman alleged enforcer for juice operator Sam DeStefano was found in the trunk of his leased auto Monday November 18, 1963. Foreman had been missing since November 14, 1963. Foreman was an ex-convict, former professional wrestler, and one time bondsman who was stabbed 4 times in the back, once in the chest, and once in the right forearm and was shot in the left hip and right arm. Chicago police investigation indicated that absence of blood in the car made it obvious that the murder took place elsewhere. Police confirmed reports that Foreman had gone to DeStefano's home on the day that he vanished.

DeStefano advised police that Foreman had talked and played cards with him for about 2-hours on the day he was reported missing. According to police Foreman was DeStefano's "front man" in the loan shark's invasion of bail bond firms and insurance agencies. Approximately one month ago Foreman's "little black book" fell into the hands of the police. According to police, this book was filled with notations linking La Cosa Nostra gangsters with insurance and bail bond firms. Police reported that during a takeover of an Oak Park insurance agency Foreman had a bitter quarrel with Felix Alderisio and this quarrel is viewed by police as providing a possible motive for the Foreman slaying."

Leo S. Foreman

Leo Seymore Foreman was born on September 2, 1921, in Chicago and was living at 4817 Neva Avenue with his second wife, Ursela and their 3-year-old child. His police record dates back to August 6, 1939, when he was arrested in Milwaukee, Wisconsin. His police record contained 20 different arrests for forgery, swindling, perjury, worthless checks, confidence game, and embezzlement. He used the aliases of Leo Wilson, Edward F. Smith and his old wrestler name of "Bull" Montana.

In June 1954, Foreman, then living at 4931 N. Lawndale Avenue, was fighting extradition to Tucson, Arizona, for violation of probation in a worthless check case from November of 1952. After his arrest on August 17, 1953, for being a fugitive, his court case was continued 6 times.

In 1955, he pled guilty to charges of confidence game and embezzlement and was sent to Joliet Prison for a year and a day. He was released on February 25, 1956.

In April 1958, a Cook County grand jury voted three confidence game true bills against Leo Foreman. Forman apparently took money from three men to whom he promised things he could not get done. He promised one of his childhood friends, named Nathan Sherman that he could get Sherman his city truck driver job back for $200, which he did not. Then he promised a Clyde White that he could get him a press card for photographers through a newspaper reporter for $100, which he did not and he promised a Tom Cox that for $550 he would "take care" of a personal injury suit against Cox for $5,000 and failed. In October 1963, he was arrested for impersonation of a bondsman and released. Foreman would later jump his $7,500 bond.

On March 1, 1961, the FBI seized him in Freeport, Illinois and brought him to St. Paul, Minnesota to stand trial in a bankruptcy case. He was found guilty of contempt of court and sent to Sandstone Penitentiary in Minnesota for 6 months. Once free, he was arrested once again in St. Paul on a swindling charge, which caused Cook County, Illinois, to drop the confidence charges against him.

On May 26, 1963, Oak Park police went to the Vilona Agency on Harlem Avenue, an insurance company that Foreman took over from a partner of Judge Cecil Smith named Bernard Vilona. An anonymous phone call had been placed to the police that an argument was going on involving a gun. When police arrived, they found Foreman and six other men, including a James Rocco, aka James Tedeso, a convicted burglar from Minnesota. The argument was between Foreman and Rocco over the allegation that Foreman left Rocco "holding the bag" in a business deal in Minnesota. Neither would explain what "the bag" was and no guns were found. The Oak Park PD asked Foreman to pack up his business and get out of Oak Park, which he did.

An advertisement for Leo Foreman's company

TonyDark

CITY OF CHICAGO / DEPARTMENT OF POLICE   1121 South State Street   Chicago 5, Illinois   WAbash 2-474
IDENTIFICATION SECTION

ARREST RECORD OF   Leo Foreman

DATE   12-14-62

DATE OF BIRTH   9-2-21

NAME & ADDRESS	C.B. NO.	DATE OF ARREST, ARRESTING OFFICER & DIST., CHARGE, DISPOSITION
Leo Wilson	399632	Arr.Milwaukee,Wis.Aug 6 39 susp. fugt. worthless c T.O.T. P.D. Chgo,Ill.
" Forman	D52885	Sept 1 39 90 days H of C & $1. Att.to commit a cri Judge Dougherty.Offs.Ryan & Bernacchi,35th Dist. Feb 18 47 Inv.Off.Seyferlich & Co. S.A.S. Sept 8 47 1 yr. prob. O.M.F.P. (checks).Judge Beam.Offs.McGough & Powell, 24th Dist. Jan 10 51 Inv.Off.Smith & Co.DB. Nov 6 52 Tucson,Ariz.Perjury. Aug 17 53 t.o.t. Off.Simmons & Co. Joliet,Ill. PD. fugt. con game (checks).Off.Allman & Co. DB. Oct 6 53 Inv.Off.Bartosh,S.A.S. Sept 30 54 Inv.Off.Murphy S.A.O. Oct 9 54 Arr.Off.Sgt.Rusin & Co. S.A.O. Indicted by Oct.term 1954 G.J. Feb 16 55 Joliet Pen #36910 con game 1 yr. 1 yr 1 Plea Guilty,Embezz. 1 yr. 1 yr. 1 day Plea Guilty. Disch. Feb 25 56 Exp. of Sent. Feb 19 57 Inv.Off.Bartosb & Co. S.A.S. Mar 17 59 Bond Forf. SOL ea. con game (3) Judge Burman. Apr 17 62 Reinstated & nolle Prossed. con gam (3) Judge Drucker.
Leo S. Foreman 4847 N. Harlem Ave.	1174073 1386453	Dec 14 62 Off.Northfell OCD. - 6 Feb 63, 193-1. X Parte Jdg. Chelos. 22 Oct. 63. Martis 5th. Impersonating Bondsmen Released. - 18 Nov.63 Crime Lab. FP Case # 12975-63 H-294- The above was found dead in the trunk of a 1963 Oldsmobile Lic. FA 5792 Ill. 63 on the street in front of 5208 W. Gladys St. Occurred 2100 Hrs. 18 Nov.63. 15th. Dist.

204

On the day they found Foreman's body in the trunk of his rented car, his wife, Ursela, told the police she had notified the police four days after Foreman failed to return home. The police asked why she waited so long to report him missing and was told that Foreman would often disappear for a day or two but then would always come home. She added that he would always call to say he would not be coming home, but had not called which was what led Ursela to contact the police. She told the police that her husband was deep in debt to Sam DeStefano and that he had recently withdrawn their $2,000 savings from the bank to pay someone off. She added that she, herself, was in desperate need of money and began carrying a pistol because of DeStefano. She also added that the business they owned, LeFore Company, was an insurance company and a truck-leasing firm. The homicide report stated:

"*Mrs. Foreman was interviewed after which she have a signed statement the gist of which indicates an association with Sam DeStefano on part of her husband in that the victim owed Sam DeStefano money that was provided by DeStefano for bond purposes relevant to her husband. Mrs. Foreman stated that she had done some sewing for Mrs. DeStefano. She stated she last saw her husband alive at about 6:00A.M., on November 14, 1963 in the bedroom of their home at 4817 North Neva. She was unable to provide any information relative to any harm that might befall her husband.*"

Ursela, Leo's brother Ruben Foreman and Samuel "Mopsy" Cavallo went to the Cook County morgue to identify the body. Ruben Foreman was an operator of a filling station on the Northside of Chicago and told police that his brother had borrowed several thousand dollars from him over the last 2 years and never paid any of it back.

Sam Cavallo was office manager for the LeFore Company and was one of the last people to see Foreman alive. Cavallo was free on bond himself, waiting for his hearing on charges of grand theft arising when he, Leo Foreman and Rodger Anderson were arrested in September 1963 while transferring $40,000 worth of high-fidelity phonographs and TV sets that they had stolen from a parked truck. The robbery happened right after Foreman returned to Illinois from Minnesota. Cavallo said he drove to the location of the arrest on instructions from Foreman who told him that something was going on at this location. He said when he arrived he observed two men and asked them what was going on, and then was arrested. Cavallo stated to police that he suspected Foreman of "setting him up" on the incident, but later when Foreman denied this, he discounted Foreman's implication in this incident.

During an interview, Cavallo told police that he had become acquainted with Leo Foreman in the winter of 1962. He added that he was a cement mixer by trade but was told to go and see Leo Foreman in the months he was off work for some work by a Rodger Anderson and an Andy Anderson. Cavallo was vague as to his duties after he accepted employment at Foreman's insurance company. He also stated that for a period of a month he received no salary before being given the status of office manager of the company. Others associated with the LeFore Company were Don F. Manin, Bob Dohner, Stan Leavitt, Barbara Rucker, Daniel Laveris, Morris Atlas and Foreman's secretary, Connie DeGrazio.

Cavallo said that on November 14, 1963, at about 1:30 pm, Leo left the office carrying a brief case saying he was going out on business. Connie DeGrazio had made an appointment for Foreman with an attorney named George Leighton, but it was not known if the appointment had been kept. Not hearing from Foreman, Cavallo stated that he became concerned and believed that Foreman might have been arrested. He made daily inquiries by means of telephone conversations and personal appearances with Sam DeStefano, the personal appearances being at the home of DeStefano allegedly to determine the reason for Foreman's absence from his own home and place of business. The discussions focused as to the reason why Foreman had dropped out of sight without leaving some word as to his whereabouts. Cavallo stated to police that DeStefano asked him if he knew of any reason for Foreman's absence. Cavallo told DeStefano that he could not account for this situation. Cavallo persistently denied that he was advised or instructed by DeStefano as to what further action he should take in this matter.

A reporter went to Sam DeStefano's house and interviewed him from his bedside since DeStefano was recovering from a recent surgery. He told the reporter, "*Leo didn't owe me a dime. He liked to put up a big front and hang around with certain people in order to be in the limelight. But he was harmless. Leo told me he had been beaten by Kensington police about a month ago. He came to me a few weeks ago and said he was being trailed by detectives wherever he went and he thought it was because he was about to sue the policemen who had beaten him."*

DeStefano said to police, *"I knew Foreman for about four years. We never had any business dealings. He came to see me just to wish me a quick recovery. We played cards for awhile, then he and Cavallo left."*

That same day an anonymous call was placed to Sgt. Donald Kelley at the Shakespeare Avenue homicide detail telling him, *"Foreman was an informer. That's why he got it. He was a rat!"* and hung up the phone.

The next day the newspapers focused on how Foreman was known as a bumbling hoodlum who was always raising schemes that attracted the attention of law enforcement agents. One police officer called him a "bumbling sharpie" and "self-styled fixer" whose fixes were subject to question. The "Foreman" act was laid out. He would hang out at the courtrooms walking up and down the corridors searching for distraught defendants. When he found one, he would engage in conversation getting the defendant to tell his story and his problems. Then Foreman would promise the defendant to "fix" his case for a fee. Once the defendant agreed Foreman would walk into a judge's chamber and pretend to talk to the judge to fix the case but would actually ask whoever was in the room what time of day it was, how they were doing, or where the bathroom was. He would then walk out of the chamber and tell his new client everything was good and to just pay him once he was free. Later Foreman would sit in the courtroom of his new client and wait to see if the defendant would win his case and was acquitted or if he would lose his case and go to jail. If he won, Foreman would walk up to the guy and say, *"See, I told you I would take care of it. I got you off the hook, now pay up,"* and he would be paid because the defendant believed he had fixed the case. If the guy lost Foreman would simply slip out of the courtroom and call it a day, knowing the victim was going to jail so he didn't have to worry about the angry client coming after him.

The papers also focused on a $10,000 loan Foreman made from Sam DeStefano in 1959 and discovered that Foreman met with Sam DeStefano three or four times a week. Police were searching for a hoodlum seen at DeStefano's house right after the murder named George Boulihanis.

More FBI Reports
11-20-63
File 62-9-9-1400

"Conference held yesterday by Agent, this office, with Captain William Duffy, Director, Intelligence Unit Chicago PD, and Deputy Chief of Detectives Michael Spiotto. Cooperation was extended to the Chicago PD about our knowledge of activities and associates of Sam DeStefano, who by weight of evidence is the primary suspect in the killing of Foreman. Chicago PD feels DeStefano either killed Foreman himself or allegedly used former Chicago policeman Kenny Anderson to do so. Anderson is another known subordinate of DeStefano.

During conference, Duffy allowed the agent to completely review all entries listed in the black book taken from Foreman on October 26, 1963, when Foreman was arrested by Chicago PD. The black book contains Foreman's diary for the last 10 months as he pursued his business as bail bondsman, insurance broker, and collector of "juice" payments for DeStefano. The books show that Foreman met Chicago Municipal Judge Cecil Corbett Smith on at least half a dozen occasions during the last six months. Some of the meetings were in the chambers of Smith and one was for dinner at the Edgewater Beach Hotel. The book also shows Foreman met with Frank "Skids" Caruso, a lieutenant of top hoodlum Gus Alex, possibly about policy operation on South Side of Chicago. Book shows at least two meetings of Foreman with Lieutenant Harry Smith, a member of the Chicago PD. The book also shows several meetings by Foreman with Chicago detectives Joseph Tye and George O'Brien, presently assigned to the State's Attorney Office. In one entry, Foreman shows he contacted Attorney George Bieber to 'straighten out Tye for $2,000.'"

The book also discusses a meeting with Foreman and Anthony Ross Accardo, son of Tony Accardo; Ben Stein, labor racketeer; Kay Jarrett, Madame of prostitutes; Harry Boshes, front for Chicago hoodlums in motel field here; Chicago attorneys Mike Fumo and Bob McDonnell; Pete Cappelletti, another subordinate of DeStefano; Don Conway, former chief investigator, Secretary of State's Office; Nick Ferri, present chief investigator, Illinois Secretary of State; Morris Klein, of the Cook County Sheriff's Office whom apparently Foreman was attempting to keep in office after change of administration from Sheriff Sain to present Sheriff Ogilvie; Judge Kranz, police magistrate, Niles; William Tripp, well know policy operator on the south side of Chicago; a person believed to be Captain Nathan Klein, Juvenile Division, Cook County Sheriff's Office; Denise Nelson, probably a paramour of Foreman recently arrested by the FBI on ITSP charges; Louis Roundtree, bailiff for Municipal Court Judge Sidney Jones; Harold Parker, policy operator, south side of Chicago; and an individual possibly identical with Chicago gambler Joe Epstein.

Apparently, some of these contacts were on legitimate business in Foreman's capacity by Foreman with any federal authorities in any capacity. The book shows no contact by Foreman with any federal authorities in any capacity.

It is noted that Sandy Smith, reporter of the Chicago Sun Times Newspaper, confidentially advised that immediately after the agent left Duffy and Spiotto, he met with Smith for a lengthy period and was shown contents of the book. This is the basis for the entire front page of the Chicago Sun Times this date captioned 'Little Black Book, Municipal Judge listing in slain hoodlum's diary,' an exclusive by Sandy Smith. Smith advised, confidentially, that he was allowed to write the story about the contents of the book and investigation of the Chicago PD with the only condition that he not name Chicago PD officers described by Foreman in the book.

The Chicago PD interviewed DeStefano in his home on November 19, 1963. DeStefano was uncooperative and no leads were obtained. The Chicago PD also interviewed Carol Smith, paramour of Foreman, also mentioned prominently in the book, without positive results. The Chicago PD attempting to locate Kenny Anderson, above."

Once back in the Chicago area, Foreman and Sam "Mopsy" Cavallo walked into the Kensington District police station on October 22, 1963, to make bond for a man who was arrested for suspicion of receiving stolen goods. The man arrested was Fred Harvey, an ex-convict who was known to be friendly with Sam DeStefano. Harvey operated an insurance office on Stony Island Avenue in Chicago and admitted under police questioning that he had "fenced" stolen goods in the past. Foreman arrived, claiming he was a bail bondsman and was there to pay Harvey's bond. When Police Commander Edward Egan, questioned Foreman, informing him that ex-convicts could not be licensed bondsman Foreman changed his story saying he was acting on the behalf of a sister who was a bondswoman. Police detained Foreman and Cavallo and took Foreman's little red book full of his appointments and Cavallo's little black book mentioned above."

Some of the pages listed the following:

> Jan. 9, see Sam DeStefano this morning, he wants to see me bad.
> Jan. 14, see Sam D. today for sure, important.
> Jan. 17, see Sam D. important.
> Feb. 25, get in touch with Sam D. I gave him $1,000.
> Mar. 5, I gave Sam D. $700.
> June 5, meet Bob McDonnell and Judge Smith about DeStefano.
> June 17, meet Judge Smith, McDonnell Edgewater Beach Hotel.
> July 22, Bob McDonnell on payroll for $400 a week.
> Aug. 19, be down at Judge Smith's courtroom.
> Sept. 10, call Judge Smith, ask about the Gagliano case.
> Sept. 10, pick up driver's license for Anthony Accardo Jr.
> Oct. 22, Tony Accardo Jr. traffic court.

Another FBI Report
11-22-63
File 62-9-9-1401

"In connection with the Leo Foreman murder and little red book of Foreman seized by police authorities prior to his death, an article appeared in a Chicago newspaper titled '*Many Named in Slain Hoodlum's Diary.*' The book contained the name of Lieutenant Harry Smith, head of O'Hare International Airport Police Detail, and when questioned by the newspaper reporter regarding this, Lieutenant Smith admitted that Foreman visited him twice in an effort to seek aid in building a bonded messenger service with clients at the airport. Lieutenant Smith also furnished the following information to the reporter; "On one occasion he said Foreman entered his office while an FBI agent was there. Foreman began bragging about his various business interests. The FBI agent told Foreman, '*Why don't you give me some of the real information you have on Sam DeStefano and some of the others?*' '*I'm not a snitcher,*' Foreman replied.

The above incident was a chance meeting with Foreman by Special Agent Raymond F. Hogan on 10/20/63. At this time, Agent Hogan was on official duty at O'Hare Field to arrange details for Attorney General Robert Kennedy's return flight to Washington DC. While at the Security Office at O'Hare Field, Lieutenant Smith came in and was accompanied by Foreman at which time Smith introduced Foreman to Agent Hogan as a former bondsman. Foreman mentioned a few people with whom he was associated, among them Sam DeStefano. At this time, Foreman indicated that he would not furnish any information to the FBI even if he had such information. Since this meeting, Foreman has not been contacted by Agent Hogan or any other agents of this office."

FBI Report
11-22-63
File 62-9-9-1405

"Following is a summary of developments since the body of Leo Forman was found in the trunk of his leased car. The body was found approximately eight blocks from Sam DeStefano's house.

Several months ago, when agents attempted to interview Pete Cappelletti, another henchman of DeStefano, DeStefano anticipated another attempt to interview Cappelletti on the next day. When agents failed to appear, he telephonically contacted an agent who has interviewed him on several occasions and indicated his frustration that agents had not appeared since he, Foreman, and one or two other of his Henchmen had been waiting for agents. Such was role played by Foreman for DeStefano.

On the morning following the discovery of Foreman's body, a conference was held by the agent who was very familiar with activities, habits, associates, and the background of DeStefano through above-mentioned interviews with DeStefano and Captain William Duffy and detective Michael Spiotto.

DeStefano operates in the sphere of juice rackets in the Chicago area and has undoubtedly committed numerous gangland type killings of delinquent debtors, including Arthur Adler, former nightclub owner, in Chicago. It is noted that this office conducted lengthy investigations into this situation and considered DeStefano as probably the killer.

Some indications that Milwaukee Phil Alderisio possible killer in this situation since he apparently had an argument within the past several months with Foreman. However, DeStefano considered primary suspect.

During a conference with Duffy and Spiotto, an agent completely reviewed all entries listed in the book of Foreman's. This case has received tremendous publicity by all news media in the Chicago area, with particular emphasis on involvement of Judge Cecil Corbett Smith. Judge Smith has submitted to interviews and has admitted a 20-year association with Foreman. The press has developed information that Foreman was visited by Smith on at least two occasions while Foreman was in Joliet State Prison. According to the press, Smith voluntarily submitted to a lie detector examination in Memphis, Tennessee, on November 21, 1963. He denied any participation in the killing but in response to questions as to whether he had ever taken a bribe to fix a case, he is reported to have replied that he could not recall and then stated that he may have received gifts after cases were closed. When asked whether Foreman ever procured a woman for him, Judge Smith responded that Foreman might have introduced him to a woman but that he did not request Foreman to do so. The case has been the subject of editorials criticizing Judge Smith, Mayor Daley's Democratic Organization of which Smith was a member, and Chicago PD for not knowing the connections of Smith with Foreman and not having solved the killing to date. All newspapers were clamoring for impeachment and disbarment of Judge Smith.

Since the discovery of Foreman's body, DeStefano has submitted to numerous television and newspaper interviews. He apparently has developed animosity towards Judge Smith since he referred to him as a hoodlum and has advised anyone who will listen that he is out to break Judge Smith's back. It should be noted that DeStefano is a mental case and has a tendency to talk to anyone who will listen. He made at least one telephone call to the Chief Justice of the Municipal Court, who previously has been quoted saying that he did not intend to discipline Judge Smith. DeStefano completely lost his temper due to this statement and called the Chief Justice numerous obscene names. He furnished the Chief Justice instances showing the association of Judge Smith with Foreman and DeStefano. Because of this phone call, the Chief Justice reversed his position and has barred Judge Smith from this courtroom.

In regards to Judge Smith, it is noted that Chicago sources and informants have not previously furnished information showing involvement of Smith with the hoodlum element. It is noted that Municipal Court Judges handle only misdemeanors, traffic violations, and relatively minor situations.

Mayor Daley has been quoted saying that Smith's associations are in conflict with rules of ethics and that he has committed a great offense against the bench society and the community.

Virgil Peterson, Chicago Crime Commission, also criticized Smith for associations with Foreman. The Chicago Bar Associations announced that its judiciary committee would make an investigation into this situation involving Judge Smith. It is noted that Smith is a Democrat who has been a municipal court judge since 1932. It is noted that Chicago crime reporter Sandy Smith confidentially advised that he was given access to the diary of Foreman the afternoon following discovery of Foreman's body. This led to Smith's exclusive stories constituting a scoop from him over other Chicago newspapers. Information received on this date indicated this has caused a furor among editors of other newspapers who bitterly complained to Police Commissioner O.W. Wilson on the afternoon of November 12, 1963, over 'preferential treatment of Smith.' As a result, Wilson ordered Deputy Superintendent Morris and Captain Duffy to make complete contents of the book available to all newspapers without regard to Chicago police officers and all others named in the book. Morris and Duffy protested bitterly to Wilson on grounds that such disclosure would jeopardize the investigation of the murder and jeopardize innocent individual's named in book. However, the protest failed and complete contents of the book were given to all newspapers on the afternoon of November 21. As a result, all newspapers are having a field day interviewing the hundreds of people named and speculating as to the reason for their associations with Foreman. In this regard, it is noted that there is reference in the book to 'see that Denise contacts FBI and changes her address.'

Later in the book an entry is made showing Foreman represented one Denise McCarthy in Federal District Court here as bondsman. Obviously this reference refers to Denise Nelson, aka Denise McCarthy and Carol Smith, who was arrested by this office on ITSP charges and was recently convicted in Federal Court on this charge. To date, no newspaper has mentioned either above entries.

It is noted that Chicago PD feels very strongly against Judge Smith due to the fact that Smith, in their opinion, allowed complete mockery of justice earlier this year when DeStefano was tried for a traffic violation in his court, which occurred while, he and top hoodlum, Willie Daddono, were under surveillance. Judge Smith allowed DeStefano to represent himself which caused a 'three ring circus' widely carried by news media and allowed DeStefano to cross examine two Chicago police officers for three days and for a total of 12 hours during which time Smith allowed DeStefano to bring up many matters contrary to all rules of evidence. Smith then discharged DeStefano, but fined DeStefano $200 for contempt of court. DeStefano is quoted in papers saying he made a formal complaint against Judge Smith to the Chicago Bar Association for holding him in contempt of court and fining him $200. According to DeStefano, Judge Smith offered to pay the fine himself if DeStefano would withdraw his complaint.

Another individual prominently mentioned in the book is DeStefano's [Blacked out by Government]. This PCI informant advised that on November 14, 1963, that he received a phone call from DeStefano who advised him that his 'fat friend,' Leo Foreman, was dead. DeStefano informed him that Foreman was killed for two reasons; one, that he owed DeStefano $7,000 on juice loans, which he refused to pay; second, that Foreman was an informant for the FBI in Chicago. PCI stated that DeStefano indicated Foreman was severely tortured prior being killed.

The informant stated he saw a car resembling Foreman's 1963 red Corvair rented from Courtesy Motors, Chicago, on that day on Hamlin Avenue, just south of Madison Street. The informant advised that Mrs. Leo Foreman had notified the Chicago PD that Foreman was a missing person since November 14, 1963.

DeStefano admitted playing cards with Foreman on the day he disappeared. The informant also advised that he observed Chicago top hoodlum Chuckie Nicoletti, a known hit man, at the home of DeStefano on November 13, and believes Nicoletti was possibly responsible for the murder. The informant states that about 3 months ago at DeStefano's house, Foreman, Nicoletti, and DeStefano had a conversation concerning Foreman's allegedly being related to Senator Hubert Humphrey of Minnesota; and through this relationship, Foreman was to attempt to obtain a presidential pardon for Julius 'Ju Ju' Grieco, who is serving a 15 year sentence at Leavenworth Prison after being convicted at the U.S. District Court, Chicago. The informant stated it was later determined by Nicoletti that Foreman was not a relative to the Senator and he was

unable to cause Humphrey to take action. The informant stated that
Nicoletti became highly incensed at Foreman's lying.

The informant stated that he learned that Joe Stein, who is the
owner of an unknown loan company and whose partner is Milwaukee
Phil Alderisio, that he had in the past loaned Foreman money and that
Foreman along with three or four unknown individuals had given Stein
a hard time about paying the debt. The informant stated that a short
time later, date not known, Alderisio walked into Foreman's office and
had an open dispute with Foreman. At this time, Foreman drew a gun
on Alderisio and caused Alderisio to back down."

FBI Report
11-22-63
File 62-9-9-1409

"Concerning the murder and book of Leo Foreman, Carol Jean Smith,
aka Denise McCarthy, aka Denise Nelson, was arrested on March 15,
1963. The prosecution authorized violation Section 2314, title 18, U.S.
Code. Carol Smith failed to appear in court on August 9, 1963, and a
warrant was issued.

Leo Foreman, LeFore Company, was contacted by FBI Agent Carlton
H. Wolfarth on August 22, 1963. He advised the whereabouts of Mrs.
Smith. Smith was arrested seaside, in California, as a result. Foreman
claimed he paid Smith's way to California to be with an ailing child. It
was not her fault she did not appear. He stressed he would only furnish
this information, nothing else. Foreman, therefore, was not made a PCI
informant.

Smith was sentenced November 8, 1963, and SA Wolfarth asked her
if Foreman was involved with counterfeit checks or money orders. She
advised he was not.

Foreman telephoned SA Wolfarth November 13, 1963, saying he had
heard about the inquiry on him. He desired that he should be contacted,
rather than someone else; no arrangements were made to interview
Foreman.

The president of Plaza Drive In Bank, Norridge, November 13, 1963, advised on October 7, 1963, that two stolen Amexco money orders were deposited into the LeFore Company bank account in the amount of $100 each. These money orders were not honored by Amexco. LeFore Company checks were made payable to Leo Foreman for the amount of $1,000, dated October 21, 1963, but lacked funds for payment.

For the information of the bureau, the Chicago PD is aware of the recent argument between Foreman and Phil Alderisio. No information concerning Charles Nicoletti is presently being disseminated to the Chicago PD at this time in view of the danger to the informant's life and due to the fact that DeStefano informed the informant of Foreman's murder."

FBI Report
11-22-63
File 62-9-9-1410

"Concerning the murder of Leo Foreman, George Cecil Smith was removed from his bench on this date by Chief Justice Bowe. Bowe arrived at his decision following a midnight phone call from Sam DeStefano who, according to Judge Bowe, punctuated his language with shrieks and a variety of strong oaths telling Chief Justice Bowe the derogatory information about Smith. According to the Chicago press, Judge Smith contacted the Chief of police in Memphis, Tennessee, and the agent in charge of the FBI in Memphis, in order to be referred to a polygraph operator in order to answer questions concerning his association with Foreman and DeStefano. The SAC in Memphis was contacted and absolutely states that there was no truth in the statement that he recommended a polygraph operator. He knows no polygraph operator in Memphis. This is another example of irresponsibility on the part of the Chicago press.

No information was available to Chicago PD or any other source at that time concerning results of that lie test. Smith obviously was attempting to clear himself of involvement with Foreman and to refute allegations being made against him in the Chicago press and on TV by DeStefano.

Judge Smith is quoted as saying that DeStefano had contacted him repeatedly by telephone in Hot Springs and on the last occasion completely lost his temper in threatening to get Judge Smith through the newspapers.

DeStefano had submitted to interviews since Foreman's discovery by the press and TV here. He had gone to great lengths to furnish derogatory information concerning Judge Smith.

Contact was being maintained with Captain Duffy, Intelligence Unit. Duffy advised that Superintendent Wilson authorized dissemination of the complete contents of Foreman's black book to all papers. It is noted that only Sandy Smith of the Chicago Sun Times had such cooperation. Smith obtained such cooperation on a confidential basis from Captain Duffy. Chicago PD had no success to date in solving this crime although all officers involved continued to agree that DeStefano is responsible either by direction or by his own hand."

FBI Report
11-22-63
File 62-9-9-1432

"Chicago received information on November 21, 1963, from a Chicago informant who had furnished reliable information in the past to the effect that the informant had been talking to an individual known to him as "Pix," an associate of DeStefano and Foreman. " Pix" reportedly indicated he was aware prior to Foreman's death that he was to be killed and heard about his death two hours after the killing and before the body was found. "Pix" allegedly said that DeStefano had asked him for Carol Smith's address in California. "Pix" further indicated that Carol Smith and Judge Cecil Smith were going to be killed. Chicago brought this information to the attention of Lieutenant Edward Barry of the

Chicago PD. He requested that local authorities in the area where the intended victims were to be advised that their lives might be in danger. Chicago promptly furnished the above information to San Francisco and Memphis for relay to local authorities.

Memphis advised that Judge Smith departing today for New Orleans and is being afforded protection by Memphis PD while in that territory."

Judge Cecil Smith admitted a 20-year friendship with Foreman that began after Foreman returned from Arizona and was able to get Smith a car. Smith said he was a good friend of Foreman's mother and that when Foreman was in trouble in Minnesota Smith drove up two times, once in 1961 and once in 1962 to help him with bond, and to help Foreman in getting business for his trucking business. The trucking business owned by Foreman in Waverly, Minnesota was called Smith Trucking Company and was under Foreman's alias Edward Smith. Both times Foreman gave Smith a check to cover his travel expenses and both times the checks didn't clear the bank. Smith said about Foreman, "*I've known Foreman and his family for 20 years. I went to his mother's funeral. I knew him when he was writing bail bonds in the Municipals court 15 or 20 years ago. He thought a great deal of me. I performed his wedding ceremony, if I'm not mistaken. He was just a big kid at heart, but he had ideas of being a big shot. He got the wrong ideas. He associated with some wrong people.*"

When asked why he placed a phone call to the police to have them give Foreman's pocket book back he said, "*I'd like to get the book back for Foreman, I've always been a friend of policemen, you know that. He is a good boy. He's a con man, but a good man. He is a little mixed up, but he's still a good boy.*"

A reporter went to DeStefano's house for an interview concerning DeStefano's knowledge of the Judge Smith case. There Sam DeStefano produced two checks that he said tied Judge Smith to Foreman's operations. DeStefano said, "*This guy Leo needed Judge Smith to operate. He was known by many people as Edward Smith and they thought he was Judge Smith's son. To the best of my knowledge, Leo didn't have any clout with any other judge. I had dinner with Judge Smith at the Germania Club,*" *with my two daughters and with Leo Foreman and another girl. The bill was about $35. I offered to pay, but Judge Smith signed the bill."*

The reporter asked DeStefano when he first met Leo Foreman, his answer was, *"Judge Smith called me one time and asked me to go for $2,000 for this Leo Foreman, who he said was a very good friend of his. He said Foreman was finishing out a prison term but had to come up with $2,000 for a fine. I didn't like the way this Foreman sounded but his brother, Reuben, came to see me. We dickered awhile and when Reuben said he could come up with $1,000, I said I'd go for $1,000. Leo finally paid me back."*

The reporter asked Sam why Leo was killed; he replied, [sic] *"There's a thousand reasons why he could have been killed. I don't know the exact one. He was the kind of guy who would take money from an individual and tell him, 'Everything is taken care of.' Then the poor individual would go to jail. Leo would take money even when he didn't have any clout. He took their money and never produced. You know there's no future for a guy like that."*

FBI Report
11-28-63
File 62-9-9-1417

"Concerning Leo Foreman's Murder, Judge Cecil Smith was summoned to a hearing by Cook County State's Attorney Daniel Ward and key members of his staff for six hours on November 26, 1963. Following the conference, Ward declined to announce results but advised the press that Judge Smith had been responsive to questions but he would return this date for additional interrogation. The purpose of the hearing is to ascertain involvement of Smith with Foreman, Sam DeStefano and other members of the hoodlum element.

The intelligence Unit, Chicago PD, on this date turned over to this office all information, which they have obtained from an informant close to DeStefano and Foreman. The informant is presently a member of DeStefano's group who has engaged in several hijackings and burglaries masterminded by DeStefano and carried out by his group. One item of interest concerns a contemplated robbery of Broadway Bank in Melrose Park, which is subject of separate airtel. Chicago PD advised of a discussion between Chicago top hoodlum Milwaukee Phil Alderisio and DeStefano, having to do with real estate property involving a value of $50,000. According to this informant, this deal involved Foreman who had failed to accomplish something. At the conclusion of the conversation, either DeStefano or Alderisio said, 'we can always get the Saint to take care of it.' This apparently is in reference to Chicago hoodlum Vincent "The Saint" Inserro. The informant observed a meeting between DeStefano and Alderisio at the Armory Lounge at the time when DeStefano apparently was in conference with Sam Giancana. The informant knows of many other dealings between DeStefano and Foreman and would guess that Charles "Chuck" Crimaldi, a most vicious thug employed by DeStefano, may well have killed Foreman.

An FBI informant advised that he be acquainted with an individual who happened to be in the office of the insurance company where Leo Foreman worked in Oak Park, Illinois in November of 1963. This individual advised that during this month, Sam DeStefano visited Foreman and engaged in a violent argument during which time DeStefano threatened Foreman. This argument involved money owed by Foreman to DeStefano, apparently a substantial amount. Shortly thereafter, the body of Foreman was located and shortly after that, the individual who was privy to the caller stated substantially as follows: 'The roof is going to fall in on Foreman. Don't worry, your troubles with him are over.' This individual indicated that he felt that obviously DeStefano and his associates were involved in the murder of Foreman. It is noted that considerable information concerning the association between Foreman and DeStefano had previously been reported."

In a twist on November 28, 1963, Sam DeStefano contacted the police and asked for police protection when he received phone calls from unknown individuals threatening him and his family with bodily harm unless he lay off Judge Smith. He requested bodyguards for himself and his two teenage daughters.

On January 15, 1964, Judge Cecil Smith sent a letter to then Governor of Illinois Otto Kerner stating his resignation, writing, *"On the advice of my doctor I hereby resign my office as an associate judge on the Circuit Court."*

Days earlier a story was released saying the mob might have killed the wrong "rat." The report stated that the only information the mob had was that an "insurance man" was talking to the feds and they assumed it was Foreman. Even though Foreman was giving information, the mob soon found out that an insurance man named Lewis Barbe was talking to the feds about an insurance fraud case, involving mobster Marshall Caifano. Two weeks after Foreman's body was discovered, Caifano was indicted from the information provided by Barbe against Caifano for attempting to defraud $48,000 from an insurance firm.

Only about 20 people showed up to Leo Foreman's services, headed by Rabbi Moses Mescheloff of Congregation of Kings of West Rogers Park.

A reporter asked Sam DeStefano when did he see Leo Foreman last and how did he look to him? DeStefano answered, *"He looked like he didn't have a worry in the world."* DeStefano paused and smiled, *"But I'm not going to tell you when was the last time I saw Leo, I won't tell the police either."* Stunned, the reporter asked, *"Wasn't he here in your home on Monday, November 11, a week to the day before his body was found?"* DeStefano answered, *"That's right, but that was not the last time I saw him. And I'm not going to tell you when that last time was."*

Nine years later in September 1972 mob rat Charles Crimaldi was granted immunity to testify as to who killed Leo Foreman and why. Crimaldi's first story said that Sam DeStefano and his brother Mario called Foreman on the phone on the night of November 14, 1963, telling him to come over to Sam's house because he had some stolen diamonds he wanted Foreman to fence for him. When Foreman arrived, Sam and Mario put a gun to his head, forced him into his car, and drove to Mario's house at 2613 South Mayfair Avenue in Westchester, Illinois. Once there, Charles Crimaldi and Anthony "The Ant" Spilotro drove to the house to assist in dragging Foreman into Mario's nuclear fallout shelter that was located in the basement of his home. Sam grabbed a baseball bat and hit Foreman over the head knocking him to the floor, causing him to black out. While Foreman was unconscious, Sam ordered that Foreman's shirt and jacket be pulled over his head and his pants be lowered to his knees.

There are other reports that list slightly different accounts of what happened. One states that Crimaldi and Sam DeStefano played cards with Foreman at Sam's house before they went to Mario's house in Westchester. He added that, once the four killers reached Mario's house, Mario asked Foreman if he wanted to see the work he had done converting his old bomb shelter into a sauna bath. When Mario, Crimaldi, and Spilotro were down in the shelter they made sure Foreman entered the room first. Then Mario and Crimaldi pulled their guns out and shot Foreman at close range near his head and neck. Crimaldi said another shot came from behind him, from Tony Spilotro, hitting Foreman and making him fall to the ground moaning, *"Oh my god, oh my god."* Mario picked up a butcher knife and stabbed him a few times, Crimaldi added, *"I kicked him, Tony kicked him, and then Mario gave Tony the knife, and Tony stabbed him. Leo was still moaning."* Sam came down dressed in his pajamas with a gray overcoat covering him and threatened to castrate Foreman with his pistol. Foreman pleaded, *"Please don't."*

Sam began to curse at him screaming, *"You thought you'd get away from me. I told you I'd get you. Greed got you killed, over diamonds."*

Crimaldi's testimony about what happened next is as follows:

Question: What was Leo doing at this time?
Crimaldi: He told Sam, please Unk, oh my god.

Question: Unk, What is the significance of Unk?
Crimaldi: Leo used to call Sam his uncle when they were on good terms and everything. Supposedly because he, "Foreman," didn't have any family. (Crimaldi then went on to say DeStefano cursed at Foreman a bit more before shooting him in the buttocks.)

Question: What happen then?

Crimaldi:	Mario then stabbed him a few more times and Leo kind of stopped moving.
Question:	Did you see anyone do anything with regard to Leo's arm?
Crimaldi:	Yes. Mario cut a piece out of it.
Question:	What do you mean by cut a piece out of it?
Crimaldi:	With a knife.
Question:	He just gouged a piece of flesh out?
Crimaldi:	Yes.
Question:	Was this before or after or after they killed him?
Crimaldi:	After.
Question:	What happen then?
Crimaldi:	Sam said he was going and that we know what to do with Foreman, he would talk to us later.
Question	Did Tony Spilotro do any of the cutting? In other words, they were taking turns cutting him?
Crimaldi:	Yes.
Question:	After Sam left, what happened then?
Crimaldi:	We took off Leo's coat and suit coat and that's when Mario cut his arm. And then, that's when we were going to take him out and put him in his car, carry him out. We dragged him out and threw his cloths on in the car.
Question:	When you last saw Leo Foreman in the bomb shelter, after he was dead, when you carried his body out, did you notice something unusual about Leo Foreman's face?
Crimaldi:	He had a smile on his face.
Question:	What comment was made about his face, that he had a smile?
Crimaldi:	Sam said look at him, he's laughing at us, and felt like he was glad he died.

The court report of the events is slightly different from the two other reports, the report reads as follows:

"Leo Foreman owed money, a considerable amount of money to Sam DeStefano's loan shark racket. Because of a recurrent failure to pay off his debts, which were being compounded daily by astronomical interest rates, it was decided that Leo Foreman had to be eliminated.

On the afternoon of November 14, 1963, Leo was invited to the home of Mario DeStefano for the purpose of making some kind of "deal." Having been cleverly induced into DeStefano's home, the stage was set for the murder of Leo Foreman.

Assuming the role of generous host, Mario DeStefano took Leo and another visitor (Charles Crimaldi) on a brief tour of his house. Mario then suggested they go down into the bomb shelter (where Anthony Spilotro was waiting). Leo agreed, and the trio set off winding their way down a series of right-angled stairwells towards the underground bomb shelter.

Having rounded the final turn, the mood of amicability suddenly changed as Charles Crimaldi shoved Leo down the last few stairs. Simultaneously, Crimaldi, Spilotro, and Mario DeStefano drew their guns and fired at the figure of Leo Foreman. Foreman was hit by a number of bullets, but he was alive and conscious begging for mercy. Although Crimaldi wanted to kill Leo, to put him out of his misery, Mario cautioned him not to.

Mario then produced a butcher knife. He knelt down beside the prostrate figure of Leo Foreman and stabbed him a few times. Crimaldi and Spilotro then kicked Foreman several times. Although he was bleeding profusely, Leo Foreman was still alive and conscious.

At that point, Sam DeStefano appeared at the top of the stairwell, wearing his pajamas. Sam walked down the steps and over to Foreman who was still moaning. After cursing at Foreman, Sam pulled down the front of Leo's pants, grabbed his penis, and threatened to shoot off Leo's testicles. Again, Foreman begged for mercy.

Sam then went behind Leo, stuck his revolver into Leo's anus, and pulled the trigger. Since Leo was still alive and moaning, Mario again picked up the butcher knife and plunged it repeatedly into Foreman's body until the moaning stopped. Mario then cut a piece of flesh out of Leo's arm.

Foreman's body was carried upstairs and placed in the trunk of his 1963 Oldsmobile and driven to 5208 Gladys Street in the city of Chicago."

Between the three different reports of the way things happened that night the end was all the same-Leo Foreman was killed and dumped.

Years later when Mario sold his Westchester home, that opened the door for Chicago police crime laboratory technicians to get into the basement and bomb shelter to process the scene. Found were microscopic blood specks, wood chips and cement particles from the floor and walls. Those specks were compared to particles found on Foreman's clothes. The wood chips and cement pieces matched.

Crimaldi said that Foreman had escaped death many times by other mob bosses. Two times Felix "Milwaukee Phil" Alderisio gave the order to kill Foreman. The first order to kill him was for two reasons; first, the failure to pay $1,000 owed to Alderisio from free lancing juice loans; and, second, Foreman failed to deliver on a tractor-trailer full of stolen appliances from Sears, Roebuck & Company. Foreman was responsible for hiring two other hoodlums to assist in this robbery; the two other hoodlums were caught and arrested. Alderisio gave the contract to kill Foreman to Vincent "The Saint" Inserro. However, fearing too much heat being placed on the mob for Foreman's murder, Alderisio called off the contract. Sometime later, Alderisio called Foreman for a meeting at Alderisio's home when Foreman then owed $28,000 to Alderisio from his independent juice loan operations. An argument broke out between the two when Alderisio told Foreman he had to shut down his operations. Outraged with that request, Foreman told Alderisio to *"get lost"* and to *"fuck off."*

Sometime after the disagreement with Alderisio, Foreman continued his operations and in turn also refused to pay back money owed to Sam DeStefano. According to Charles Crimaldi, after that refusal to pay,

Sam DeStefano and Crimaldi drove to the Armory Lounge where they were given the contract to kill Leo Foreman by Sam Giancana.

Anthony Spilotro was put on a plane in Las Vegas bound for Chicago, under arrest. During the plane flight, the officer escorting Spilotro engaged in casual conversation about the Foreman murder. His report is as follows:

"During a return flight from Las Vegas, Nevada, to Chicago, Illinois, Special Agent William O'Sullivan initiated casual conversation with Anthony Spilotro concerning living conditions in Las Vegas, and Spilotro's business enterprise of Anthony Stuart LTD.

Spilotro stated he was renting the house at 2612 Siesta for $350 per month. He was preparing to purchase a lot and build his own home.

As of September 1, 1972, Spilotro has his business, Anthony Stuart LTD., 2880 Las Vegas Boulevard South, Las Vegas, put in trust in favor of his 6-year old son, Vincent. Spilotro fears that he might lose the business because of his indictment for murder. Spilotro related that his business was going very well and sales were steadily increasing. He is paying $2,000 per month rent on the gift shop. The shop was initially set up as a corporation by Spilotro's attorney, Oscar Goodman of Las Vegas. The name Stuart in Anthony Stuart LTD, is his wife Nancy's maiden name.

The conversation changed to the instant case and Spilotro said that he would swear on the eyes of his son that this case was a frame. He said he would like to know what the "Rat" (Charles Crimaldi) was promised in consideration for his (Crimaldi's) testimony. Spilotro stated he knows very little about Crimaldi, that he has never had coffee with him (implying a friendly relationship), and he has met Crimaldi only about six times in his life.

During the ride from O'Hare Airport to the Cook County State's Attorney Office, Spilotro read an article published in the 'Chicago Today Newspaper' concerning Crimaldi's testimony before the Cook

County Grand Jury on August 25, 1972. Prior to reading the article, Spilotro asked if Crimaldi had been granted immunity. The response was affirmative. Near the end of the article Spilotro exhaled a sigh of depression, returning the newspaper, and said nothing further concerning the case."

At the bond hearing for Tony Spilotro in September 1972 a trembling Charles Crimaldi gave the following recollection as to the events of the killing, "*Mario pulled a gun, I pulled my gun. We fired, Tony was in there too, and he fired. We fired together. Then Mario took a butcher knife, cut Leo's belt, and took down his pants. Then Sam came in, he threatened to shoot Foreman in the groin, but then shot him in the buttocks. Tony stabbed him a few times, then cut some skin from his arm. I told you I'd get you for this screamed Sam.*"

After more questioning, Crimald did admit that he lied to the police in December of 1963 when they came to question him about the Foreman murder. His 1963 interview with Sgt. James Fitzgerald was as follows:

December 27, 1963

Question: What is your name, address?

Crimaldi: Charles Crimaldi, 831 S. Carpenter Street.

Question: What is your business or occupation?

Crimaldi: I am a plumber, employed by Frank's Plumbing for the past 3 months.

Question: What is the extent of your education?

Crimaldi: I went to 3 years high school.

Question: Do you know where you are now and why?

Crimaldi: Area #5 Homicide for the investigation of Leo Foreman.

Question: Do you wish to give a statement free and voluntary relative to this investigation?

Crimaldi: Yes.

Question: Did you know Leo Foreman?

Crimaldi: Yes.

Question:	Tell us the circumstances in which you were acquainted with Leo Foreman?
Crimaldi:	I met Foreman at a friend's house, Sam DeStefano, about a year and a half ago. Foreman was a guest at DeStefano's home. Sam DeStefano introduced him to me and stated that Foreman had just came home from Minnesota.
Question:	You stated that you are a friend of Sam DeStefano's, how long have you known Sam DeStefano?
Crimaldi:	About 15 years.
Question:	Under what circumstances do you know Sam DeStefano?
Crimaldi:	My mother went to school with his wife and it has been a close relationship with the family since.
Question:	After your first meeting and introduction to Leo Foreman, did you see him thereafter?
Crimaldi:	Yes, I saw him numerous times at Sam's house.
Question:	How often do you see Sam DeStefano and for what purpose?
Crimaldi:	I visited Sam almost every night strictly for friendship purposes.
Question:	On these numerous visits to Sam DeStefano's house you stated that you saw Leo Foreman numerous times present, did you inquire of Sam DeStefano who this man Foreman was and what his frequent visits to Sam meant?
Crimaldi:	No.
Question:	Did you meet Leo Foreman at other places?
Crimaldi:	I met Leo Foreman at his office on 7000 West on Belmont about 8 months ago, for the purpose of getting auto insurance, but his price was too high, so, I went to a different person.
Question:	Did you see Foreman on any other occasions?
Crimaldi:	Yes, I met him in traffic court with Sam, under Sam's traffic violation.
Question:	Do you know what the purpose of Foreman's frequent visits to Sam DeStefano's house was?
Crimaldi:	No.
Question:	Have you ever had the occasion to borrow money from Sam DeStefano or Leo Foreman?

Crimaldi:	Yes. I borrowed money from Sam DeStefano, $1,600 for the purpose of my car, the 1962 Rambler I am presently driving. I never borrowed money from Foreman.
Question:	Can you account for your activities on 14 November 1963?
Crimaldi:	Yes, I got paid and went by Sam DeStefano's house at night.
Question:	Can you account for your activities on 15 November 1963?
Crimaldi:	Yes, I went to work and went bowling at night at G&L Bowling Alley at Chicago and Pulaski Avenues. I finished bowling at 1 A.M.
Question:	Can you account for your activities on 16 November 1963?
Crimaldi:	I think I worked that Saturday and went by Sam's house at night.
Question:	Can you account for your activities on 17 November 1963?
Crimaldi:	I was probably at Sam's house all day.
Question:	Can you account for your activities on 18 November 1963?
Crimaldi:	I worked at 32 N. Central until 4:30 P.M., went home, ate, changed cloths and went to Sam's house. I stayed at Sam's house until 1:30 A.M.
Question:	Did anything unusual occur on the date?
Crimaldi:	Yes, the murder of Leo Foreman was broadcasted over the television.
Question:	Is there any other particular reason for your staying until 1 A.M. on the morning of the 19th?
Crimaldi:	Yes, I was waiting for the late news broadcast, which I heard at 1 A.M. and at this time Sgt. D. Kelly of Area #5 Homicide was there.
Question:	Do you perform any service or work for Sam DeStefano?
Crimaldi:	No.
Question:	Have you ever performed any service or work for Leo Foreman?
Crimaldi:	No.
Question:	Do you know Sam Cavello? If so, under what circumstance?
Crimaldi:	Yes, I met him at Sam's house with Leo Foreman.
Question:	When did you last see Leo Foreman alive?
Crimaldi:	Sometime last summer.
Question:	Would you submit to a lie test of any knowledge of the Foreman murder?
Crimaldi:	On the advice of my attorney.
Question:	Previously I asked you if you would submit to a lie test, you said you would, what caused you to change your mind?

Crimaldi: I believe I should consult my lawyer first.

Question: If after reading this statement and finding it to contain only what you have told us, will you sign it? Will you initial it?

Crimaldi: No.

When Crimaldi was asked about turning government informant in 1973, he told the court that he had been paid $200 a week cash between April and September 1973 and was being paid $300 a week in cash for his testimony and information by the U.S. government at that moment. When Crimaldi said that, gasps from the second row of the courtroom filled the room.

Foreman tried to outwit the mob and DeStefano and lost, but as one informant said, "At least he died with a smile on his face, possible knowing his killers would be caught." The conclusion of this story is further in this book.

Leo Foreman

Chapter Twenty-Two

DeStefano Listed as a Suspect

In August of 1961, Sam DeStefano was listed as a suspect in and questioned concerning the murders of:

Drury Murder

DeStefano's name resurfaced in November 1950 during the murder investigation of Chicago Police Lieutenant William Drury. On September 25, 1950, Drury was putting his automobile in a garage near his home when he was assassinated by unknown hoodlums. During the probe, investigators learned that Charles DiUmberto, aka DegliUmberto, a New Jersey hoodlum whose first wife was a relative of mob boss Charles "Lucky" Luciano, confessed that an Anthony Rotondo had admitted killing Drury for $9,000. DiUmberto told investigators that while he was in Leavenworth Prison on a forgery conviction, he witnessed Sam DeStefano act as a "go-between" for mobsters Paul DeLucia "Ricca" and Louis "Little New York" Campagna, who were serving prison terms, to arrange the murder of William Drury with Anthony Rotondo. When DeLucia was asked if he knew Sam DeStefano he replied, *"I don't know what his business is. We met when we were in jail together at Leavenworth. I don't see him often."*

When DeStefano was interviewed, he admitted that while in Leavenworth, he met Paul DeLucia and Louis Campagna and that he knew Rotondo. He claimed Rotondo was a "moocher" who might concoct any kind of story to "bum" some money from someone. He admitted that he had met DiUmberto and Rotondo in Chicago a few weeks ago around the time of the murder but Sam added that Rotondo had just "mooched" $50 from DeStefano on the basis of their acquaintance in prison.

When DeStefano and DiUmberto were brought face to face, DeStefano asked him, *"Why do you want to do this to me? All I ever did for you was to feed you and try to help you."* Both DeStefano and DiUmberto refused to take lie detector tests, while Rotondo was arrested in Baltimore and questioned. DeStefano remains a suspect in the murder of Drury.

Ralph Del Genio

Ralph Del Genio was a city of Chicago truck driver and civil employee who doubled as a burglar and thief. Also known as Ray Devon, Del Genio was sponsored in his city job by mob labor boss Frank "Frankie X" Esposito. Del Genio's beaten and bruised body was found in an abandoned car on June 20, 1961.

The abandoned car was found on Wells Street in the city of Chicago and was towed to the city pound after a few days. At the pound, a worker discovered that the rear seat of the car was removed and tossed in the trunk and in its place was the murdered body of Ralph Del Genio, which was covered by a blanket.

Del Genio's son, Fred Del Genio, was a known syndicate burglar under the control of the Kringas family. Gus and John Kringas were under the control of mob boss Sam Giancana. Ralph's daughter, Dolores Marcus, was once the sweetheart of mobster Agostino "Gus" Amadeo who was killed in a shootout with police in 1954.

Police discovered that Ralph Del Genio was acting as a "juice" collector, calling himself an "agent" for "juice" bosses. It was also discovered that Del Genio was in debt to Cicero syndicate "juice" bosses for some $23,000.

Once investigators discovered this and the coroner's office said Del Genio had been kicked and beaten to death, they headed to the house of Sam DeStefano for questioning. DeStefano did admit to detectives that he knew Ralph Del Genio but denied he knew anything about his murder.

One of the other people sought for the murder of Del Genio was William "Action" Jackson who was viciously murdered weeks later. The murder has never been solved and simply "went away."

The M & M Murders

The bodies of William J. McCarthy and James Miraglia were found stuffed in the trunk of a car on May 14, 1962. The car was parked in front of the building at 3855 W. 55th Place for about two weeks before the police discovered the slain bodies. McCarthy's throat was slashed from ear to ear, while Miraglia had been strangled.

The day their bodies were found both Miraglia and McCarthy were supposed to report to federal marshals to begin serving a 2-year prison sentence for robbery. On January 17, 1961, Miraglia and McCarthy used baseball bats to rob Rudolph Churan of $5,000.

Miraglia had been reported missing by his wife Rita on May 4, 1962, while McCarthy was reported missing by his wife Betty on May 2, 1962. Police speculated the reasons as to why the two were murdered:

1. Reports suggested that they might have robbed a syndicate handbook.
2. They had been giving information to the government about hoodlums and syndicate operations.
3. It was connected to the killing of Miraglia's father. On August 13, 1959, two masked gunmen in the Orange Lantern tavern shot John M. Miraglia, a minor hoodlum, to death.
4. Both McCarthy and Miraglia held back loot from various burglaries from other members of their robbery gang.

FBI agent William Roemer Jr. went to the house of Sam DeStefano to interview him when the FBI discovered that both McCarthy and Miraglia had been on "juice" to DeStefano. According to FBI reports, Sam DeStefano, Tony Spilotro, Charles "Chuckie" Nicoletti, and Felix "Milwaukee Phil" Alderisio picked up McCarthy and tortured him as to the whereabouts of Miraglia. Refusing to talk, McCarthy's head was placed in a vise and squeezed until his eye popped out. McCarthy told them how to find Miraglia and begged to be killed. His throat was slit to put him out of his misery. This is the incident made famous in the movie "Casino" starring Robert De Niro, Joe Pesci, and Sharon Stone. When the four found him, Miraglia told his killers he knew he was going to die and asked for one favor, to be strangled to death so his wife could collect the insurance money. After this murder, Nicoletti and Alderisio moved Tony Spilotro out of DeStefano's crew and into the outfit as a hit man.

L.C. Smith

On June 13, 1961, the body of L.C. Smith, an African American, was found shot to death in his car at 161 W. Monroe Street in Chicago. Smith had been shot five times in the head. A witness said that at 4:30 in the morning Smith was kidnapped by four white men who forced Smith into his own car and drove off with another car following them. His body was found at 7:15 a.m. the same day. The witness identified a Cicero hoodlum named Michael LoSurdo as one of the kidnappers. LoSurdo had been arrested a month earlier at a syndicate gambling joint on Cermak Road in Cicero. LoSurdo was arrested on kidnapping and murder charges but was released on a no bill. Later reports stated that Smith was involved with "juice" men and Sam DeStefano was listed as a possible suspect. The murder is still unsolved.

Theororos Sampaniotia

Theororos Sampaniotia, a Cicero gambler, was found shot to death in an abandoned garage at 642 Blue Island Avenue in February 1961. He had been shot five times. Found in his pocket was a pen from one of the Cicero gambling establishments he was known to frequent. Police discovered that Sampaniotia had been attempting to shake down syndicate gambling joints in Cicero. There was a report that he fell behind on his "juice" loan payments and Sam DeStefano was investigated as a suspect. The murder is still unsolved.

Michael DeMarte

Michael DeMarte was known as a minor hoodlum who made his way as a bookie who would gamble away all his winnings. Being connected to some top hoodlums, DeMarte was in the lower levels and was expendable. In 1960, he had lost all his money, both in betting and paying out bets, and had to go on "juice." When time came to pay up, he fell behind and fell out of favor. It was time to make an example of what happens when you fall behind in your payments.

On November 15, 1960, DeMarte was walking up to his house when three syndicate men pulled up in a car, jumped out and shot DeMarte in the head. As he lay on the ground dying, the two gunmen unloaded their guns into him with what they called "insurance" shots, to make sure he was dead. Sam DeStefano was investigated as having a hand in his murder. The murder is still unsolved.

Carl Wiltse

Carl Wiltse was born around 1934 in Chicago and had dreams of running his own big-time syndicate burglary crew. His dream ended on August 2, 1961, when two assassins climbed up the back porch of his apartment and slipped through the back window. Wiltse sat in his chair watching TV while the two hoodlums opened fire killing him with two shotgun blasts.

Police suspected that the killing was in connection with a dispute with his fellow burglars and that his death was linked to the murder of his associate, burglar Michael Joyce, who was killed a week earlier. But when Wiltse's lawyer Robert J. McDonnell came forward to tell the police that he had heard that Wiltse was "talking too much" to the wrong people, police immediately began to look into Wiltse's connections to Sam DeStefano. Detectives received information that Wiltse was killed because he fell behind in "juice" loan payments.

McDonnell said that his client had appeared in court on a burglary charge all bruised and battered. Wiltse told McDonnell that mob enforcers had attacked him a few days before his death. The goons knocked Wiltse to the ground near his home at 855 N. Wolcott Avenue, took his head, and pounded it into the pavement while threatening to kill his wife and five children.

Arrested were four of Wiltse associates, Stanley Kozienec, Robert "Whitey" Proszowlicz, Thomas Higgins, and Rich Machowski. All four passed lie detector tests and were released. Sam DeStefano remained a main suspect.

Shelby Faulk

On June 14, 1961, Shelby R. Faulk was found shot to death in his white Cadillac. His car was found in an alley behind 7304 Union Street, blocking the garage of the home. Faulk's head was hanging out of the front window on the passenger side of the car. He had been shot once in the chin, chest, and left ear. The night Faulk disappeared he was to meet with a Nolan Mack and had $7,000 in cash on him so the two could purchase 6 kilograms of heroin. All that was found on his body was 62 cents in change.

Hours after discovering his lifeless body, police went to his home at 7120 Emerald Avenue where they discovered a dice game in progress. Arrested were his brother, his wife Geraldine, his brother-in-law Lawrence, and 16 other gamblers.

Shelby Faulk was known as a south side drug pusher and ex-convict. In 1949, he was arrested for carrying a gun. In 1950, he was sentenced to 1–2 years in prison for manslaughter in Nashville, Tennessee. In October 1952, he was sent to state prison for being in possession of gambling equipment; and in June of 1955, he was sentenced to 2 to 3 years for possession of narcotics. In April 1959, he was found not guilty for possession of drugs, and in November 1960 was found not guilty on a sale of narcotics charge. Shelby Faulk had been seen meeting with Sam DeStefano shortly before his death.

Lester Belgrad

On December 7, 1960, the body of Lester Belgrad, a jewelry salesman who had been arrested many times, was found face up in the back seat of his automobile with three bullet holes in his head. The car was parked in front of 1651 West 13th Street.

Belgrad's wife, Mrs. Frieda Mix, said her husband had left their home at 2626 N. Richmond Street at about 10 p.m. on December 6 and never returned home.

Belgrad had been arrested in the past on a charge of selling gold plated police stars. After his death, an informant told detectives that nine wealthy men with mob ties were robbed by two men who posed as policemen. These men refused to go to the police to report the robberies saying they would handle the situation mob style. One of the men robbed was believed to be mobster Marshall Caifano who was beaten and robbed in the months before the murders. Sam DeStefano was listed as maybe having a hand in the set-up of this murder.

Frank Del Guidice

The body of known burglar Frank Del Guidice was found in his auto, shot twice in the head, on December 12, 1960. Del Guidice, with an arrest record dating back to 1933, was partners with hoodlums Lester Belgrad and Richard Fanning. His car was found parked in front of the building at 1705 Ohio Street in Chicago.

Fanning, Del Guidice and Belgrad had been seen together in the past weeks leading up to the murders and were suspected of robbing syndicate hoodlums.

Richard Fanning

Richard Fanning was known as an ex-convict with a reputation as a syndicate burglar. He was found stabbed to death in his car, parked in front of the building at 3565 Wells Street in Chicago. This was the third killing in 5 days with members from the same burglary crew.

Police learned that his killer tortured Fanning for information. His wrists were severely bruised, his groin had been mutilated, and spikes had been driven under his fingernails. It is believed that he gave up his two associates, Lester Belgrad and Frank Del Guidice. Because of the way he was tortured, detectives focused on Sam DeStefano as having something to do with his murder.

John Hennigan

John Hennigan was a former FBI and state's attorney's office informant ratting on the Chicago mob who was killed in front of his home on November 16, 1961. While Hennigan sat in his parked car in front of his home at 2641 W. 25th Street, a gunman opened the driver's side door and shot Hennigan in the groin with a 12-gauge shotgun.

Found on Hennigan were telephone numbers and addresses of three Cicero gambling joints that were known to provide "juice" loans from Sam DeStefano to its customers after they lost all their money. Also found in Hennigan's pocket was a receipt from the mob's Casa Madrid in Melrose Park and a business card from a loan company.

Hennigan had a police record dating back to 1937 with 10 arrests for passing bogus checks, armed robbery, forgery, postal violations, and burglaries. His only conviction came for a charge of carrying a concealed weapon. At the time of his murder, he was out on bond for robbing a Russell Mack in a tavern located at 2600 West 25th Street. He also took $200 in cash belonging to Marion Wetzel, the owner of the tavern.

Among some reports it's speculated that Hennigan may have made a deal to become an informant for the Illinois State's Attorney's office and that's the reason he was killed. However, many at the time believed that he was killed by Sam DeStefano.

Albert Testa

Al "Transon" Testa was known as a small-time syndicate gambler and burglar. The tinny gangster that stood at 4 and a half feet in height was found in the alley at the rear of 1031 N. Francisco Avenue in Chicago on October 8, 1961, with two bullet holes in his head. Not dead but in a coma, Testa was taken to the hospital where he later died without naming his killers but was able to tell the police he was dumped from a car.

The pint-sized ex-convict, born around 1913, made his mark in the 1930's as a burglar who could fit into small windows. He was arrested for rape, burglary, and larceny charges. He entered Illinois State Prison in Joliet on April 22, 1943, for his rape conviction. In August 1947, he was arrested for robbing a drunken man while the two were at the old Pleasure Club at 3106 Madison Street in Chicago. The drunken man, Philip Aiello, said that Testa and two other hoodlums put him in an automobile after he became intoxicated and robbed him of $29 and a gold ring. When Testa was placed in lock up, a police guard had to be on hand 24 hours a day since Testa could squirm through the bars of his cell. In 1948, Testa was sentenced to 2 years in prison for counterfeiting.

In June 1960, Testa was arrested with Anthony Pamillo at the saloon located at 931 S. Western Avenue for taking horse bets.

Sometime after, Al Testa and his partner, burglar Philip Polito, were arrested and questioned in the murders of William "Action" Jackson and Herman Posner but were released.

The pint-sized Testa was called "the Midget" by the hoodlums who knew him but gained his nickname of "Transom" because he used transoms to enter places he burglarized.

Testa's downfall came after he met an 18-year-old striptease dancer that he fell in love with and began to bring around to all the mob hangouts. The dancer soon became a favorite of mobsters William "Potatoes" Daddono, Sam and Chuckie English, and Rocco Infelice. After a few months the, dancer went to the police to rat out everything she had learned about the mobsters she became friendly with. It was believed that Al Testa was blamed for bringing her around and was punished for it.

Phil Polito and John "Donkey Ears" Wolck were arrested and questioned for the murder; both were released. Police also were looking for Daddono, the English brothers, Infelice and Sam DeStefano for questioning. The murder is still unsolved.

Ralph Probst

One story concerning Mad Sam DeStefano's trips to the hospital in January 1967 for stomach pains may have led to the murder of Cook County Sheriff's Police Officer Ralph Probst, who was one of the officers assigned to handle Mad Sam while in the hospital. On April 10, 1967, Probst was watching the Academy Awards on television with his wife, Marlene, in their home at 8802 Corcoran Road in Homewood. Probst had walked to the kitchen for a drink of water, and then moments later, his wife heard a shot and glass shattering. When she reached the kitchen, her husband was on the floor, dead in a pool of blood. Probst had been shot in the back of the head by a .41 caliber Magnum pistol, then a rare weapon. The killer, who had been standing outside on the driveway, fired the shot through the window when Probst entered the kitchen.

Just three months earlier, Probst had had a run-in with Mad Sam at the hospital. The run-in left a sore spot in DeStefano's mind. Probst's partner, Officer Bob Borowski, said, "*Sam had a big fancy Chinese dinner brought in and baskets of fruit all over. Ralph sent the food back and put on the handcuffs. … And Sam didn't like that. Not one bit.*" Another officer named Jerry Harmon added that Mad Sam told Probst, "*You'll be very sorry you treated me this way.*"

Sam DeStefano was listed as a suspect, but no evidence other than the run-in was uncovered. It's not clear if Mad Sam had anything to do with the murder but what happened was that another person had crossed DeStefano's path and was killed. In 2001, a plea was made by to the public for any information concerning the murder. It remains unsolved.

Al Brown

Mob gunmen shot a syndicate burglar named Albert Brown to death on November 4, 1961, as he stepped out of his car. His body was found in the parking lot of the Lonergan Die Company at 4651 Arthington Street in Chicago. When people from the company heard the shots, they ran outside and found Brown's body lying face down on the ground with his legs halfway under his car with the engine running. He had been shot four times in the head and chest. The gun used was a 7.65mm Italian Beretta automatic pistol, which was found 60 feet from the body, in the weeds.

Brown had just been convicted of breaking into a company and attempted to break into the safe in May 1961. He was sentenced on October 31, 1961 to 5 to 10 years in prison but was out on an appeals bond when he was murdered. Sam DeStefano was mentioned in the murder investigation.

John Arthur Powers

On March 31, 1961, John Powers was about to enter his basement apartment at 3639 Dickens Street when he was shot five times. Before his death, he boasted that he owed $1,800 to the "outfit."

Police learned that Powers was desperate to make his "juice" loan payments to mob loan sharks and to pay up on his outstanding loan with Sam DeStefano. Powers staged a robbery of a syndicate horsebook in Cicero. For this, he was killed.

Months later a smalltime hoodlum named Eddie McNeil bragged that he was a close friend of many mob hit men. Being so close to these killers McNeil began to tell people he, too, was a mob hit man and bragged to a dice girl trying to impress her that he killed his "pal" John Powers on orders from the mob. Word got out that McNeil was telling people he was a mob hit man. His body was found on May 15, 1961, in an alley behind the building at 3441 Fullon Street. He had been shot six times. Detectives received word that McNally had been on "juice" to Sam DeStefano at the time of his death, a debt that was never repaid.

Michael Joyce

Known as a big time syndicate burglar and safecracker, Mike Joyce had been arrested many times for stealing furs and jewelry from homes and apartments, vagrancy, and narcotics, and was questioned in the murder of Charles Gross, an acting 31st Ward committeeman in 1952.

On July 29, 1961, Joyce's charred body was found in a burning car in front of 819 N. Harding Avenue. As firefighters extinguished the flames, they could see that Joyce was in a kneeling position and had been shot once in the head and once in the abdomen. Joyce operated in the area of Chicago that was under the control of Nick and George Bravos. Many times, when his career would hit a snag in the road, he went to the "juice" men for a loan. According to the Chicago Police, Joyce fell behind in his payments to the Bravos brothers and Sam DeStefano and ignored the usual threats from the "juice" collectors to make good on his loans. When they set him on fire, it sent a message to all the other "juice" victims who ignored threats against them, the message being, *You will burn if you think we are joking.*

Chapter Twenty-Three

That 70's Sam

On June 9, 1970, Mad Sam got out of his hospital bed in Statesville prison and went before a parole board asking for his release. He was denied parole.

While Sam remained in prison, his brother Mario was still working the rackets when in November 1970, a young off-duty police officer and his fiancée walked past the North Western Avenue emporium banquet room of a pizza place and were ushered into the place to peruse brochures on cemetery crypts. The young police officer, familiar with the organized crime chart, noticed that the men making the pitch to him were mobsters Mario DeStefano, Charles Nicoletti, Lennie Patrick, and Mike Patrick. The young police officer left the room and called for backup.

Mario was the owner of the Metropolitan Vault Company, which made burial vaults. Charles Siragusa and the Illinois Crime Committee launched an investigation into reports that Metropolitan Vault Company was using pressure tactics to gain control of the business. Siragusa issued an investigatory subpoena asking for the books and records of customers and prospective customers of Metropolitan Vault, Inc. The Funeral Director's Service Association of Greater Chicago, whose members at the time included Frank Annunzio, Frank Armanetti, Michael Galasso, and mobster James Eco Coli, launched its own investigation into the alleged illegal pressure tactics and ruled that Siragusa and the Crime Commission had no right or legal authority to subpoena the records or make those allegations. The Crime Commission closed the case when they found no evidence of any illegal practices.

The investigation did reveal that in May 1971 Mario was being introduced to various undertakers in the Chicago area as a sales representative for the Metropolitan Vault Company. The company employed three men who manufactured about 30 vaults a week. The vaults were sold to individual Italian undertakers. One-half of the vaults were purchased by the Salerno Brothers Funeral home on North Avenue in Chicago. The Metropolitan Vault Company was previously known as Décor-Cem Incorporated and Tri-Cote Incorporated, located at 1310 S. Cicero Avenue.

Another shocking discovery was that Mario DeStefano, a convicted murderer, had a firearms permit for carrying weapons. In September 1972, while the FBI was investigating how Mario could get a firearms license, they received word that the Chicago mob was fed up with the DeStefano brothers. They also found out that Charles "Chuckie" Nicoletti actually owed the Metropolitan Vault Company and attempted to sell the company to get away from the DeStefano's. On February 28, 1973, new owners took over the Metropolitan Vault Company.

After serving his prison sentence in Joliet prison hospital, Mad Sam was paroled on June 25, 1971. While in prison, he had suffered vascular problems and demanded to be wheeled out of Joliet in a wheelchair. However, once outside the walls, Sam jumped out of his wheelchair and embraced his wife who was waiting with other family members. In normal Sam DeStefano fashion, he turned to the gathered newspaper reporters who had showed up for a story and gave them a short statement complaining about prison life and the parole board.

As Sam settled back into life outside the cell, he filed a civil suit against John Twomey, George Stampar, and Julius Venckus from the State of Illinois. Another incident in December 1971 that outraged Sam was when general manager, John Severino, at WLS-TV station in Chicago, called for stronger gun control legislation in his editorials. DeStefano contacted Severino by telephone and let him have it, protesting for almost an hour.

The FBI interviewed one informant in September 1971 concerning Sam and Mario DeStefano. The informant told the FBI that Mad Sam had been doing too much complaining about the "Outfit" not helping him and his family while he was locked up in jail. The informant said that Sam made many enemies among the "mafia" and if he didn't stop complaining and getting publicity, he was going to be "hit." This informant also said that Sam and Mario were considered "special" members of the mob, even though in Sam's mind he was not a mobster or member of the mob. The informant also added that Mad Sam showed up at the wake of mobster Felix "Milwaukee Phil" Alderisio in October 1971. He stated that so many of the "outfit" guys were mad at Sam that they avoided him. Mad Sam was observed standing in the back with mobster Leo Manfredi.

1972 Trial

In 1972 Sam DeStefano's one time top enforcer Charles "Chuckie" Crimaldi went to work for the Drug Enforcement Agency as an undercover rat. The first target in the line of fire for the DEA was Crimaldi's old friend, Anthony "Sonny" Esposito Jr.

Crimaldi worked with DEA Agents to set up a plan to catch Esposito with drugs in his possession. Sonny's father, Anthony "Tony X" Esposito Sr., and his brother Frank "Frankie X" Esposito, controlled labor union Local 1001 of the County Municipal Employees and Foremen's Union in Chicago for over 30 years and the Chicago District Council of Labors for 15 years. Both Frankie and Tony X were members of the old "west side bloc" in politics and members of the old Democratic machine that backed Richard J. Daley for mayor of Chicago in the 1950's. Both Esposito's died in 1969 and Sonny Esposito had been slated to take over the union presidency of Local 1001 for the mob.

CHGO. P. D.
1247563

Author's Collection

Anthony "Sonny" Esposito Jr.

When the DEA enlisted Crimaldi as an undercover agent, reports say that he, Crimaldi, would not say the reason why he became an undercover agent for the DEA except that he was "doing his duty" and hated narcotics because his brother spent a good portion of his life as a heroin addict. However, one report suggested that Crimaldi and his brother, Tony Crimaldi, were running a heroin business as heroin dealers since 1966 and got caught. It was either prison or rat on his buddies. Sonny's brother Frank "Butch" Esposito testified that he would see Tony and Chuckie Crimaldi everyday in the old neighborhood between 1964 and 1967 selling heroin. He also added that Chuckie was known as a dealer and would sell his heroin through Tony Crimaldi.

So Crimaldi became a paid informant receiving around $1,600 over a few months as he spilled his information to agents. Under pressure from the DEA to give more information, Crimaldi says the DEA asked him about Sonny Esposito. Crimaldi testified that he had grown up with Sonny back in the old neighborhood but had not seen Esposito in 5 or 6 years.

Crimaldi claimed one of Esposito's men named Walter "Ike" Withers called him and asked him if he wanted Esposito to supply him with some cocaine. The DEA had information from another informer that Sonny Esposito had connections with powerful drug dealers in South America and believed that Sonny had a hand in supplying cocaine to the Chicago area.

Esposito told Crimaldi, with the conversation being recorded, that he personally did not deal in drugs but could ask around and see what he could find. After the two met at the Regency Hyatt House just outside of Chicago, Crimaldi told Esposito that he was in serious financial trouble and needed to make some fast cash.

Over a series of phone calls between Esposito and Crimaldi, Sonny told Chuckie that he didn't like this drug business and couldn't help him get any drugs.

Almost four months after Crimaldi and Esposito met, the DEA showed up and arrested Esposito, charging him with possession of 206.5 millimeters of a substance with 50 percent cocaine contact with intent to distribute.

When it was time for Esposito's trial in 1972, Charles Crimaldi was the lead witness for the prosecution. With Sam DeStefano out of prison and the Esposito family being a very close friend to Mad Sam dating back to the 1920's, he took it upon himself to try and "take care" of Crimaldi for Esposito. On the day of Esposito's trial, Mad Sam knew Crimaldi would be taking the elevator in the Federal Building in Chicago to the courtroom on the top floors. So he and another hoodlum, close to both DeStefano and Esposito named Edward "Eddie" Speice, waited for Crimaldi to show up so they could "have a word with him."

1) The official DEA report on the incident is as follows:

"On Tuesday, February 22, 1972, at approximately 10:30 a.m., Group Supervisor James P. Braseth and Government witness Charles Crimaldi entered the north middle express elevator of the south tier of seven express elevators in the Federal Building, 219 South Dearborn, Chicago, Illinois. Group Supervisor Braseth and Mr. Crimaldi were the only occupants of the elevator at this time.

When the elevator stopped at the second floor, organized crime members Sam DeStefano, Edward Speice, and two males unknown to Crimaldi who turned out to be Mike Polesti and Leo Parent, entered the elevator. DeStefano approached Mr. Crimaldi, glared at him, and stated, *"My eyesight is dim, but I think I know you."* Mr. Crimaldi did not reply. DeStefano then stated, *"My memory is fading too. It must be old age."* Mr. Crimaldi again did not reply and DeStefano continued stating, *"I hear your eyes are dimming and your memory fading permanently this week."* Mr. Crimaldi still did not reply.

At this time, the elevator stopped at the 14th floor and one of the males unknown to Crimaldi got out. The man was visibly upset as if he realized how DeStefano was threatening Crimaldi. When the elevator stopped at the 14th floor, Group Supervisor Braseth moved to his right and stood between Mr. Crimaldi and DeStefano. There was no further conversation. Within a few seconds, the elevator stopped at the 18th floor where Group Supervisor Braseth and Mr. Crimaldi exited and then entered the BNDD Office.

Upon entering the office, Group Supervisor Braseth and Mr. Crimaldi wrote down the statements made by DeStefano. Mr. Crimaldi regarded the statement of DeStefano as a direct threat on his life and a warning not to testify against organized crime member Anthony Esposito Jr., a close friend of both DeStefano and Speice."

2) Another report regarding the incident involving Edward Speice is as follows:

"When the elevator stopped on the second floor, Edward Speice entered first and turned, stating *"Hurry up, look who's here."* DeStefano then entered the elevator. After DeStefano threatened Mr. Crimaldi, Speice stated to Mr. Crimaldi, *"Done any fishing lately?"* Mr. Crimaldi interpreted this statement as meaning they wanted to use him as fish bait.

Mr. Crimaldi was scheduled to testify against Anthony Esposito on February 22, 1972, before the Honorable Judge Thomas R. McMillen. It was later determined by Group Supervisor Braseth that DeStefano and Speice proceeded to the 21st floor and entered the court of Judge McMillen.

Sam DeStefano was wearing black and white bell-bottom trousers with a black shirt and black trench coat. Speice was wearing dark trousers with a white turtle-neck sweater and a brown leather coat."

3) Charles Crimaldi's statement of what occurred in the elevator:

"On Tuesday, February 22, 1972, Group Supervisor Braseth and myself got on the elevator in the Federal Building. As the elevator stopped on the second floor, Sam DeStefano and Edward Speice and two other men I didn't know got on. DeStefano walked up to me and staring at me said, *"My eyesight is dim, but I think I know you. My memory is fading too. It must be old age. I hear your eyes are dimming and your memory is fading permanently this week."* During the time DeStefano was talking to me, I made no remarks to him.

The elevator then stopped at the 14th floor and one of the two men got off. As he got off, group supervisor Braseth moved over and stood between DeStefano and me. DeStefano didn't say anything else and when the elevator stopped at the 18th floor, group supervisor Braseth and I got off and went into the BNDD Offices.

At this time, group supervisor Braseth and I sat down and wrote down the statement DeStefano made. I took his statement as a threat to my life. Many people have told me DeStefano is trying to kill me and I believe this threat was a warning not to testify against Anthony Esposito."

However, Crimaldi wrote in his book that when he and Braseth exited the elevator he, Crimaldi, had time to tell off DeStefano in a rant that equaled one of Sam's crazy lashings. After this rant that took at least a minute, Crimaldi claims he said it so quiet that only Sam could hear. He added that when he was done "scaring" DeStefano, as he put it, DeStefano turned to Ed Speice and said, *"Come on Eddie, let's get the fuck away from these goddam animals."*

On March 2, 1972, Sam DeStefano and Edward Speice were arrested and charged with threatening a government witness. Bond was set at $15,000 each but proved laughable bond to DeStefano when he pulled out his wad of $1,000 bills and paid the bond for both.

DeStefano and Speice said they went to the Federal Building that day to see how the trial on Mike Polesti was going. DeStefano and Speice met up with hoodlum Leo Parent who was also at the building and they accidentally ran into Charles Crimaldi in the elevator.

Sam DeStefano demanded an immediate jury trial and was granted one. He pleaded not guilty before the judge and in a 15-minute speech, he declared, *"I was framed. I can afford a lawyer, but I want to represent myself to clear my name."*

DeStefano informed Judge Richard B. Austin that he was going to subpoena ten members of Crimaldi's family, including the former husband of Crimaldi's present wife. When Judge Austin commented it would be hard to serve all those subpoenas that day DeStefano replied, *"If the marshals can't find them, I'll send out people to find them myself."*

Then DeStefano asked that his bond of $15,000 be lowered to $10,000 because, *"Pimps, hijackers, whore masters, and dope pushers all are released on lower bonds and he has been fighting drug traffic in this country for the last 35 years and was a law-abiding citizen."* DeStefano then went into the events that happened at his home when agents came to arrest him, *"I was compelled, your honor, under force and threats, by these same agents that sit over there, and especially James P. Braseth. He threatened me many times during the course of this arrest. He came into my house, after me letting him in because I took his word that he had a warrant. He came in there to perform* a Hampton-Clark by Hanrahan. He came in there to kill me, and I can prove that statement. He knew my wife left. He could have arrested me on the 29th when the warrant was issued. He could have arrested me in the daytime, but they waited until my wife left for the hospital at 4:30, their usual procedure, to visit her mother. No cars were in front of my house. And he thought that I was alone, but fortunately there was a man in there that they couldn't see from the windows, and they waited until 5:30 in the dark of night, raining, about eight to ten strong, ringing the bell. I immediately went, and how do you think they found me, your honor? In my pajamas, my wife's apron, cooking supper for when she comes back from the hospital.

Who are you? I asked

Government agents, we come to arrest you.

Have you a warrant?

Yes!

What are you arresting me for?

Well, we have a warrant for your arrest.

I said, "If you have a warrant, this is very simple. I don't run, one of you can go to my other entrance."

The judge interrupted DeStefano asking, "What has this got to do with your bond?" DeStefano answered, "Why should I be treated this way your honor?" DeStefano went on to explain that he let the agents in on their word that they had a warrant but didn't have a warrant. He then complained about how he had to spend the night in prison in his pajamas. After more arguing, the Judge agreed to lower his bond.

The nickname for the trial became "The Court Circus." First, the lawyer for Edward Speice, named Frank Oliver, asked the judge for a separate trial knowing DeStefano was going to conduct a crazy trial. He was denied. DeStefano started off by telling the jury that he was willing to die for his principles. He then repeatedly swallowed pills from different pill bottles set up on his table. He told the jury, "If you send me to prison, you'll send me to my death, but that's all right." He then paused and began to cough as loudly as possible. He made his way over to the trashcan in the courtroom, and spit into it several times. He turned to Judge Austin and asked for a recess, which was granted. Once the jury was removed from the courtroom DeStefano walked over to the long table being used by government attorney's Jim Thompson and Michael Fitzsimmons, took off his yellow clip-on tie and brown suit coat, and lay down on top of the table to get some rest.

DeStefano's opening statement to the jury was as follows:

"Ladies and gentlemen of the jury, first I want to apologize. Maybe I misunderstood co-counsel in this case, and the misunderstanding was a certain date but I understood him to say the 22nd of the indictment, and so I possibly made a mistake, I do not know, my mind is confused. We felt and we witnessed a man of 63 years of age and very ill. I am going to try to take just a few moments of your time. I am very meticulous. I am very what they call a perfectionist, and it is a dangerous thing to be a perfectionist. I like everything just so. That includes this trial and the way I live at home with my wife and three children, nieces, nephews, et cetera. I like everything just so, although I can honestly state I don't make their life hard because I am a perfectionist. I allow for that and I only ask them not to touch my cigarettes and my glasses, where they are, and I know where they are at.

Any statement at any time that I will make to you, you can bet it will be an honest statement. I might make a human error that is possible. I am not infallible, but I will give you the facts of this case. I have no intention to make an opening statement because I have nothing to prove to you people. It is up to the great State's Attorney, Mr. Thompson, the power of the American Government, to prove that Sam DeStefano and Eddie Speice are guilty beyond a reasonable doubt.

Now, I want to make this as short as possible. First, I am very exhausted. I have a false aorta and arteries. I have undergone two of those operations and many other diseases.

Now, this charge began on this incident, began on February 22nd. This incident in the elevator happened on February 22. The dates are very, very important for you to decide whether it will be a guilty verdict or a not guilty verdict. On the 29th Agent Braseth went before one of our Magistrates Balog and got a complaint for the arrest of me and my co-defendant who I slightly know for a few months, Ed Speice.

Now, on the 29th, it being the leap year, I hope you unmarried girls got your shot in, but on the 29th, after he got this, I don't exactly know the time, but let's assume it had to be in daylight, I lived in the same residence at 1656 North Sayer Avenue with three children who are now school teachers for the past 20 years. I ask you to bear in mind, why didn't they come there to arrest me that day or notify me? They knew I had a civil case going in this building. But they come on the evening of March 1st, in the dark of night, raining and muddy. At no time before they got this complaint did they come and say, '*Sam DeStefano, what were you doing in this building?*'

Now if I may shout, I want you to forgive me because that is righteous anger. I repeat, as sick as I am, I will shout. I can't help myself. I will shout until I drop dead on this floor, but I want you to hear that testimony on that stand and then judge Sam DeStefano and then judge Edward Speice. I thank you. I trust you will give me a fair trial. This is all I ask. I called this trial immediately with no continuance or anything, and the judge and the prosecutor will verify that usually these take months, but I demanded a trial yesterday when I was indicted, I believe, the day before. This is unheard of, to go to trial so fast, but this was on my demand. That is what you call justification, righteousness, righteous anger, and I want you people to remember this and judge me as I am. If you send me to prison, you will send me to my death, but that is all right, I am willing to die for my principles."

At the trial, the government attorney, James Thompson (who would later become governor of Illinois), stated that when DeStefano asked Chuckie if, "*He had done any fishing lately?*" that meant DeStefano was forecasting prophecy that Chuckie would be cut up into little pieces and thrown in the river.

When DeStefano questioned DEA agent James Braseth, he asked him "*Why are you trying to frame Sam DeStefano into the penitentiary?*" Thompson objected time after time to the questions DeStefano was asking. At one point, DeStefano grabbed a roll of toilet paper and threw it in the air screaming, "*Your whole testimony is worth this...after it's been used!*" Once DeStefano tossed the toilet paper in the air, Judge Richard Austin called a recess. DeStefano, protesting, demanded that the toilet paper be admitted into evidence. The judge refused and walked off the bench.

DeStefano asked agent Braseth what Charles Crimaldi did for a living, Braseth answered, "He said he was employed by you as a juice-loan enforcer." Mad Sam objected asking loudly, "Juice? What kind of juice? Orange Juice? Electric Juice? Pineapple Juice? What Juice?" Braseth replied "Money lender." DeStefano laughed and pulled out a wad of money from his pocket and showed it to Braseth asking, "Do you want to borrow some money from me?" Jim Thompson interrupted, "Maybe he can't afford the rates." DeStefano then pointed out to the court that he was the manager of his wife's bond business.

Among other acts of craziness, DeStefano said that, "There are only two great lawyers in this world, me and Perry Mason, and Mason isn't available!" He accused Jim Thompson of setting the case up so he could look like a big man and run for governor of Illinois. He would walk up to the jury box, pound his hand on the railing, screaming, "Where's my medications, somebody get me a heart pill!"

He continuously screamed he needed his medication for his bad heart, poor eyesight, anemia, and bad hearing. He once again asked for a recess then reclined on the prosecution table and placed a handkerchief over his face to get some rest.

DeStefano still tried to call Chuck Crimaldi's entire family as witnesses. Chuckie, himself, was reportedly too afraid to appear at the trial because of what DeStefano might do to him as he sat in the witness booth. When Thompson volunteered Edward Speice's lawyer, Frank Oliver to question Crimaldi over the telephone, DeStefano replied, "I refuse! These are vicious people we're dealing with. The government! I would be talking on the phone while someone held a machinegun in his ear." DeStefano demanded that he had a constitutional right to face his accuser.

Crimaldi's uncle, Pat Stompanato took the stand as a character witness for DeStefano. Stompanato gave glowing accounts saying Sam DeStefano was an upright businessman and a "friend of the family." At one point Stompanato spilled a carafe of water on his suit. Thompson said, "Mr. DeStefano, your witness is all wet." DeStefano turned and was ready to object to Thompson until he saw that Stompanato's suit was wet. DeStefano paused and replied, "*Let the record show that it was a jug of water that the witness was all wet about.*"

Speice's lawyer, Frank Oliver had had enough of DeStefano. He requested that his client have a separate trial on grounds that he did not want to be part of that "circus" anymore and that Edward Speice had sat quiet throughout the trial and that DeStefano had created "*a noisy, tumultuous, disorderly trial*" and "*This trial has been a monument to disruption.*" When Oliver made the request, Sam jumped to his feet and told Oliver that he was "*egotistical paranoid.*" Oliver criticized Mad Sam for taking his shoes off in the courtroom to which Judge Austin commented at that point, "*As long as he doesn't take his pants off.*" DeStefano angered by Oliver's comment told the judge he has obeyed the orders of the judge and said, "*Tell me to stand on my ear and I'll stand on it if I can.*" Oliver then asked the judge for permission to leave the courtroom to take a pill. Judge Austin replied, "*Ok. And if you find a pill out there for me, bring it back, won't you please.*"

Eddie Speice took the stand and said he knew Chuck Crimaldi for some 25 years after first meeting him as kids in 1947. He added that he didn't really get to know him until the two were both inmates at the Illinois State Penitentiary in Pontiac around 1952.

Eddie Speice said he only knew Sam DeStefano since around 1970 and that DeStefano was going to finance a Toyota car dealership with him and the two were going to be partners.

His recollection about entering the elevator was that when he entered the elevator he saw Chuck Crimaldi standing in the corner trembling and vibrating. His face was red and his head was shaking up and down, that's when Sam DeStefano walked into the elevator.

Speice said that Mike Polesti turned to him and asked him, "*Have you done any fishing lately?*" because when Speice worked in the prison hospital as a surgical nurse he would talk to Polesti about how much they loved fishing.

Speice also added that he often heard Sam DeStefano say, "*My eyes must be dimming and my memory must be fading*" when he saw someone he didn't recognize or believed he should know.

The elevator stopped on the 18th floor and Agent Braseth grabbed Crimaldi's arm and escorted him out of the elevator. He said Crimaldi's face was flushed and red and it looked like he was going to throw up. They rode the elevator up to the 21st floor where Speice, DeStefano, and Michael Polesti got out. According to Speice, DeStefano turned to Speice and said, *"Did you see that nut in the elevator? It looks like he was going crazy. He either jumped a bond of mine or he must owe me money."* Speice replied, *"You are putting me on?"* DeStefano: *"What do you mean putting me on?"* Speice: *"You didn't recognize him?"* DeStefano: *"No, I didn't recognize him."* Speice: *"It was Chuckie."* DeStefano: *"Chuckie who?"* Speice: *"Chuckie Crimaldi."* It was Speice's testimony that DeStefano didn't even realize that the person in the elevator was Charles Crimaldi.

Speice then said that DeStefano suggested they go back to the 18th floor and speak to Crimaldi, which they did but could not find him.

A county clerk named Raul Martinez was called to testify and said that Sam DeStefano approached him the day of Esposito's trial and asked him to, *"See what you can do for the kid. He's a good kid."*

Other people called to the stand in DeStefano's trial were Sonny Esposito who claimed he never met DeStefano before his trial. Hoodlum Louis Tragas testified that as he sat outside Esposito's courtroom on that day he overheard one of the DEA agents telling Charles Crimaldi that the government was trying to frame DeStefano. Tragas testified that he put his ear to a door after seeing Charles Crimaldi being rushed into a room. He listened in on the conversation and said he heard Crimaldi say, *"Listen, Tony [Esposito] didn't give me that dope. I planted it there, I framed the guy."* Then one of the DEA agents told Crimaldi, *"Don't worry about it. We will still go through with the same deal."* Then Tragas said someone said, *"Well, what about Sam [DeStefano]?"* The agent replied, *"Don't worry about Sam, we will think of something to arrest him for later. We will put him away. Nobody can stop us when we get him down here; we know what to do with him."* He said he heard Crimaldi ask why was Sam in the building anyway and was told by an agent, *"Don't worry, we'll think of something to arrest him for."*

When DeStefano questioned Tragas he asked, "*Do you mind if I call you Louie?*" Tragas replied, "*Sure, if I can call you Sam.*" DeStefano answered, "*Call me counselor, I am an officer of the court. Out in the lobby you can call me Sam.*" A month after the trial Tragas was indicted by a federal grand jury for alleged perjury in the DeStefano trial.

Charles Krulik, an ex-convict specializing in burglaries, testified that he was familiar with gangland jargon and that he had never heard the expression, "*done any fishing lately*" in the underground. Attorney Frank Oliver asked Krulik, "*In the world of criminals and rascality how would you refer to a gun?*" "*A rod or a heater,*" answered Krulik. Oliver, "*And in your milieu, how would you say murder?*" Krulik answered, "*It depends on what degree.*" Oliver, "*What about the phrase, 'done any fishing lately?'*" Krulik answered, "*It means with a rod and reel.*" Oliver, "*So in your whole disreputable career as a burglar, you never heard that phrase, 'done any fishing?'*" "*Only in harming a fish,*" replied Krulik.

Charles Martin Krulik, born on September 4, 1927, was burglarizing homes at the age of 16. His first arrest was at the age of 17 in 1944 for burglary. In 1954, he was the victim of a robbery when he was working at a United Parcel garage in Maine Township. Three gunmen wearing masks tied Krulik and burned open the safe containing $5,000. It was suspected that Krulik had a hand in the robbery but it was never proven. Throughout his criminal career, he served time in prisons in Florida and Joliet Prison in Illinois. Eight months later, after he testified in the DeStefano trial, on November 24, 1972, two men were walking alongside Algonquin Road near the Tri-State Tollway in Maine Township when they discovered a murdered body buried in a shallow grave. Days after the body was found, an anonymous telephone call was received by the police telling them to check dental records of Charles Krulik and match then to the body. They were positive; the murdered body was Charles Krulik.

One thing that angered Sam during the course of his trial was the continuous references to the fact that everyone kept saying they were afraid of Sam DeStefano. In an effort to prove that false, Sam DeStefano called Shirley Esposito to the stand as a character witness.

Shirley Esposito was the wife of Anthony "Sonny" Esposito Jr. and was involved in the union offices of Local 1001 in Chicago.

He asked her, *"Shirley, have you any reason to be frightened of me?"* *"No"* she answered.

DeStefano: *"Have you known, to the best of your knowledge, of any Esposito, including your husband's uncle Frank Esposito, his father Anthony, to his grandmother, to his grandfather and all of his relations of being frightened of me?"* *"No"* Shirley said once again. With that statement DeStefano rested his case.

DeStefano's Closing Argument

When it was time for Sam to give his closing arguments, he spent his allowed 45-minutes talking about the mistakes that the DEA agents made in his and Esposito's case. When it came down to how the jurors should vote, he said the following:

"When a man is unjustly accused of a crime, this is what you call just anger. When he knows he is being framed, how does a man act? What is he to do when he knows the power of the government, and he's a lonely person fighting with the co-defendant that has no power? How am I supposed to act? Why, just the thought of it angers me right now, and I believe you can see it in my eyes. Yes, I am angry. I have been angry for days, and I have been working day and night to attempt to prove they are framing me.

I want to apologize for my behavior, but anything I did in here, I had permission of the good Judge Austin. For example, let's take my booties. I wear them because of my arteriosclerosis. If I wear shoes too long, I am in terrific pain. I am under terrific medication.

I have attempted to introduce as evidence my medical history. I am the only man in the history of this government, in this country or the world that had gone under two severe arteriosclerosis operations with the false aorta and artery below the groin.

I want to apologize to you people. I am not an attorney. I don't know the procedures here. I have been a student of cases that I read in the papers, such as where they frame people such as the Father Berrigan

257

trial where the government witness demands $50,000 tax-free and all expenses. That is your money and my money. It is those good people's money out there. And the Narcotics, Dangerous Drugs Division is known as the biggest agency of framers in the history of the world.

As I told you, or if I haven't, I only have an 8th grade grammar school education, otherwise my education comes from the ordinary day-to-day of life until I'm 63 years of age. As a boy, I was interested in law. Unfortunately my parents were immigrants and I couldn't go to school and I had to hustle newspapers and shine shoes.

Do I frighten any of you jurors when I scream and holler? I don't mean to, but I am an innocent man fighting for my life. And I repeat, if you believe that Sam DeStefano had the ignorance to do such a thing in such an elevator, then you have only one verdict to bring in, a verdict of not guilty or reason of temporary insanity. Your verdict has to be not guilty or that. Thank you."

After the 5-day trial, Sam DeStefano was found guilty and sentenced to almost 4 years in prison and a $5,000 fine. Edward Speice was also found guilty and sentenced to 2 years in prison. DeStefano was released on a $25,000 appeal bond and Speice was released on a $10,000 appeal bond. When DeStefano's wife, Anita, put up the bond, Sam was reminded to *"be sure to pay her fee."*

DeStefano did get an attorney to handle his appeal. Attorney Julius Echeles filed a motion of acquittal arguing that the judge did not allow DeStefano to subpoena Charles Crimaldi.

After the trial, DeStefano admitted his behavior was "bizarre" and said, *"I happen to be a fellow who possibly has a big mouth and don't know when to keep quiet, but I know in my heart of hearts that I did not commit this so-called crime."*

The reporters fired questions at Sam:
Q) Why do they say you're involved in juice?
A) *I've never been in the juice racket. I've never been in business illegitimately.*
Q) Are you still in pretty good with the boys?
A) *I have no boys.*
Q) The mob Sam.

A) *The only mob I have is Anita, my wife, John, Sandra, and Janice, my children. My kids are all school teachers.*
Q) What about your trial Sam?
A) *I've been framed.*
Q) What would you like to do?
A) *I plan to devote the rest of my life to teaching youngsters the law at my home. I know as much law or more law than any lawyers or judges.*

Days after being convicted, Sam walked into the Illinois Revenue Department offices to pay $1,038 on the tax from his new 1972 Rolls-Royce Sedan that he purchased for his wife in Zionsville, Indiana. The car cost $27,450, which it was believed DeStefano paid for in crisp $1,000 bills.

More trouble came in the form of a Grand Jury charge in July 1972. The Grand Jury filed charges against Sam DeStefano for knowingly receiving a Dakin Double-Barreled shotgun and a Smith and Wesson 22. Caliber revolver on June 26, 1971, the day after he was released from prison. Since DeStefano was a convicted felon, he was not permitted to have any firearms in his possession. He was charged with illegal possession of firearms. On September 15, DeStefano plead not guilty when arraigned before Federal District Judge William Bauer.

On March 29, 1973, a federal grand jury indicted DeStefano on a perjury charge for lying in court. DeStefano had said that the guns belonged to his wife and family when he was caught with them. The government said that it was a lie because DeStefano filled out the gun ownership applications forms and then forged his wife's signature.

Chapter Twenty-Four

The Ghost of Leo Foreman

A month later, a joint investigation between the FBI and the Cook County State's Attorney's office re-opened the murders of William "Action" Jackson and Leo Foreman. The reason was that Charles Crimaldi told authorities that he was present at both murders and was given immunity to testify. After the grand jury held hearings, Sam DeStefano, Mario DeStefano, and Anthony "The Ant" Spilotro were targeted as the killers and a list was published of who was to be called to testify. They were attorney Robert McDonnell, ex-Chicago policeman Kenny Anderson, Peter Cappelletti and former Judge Cecil Corbet Smith.

On August 31, 1972, Sam DeStefano was arrested outside the Cook County Courts Building when he was arriving to turn himself in on the indictment of murder. Mario DeStefano turned himself in to police later that night while the FBI and Nevada authorities arrested Anthony Spilotro in Las Vegas. However, Spilotro was freed on a $10,000 bond, which left Illinois authorities shaking their heads in disbelief with Illinois State's Attorney Edward V. Hanrahan saying "incredible."

Both DeStefano brothers spent the night in Cook County jail and were brought in front of the judge. As the brothers entered the courtroom, Sam's wife, Anita, began to cry as Sam blew a kiss to her. Mario's wife, Mary, and his two daughters, Rosalie and Carmine, sobbed as he embraced them with a hug. Sam turned to his sister-in-law and told her, *"I'll have your husband on the street faster that you can blink your eye."*

Sam went in front of Judge Saul Epton and told him that he and his brother need to be allowed to be released on bond because both had heart ailments and wouldn't receive proper treatment in County jail. Sam made an argument that they should be released since Anthony Spilotro had been released on bond in Las Vegas and a Communist at the time named Angela Davis had been charged with murder and was released on bond. What Sam didn't know was that the Illinois State's Attorney's Office had contacted Las Vegas and had Spilotro arrested again on a charge of being a fugitive of justice and was being held in the Clark County Jail.

Sam told the judge, "*Excuse me sir, I'm prepared to argue the motion now. This is a case that goes back nine years, that has no substance to it. This is a nine-year-old case built up out of straw by Mr. Charles Siragusa.*" The judge stopped DeStefano by saying, "*You have been living with this case for nine years, I have had it for nine minutes.*"

The case was continued and the DeStefano boys were lead out of the courtroom back to jail. On the way out, Sam turned to the news reporters and asked, "*Did you boys get a good story? I'll give you plenty of action.*"

While Mario sat in Cook County Jail, he wrote the following letter to Judge Saul Epton:

"*Your Honor, you no doubt have read the newspapers over the weekend, the same as I and millions of other citizens. After reading these vicious attacks by the news media, one can only feel that this was a vicious conspiracy to prejudice our chances of having a bond set in this case. In one particular article published in the Chicago Sun-Times of Sunday, September 3, 1972, the States star witness was supposedly attacked by a gunman who emptied his gun at the witness as he was entering his home one evening. I cannot believe that this ever happened Your Honor, and if Your Honor will please take the time to check this out with the Police District in which this supposed act had occurred, Your Honor will find that no such thing had ever taken place and that no report of this supposed attack was ever filed with the Chicago Police Department. Your Honor knows, I know and the citizen on the street knows that if such an attack ever happened to anyone of us or if any one of us had seen such an attack take place against another citizen it would be our just duty to call the police and report such an attack. We also know that it would be the just duty of the attending police officer of that particular police district to make a written report of that supposed attack. If Your Honor will please take the time to check these particulars out, your Honor will find that no such written report exists in the books of the Chicago Police Department because no such supposed attack ever occurred. All this adverse publicity was published over the weekend for the sole purpose of hurting our chances of having a bond set.*

I am an ex-convict your honor and I have been out of prison over twenty-two years. I have been in no trouble in all of those twenty-two years, other than a fine for supposedly illegal voting and that shouldn't have been because being born here in the State of Illinois, I took it for granted that I was a citizen of these United States. After my marriage, my wife and I registered and voted in the district in which we lived, just like any other ordinary citizens would do at election times. However in 1964, fourteen years after my release from prison, I was indicted by Mr. Charles Siragusa of the Illinois Crime Commission for illegal voting because I had failed to have my citizenship restored to me when I was released from prison, something no one; either at the prison when I was released, nor at the Chicago Parole Office when I reported to them. So therefore, I was indicted and fined on a supposedly vote fraud charge. That is the extent of any trouble I have actually been charged with in the twenty-two years I have been home from prison.

I have been married for over twenty-one years and have a wonderful and devoted wife who is a cancer victim and who needs me terribly much at home, for I am her sole support. We have three beautiful and wonderful children. Our oldest is majoring in Psychology and is entering her third year at the University of Illinois at Urbana. Our son, who is just eighteen years of age and who has just graduated high school this past June, will be entering his first year in college. Our little girl, who is fourteen years of age, will be entering her first year in high school. I am their sole means of support.

When I was released from prison, I went into the restaurant business. I was a success in that business and was at one location for over nineteen years. However, due to spending many, many hours in my restaurant; (I did all of my own cooking and many other chores pertaining to the business), I began having heart attacks. I have had two heart attacks, my first in 1964, and my second in 1967. I am also a victim of arteriosclerosis and have been taking a drug called "Questron" which was introduced to the medical world by Doctor William Weaver of Atlanta, Georgia. When this drug was first brought to the attention of the Surgeon General at Washington, the United States Government sponsored a program conducted by Doctor Weaver, and I was one of the few who became a guinea pig in those experiments. I am still taking "Questron," for it has helped me greatly, but I have not had any since I have been here. The restaurant business required many, many hours of attention and because of that fact and also my condition, my wife and I decided to sell our restaurant and property and enter into a new and less trying business. So in August of 1970, we went into manufacturing Burial Vaults. Our plant is located at 10205 West Pacific Avenue in Franklin Park, Illinois. I am the sole operator of this plant. Although I have three employees, I still do just about everything there is to do there, except for the mixing and pouring of the cement. I am plant manager, I do all of my own book keeping, send out the monthly invoices, make up the payroll, drive a big truck in which I deliver the burial vaults to the various cemeteries throughout the city and suburbs, and I even go out to sell. I am needed there greatly, for at present my wife and son are there trying to do the best they know how, but soon my son will and must go to school; then what shall my family do for support?

Your Honor, I am one of many businessmen who are members of Chance, Inc., an organization founded by the Inmates of Joliet Penitentiary who are dedicated to helping inmates find jobs and stay out of trouble when they are released from prison.

My wife and I own Metropolitan Vault, Inc., and we also own our home. Also Your Honor, you must take into consideration that after learning of my indictment, I called my home and spoke to the Officers who were there with the arrest warrant and told them that I would give myself up within two hours. I kept my promise for within two hours after I spoke to them, I met my attorney in front of the Criminal Courts Building and we both walked into the State's Attorney Office where I turned myself in. These are true facts, Your Honor, and I pray that justice will prevail and that I can be released on bond, Thank you, Your Honor.

Sincerely,
Mario DeStefano
Cook County Jail

At the hearing on September 6, DeStefano told the court that it was impossible for him to kill Leo Foreman because he was recovering from an operation on his bowel and it would have been imposable for him to kick, punch, stab or shoot Leo Foreman in that condition. DeStefano acting as his own attorney once again called his wife, Anita, to the stand for questioning. Anita testified that Sam had his operation at West Suburban Hospital on October 27, 1963, and returned to that hospital for two more operations two months later. Anita described her husband as *"on the doorstep of death."* Sam then called his bodyguard, Joe Valicento, to the stand asking the same questions. Valicento testified that he had to carry Sam *"from chair to chair because he couldn't walk"* in November 1963. Sam added that on the night of November 18 when Foreman's body was found, the police came to his house and questioned him about the murder. Sam showed the police his scars and stitches from his surgery.

He then called the surgeon that operated on him in 1963, Dr. Joseph Moles, to the stand to testify. Doctor Moles testified that it was "possible" that DeStefano could have been able to leave his home that night when questioned by the assistant state's attorney Robert Novelle. When DeStefano questioned the doctor he added that it was "not probable" that DeStefano would have left his home, *"It would not have been in his medical interest,"* added the doctor.

After winning a change of judges, the DeStefano brothers won a chance to convince the new judge, Robert Collins that the two should be allowed to be released on bail. During the September 20 hearing, Judge Collins ordered that Charles Crimaldi had to appear in person to testify in this case.

Two days later Judge Collins denied bail for Sam and his brother on grounds that the defense did not refute presumption of guilt. However, Judge Collins did grant bond to Tony Spilotro, allowing him a $50,000 bail for his release.

Angered by the ruling that Spilotro was allowed to be released on bond and the DeStefano brothers were not, DeStefano filed a complaint with the Illinois Appellate Court. After a hearing, the Appellate Court ruled that the two should each be freed on a $100,000 bond. The $20,000 was posted and Sam and Mario were allowed to go home to prepare for their upcoming trial.

The FBI discovered that on September 14, 1972, the DeStefano brothers and Spilotro went to the Outfit for help in their case and were turned down. The informant said that the DeStefano's had been "dumped" by the Outfit and it appeared the DeStefano's had more trouble with the Outfit than they did with the murder charge against them. One source said that Tony Accardo was personally fed up with the DeStefano's and Spilotro who he described as "mad killers." The situation got worse in October 1972 when Paul DeLucia, "Paul 'The Waiter' Ricca," died. Another informant described the situation as, *"The DeStefano brothers no longer have a buffer between them and the Outfit. The Outfit became disenchanted with Sam and Mario either because of their methods or because the DeStefano's were infringing upon others in their illegal activities."* The report ended with the informant saying that the DeStefano brothers felt that their lives on the street were in jeopardy because of DeLucia's death.

Many months later, the Illinois State Court of Appeals upheld the conviction of Sam DeStefano for threatening Charles Crimaldi in the federal elevator in 1972. That same court ruled that Edward Speice was to be given a new trial because of DeStefano and his actions during the trial.

Chapter Twenty-Five

Bye Bye Sam

Enough was enough; Sam had to go, FOR GOOD! With the death of top mobster Paul DeLucia in October 1972, Sam's days of being protected were over. Throughout the 1960's many requests were made by mob boss Sam Giancana to get rid of DeStefano, but all requests were denied by DeLucia. With DeLucia gone, there was no one left to save Sam.

In April 1973, the order was given that Sam DeStefano was to be eliminated once and for all. He had three open court cases against him, the Leo Foreman murder indictment, the possession of guns and perjury charges from that case, and the pending appeal of his conviction for threatening a government witness.

According to investigators and underworld informants, the details of Sam's last days alive were compiled. One report stated that on April 14, Sam DeStefano received word that the hiding place of Charles Crimaldi was found

Sam DeStefano's house at 1656 Sayre, Chicago Illinois (Author's Collection)

and they had an opportunity to kill him before he could testify against Sam in the Leo Forman murder trial. With that news, Sam told his crew that they would go and kill Crimaldi. Therefore, investigators believed DeStefano might have been waiting to be picked up by his goons to go and hit Crimaldi.

The details of the day, given by his wife, Anita, was that Sam woke up on April 14, and was told by Anita that she was going to see her sick mother that morning. Sam was fine with that and told her to leave the garage door open because he wanted to clean the garage. When Anita and DeStefano's bodyguard, Joseph Valicento, left the house at 9:40 a.m., Sam was dressed in all black clothes, which he called his work clothes, walked into his garage, and began to sweep it out. At around 10:30 a.m. two neighbors heard two shot's coming from DeStefano's house One said he thought it was a car backfiring and didn't make anything of it.

Around 11:15 a.m., two Chicago police investigators, named Thomas Spanos and James Turney, went to DeStefano's house to discuss a burglary of DeStefano's house that Sam had reported to the police on April 5. The report stated that DeStefano said the burglars had keys to his house, knew exactly where the secret shut-off for the alarm system was, and shut it off. He told police that he somehow frightened them away as they fled out the back door and into a black car parked in the alley behind his house. As the detectives drove up to Sam's house, they noticed three excited men standing in his driveway. One of the men who was known as a DeStefano associate screamed to the police car that, *"Sam's been killed."* As the police entered the garage, they discovered the lifeless body of Sam DeStefano on the garage floor. DeStefano had been shot once in the chest and once in the arm by a shotgun. The first blast from the shotgun was so powerful that it blew DeStefano's left arm right off his body throwing it to the back of the garage. DeStefano's body was lying on his back right next to the stairs leading into the house with his legs spread-eagled toward the street. The arm was severed right above the elbow and two shotgun shells were found on the floor of the garage. The broom was placed against the wall and his black-rimmed glasses were lying in the center of the garage, knocked off his face from the blast.

Around noon, Anita arrived back home and was terrified to see all

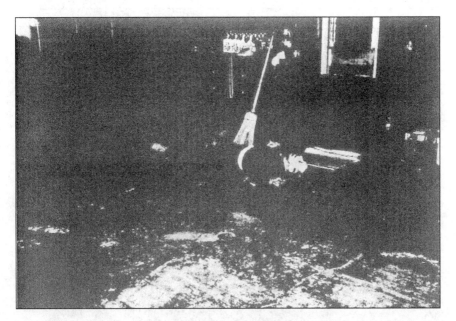

Side shots of Sam Destefano's body
(Chicago PD photo)

Sam lying dead on his garage floor (Chicago PD photo)

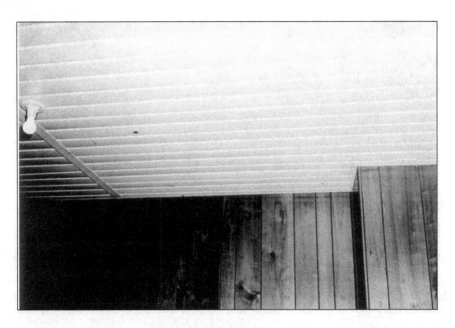

Blood spots on the celing and splatter on the walls in Sam's garage
(Chicago PD photo)

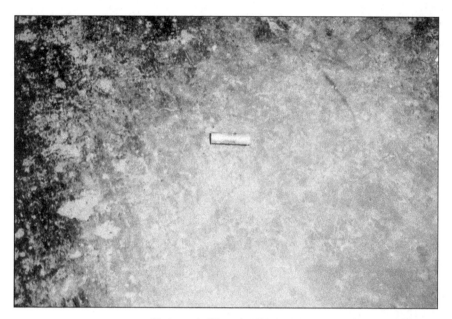

Shotgun shell found at the scene
(Chicago PD photo)

Another shotgun shell

the police and the 150 spectators that had gathered around the block to get a peek. Accompanied by a bodyguard, she was rushed into the house screaming, *"Where's my husband?"* Sometime later, Anita appeared outside once again, screaming to reporters and the police, *"You people killed him! Take every picture, make sure you don't miss a goddam thing!"* The neighbors said they noticed a gold-colored car with its hood up parked near DeStefano's house, which police believed were the killers watching the house. After the two shots, another neighbor noticed a white car speeding down the wrong way on Sayre Avenue away from DeStefano's house.

As information in the investigation leaked out, many angles of the murder and a list of suspects was put together. Among the first things investigated were:

1. The murder was in retaliation for the murder of Louis Fazio on September 27, 1972. Fazio, a Milwaukee, Wisconsin restaurant owner and close friend of DeStefano's, was going to give crucial testimony linking the murder of William "Action" Jackson to Sam DeStefano.
2. Police picked up Mario DeStefano and interrogated him, asking if he set up the hit on his brother. Police learned that a riff had developed between Sam and Mario concerning the up and coming Foreman trial. Mario was scared of what crazy antics his brother would pull and did not want to go down with the ship. He successfully won a ruling allowing a separate trial with Sam's being held first, Anthony Spilotro, and Mario's second. Mario denied any connection to his brother's killing.
3. The police wanted to speak with Tony Spilotro's brother, Victor Spilotro, to get an alibi. Tony Spilotro was at his boutique in Las Vegas the night of the killing.
4. Days after the murder, police noticed Sam Giancana's courier and chauffeur, Richard Cain, in town at many of the mob's hangouts. A theory was hatched that Cain may have had a hand in the murder. Mob boss Sam Giancana was hiding out in Mexico from the U.S. government and may have sent Cain to Chicago with

word that Sam DeStefano was to go and the contract was valid. Other information was told by an informant that an ultimatum was given to mob bosses by DeStefano to have Charles Crimaldi killed. If they did not kill him, DeStefano was going to "*blow his whistle*" on the mob. That angered mob bosses who agreed to the contract from Giancana. More evidence linking Cain to the involvement came 8 months later on December 20, 1973 when Richard Cain arrived at Rose's Restaurant at 1117 West Grand Avenue to meet with four unknown people. After a 10-minute meeting, two syndicate gunmen entered the restaurant making it look like a robbery was about to be staged. The unknown men that Cain was meeting with walked out of the restaurant. Cain, a waiter, some other patrons and the owner, Sam Cozzo, were lined up against the wall. The gunmen walked over to Cain and with two shots from a shotgun blew his face off. The gunmen walked out of the shop and made their get-away. One of the versions attached to the invitation was that the Cain killing was in retaliation for killing Sam DeStefano.

5.   Detectives believed that the attempted robbery of DeStefano's house on April 5 was a test run to set up his murder. The killers may have been planning the best way to kill DeStefano and may have attempted it that night. They believed DeStefano was holding back on the events that had occurred and believed that the three robbers tried and failed to kill DeStefano that night. Some items were stolen from his house. DeStefano said he and his wife had been out shopping for 45 minutes when the burglars entered his house. According to DeStefano, they turned off the security system, took one fur coat, some jewelry, and DeStefano's registered .38 caliber handgun, and went right to his secret hiding spot where he kept all his books containing his "juice" collections and customers' names and all his tape-recorded phone calls that he would use to blackmail people if he had to. Police did not believe DeStefano that anything other than his tape recordings and books had been stolen. Days later, an informant told the detectives that mob bosses ordered the robbery of DeStefano's books and tape

recordings so when he was killed the police would not discover them during the search of his house.

6. Seven days after the murder, more than one informant told the police that DeStefano was waiting to be picked up by his killers to go and kill Chuckie Crimaldi. The killers told DeStefano they found Crimaldi and it was possible to get to him. It was true that Crimaldi was in a position to be hit since he was out of jail and had only two police bodyguards assigned to him but the killers never found Crimaldi and used the false information to draw DeStefano out of his house alone. The killers pulled up into DeStefano's driveway and got out with the shotgun. DeStefano knew and trusted them so he did not believe he was in danger. They fired two rounds into DeStefano as he went to close the garage door. The reason a shotgun was used is because Sam hated shotguns. They terrified him and the thought of being torn apart by the buckshot pellets scared the hell out of him. So a shotgun was used as an extra "Fuck You" to Sam.

Right before the wake, an autopsy was performed on Sam DeStefano and it revealed that he had been suffering from acute malnutrition.

The wake was held at Galewood Funeral Chapel. The next day his body was driven to Queen of Heaven Cemetery in Hillside, Illinois, with a small ten-car procession and private services were held before his entombment. As police detectives gathered to write down license plate numbers, they noticed not one mobster attended the services.

(Author's Collection)

(Author's Collection)

A month later, an informant told the FBI the following concerning the DeStefano murder:

"Chicago source now advises that Anthony Spilotro felt very strongly that his indictment with Sam DeStefano and subsequent trial with him would 'pull him down.' In view of what he felt was severe liability this regard, Spilotro reportedly made contact with Anthony Accardo, elder statesman of organized crime, and obtained authorization to hit DeStefano. Source unable to advise whether Spilotro actually participated in DeStefano's killing."

The murder of Sam DeStefano was the 1,012th gangland killing in Chicago since 1919.

In the end

A month after Sam's murder, the Leo Foreman murder trial went on as scheduled. Mario DeStefano and Tony Spilotro hired attorneys Harry Busch and Frank Whalen to defend them. During the trial, Charles Crimaldi once again testified about the murder.

At one point, the trial was stopped by a rumor that one of the jury members had received either a threatening telephone call or a cash bribe to vote not guilty. When the judge questioned the jurors, no one admitted to being contacted and the trial continued.

Chicago Police Crime Laboratory technicians testified that the paint chips found on Foreman's body were similar to paint found in Mario's basement. When Mario took the stand, he testified that the paint chips could not have come from his old home because his basement had not been painted until 1967, four years after Foreman's death. DeStefano's attorney Harry Busch even called the contractor, Ciro Paoletti, to the stand to testify that he refinished the floor of Mario's basement in 1966, six years before the police found their evidence. Paoletti described the bomb shelter as, *"The entrance to the bomb shelter was small, bump your head. I'm five foot four and I have to duck my head. We made it so you don't bump your head. It was a damp place. It had a bad pitch, I had to put concrete around to give the floor proper pitch. The floor was rust color from seepage, it was not painted, it had never been painted. There was asphalt tile before; I could see the glue from the tile. You'd be nuts to paint it, it was too damp."*

Spilotro's brother, John, was called to the stand and testified that he and Tony were buying furniture at the time of the murder.

After eight weeks, the murder trial went to the jury. State's Attorney Daniel Wolff's closing argument said that Leo Foreman's mutilated body was meant as an example to others who might become informants or for revenge on juice loan debts, *"It was a case that he had the money and wasn't paying it back."*

During the closing argument, Mario's wife, Mary DeStefano, ran out of the courtroom-crying saying, *"I can't listen to these lies anymore."*

After nine hours of deliberation, the jury of seven women and five men found Mario DeStefano guilty of murder. However, they found Tony Spilotro not guilty, causing him to nod at the jury and mouth a "thank you" to them. John Spilotro made a statement to the press saying, *"We knew there was a liar on the stand,"* referring to Charles Crimaldi.

Mario was taken from the courtroom and sent back to prison, awaiting sentencing. The prosecutor asked for a sentence of 70 to 110 years in prison. On August 23, 1973, Mario was given 20 to 40 years in prison.

Three months later, Circuit Judge Robert Meler ruled that new evidence in the Foreman murder case was presented and Mario DeStefano was allowed to be released from prison on a $100,000 appeal bond. The new evidence was that on October 22, 1963, almost one month before Leo Foreman was killed, Foreman was arrested by the Chicago police at the Kensington District police station for posing as a bail bondsman. After the arrest, Foreman was taken to a secure area and beaten by the police officers. After the beating, Foreman went to the office of Judge George Keighton, who was then a private lawyer, and said he wanted to file a lawsuit against the Chicago Police. The "new" evidence was that the police officers that he had threatened to file a lawsuit against might have murdered Leo Foreman.

Mario's freedom did not last long; he was released and brought back to prison all in a twenty-four hour period. The Chicago newspapers had a field day wondering how a twice-convicted murder could be released from prison.

His freedom finally came on Christmas Eve 1973 when Mario DeStefano was released from prison once again on an appeal bond. As he walked to his car, he was greeted by his happy relatives, turned to the media, and screamed, "Merry Christmas" before entering his car and driving off. State's attorney Bernard Carey's statement was a little different saying Mario's release was, *a travesty of justice.* The Illinois Supreme Court ruled on Mario's release in January 1974, agreeing that the twice-convicted murderer could stay out on his $100,000 bond while he sought a new trial.

Even Charles Crimaldi had something to say about DeStefano's release from prison, *"It looks like Chicago has a long way to go before it cleans its own house. So here's the joke, I gotta hide and DeStefano is free to look for me."*

While he was out on bond, Mario DeStefano's name appeared in the murder investigation of mob boss Sam Giancana in the summer of 1975. The state's attorney's office received word that Mario DeStefano was working as Giancana's part-time bodyguard and wanted to question him about the murder. They found him in the hospital where he had been since June 15. He was listed in critical condition at Rush-Presbyterian-St. Luke's Medical Center after surviving several multiple heart attacks four days before the Giancana murder. Mario was even subpoenaed to appear before a grand jury on the Giancana murder. But it was later determined that Mario could not have been working for Giancana because of his illness and the fact that mob bosses didn't want anyone working with any member of the DeStefano family.

After his brother Sam was killed and he was released from prison, Mario was ordered to stay out of syndicate business, according to FBI documents. He stayed in touch only with mobster Joey Aiuppa. The FBI in Chicago had opened a case against Mario DeStefano in July 1972 entitled "Mario Anthony DeStefano, case number 92-2029." The file contained the information that, as of 1972, Mario DeStefano was in touch with and seen meeting with mobsters Jack Cerone, Tony Accardo, Joey Aiuppa, Paul DeLucia, Vincent Inserro, Leo Manfredi, Charles Nicoletti, Tony Spilotro, and James "Turk" Torello.

In July 1975, the Illinois Appellate Court overturned the 1973 murder conviction and ordered a new trial. It was not to be because Mario entered the hospital once again on August 8 and died on August 12, 1975, from carcinogenic shock from ischemic cardiomyopathy.

(Author's Collection)

His wake was held at Granata & Massey Funeral Chapel at 1857 N. Harlem Avenue in Chicago and he was buried in the mausoleum at Queen of Heaven Cemetery in Hillside, Illinois.

With Sam gone, his wife, Anita, died in 1987 and is buried next to her husband. His son, John, moved to Denver, Colorado, where he graduated from Regis Catholic College in June 1967. He obtained a job as a teacher in a junior high school and was attending classes to obtain his masters degree in the late 1960's. He married and had two sons. Both of Sam's daughters, Sandra and Janice, went into teaching in the late 1960's.

Mario DeStefano's wife, Mary, also died in 1975, and his son, Sam

DeStefano, who he named after his big brother and father, followed in his family's footsteps.

In 2001, Mario's son Sam "Little Sam" DeStefano was reported to be an alleged member of an outfit-sponsored jewelry theft ring that was allegedly run by William Hanhardt, one-time Chicago Police Department chief of detectives. DeStefano specialized in multimillion-dollar jewelry robberies while running the Rush Street Jazz Club and the Back Room Club with Annie Spilotro, the wife of Michael Spilotro. He did tell a judge one time that he left organized crime in 1994 to open a construction company. The young Sam DeStefano married his girlfriend, Karen, a one-time cocktail server at the old mob hangout, Gianotti's Restaurant on Cumberland Avenue. However, the love affair ended when Sam met a younger woman and the two divorced. Sam then went on to marry the other woman, Cynthia.

In October 2000, Hanhardt was charged with leading a crew of jewelry thieves with connections to the Chicago mob. Members named as being connected to this crew were Joseph Basinski, listed as the right-hand man to Hanhardt; Guy Altobello; Paul "The Indian" Schiro, known as an alleged mob enforcer who was later charged in the "Family Secrets" indictment; James D'Antonio, and Sam DeStefano were mentioned as allegedly taking part in helping out with the surveillance of their scores and assisting in the robberies.

When the criminal court case against Hanhardt began in October 2001, one of its key witnesses spilling the goods was Karen DeStefano, the ex-wife. Allegedly, the reason was Karen DeStefano demanded that Sam give her half of her share of goods in the divorce. She especially wanted some jewelry that had been given to her by Sam that was from the robbery of a Hyatt Hotel. Sam said no. The first mistake was that Sam put a safe deposit box in Karen's name and put some stolen jewelry, car and telephone bug information and his fictitious driver's license in it for safe keeping. The second mistake was Sam brought his new girl friend Cynthia to court flaunting her in front of Karen. Scorned, Karen decided to have a talk with the FBI and everything she told them turned out to be true. Sam DeStefano pled guilty and was ordered to help pay back $5 million in fine watches, jewelry, and gems taken in eight robberies nationwide. Sam DeStefano was sentenced to five years in prison and according to the Federal Bureau of Prisons, a Sam DeStefano born in 1955 was released in January 2007. William Hanhardt attempting suicide by an overdose of prescription pills. After he recovered, he pled guilty and was sentenced to 16 years in prison.

In a final tribute in 2003, the Chicago Tribune newspaper listed Sam "Mad Sam" DeStefano as one of the top six "most evil Chicagoans of all time." Among those listed with Sam were John Wayne Gacy, who killed 33 young men between 1972 and 1978; Richard Speck, who killed many nurses at his town home in 1966, and Henry Holmes, who confessed to 47 murders by strangulation.

Chapter Twenty-Six

DeStefano's Boys

Sam DeStefano relied on his crew of hoodlums to make his daily pickups and enforce his laws. In 1964, the FBI became very interested in who made the list as "DeStefano's men." A report dated 12-30-64 said:

"Information has been received indicating that perhaps the leading shylock in the Chicago area is Sam DeStefano. DeStefano lends a great deal of money to individuals who do not have a proper credit rating so that they can obtain money from legitimate financing sources. Usually the interest charged on loans made by DeStefano is 'six for five'. DeStefano has a battery of collectors, who, like DeStefano, are noted for inflicting physical violence to the persons of the delinquent debtors. Among these underlings of DeStefano are: Tony Spilotro, Sam Gallo, Mario DeStefano, Art Pascucci, Peter Paul Cappelletti, Alfred "Al" Zaccagnini, Vito Zaccagnini, Charles Crimaldi, and the Bastone Brothers."

Charles J. Crimaldi

"I'll throw acid in your face, your mother's face, if you don't pay us. Now, if we come looking for you, you're in trouble because every hour we spend looking for you, we could be meeting somebody who wants more money. It's costing us money to find you."

Those were the words of Charles "Chuckie" Crimaldi in the 1970's after he turned government informant and sent some of his life-long friends and associates to prison.

Born Charles John Crimaldi in Chicago, he got his start pulling off hijackings, burglaries, armed robberies, and bank robberies. For a legitimate job, he made his way as a part-time journeyman plumber and bartender. Known as Chuckie Crimaldi to his associates, he was born to John "Cuono" and Louise Crimaldi in 1932. His family consisted of his brothers Guy Crimaldi, born around 1928, and Anthony "Tony" Crimaldi, born around 1930, and two sisters named

Madeline and Theresa. His father John "Cuono" Crimaldi was a laborer listed as being on a paving crew and a cement fisher. John lived with his wife, children, his brother, Antonio, and his family at 4514 Congress Street in Chicago. According to records, Antonio came to America from Italy in 1910, with his brother following in 1920. When John Crimaldi died in 1935 at the age of 31, it was up to Chuckie's older brother Guy to help straighten out an out-of-control Chuckie. At a very young age during World War II, Chuckie and his brother, Tony would steal butter and other items in short supply because of the war effort and sell them on the streets.

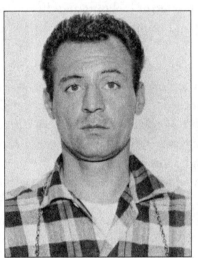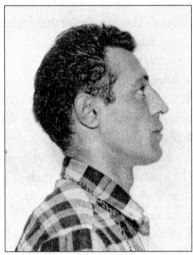

A young Charles Crimaldi attended St. Mathews Parochial School from January thru June 1947 and Tuley High School from October 1947 thru June 1948. His attendance was listed as poor and was mentality listed as average. He was transferred to Montefiore School in 1948.

He was well known in the Juvenile Court system in Illinois being in the Intake Department on eight occasions between 1945 and August 1950 with many dismissals. Among of the incidents mentioned showing the crimes which Crimaldi was involved in which was on November 29, 1949, when Chuckie was taken to Juvenile Court for being with two boys who took 12 cents from a fellow classmate named William

Lang. The Assistant Principal of the Sabin Branch of Tuley High School complained that Crimaldi and his two classmates were responsible for strong-arming other children at the school for money. Crimaldi denied taking part in the beating but did admit that he had been in the vicinity when a boy named Ron Chesney beat up William Lang. Crimaldi was placed under special supervision.

Seven months earlier in March 1949 Chuckie was arrested with Fred Weidman, Ronald Chesney, George Fine, James DeVenturi, Daniel Zegan and William Gnatek. All were charged with burglary. Chuckie and Fred Weidman entered the home of Gnatek's grandmother while the other boys, including Gnatek himself, acted as lookouts and they robbed the house. The gang took war bonds, old coins, a ring, two watches, and $100 in cash.

Another incident around the same time was when Crimaldi, Weidman and DeVenturi tried to break into the home of Joe Searson at 908 N. California Avenue but found out that the family was still at home causing them to abort the robbery. Crimaldi had robbed the house once before with his brother, Tony, and a Robert Kamien. In that robbery, Crimaldi took a revolver, a watch, a ring, and $1.33 in cash.

The rest of his juvenile record listed an arrest in February 1945 for the burglary of Crimaldi's aunt's house, an arrest on June 1, 1945 with his brother Tony when the two broke into the house of John Nowaj and took two guns and a hunting knife. On December 23, 1948, Crimaldi appeared in court as an accessory to a burglary with Edward Stern. Crimaldi told the court that he had been staying away from his home and was difficult to supervise due to non-cooperation of his mother. Chuckie was sent to the Illinois Training School for boys and on March 15, 1949, he was committed to the Chicago Parental School.

According to Crimaldi, he was taught how to rob taverns the right way by two hoodlums who he called John Stoloski and Anthony Stamps. It's not known if this was their real names. Together the three robbed many taverns until the gang broke up months later. Crimaldi would learn what it took to be a successful hoodlum in Chicago.

When Crimaldi would talk, it was not known which version of a story you would get. When you spoke to people who knew him and you saw the information given to law enforcement agencies from Crimaldi, the story often changed. One example involved his personal life. According to a Government investigation into the life of Charles Crimaldi in 1950, he told the investigators that he, then eighteen-years-old, married his 17-year-old girl friend, Rose Mary Coletti, on August 12, 1950. The two were reportedly expecting their first baby at the time. However, when Crimaldi wrote his biography *"Crimaldi, Contract Killer,"* he said Mary was just a girl friend and his first wife was named Roxanne. After he divorced Roxanne in 1961, he would later marry his second wife Janine and go on to have four children.

Back in 1950, Chuckie told the police that he lived with his wife Rose Mary at her parent's apartment at 2724 W. Chicago Avenue, which was the back room of a commercial store. Between February and September 1950, Chuckie Crimaldi was listed as working as an assembler at the United Manufacturing Company located at 3401 N. California Avenue. He was terminated because of too much absenteeism. His wife worked at the old Woolworth's Store as a clerk for $0.80 an hour.

Once Crimaldi was done with the Juvenile Court system and his police record was wiped out, he continued his criminal ways. In September 1950, he was arrested with William Lengyel and Joseph Trychta when the three took a jacket, a pair of slacks, a pair of shoes, and a shirt valued at $29. On October 9, 1950, Crimaldi and Louis Stamas were arrested for breaking into the house of Joseph Kartholl. The two took watches, a telephone, a rifle, two revolvers, two pistols, a radio and a suitcase all valued at $400. Chuckie confessed to the crime.

Years later, one robbery that went wrong involved Chuckie, his brother Tony and an old woman. There was an old woman who owned an apartment building on Washington Boulevard in Chicago who collected her rent on the first of every month. A perfect victim to rob, the Crimaldi brothers kicked in the door to her basement apartment to steal the rent money. The problem was the old woman had a bad heart and everyone in the building knew it except Chuck and Tony. When Tony kicked the door down, it made a loud noise that sounded like someone hitting the floor. Once inside Chuckie made the old woman lay on the bed where they tied her hands and placed a handkerchief over her face so she could not see what was going on. The people living upstairs heard the loud thump and thought the old woman had hurt herself. They made their way downstairs and banged on the door to see if she was okay. Trapped with no way out, Chuckie and his brother hid in the apartment. When no one answered the door, the neighbor called the police. The Crimaldi brothers were discovered hiding and arrested. On the way to the Filmore Police Station, Crimaldi asked the cops if he and his brother could buy their freedom. The police officer asked Chuckie if he could come up with $3,000 in an hour for their release, Crimaldi told the cop to pull over at a pay phone and he would see what he could do. Crimaldi then placed the call to Sam DeStefano and explained what happened. DeStefano demanded that the officer get on the phone so he could talk to them. After a few minutes on the phone, the officer removed the handcuffs and told the brothers that everything was taken care of. They continued to the police station and once inside, Chuckie and Tony were handed different clothes from a locker and told to change because people were on their way to identify them. Once in the police lineup, with different clothes on, the people could not identify the Crimaldi brothers. Moments later, the two were released and all charges were dropped.

His luck changed on December 18, 1950 when Crimaldi was charged with burglary and given 60 months probation. On August 31, 1951, he was arrested and charged with burglary and larceny of a motor vehicle in Elmwood Park.

<u>File Card</u>
Charles J. Crimaldi
AKA Chuckie Grimaldi
Born: September 6, 1932
Died: Entered witness protection program, Unknown

<u>Crimaldi's known arrest record</u>

September 1950	Burglary
Oct. 9, 1950	Burglary
Dec. 18, 1950	Burglary 5 years probation
Dec. 18, 1950	Armed Robbery, 5 years probation
Sept. 7, 1951	Fugitive, Burglary

Sept. 20, 1951	Warrant violation of Probation
Oct, 6, 1951	Burglary
Dec. 27, 1963	Murder Investigation "Foreman"
October 1964	Bribery

Known Addresses

S. Carpenter Street, Chicago (1939)

Walton Street, Chicago (1942)

2724 W. Chicago Avenue (1950)

238 S. Leavitt Street (1951)

831 S. Carpenter Street, Chicago (1964)

2220 North Lorel, Chicago (1970)

Crimaldi quote

"I've broken arms and I've broken legs and I've watched a man die with a knife in his throat. But most of them had it coming. So what difference does it make? I've got no regrets."

A report dated October 6, 1951, contained the information on Charles Crimaldi's arrest in Elmwood Park by Officer Peter Rice. Under the name of Charles Grimaldi, he was arrested for burglary along with his brother Anthony Grimaldi of 328 S. Leavitt Street, a Robert Lutz of 1937 N. Francisco Avenue and John Pingitore (Pigitore) of 825 N. Maplewood Avenue.

Charles Crimaldi plead not guilty to the burglary, had the jury waived and the testimony was heard. He was found guilty of burglary and sentenced to five years probation. However, he was also found guilty of armed robbery and sentenced to 4 to 10 years in the penitentiary. Lutz, Pingitore, and Anthony Crimaldi all plead guilty to the burglary. In addition, Pingitore, Lutz, and Anthony Crimaldi each plead guilty to larceny of a motor vehicle where Charles Crimaldi was found not guilty on his charge of larceny. Lutz, Pingatore, and Tony Crimaldi were charged with stealing eight tire tubes, six car batteries, seven tires, four hammers, twenty-five wrenches, three socket sets, two break pliers, one electric polisher, one electric sander, and one electric drill.

Chuckie was sent to Joliet Prison for a short stay before being transferred to Pontiac Prison in Illinois. That is where his life would change forever-that is where he met Sam DeStefano. Crimaldi awoke one morning in his cell with word that Sam and Chuckie's mother were there to visit him. According to Crimaldi, Sam contacted his mother because talk on the streets of Chicago was that Chuckie was a "stand-up-guy" and that he took the rap for his brother. Sam was scouting men to work for him in his rackets and wanted Chuckie to become one of his goons when he was released from prison. Sam told Chuckie that he was working on getting him out of prison early and that he had a state reprehensive from the old 21st Ward in Chicago handling it. According to Crimaldi, that man was Clem Grover, a Republican committeeman on the pad with gangsters. Allegedly, after Grover could not help DeStefano in his request to free Crimaldi early from prison, two masked men hiding in the shrubs grabbed Grover as he walked from his garage to his house. Looking out of the second story window at the time was Grover's wife, Amelia, who witnessed her husband being kidnapped. One of the rumors is that his body was dumped into a hole under the Roosevelt Expressway in Chicago and covered up with cement.

Sam had one request for Crimaldi while he was serving his prison time. Read the bible, dictionary, and any books he could get his hands on. Learn to speak proper English, understand business books and psychology books, and learn how to manipulate people so that when he was out and working for Sam he could use those skills to control people. Sam was giving advice that he used himself while he was in prison in Wisconsin, when all he had to read there were the Bible and the dictionary.

Sam's thinking was "learn while in prison and practice it on your fellow inmates." If you got caught doing something wrong in prison, it would just add days or weeks to your sentence or days in the "hole" as they called it. But if you practiced out in the real world and got caught, then it's years back in prison. It was then that DeStefano encouraged Crimaldi to learn how to be a plumber. Not so he could learn how to unclog a pipe, but to understand how to use pipes, furnaces, heaters, and gas lines as weapons against his enemies.

Crimaldi took Mad Sam's advice and learned how to become a better criminal. He was released from prison in October 1954 and went straight to work for Sam DeStefano. After Crimaldi spent years as the plumber of the prison, Sam placed a phone call to the Plumber Union hall and told Chuckie to go down there so he could be placed in the union. Crimaldi explained in his book that he was offered an apprentice position as a plumber but turned it down and left the hall. When Crimaldi relayed the story to DeStefano, rage filled his body and he took it as a personal slap in the face towards him from the union. So he called his old mobster friend Joey Glimco, then president of the Taxi Cab Union Local 777 in Chicago, and asked a favor to have Crimaldi placed in the union. The next day Crimaldi received a phone call from Steve Bailey, who was then president of the plumber's union, and was given a union card.

In the 1960's police had Chuckie Crimaldi listed as hanging out at the corners of 13th Street and Cicero Avenue in Cicero, and Delaware Place between Rush Street and Ernst Court in Chicago. He was also a staple on the Mannheim Road strip running through Stone Park, Illinois. The strip was dubbed "little Vegas" in attempt to get top name entertainment in the mob-owned clubs on the strip. He was also using his home as a place to "work over" his victims behind on their "juice" payments.

After Crimaldi had gotten a divorce, he spent most of his time working for Sam. In addition to his collecting and "juice" activities, Crimaldi said he was running a theft ring and pulled off a few robberies including jewelry stores and a bank robbery. According to Crimaldi, Sam made him become a bartender so the "juice" payments could be dropped off to him while he worked.

In 1968 while Sam DeStefano was in prison, his wife Anita decided to close down Sam's loan business and blamed it on Crimaldi. Anita, who believed that the "juice" racket is what turned her husband into an animal and sent him to jail, wanted out and knew this, was the perfect opportunity to get out. Since Sam was in prison and Crimaldi was the only one out there collecting the money for Sam, she told Sam that Chuckie had quit collecting and she was closing up shop. This caused a falling out between DeStefano and Crimaldi, which lead to Chuckie quitting his employment. So Crimaldi went out to the six or so people he was collecting "juice" payments from for DeStefano and told them they didn't have to pay anymore because Sam didn't have anyone to enforce it while he was in prison. Then when Sam was released from prison and he went looking for all his money owed to him, they could just tell him that, *"Chuckie said we didn't have to pay until you were out."*

Because of this, DeStefano sent word out from behind bars that a contract was being placed on Crimaldi's head. A few weeks later, Crimaldi was driving home on Pulaski Road around 12:30 at night when another car pulled alongside him and opened fire blowing out his back window. Crimaldi forced the other car to stop, jumped out with a baseball bat, and dragged the driver of the other car out to the ground. He told the hoodlum to tell Sam to *"send someone better than him because when they come after me, they're coming after him."*

Later Crimaldi found out from a friend in prison serving time with DeStefano that after that incident another hired killer was sent out to a known hangout place of Crimaldi's but could not find him to kill him. That information made Crimaldi re-think his steps and learn new tactics.

Chuckie Crimaldi now had to find someone new to collect for so he went to work for some Cicero hoodlums collecting "juice" for about a year.

One of the more fascinating stories from Chuckie Crimaldi was his alleged involvement in a plot to kill Cuban President Fidel Castro in the 1960's. This operation was allegedly launched by the Central Intelligence Agency of America (CIA). On March 17, 1977, Charles Crimaldi told government agents that he was present with Chicago mobsters Sam Giancana and John Rosselli at the time when the assassination of Fidel Castro was planned and attempted. He also added at the meeting that he had information about the possible link between the plans to assassinate President John F. Kennedy.

Crimaldi said that the first meeting to discuss the plot to murder Castro was held at Sam Giancana's headquarters on Roosevelt Road called the Armory Lounge. Present at this meeting were Sam Giancana, Sam DeStefano and a person known to him as Melisi, who he believed was John Rosselli. The reason for the mob getting involved was to mitigate the prison sentence, which Sam DeStefano was facing at the time. DeStefano was told that he could get relief from his sentence through cooperation in this murder plot. According to Crimaldi, Sam Giancana's plan was to send DeStefano and mobster William "Wee Willie" Messino, who was also facing a lengthy prison sentence, to South America to hide out until plans could be made to get the two onto the coast of Cuba. Once there, the two would kill Castro and when they came back home to Chicago Giancana would be able to make their prison sentences go away. Crimaldi said that the CIA made contact with Sam Giancana though James "Jimmy" Hoffa, then president of the International Teamsters Union.

The second meeting was held during a funeral in Chicago where Crimaldi, Giancana, DeStefano, and Paul "The Waiter" Ricca (De Lucia) discussed the Castro plot. Ricca told Giancana he was not to undertake any part of the Castro assassination. He explained that the Chicago mob was going to be used as patsies either way, whether they failed or succeeded. Giancana, DeStefano, and Crimaldi heeded this advice and did not go through with the plan.

It was added that the morning of this interview, Chicago mobster Charles Nicoletti was killed in Northlake, Illinois. Crimaldi had stated that Nicoletti was allegedly part of this assassination plot and stated that all the people involved in that plot would be killed including Miami, Florida mob boss Santo Trafficante.

The following is another report dated April 11, 1977:

"Jack Moriarty and I spoke with Charles Crimaldi personally, along with John Kidner, the author of Crimaldi's book, and Sandy Troup at the National Press Building yesterday. We talked to Crimaldi for about one hour and he seemed willing to meet with us again. One of the major reasons for meeting with Crimaldi was to verify that he is, in fact, the person he claims to be, so that we can give his story the proper amount of credence. Jack and I posed several questions and obtained information from which we can check his official files and contacts in order to verify what he told us. Crimaldi, in fact looks like a Mafia hit man, which he claims to be: he is about 5'7" tall, weighs about 135 pounds, has a scar on the left side of his face, a tattoo on his hand, blue eyes, and is right handed. He gives his birth date as September 2, 1936, and looks approximately the age, which he claims to be. He has slightly thin and graying hair and acts fairly nervous when spoken to. In order to verify the details of his life, we have to obtain the names of several contacts in the DEA who are aware of his activities during the past few years. In particular, Agent Jim Braseth who had guarded Crimaldi since approximately 1970, and may be contacted at the Minneapolis office of the DEA. In addition, James Gallagher, who is employed in a high level position in crime control in Illinois, is quite familiar with Crimaldi when he testified as the trial of Anthony Esposito in Chicago, where Crimaldi detailed activities of the syndicate in that city. Crimaldi is also working for the FBI presently and is usually accompanied by two FBI Agents. While with Crimaldi, we discussed principally three topics: 1) his involvement with and the arrangements made for the Mafia's assassination of Castro; 2) his knowledge of Charles Nicoletti, who was murdered last week in Chicago and was also involved in arrangements for the Castro assassination; and 3) his knowledge of Jack Ruby.

Concerning that Castro assassination, Crimaldi related essentially the same story that's in his book and what he had told us before. He added that he didn't know of any later attempts on Castro's life undertaken by members of the Chicago Mob and had no further contact with the Castro assassination. He was, however, approached by the CIA later and asked to enter their employment. But remarked several times about the CIA involvement with the Mob, including their involvement with the Castro assassination. It is his knowledge that James Hoffa was the person who arranged the Castro assassination with Sam Giancana. He does not believe, however, that Hoffa was involved in the Kennedy assassination.

Concerning Charles Nicoletti, who was killed last week in Chicago, Crimaldi said that his death was probably due to his involvement in the Castro assassination. Crimaldi said that Nicoletti was well liked and respected by members of the Mob in Chicago and that he doubted that there was any internal reason for his death; thus, he believes that the CIA ordered his death because of the Castro Assassination plot.

He does not know of any involvement that Nicoletti had with the Kennedy assassination. We asked him if it might be worthwhile to subpoena personal records of Nicoletti in the hope of finding notes of his involvement in the CIA. Crimaldi said that it was doubtful that Nicoletti had notes but that it is possible that some records have been preserved. More important, Crimaldi said that Giancana definitely had records and notes, which were taken, out of his home after his death by the Illinois Crime Commission. He is convinced that these personal records should be consulted and he is positive that these records are in the possession of the Illinois authorities and can be obtained by us. Finally, concerning Jack Ruby, Crimaldi had no personal knowledge or contact with Ruby. After Ruby shot Oswald, however, he was privy to several conversations concerning Ruby by members of the Chicago Mob. They described him as a 'punk,' therefore leaving the impression with Crimaldi that no reputable underworld figure would have had any contact with him. He suggested that only one person in the Chicago area, Joey Glimco, had any personal contact with Ruby. Glimco, who is head of the Taxi Cab Union in Chicago, is alive and living in Chicago and can be contacted. Crimaldi warned us, however, that Glimco is evasive and very shrewd, and he doubts that we could obtain information concerning Ruby easily from him.

Crimaldi gives as his reason for talking with us his opinion that the more publicity he obtains, the harder it will be for the Mob to eliminate him; he feels that once all of the information which he has is in the public domain, there will be little reason for killing him."

Crimaldi said that everyone involved in this meeting with the CIA was killed. Sam "Momo" Giancana, John Rosselli, Sam DeStefano, Charles Nicoletti, and Jimmy Hoffa all met their end by being shot to death, except Hoffa whose body has never been found. Crimaldi was the only one left alive with this information.

Charles Crimaldi disappeared from mob trials and providing information. It is not known, or may never be known, if he is still alive or dead or even still in the witness protection program. Crimaldi spoke of himself as a mob killer with a conscious. He said he was a man who, at every turn, tried to stop Sam DeStefano from killing his victims, a

"Robin Hood" when it came to drugs and drug dealers. But those who knew him before he turned government rat knew him as a liar, con-artist and killer. He only became a government rat when he got caught and was facing many years in prison. Charles Crimaldi only cared about one thing, himself.

Sam Gallo

Sam Joseph Gallo was born around 1921 in Chicago and became one of Sam DeStefano's lieutenants by the end of the 1950's. One report stated that Sam Gallo was a nephew of Sam DeStefano or related to him in some way.

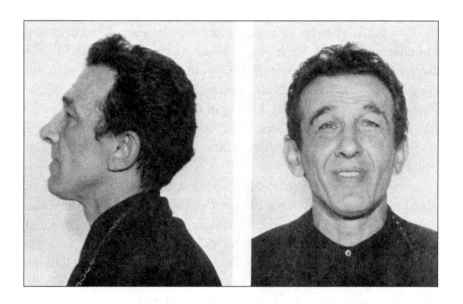

In 1956, Sam Gallo was listed as a one-time taxi cab driver and newspaper circulation driver with no criminal record. He was married to his wife, Antoinette, and they had two children. During the years, he was involved in crime, Sam Gallo could usually be found at Central and North Avenue in Chicago, or Harlem and Lawrence Avenue in Harwood Heights.

Sam Gallo was the brother of a minor hoodlum named Carmen Gallo Jr. Reports of Carmen Gallo stated he was born around 1930 and had a police record dating back to 1948 when he was arrested for tampering with an auto. Later that year he was also charged with accessory to rape. In 1949, he was arrested three times for minor offenses and in August 1950, he was arrested with James Pellegrino and Fidel Hernandez when the three were sitting in a parked car at Lexington and Laflin Avenues in Chicago. The Chicago PD noticed the three sitting there and pulled up to the car to question them. Found in the trunk were 32 counterfeit $10 bills. The three were arrested and after the trial, Carmen was acquitted of that charge.

Both Sam and Carmen Jr. were the sons of Carmen Senior, who died in September 1964 and either Bessie Grippoli or Bettina Groppola, both are listed as his mother. Listed as Sam's and Carmen's siblings are Madeline, Dominic, Mary and Jean.

On August 7, 1956, the body of Carmen Gallo was found in a ditch in Will County, Illinois on Naperville Road about a half mile from Route 66. His mouth was tapped shut with four-inch tape, his legs tied with rope, his wrists were bound with tape, and he was shot four to six times in the back of the head.

When interviewed, Sam Gallo told the investigators that the two had spent most of the night at their parent's house and that Carmen had driven him home late at night. The next morning, Carmen's car was found parked in front of his house on Lexington Avenue while his body was found in the ditch. At the time, Carmen was listed as working as a cab driver and was to be married within two weeks of his murder. The murder has never been solved.

In December 1956, Sam Gallo was shot in the right ankle by gunmen and was in the hospital under a police guard. He told the police that he left the Tip Top Snack Shop on Franklin Street in Chicago and started walking to his job as a circulation driver for the old Chicago American newspaper when a black Ford sedan pulled up next to him and someone in the car shot him in the ankle. Police conducted an investigation but could not understand why Gallo was shot.

On May 30, 1958, they found out why. The body of Dominick "Little D" Albano, an ex-convict who also went by the names of Mike Sipari and Vincent Costa, was found shot to death. It was learned from Dominic's brother, Anthony "Little T" Albano who was serving a sentence in Joliet Prison, that Dom, Carmen Gallo, Joseph Restagno, Sam Gallo, Thomas Kaskas, and Peter Salanardi were all part of the same stick-up gang. Joseph Restagno was found dead near Carpentersville on July 17, 1956 and Peter Salanardi, who was listed as a New York hoodlum, was found shot to death in his car a few days later. Thomas Keskas's tortured body was found shot to death on July 21. The reason for their deaths was that the gang had been robbing handbooks located in Cook County, Illinois and parts of Indiana. One report listed that the gang robbed a Cicero handbook of $80,000, which angered the Chicago outfit. It's not known if Albano escaped mob vengeance but it didn't matter. On April 26, 1958, Albano was a companion of John McGann when McGann was shot while trying to rob a doctor. Two days before this robbery, a Dr. Carl Champagne was robbed. Carl Champagne was the brother of mob lawyer Anthony V. Champagne, who was a close friend of Al Capone, Paul Ricca, Tony Accardo, and Sam Giancana. One month later, Albano was killed mob-style. It was not known if Sam Gallo escaped a mob hit or was just shot in the ankle as a warning. It was also mentioned that Sam DeStefano may have stepped in and saved Gallo's life.

In December 1962, Sam Gallo was driving his car on North Avenue when sped across the intersection and threw a red light. Unknown to Gallo, two undercover police officers were sitting in their parked car watching the intersection and pulled Gallo over. As the police officer walked up to the car, Gallo asked why he was being pulled over. The police officer said, *"You ran a red light."* Sam Gallo smiled and said to the police, *"Let me take care of this."* Gallo handed the police officer a bag containing $3,910 in cash. Gallo told the police officer, *"Take this, but give me $500 back for Christmas... ok, take all the money, but let me go."* The police officer smiled and pulled Gallo out of his car and placed him under arrest for bribery. While the police officer searched Gallo, he found another $1,800 in cash, a list of people on "juice" and a bunch of canceled checks in his pocket. Under the driver's side seat in the car was a canvas money pouch marked Midwest Bank and Trust Company on it, from 1606 N. Harlem Avenue in Elmwood Park. When Gallo was taken to the Central police lock up, he told the police that he had borrowed the money for a down payment on a restaurant. The police did not believe him; they already knew he was a "juice" collector for Sam DeStefano. The police asked Gallo if he wanted to make a formal statement. He replied, *"Do you want me dead?"*

From the twelve canceled checks found in his car, the detectives figured out that Gallo was part of an attempt to swindle $200,000 out of the American National Bank and Trust company located at 33 N. La Salle Street in Chicago. Other hoodlums involved and wanted for this swindle were Vito and Al Zaccagnini, two brothers working for Sam DeStefano as "juice" collectors, James Kennedy, Robert O'Casey, Harry Rubin, and Robert Whitlock, with alias of James Farrell and James F. Doran.

Harry Rubin was arrested and charged with grand theft. James Kennedy was arrested but stated that he was an employee of the American National Bank and Trust Company and admitted that he approved large withdraws from fraudulent accounts. Robert O'Casey was arrested as he tried to withdrawal over $7,000 from one of the fraudulent accounts from the bank. It was learned that this group was the same gang that swindled $25,000 out of a Berwyn bank in 1961.

Rubin said he came up with the plan when he met James Kennedy who was a business machine operator. From there they brought in Sam Gallo, Vito, and Al Zaccagnini to help with the plot. Rubin said that he was unaware that the plot to bilk the American National Bank was underway and he was being double crosses by the other members of this gang. He found out when he ran into Kennedy the day after Gallo was arrested by the police for running the red light and he was caught with all the checks. Kennedy said to Rubin that day, *"I hope he didn't have the checks from the bank on him when he was arrested."* It was then that Rubin knew he had been double-crossed. The plot was stopped after Robert O'Casey was arrested for trying to withdraw the money. When Rubin confirmed that the gang was made up of seven men, the police made the connection that it was the same gang that also defrauded $25,000 out of a Melrose Park bank.

Rubin explained to the police how the swindle worked. The gang opened two accounts at the American National Bank with several hundred dollars in each account. Kennedy was then instructed to take checks, deposit them in large accounts in the bank, and pass them on to other gang members before processing them. Then some of the other gang members would copy the signature of the depositor and the code number from the check. With this, they would make up forged checks and deposit them in their accounts and withdraw the money once it cleared. The plan was to open fourteen more accounts and steal around $300,000 within ten days before moving on to a new bank.

Rubin then said that he was on "juice" to Sam Gallo and that he had met with Gallo each week in a hamburger shop on the 100 block of North Wacker drive to pay his 11 percent "juice" on his original loan of $500. He also added that on two occasions he had to meet with Sam DeStefano to make the payment. Oddly enough, when the police searched Rubin's apartment, they discovered an address book with over 500 top hoodlums in Chicago and Los Angelis written in it.

Sometime later, a Mrs. Ernestine Carr was arrested for working with the gang in the Melrose Park Bank swindle case. Mrs. Carr worked at the Bank of Broadway and helped the gang swindle the $35,000. In this case, the person responsible for the irregularities was Paul Zima. Zima, who from 1959 to 1962 was a Vice President in charge of installment loans at the Bank of Broadway, was the person who approved all the loans for Sam Gallo in the kickback fraud.

Paul William Zima was born on October 19, 1906 in Chicago. In 1960, he was listed as living in Twin Lakes, Wisconsin, owning the Proprietor, Wonder Bar & Bowling Alley in Kenosha. He was arrested on November 22, 1963 for permitting minors to loiter in his tavern and selling liquor to minors.

Sam Gallo's 1963 police record contained the following listings:

Agency	Name	Date	Charge
Army	Sam Gallo	9-10-1940	Registration
City Chicago	Sam Gallo	2-10-1948	Pub Veh Lic Chi.
Chicago PD	Sam Gallo	12-10-1956	Shot, Investigation
Melrose Park PD	Sam J. Gallo	5-15-1962	Theft
Chicago PD	Sam J. Gallo	12-12-1962	Bribery Traffic Viol
Chicago PD	Sam J. Gallo	12-20-1962	Theft by deception
Cook Co. Jail	Sam Gallo	4-8-1963	Theft
Cook Co. Jail	Sam Gallo	9-13-1963	Theft
Joliet Prison	Sam Gallo	9-13-1963	Theft, Bribery

Known Addresses
516 or 506 South May Street, Chicago (1950's)
829 North Richmond Street, Chicago (1962)

Known Employment
Driver, Chicago American Newspaper (1950's)
Little Palms Inn, 760 S. Kedris, Part owner

In April 1969, Sam Gallo, then living at 1840 Long Avenue, was arrested for threatening a newspaper circulation truck driver. Gallo, mentioned as being the main "juice" man for Chicago newspaper truck drivers, confronted a man who took out two $250 loans and was late on his payments. The truck driver added that he had already been beaten twice before he went to the police and complained. Arrested with Gallo were Ralph Casale, Mario Dispensa, Andrew Suba, and Frank Tenuta.

During the court case, Ralph Casale refused to testify and was threatened with six months in prison for contempt. After being granted immunity, he final agreed to testify.

With Casale off the hook and Andrew Suba dying while awaiting trial, on April 16, that left two trials to be heard. The first trial was for Frank Tenuta and Mario Dispensa who were charged with conspiracy, criminal usury, and battery. At the trial, the main witness to testify against them was the truck driver, Donald Doyle. Doyle testified that he borrowed $200 from Mario Dispensa and wound up paying him $1,100 in interest.

He added that the person who beat him twice was Andrew Suba, who was a mob associate and worked for the Chicago Tribune newspaper delivery department. One of the terrifying stories told was how Dispensa and another hoodlum went to the victim's house and invited him for a ride to discuss his loan. The victim was taken to a forest preserve section near Glenview, Illinois, where a gun was placed to the victim's head. He was told that this would be the last chance and if he did not come up with the money to make his payments, *"It would be all over"* for him. Both Mario Dispensa and Frank Tenuta were acquitted of all charges after the testimony of Doyle raised questions about his credibility. When it was read in court, Doyle broke down into tears because he knew Dispensa would be back on the street looking for him.

Mario J. Dispensa was born around 1939 and was listed as a Chicago mob "juice" man working mostly around 31st Street and Princeton Avenue, 22nd Street and Wentworth Avenue, and 26th Street and Wallace Streets in Chicago. In 1964, he was convicted of criminal trespass and was given one year of probation. On August 2, 1971, Oak Forest police arrived at The Hut Drive-In Restaurant located at 15906 Lockwood Avenue. Flamed were shooting out the windows as a roaring fire had broken out in the drive-in. The police found two men on the ground, dazed and screaming in pain. The two men were Mario Dispensa and Anthony Rocco. Rocco was an ex-Chicago Police detective who had been fired from the Chicago PD in 1970 when he allegedly offered to

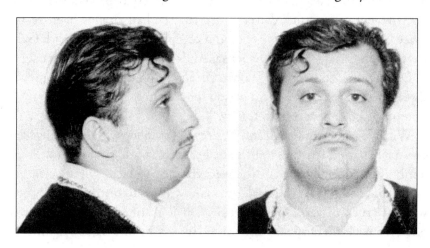

return a gun taken from a criminal suspect in return for money. The two were taken to the hospital with over 70% of their bodies burned. It was an arson attempt gone wrong. The drive-in was owned by a Bruno Bertucci who was listed as being an organized crime associate. Bertucci admitted knowing the two of them, but said he had no idea why Dispensa or Rocco would want to burn down his restaurant. He declined to comment on a report that said Bertucci and Dispensa were seen together at a Chicago social club on West 31st Street. The report said that the two met frequently with mobster James "Jimmy the Bomber" Catuara. Police said they found gas cans and rope soaked in gasoline on the scene. The fire was ignited from two stoves inside the drive-in and the fumes from the gasoline ignited while Dispensa and Rocco were pouring the gasoline on the floor. The next day Mario Dispensa died from his injuries.

On August 4, 1970, Sam Gallo did not have the same luck as the other defendants. He was found guilty and sentenced to 3 to 5 years in prison. This conviction was the first under a new law that had been passed in 1967. The law provides penalties up to imprisonment for five years and a $5,000 fine for charging more than legal interest rates. Donald Doyle testified once again saying that he borrowed $300 from Gallo and he demanded $1,250 in return for interest on the loan. Gallo denied during the trial that he had ever threatened Donald Doyle and said that he lent the money as a friendly gesture. After being convicted, when Gallo was asked if he had a statement to make, he said, "I think no comment would be best." As deputies handcuffed Gallo, his wife Antoinette started crying and told the deputy, "You don't have to put those things on him, you big slob."

Once Gallo arrived at the Joliet Penitentiary Diagnostic Center, he was greeted with open arms by mobster George Bravos and was escorted to the section of the prison controlled by the "mob." Thus began his incarceration.

In 1972, Sam Gallo was offered immunity to testify against Sam DeStefano in the Leo Foreman murder trial. Gallo refused and was found in contempt of court and ordered to serve 17 months in jail after he was finished with his 3 to 5 year sentence. At the time of his death in September 1983, he was listed as having a daughter named Nina Marie and a son Carmen Sam Gallo. Sam Gallo is buried at Queen of Heaven Cemetery in Hillside, Illinois.

Peter Cappelletti

When Sam DeStefano talked about "Cappy," he was talking about Peter Paul Cappelletti. One report states that Cappy was born on December 25, 1920, in Chicago. However, during one arrest Cappy gave the police his birthday as being December 24, 1922. Cappelletti also used the nickname of "Rocky" and was listed as living at 2450 North St. Louis Avenue.

Not much information could be found on who his parents were but confirmed reports state he at least had a brother named Michael and two sisters Clara and Marge.

One report in 1962 mentions that a Peter Cappelletti, living at 2450 N. St. Louis Avenue, had one of his brothers killed in a freak accident. According to this report, Joseph Cappelletti, of 5306 Jackson Blvd., had a job working for the Chicago Park District as a labor. His boss, Matthew Sweeney, ordered Cappelletti and another worker Ronald Thierer to load nine 300-pound concrete slabs onto a truck so Sweeney could use them for his patio at his home. According to Thierer, he and Cappelletti got onto the back of the truck after the slabs had been loaded when one of slabs began to fall over. Both men grabbed it and held it up. At that point, the truck began to roll from the curb and the other slabs began to fall. Around 2700 pounds of concrete fell on Cappelletti crushing him. Sweeney was ordered to have the slabs broken up before moving them and have them brought to the city dump. Sweeney violated regulations by having park employees loading material for his own use and by having a private truck on park property for personal use. Sweeney was fired from his position for the incident. However, he landed on his feet. His brother, Theodore A. Swinarski, an associate clerk of the Circuit Court and a 12th Ward Democratic Committeeman sponsored his brother Matthew for a job as a supervisor in the City of Chicago's department of sanitation. An investigation discovered that Sweeney had his last name legal changed by court order from Swinarski to Sweeny. Also discovered was that he owned a trucking business who rented his trucks to the city of Chicago and to the sanitary district under the name of Sweeney and the Dee N. Dee Trucking Company. In 1956 Sweeney was a witness before a grand jury investigation on charges of collusion in bidding on city truck hire contracts.

The file on another brother, John Cappelletti, stated he was a Sergeant of the Willow Springs county highway station in 1944. A year later in 1945 Cappelletti was appointed as lieutenant when Lt. Peter Madura and Lt. John Burns of the county highway police were suspended when four illegal slot machines were found in their vicinity. In 1962, he was listed as head of the stolen auto unit of the Bedford Park Sheriff's police. In 1963, John Cappelletti was listed as being a chief investigator of the legal department's investigative staff.

Peter Cappelletti was marred to Verna Mae Kelley, also known as Verna Garrick, who died in January 1995 in Las Vegas. The two had five children, Carla, Paula, Joseph, John and Peter Jr. There is another child named Michael who was listed as being 20 years old when Verna was 34 years old. One report suggests this was a child from either another marriage or another woman.

His early arrest record contained only two arrests, one for gambling on the street around 1940 and another for disorderly conduct around 1941. Both cases were dismissed. He was listed as being active in "Juice" on the corners of Halsted Street and Irving Park Road in Chicago, and Cicero Avenue and Cermak Road in Cicero in the 1960's.

According to one report, Peter Cappelletti was the brother-in-law of Sam DeStefano. Information on Cappelletti states that he attended John Marshall High School in Chicago and was in the U.S. Army from January 13, 1943 to October 27, 1945, when he received an honorable discharge.

He was known as one of two main bail bondsmen who operated under Sam DeStefano in the early 1960's. Cappelletti operated Cappy's Bail Bond Service with a Sol Manno who assisted Cappelletti while running another location. Both of these men were licensed agents working for Harry Shore, a bondsman who had an office located at 26th and California in Chicago, right next to the Cook County courthouse. The legal papers for the bail bonds business were in the name of Anita DeStefano and she was listed as a partner with Cappelletti.

One story of a George Willis shows how getting involved with "Juice" men could become a re-occurring nightmare. George Willis was born in Chicago on October 15, 1917, and lived at 2941 West Belmont Avenue, Chicago, Illinois. He made his living as a cook and by bad luck met Al Zaccagnini. Willis did have a criminal record with an arrest on September 4, 1936, in Chicago Heights for bogus checks.

Willis became a business partner with Alfred Joseph Zaccagnini, brother to Vito and known Al "Cowboy" Zaccagnini. Listed below is the story of how Zaccagnini and Cappelletti squeezed the money from Willis and a good example of how they operated. The story is told by Willis himself:

"In late 1959, while employed as a cook at the Sugar and Spice Restaurant at 3203 North Clark Street, I became friendly with Al Zaccagnini. After becoming friendly with Zaccagnini, he asked me if I know of a part-time cook, as he, Zaccagnini was opening the 901 club at 901 North Cicero Avenue. I told Zaccagnini that if he was looking for part-time help, that I would be interested, and Zaccagnini told me that he would hire me as a part-time cook at $3 an hour. In October 1959, I went to work part-time for Zaccagnini at the 901 Club as a cook. I also kept my full time job as the Sugar and Spice Restaurant.

In January 1960, Al Zaccagnini made me an offer to come into the 901 Club as a partner. I agreed and Zaccagnini informed me that in order to buy in, I would have to put up $2,500 in cash. I told Zaccagnini that I did not have that kind of money and Zaccagnini said that he could obtain a loan at the Bank of Broadway in Melrose Park, Illinois. I told Zaccagnini that if I could get this loan, I would be happy to come into the 901 Club as a partner. A few days later, Al and I went to the Bank of Broadway and talked to Paul Zima, the loan officer, who was a friend of Zaccagnini's and I applied for a $2,500 loan. This loan was approved and the loan was disbursed as follows: $1,000 into a checking account in the name of the 901 Club. Any checks drawn on this account had to be signed by myself and Al Zaccagnini. Zaccagnini told me that the other $1,500 was needed for immediate expenses and that Zaccagnini received this money in cash. This loan was to be repaid to the Bank of Broadway at the rate of $30 per week and the bank required three signatures on the note. The other person on the note as well as Zaccagnini and myself was a Joe Ross, another friend of Zaccagnini's.

The 901 Club was in business for about five months and then business began to fall off. Zaccagnini and I had an argument regarding the running of the Club and in July 1960, Zaccagnini sold the club to a Paul Perkins for an undisclosed amount of money. After Perkins purchased the 901 Club, I worked for him about two weeks and then quit.

After 'pulling out' of the 901 Club, Zaccagnini later re-contacted me and informed me that I would still have to make payments to the Bank of Broadway on the $2,500 loan. I continued to pay on this loan, which amounted to over $900, and had continued to pay on this note up until the time Paul Zima was fired from the Bank of Broadway. To date, I have never heard from the Bank of Broadway regarding this loan.

In April 1961, I went to work as a cook at the Spaghetti Inn at 3232 North Cicero. This restaurant was owned by Gus Kostos and later by Sam Paboukos, and was managed by Ann Zaremba.

After working at the Spaghetti Inn, I became aware that Paboukos was on "juice" for over $2,400 to Al Zaccagnini and Sam Gallo, who are both "juice" collectors for Sam DeStefano. Over a period, I noticed that Zaccagnini and Gallo were getting Paboukos in deeper on "juice" in order to muscle into the business. Gallo and Zaccagnini were constantly hounding Paboukos for "juice" payments.

Sometime in June 1960, during one of their numerous visits to the Spaghetti Inn, Al Zaccagnini and Sam Gallo contacted me regarding the balance of the 901 Club loan at the Bank of Broadway. Zaccagnini and Gallo advised me that the bank had been 'pressing' them for repayment of this loan as the loan had become delinquent. I told them I couldn't understand this, because I had been making weekly payments. Zaccagnini and Gallo then advised me that I was to pay them $15 per week for what was the balance of the loan and that they would in turn make the payments to the Bank of Broadway. They never did tell me what the balance of the loan was at that time. I agreed to pay them $15 per week and continued to do so for over three months. During one of my contacts with Al Zaccagnini, it was further agreed that I would try to get a $400 loan from the Parr Finance Company in Oak Park so that the balance of the loan at the Bank of Broadway could be paid off in full. I went to the Parr Finance Company with Al Zaccagnini and Sam Gallo and applied for a $400 loan. However, this loan was rejected by the Parr Finance Company because of my poor financial credit. I continued to pay $15 a week to Zaccagnini and Gallo as previously agreed to reduce the note at the Bank of Broadway.

After the Spaghetti Inn folded, I went to work at Bruno's Restaurant at 3020 North Central. In June 1962, Al Zaccagnini and Sam Gallo re-contacted me and told me that I still owed $2,500 from the 901 Club deal. We had a big argument, however, I lost. At this time Zaccagnini and Gallo informed me that they had a contact at the Loma Finance Company in Niles, Illinois, and that they would obtain another loan for me from Loma to 'wipe' the deal clean from the 901 Club. I told them that I would think about it.

In early July 1962, I accompanied Zaccagnini and Gallo to the Loma Finance Company and applied for a $2,500 loan. About four days later, Al Zaccagnini contacted me and advised me that he had received a check from the Loma Finance Company, which needed my endorsement. Zaccagnini showed up with the check and I endorsed it. Zaccagnini did not tell me the amount of the check and merely showed me the reverse side, which required my signature. At this time, Zaccagnini informed me that I would have to make $20 a week payments to him and that he would pay Loma. I continued to pay Zaccagnini $20 a week for over 14 months. In July 1963, I was contacted by the Loma Finance Company and informed that no payments had been made on this loan and that Loma was returning this account over to a collection agency. I informed the Loma people that I had been paying Al Zaccagnini $20 a week and they informed me that Zaccagnini had never paid anything on this loan to them. I then contacted Al Zaccagnini and I asked 'What the hell was going on' and Al said, 'Don't worry about it, the loan will be taken care of.'

In August, 1962, Al Zaccagnini and Sam Gallo told me that they were in a 'bind' and told me that they were going to put me on the 'books' (DeStefano's) for a $200 loan to cover up as they had been holding out on DeStefano. They told me if I would agree to this, they would take care of Loma Finance Company and all I would have to pay would be $22 per week 'juice' to them. I agreed although I never received any $200 from either Zaccagnini or Gallo and I was just covering up for them. They further asked me 'if I was asked by anyone regarding the $200 'juice', I was to say Al put me on the 'books,'

I made two $22 payments to Al Zaccagnini and on the third week, I was contacted by Pete 'Cappy' Cappelletti and I was informed by Cappy that I was no longer to pay Al Zaccagnini and that he, Cappy, would collect from me. The next day, I saw Al Zaccagnini and told him about my visit from Cappy and Al said, 'The hell with Cappy, you pay me.' The following week Cappy showed up at Bruno's Restaurant looking for me and told me that I was now in the 'big leagues' and not fooling with Sam and Al. At this time Cappy also told me that Al had put John Finn, who was a bartender employed at Bruno's on 'juice' for $150 and that Finn had skipped and his 'juice,' (Finn's) 'was going on my book.' I beefed to Cappy about this and informed him that I wanted to see Sam DeStefano about Finn's 'juice' and when I said this, Cappy did not push me any further for Finn's 'juice.'

I continued to pay Cappy $22 'juice' per week until October 1963, when I fell one week behind. After falling one week behind, Cappy then doubled my 'juice' to $44 per week, which I continued to pay until around Christmas, 1963, when I was again late with the payment. At this time Cappy then increased the payments to $66 per week, which I paid up until February 1964, when I again fell one week behind, and Cappy increased the payments to $88 per week and informed me that it would take $880 in a lump sun to clean me off the books. I continued to pay $88 per week up until this week, and I intended to pay no more, regardless of whether or not I wind up in the trunk."

Willis furnished this statement to the FBI just incase he wound up missing. Unable to pay anymore after having every penny squeezed out of him, Willis filed for bankruptcy and listed Al Zaccagnini as a creditor and a debt owed as $200. When the FBI found out a "Juice" collector for Sam DeStefano was being served with a notice as a creditor to be heard in the U.S District Court, they investigated if Willis civil rights and a possible conspiracy were being violated. This was the last thing Cappelletti need since he was already the subject of a few FBI investigations' under DeStefano and one for the protection of a Charles Tillman Batchelor. Since Cappelletti still made threats to Willis to keep paying the "juice" loan after Willis went to Cappy to tell him that he was filling for bankruptcy. George Willis agreed to let the FBI tape his phone lines so if any threats were made to Willis for no longer paying they would be recorded and Willis could be placed into protective custody. The FBI stayed in touch with Willis on a weekly basis and no other reports of violence was reported.

In May 1964, Illinois state officials revoked Cappelletti's bail bonds license because he was listed as an accused counterfeiter and sidekick of Sam DeStefano. On May 5, at 6:01 in the morning, Cappelletti was arrested by the FBI at his home in a roundup of a counterfeiting gang. Along with 11 other mobsters, Cappelletti was indicted on charges of transporting fake securities in the form of government bonds in an alleged $500,000 swindle.

When Cappelletti was arrested, agents went to his home and found records of DeStefano's "juice" loans for the years of 1963 and 1964. These records contained the listings of their clients and the outrageous interest rates charged. Also found was an Italian-made 9mm Corto Beretta Automatic Pistol with one clip full of ammo and a threatening letter dated October 10, 1962 from someone named "F" at Cook County Jail. Cappy refused to make a statement to the FBI and placed a call to his attorney, Robert McDonald. The gun was tested and compared to many mob murders in Chicago but no match was made.

Once Sam DeStefano found out about his "juice" books being taken by the FBI, he phoned the agent at the Chicago office and demanded the books be returned to him. One informant went to the FBI right after the arrest of Cappelletti saying he had been down in DeStefano's "House of Horrors" and that Mad Sam had become a "wild man" and was ranting and raving about all the trouble Cappy could make for him by keeping "juice" records in his home rather than keeping them in his car. He added that DeStefano told him that Cappy had been cautioned regarding implicating him in any manner with the "juice" racket and that when Cappy was released on bond there would be another meeting at the "House of Horrors" where Cappy would be taken care of. He also said that the only thing Mad Sam is real "wild" about is that Cappy was the only one who could really bring Sam down with the feds. He told this informant that if Cappy was picked up again by the "Feds," Sam was of the opinion that Cappy would crack because he was a weakling in his organization and that they could not take any chances with Cappy any longer, and if that happened, Cappy must be put down, meaning killed. The informant concluded the interview saying that Cappy was on real thin ice and that he was living hour by hour as Sam was going "psycho" from the pressure of his arrest concerning the voting matter. Mad Sam believed that the feds were trying to build a kidnapping charge against him and was trying to get Cappy to "fink" and testify against him.

In the counterfeiting case, Joseph Spagnoli Jr. was named as the leader of the counterfeiting gang. Testifying in the case was an ex-convict named Gerald Lee Robinson. Robinson said that he was forced to pass counterfeit travelers checks by DeStefano hoodlum Arthur Pascucci. Pascucci made Robinson travel to Alabama, Louisiana and Florida to cash $10,000 in counterfeit checks after Robinson fell behind on his $500 "juice" loan. Another informant in the case said that Cappelletti had approached him shortly before Christmas, 1963, and asked this informant to get some checks for a friend of his. He said that this person wanted to buy $10,000 worth of checks and he was going to sell the checks for ten percent on the dollar.

Cappelletti plead not guilty and the case went to court. In January 1965, Cappelletti was found not guilty and released. In the end, everything taken from the arrest including the "juice" records was given back to Cappy with the exception of the pistol. Mad Sam decided Cappy was to live.

In May 1965, sheriff's police raided the rear of a store at 1400 S. 50th Street in Cicero and found Cappelletti and three other hoodlums holding a card game. The authorities confiscated the $500 in cash and smashed the card table with axes. The other men arrested were Mike Cannavino, Paul Parrillo, and Joe Anzalone.

In September 1967, detectives of the Chicago PD raided a fake coffee shop at 837 Irving Park Road and found a 24-hour rummy game. The Greek rummy game played with multiple decks of cards was run 24 hours a day, seven days a week by the crime syndicate. When police smashed through the door, its players scrambled. Police discovered that the players were using small sticks as money during the game so if police had raided the game, no cash would be taken as evidence and they would not lose any money. The money had been paid up in advance. Three tables were being used to play the games and they were being controlled by Peter "Cappy" Cappelletti. Also arrested with Cappy were Arthur Shafer, charged with being the keeper of the gambling establishment and Sheldon Elkin who had just been released from Joliet Prison a year earlier after serving a sentence for robbery. The others arrested as being involved in the games were Milton Pongas, Christ Kolletsos and Margaret Wolff.

In July 1970, agents of the Illinois Bureau of Investigation lead by Patrick O'Connell raided a syndicate card game at 807 W. Jackson Blvd by busting through the door with a sledge hammer. O'Connor yelled to the hoodlums playing the game, "All right, gentlemen, up against the wall with your feet spread, you're under arrest." Running the game was Joe Volturo, who asked O'Connor as he stood against the wall with his hands up, "Why tonight? Why are you guys doing this to me? Answering Volturo was vice detective C. Bernard Carey, "Gambling is against the laws of the state." There had been eight other raids on Volturo's game over five years. His games usually pulled in around $10,000 a weekend. Joining Volturo against the wall Anthony Verdone, of Melrose Park, Illinois, who was said to be Volturo's partner in the games. Also against the wall, Outfit guys by the nick names of "Barbout," "CTA Johnny," and "Calico Kid." Also against the wall was the dealer of the game, Peter Paul Cappelletti.

On April 30, 1972, Cook County Sheriff's Police raided a gambling joint at 4917 West 14th Street, Cicero. Peter Cappelletti was arrested and was described by the police as follows, *"Cappelletti is a money lender, but not a juice man. He likes to go to a game, play 15 minutes, then quit, and spend the rest of the evening kibitzing and lending money. He talks a big game. He has a big shot hoodlum relative within the Cicero group. As a moneylender, Cappelletti is a middleman, in that he is not required to collect not bankroll the juice loans. A juice man gives him a certain amount for lending purposes. Cappelletti then goes to a game where he lends the money, records the amount and to whom, and then gives this information to the juice man who is responsible for collection. The moneylender is paid a fee. He works at the dice table by calling out the numbers and returning the dice."*

<u>Also arrested that night with Cappelletti were:</u>

Peter "Katz" Miller, known juice man.
Nello Gabellini, associate of the Aiuppa group.
Sam Mancino Jr., Close friend of James "Turk" Torello.
Joseph Eterno, unknown figure from Sicily.
James Ranelli, listed as a runner for the Aiuppa group.
James Ginsburg, juice man under the control of Joey Aiuppa.
Dom Santino, syndicate gambler.
Joe Dandre, (Dandriacco) bookmaker involved in construction.
Ted Grabowy, gambler and friend of Chris Cardi.
Morris Stein, known gambler.
Charles Hruby, unknown.
Walter Magiera, known gambler.
Herbert Heinze, unknown.
Raymond Pilger, known associate of mobster Sam Rosa.
Joseph Simone, associate of the Fulco-Lincon group.
John Lombardi, alleged juice man.
Mike Arena, unknown.
George Lauris, gambler.
Walter Szymanski, associate of Tony "Buck" Ortenzi.
George Mathers, unknown.
Frank Russo, unknown.

Peter Paul Cappelletti moved to Las Vegas sometime around 1986 and was listed as a retired owner of a transport and delivery company. He died in Las Vegas in December 2001 and is buried at Memory Gardens Cemetery in Arlington Heights, Illinois.

Peter Cappelletti

Vito Zaccagnini

Vito Zaccagnini, born around 1927, was known as a lesser hoodlum under the control of Sam DeStefano. Records go back to 1948 when Zaccagnini was involved in a robbery that caused the victim to die. In June 1949, Zaccagnini confessed to police that he had set up the robbery of John Onosto, a 72-year-old shoe repairman who owned a shop at 2103 Taylor Street. While Onosto and Zaccagnini engaged in conversation one day, Onosto told him that he had saved a considerable amount of cash to close down his shoe repair shop for a month so he could go back to Italy to see his family. Figuring the cash was hidden in the shop, Zaccagnini sought out the services of two hoodlums named John Groth and Chris Iosello, aka Chris Lisallo, to perform the robbery.

Zaccagnini stood across the street and watched Lisallo and Groth enter the store. He had told the two hoodlums he could not help in the robbery until Onosto was blindfolded, since Onosto could identify him. Once the signal was given, Zaccagnini ran into the shop to see the elder Onosto on the floor, his legs, and arms bound, a piece of tape over his eyes and a towel in his mouth. All three then ransacked the place looking for the hidden money.

Zaccagnini told police that when the three left the shop, Onosto was alive and that he received only 18 silver dollars for his part of the loot netted in the robbery. When police arrived at the shop, Onosto was dead. The police believed that Onosto had suffered from bronchial trouble and the gag shoved into his mouth, helped cause his death. Zaccagnini,

Iosello, Groth and a Joseph Barbaro, a prison guard who acted as a go-between, were arrested and charged with murder. The charge against Barbaro was dismissed while the other three pleaded guilty and received 1 to 15 years in prison.

When Zaccagnini was released from prison, he went to work for Sam DeStefano. In January 1964, Zaccagnini and Frederick Lippi were arrested in Las Vegas with $67,000 worth of phony checks.

According to the FBI report on Sam DeStefano, FBI agents went to Winnebago County Jail in Rockford, Illinois on March 16, 1964, to interview Vito Zaccagnini. He had been sentenced to serve five to fourteen years in prison for forgery. Zaccagnini told the agents that he was in good with the Sam DeStefano and the Fiore "Fifi" Buccieri groups and was $14,000 deep in "juice" to DeStefano who he described as the largest "juice" operator in Chicago. He told the agents that he had not been able to make any "juice" payments for over four weeks and because of threats made by DeStefano, he feared for his life. In addition, he claimed that he was in the process of losing his family because of "juice" payments and had been traveling the country cashing counterfeit Bank of America notes and phony Series E Government Bonds. Because of this, he told the FBI that he was willing to testify in any case concerning DeStefano.

Zaccagnini went on to say that, he was in debt to five different "juice" men at one time. He first borrowed $10,000 from Sam DeStefano at 11 per cent a week interest. When he could not cover his payments, he went to mobster William "Wee Willie" Messino to borrow $1,200 to make his DeStefano payments. When he could not cover his payments with Messino he went to three Cicero "juice" men and borrowed $500 from each.

Zaccagnini also told the police that one of the quirks of being a "juice" man was that at Christmas time the "juice" men would give themselves a Christmas gift by going over their books and arbitrarily increasing any unpaid principals by 25 per cent.

Among his other claims was the time in 1963 when mob loan shark bosses planned the bank robbery of a suburban bank to help the bank officials cover up the shortage of money resulting from an under-the-table loan when they believed another mobster was going to default on that loan. The bank officials provided the mobster with alarm system diagrams and drawings of the bank's floor plan. However, the mobster had managed to make his payments and the plan was called off. Another story was in 1962 when two police officers were working for "juice" men and escorted a shipment of stolen television sets worth $100,000. He refused to name the police officers.

Vito Zaccagnini was placed in the witness protection program in 1965 an gave information to the FBI for 21 months. Most of the information was hearsay and could not be corroborated. When Zaccagnini was asked why he was turning on DeStefano, he said the following:

"I'm trying to save myself and other juice victims. They have to steal, just like I did, to pay juice to DeStefano. It will stop a lot of crime if DeStefano is convicted and sent to prison."

Dominic Carzoli

Dominic A. Carzoli was born around 1924 and was reported to be a muscleman for Sam DeStefano and a west side gambler and alleged "juice" man for the Buccieri group and mobster Joe "Gags" Gagliano. His arrest record contains an arrest for gambling and burglary.

An FBI report dated 1964, listed Carzoli as a crew boss with Tim Solomon as his muscle. In 1970, Carzoli was then living at 700 N. Christiana Avenue and was listed as a cab driver. He was found guilty and sentenced to three years in prison for threatening a Betty Smith who was an employee at a cleaning store on Chicago Avenue. Carzoli was afraid Mrs. Smith was going to tell an IRS Agent about his income. He was reported hanging out at the corners of Kedzie and Chicago Avenue and Belmont and Western Avenues in Chicago.

The Solomon Brothers

Nenos K. Solomon was known as King Solomon in organized crime. Born around 1928, he was also known as Ephraim Solomon when he was listed as living at 2150 N. Lincoln Parkway in Chicago. His arrest record dates back to 1949 and contains arrests for theft, battery, burglary, and intimidation. The area listed under his control around the 1960's was Diversey and Pine Grove Avenues in Chicago. He was also known as a former professional middleweight prizefighter who quit boxing in 1955.

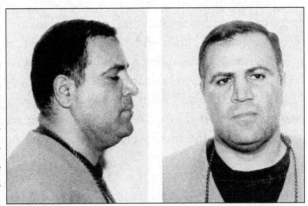

Special Agent William Roemer went to Captain William Duffy of the intelligence Unit of the Chicago PD and was told that as of 1962 Sam DeStefano had been using Nenos "King" Solomon and his brother

King Solomon

Nimrod "Tim" Solomon as "juice" collectors. Because King Solomon was a professional prizefighter it was a skill DeStefano desired in case his clients weren't on time with the money they owed. The report also stated that the Solomon brothers were very closely associated with James "Cowboy" Mirro, Rocky Infelice and Americo DiPietto. According to Captain Duffy, the Solomon brothers were reported to be arson and bombing suspects in the Chicago area. However, no information concerning any specific bombings or fires were reported. He did report that another brother to the Solomon's, known as William Sorgon, a fire and loss insurance adjustor, being involved in the activities concerning the King and Tim Solomon.

King Solomon told an informant that in order to supplement his income, he carried out "contracts" independent of the organization. In this regard, he advised that many individuals assumed that he was connected with the "outfit" and because of this, he was able to capitalize on the fear that victims have of Chicago hoodlums.

When the FBI interviewed Solomon in January 1963, he admitted he was acquainted with Sam and Mario DeStefano and that he had been a "juice" collector for DeStefano many years ago but had since developed much hatred and distrust. He recalled that once during his employment for the DeStefano's, one of his assignments was to collect a $200 loan from a taxicab driver. This individual paid him $100 of this loan and latter told Mario DeStefano he had paid the full amount of $200 to Solomon. DeStefano believed the cab driver and confronted Solomon with this allegation after which Solomon was forced to appeal to his friend, mobster Obbie Frabotta, who took care of the situation by intervening for Solomon. Solomon illustrated his hatred for Mario DeStefano by stating he would enjoy fulfilling a contract on Mario DeStefano. Solomon finished the interview by admitting at that present time he had two contracts pending for which he was to receive a percentage of the money recovered from victims and would be able to complete these contracts by putting on a display of brutality which caused fear among his victims.

King Solomon was involved in the mob's jukebox racket when it was revealed he was on the payroll of a jukebox firm. In 1968, a business executive went to the Chicago Police looking for help because he had taken a "juice." loan from King Solomon and was unable to pay. This victim was $16,000 in debt and was told by Solomon that if he did not make a payment of $3,000 he would be beaten and his legs would be broken with a baseball bat. On December 17, 1968, Solomon met with the executive in a parking lot next to a cemetery. What Solomon did not know was that Chicago Police were hiding behind the tombstones in the cemetery. They arrested Solomon on charges of attempted theft and intimidation. Nenos "King" Solomon died in October 2004.

Nimrod Timmy Solomon is believed to have been born on July 12, 1929, in Chicago and lived at 208 West Willow in Chicago. His arrest record dates back to 1949 with more than six arrests for robbery, arson, gambling, and narcotics. On February 11, 1949, four men described as "long-haired young Oklahoma bad men with luxuriant sideburns" robbed a filling station on La Salle Street of $200. The police captured Robert Oertel, who confessed to the robbery, and said the other three were Kenneth Brown, Richard Hawkins and Nimrod Solomon. When police arrested them, Solomon had the money on him. He would later be acquitted on that charge.

In 1965, Tim Solomon was under indictment and was awaiting trial on charges of arson in connection with the fire at the old Cairo Supper Club Restaurant at 4017 Sheridan Road on May 11, 1964. Also arrested in that case was the nephew of mobster Albert "Obbie" Frabotta, named William Monaco, and his associate Robert Armidano.

The assistant state's attorney would drop those charges against Solomon when it was learned that two of the women who identified Solomon at the scene getting out of a Cadillac and throwing an incendiary device through the window of the club had police arrest records. A third witness fled to St. Louis after she received threats of death if she testified. Solomon was also awaiting trial in connection with charges of theft by extortion. In that latter case from July 1964, Solomon was charged with, threatening a food chef named George Dilda. In his statement to Chicago Police Dilda said he was contacted by a man identified as Solomon, using the name of Mike Jacobs, who told him that if he did not pay some $1,200 in gambling debts that Dilda owed from betting on the horses, he would be killed. Other threats from Solomon were, *"For $50 I can hire someone to break your legs unless you pay that $1, 200,"* and *"I want that $1,200 or you're going to wind up in a sewer."*

On September 16, 1966, Solomon was arrested for transporting $52,500 in counterfeit notes from Chicago to North Vernon, Indiana. Also charged were Almer S. Linkon and George Sommer who went by the alias of Allen Nagy. Also involved in the counterfeiting were Luigi

"Cockeyed Louie" Fratto and Alan Rosenberg. However, the two were never charged since Fratto died of cancer on November 24, 1967, and gangsters killed Rosenberg in March 1967. Solomon and Sommer were found guilty, while Linkon was acquitted.

On March 2, 1967, police, armed with a search warrant, raided the home of Solomon and found a stolen tape recorder, credit card and some marijuana. However, in order to convict him for the stolen goods, the judge ordered the informant responsible for the search warrant to be identified. Rather than expose the informant, police dropped the charges

On June 22, 1968, Nimrod Solomon, William "Smokes" Aloisio, Stanley Jasinski, Ted Sullivan, Charles Bartoli and Grace Cosentino were arrested by the U.S. Secret Service for selling counterfeit United States treasury notes. In 1969, Solomon was convicted on federal charges of counterfeiting receiving 10 years in prison. It's believed he died in October of 1980.

Ed Speice

Edward Jerald Speice was born on June 11, 1931, and had been arrested more than 30 times by the time of his arrest for threatening a government witness in 1972 with Sam DeStefano. Ed Speice was a small-time burglar who had a position in organized crime through his close and personal friendship with mobster Anthony "Sonny" Esposito Jr. The two grew up together since both came from the same general area, and Speice was a member of Esposito's burglary crew.

In 1950, Speice and John Herschel were arrested for holding up a food shop. In 1952, he was arrested and sentenced to 3-to-6 years in Joliet Penitentiary for armed robbery. In 1955, he was arrested

with Theodore Kotwasinski, Dolores Zook, and his wife Patty Lou Speice, for armed robbery. In 1958, Speice was arrested with mobster Salvatore Romano, an old member of Esposito's gang and later Anthony Spilotro's gang, for burglary. Both were convicted and sentenced to prison. In 1960, Speice and Theodore Kotwasinski were arrested once again for stealing three piano organs and a television set.

Edward Speice and Sam DeStefano were arrested on February 23, 1972, for threatening Charles "Chucky" Crimaldi in an elevator in the Federal Courts building in Chicago. While Chucky was being questioned in court the fact came out that, some outstanding bad blood was held between Crimaldi and Speice. Crimaldi spoke of the time in the 1950's when Eddie Speice kidnapped his brother, Tony Crimaldi, and almost beat him to death. Crimaldi did state that the situation was straightened out, and through the years, it had been more or less passed over.

At the trial in 1972, Speice claimed that he could not obtain a legitimate job because of his extensive criminal record and had to turn to crime to stay alive and provide for his family.

Both Speice and Sonny Esposito were the subjects of a "juice" investigation by the FBI in February 1975. One of Esposito's "juice" victims went to the FBI for help but refused to testify against the two. The investigation was discontinued when both Speice and Esposito were placed under investigation in 1979 when they were involved in the planning of a new country on a piece of land between Mexico and the United States called the new "Cherokee Nation." An island formed when the Rio Grande River between Texas and Mexico reversed itself after a hurricane storm hit the golf. The river formed an island that was later purchased by a Colonel Herbert Williams. The idea was to start a new country with no taxes, legalized gambling, and a place to make their own money. Esposito and Speice were going to control the gambling operations for the Chicago Outfit and the American Mob. The U.S. Government put a stop to all the plans and the "Cherokee Nation" never got off its feet. Anthony "Sonny" Esposito Jr. died on November 23, 1985 and is buried in Queen of Heaven Cemetery in Hillside, Illinois. Ed Speice died on November 23, 1994 and is buried in Elmwood Cemetery in Elmwood Park, Illinois.

File Card
Edward Jerald Speice
AKA: Eddie
Born: June 11, 1931
Died: November 23, 1994

Known Arrest Record

Agency	Date	Charge
Chicago PD	1-28-1950	Robbery
Chicago PD	9-21-1950	Investigation
Chicago PD	1-16-1951	Investigation
Elmwood Pk. PD	8-5-1951	Burglary, ,Fugitive
Chicago PD	10-8-1951	Warrant Violation
Chicago PD	10-30-1951	Larceny, Robbery with a Gun
Chicago PD	11-1951	Assult
Joliet Prison	1-10-1952	Robbery, Burglary
Joliet Prison	5-20-1955	Paroled
Chicago PD	12-4-1955	Robbery with a Gun
Chicago PD	3-5-1956	Robbery
Chicago PD	3-15-1956	Violation of Parole
Joliet Prison	11-17-1956	Paroled
Chicago PD	5-20-1957	Investigation
Chicago PD	6-20-1957	Investigation
Chicago PD	9-26-1959	Robbery
Chicago PD	1967	Burglary
Chicago PD	1969	Parole Violation
Chicago PD	1970	Parole Violation
DEA	3-10-1971	Treating a Government Witness
Chicago PD	5-7-1994	Weapon Charge

Edward J Speice

Mickos Polesti

Mike Polesti was listed as an ex-convict enforcer for Sam DeStefano in the 1970's while working as an auto salesman at Allstate Motors located at 1529 Mannheim Road, Stone Park. He used many different spellings of his name, his Greek spelling Mickos Polasta and his American spelling Mike Polesti.

His relationship with Sam DeStefano came through Edward Speice. When Speice was in the penitentiary, Mike Polesti was a technician in a Malatia Hospital for the U.S. Army.

Anthony Spilotro

Anthony John Spilotro was born on May 19, 1938 on the far west side of Chicago. Known as "The Ant" to his mob buddies, Spilotro lived at 1102 South Maple Avenue in Oak Park in the 1960's. Listed as the places Tony could be found were Lathrop Avenue and Roosevelt Road in Forest Park, Stanley and Harlem Avenues in Berwyn, and the Voyager Motel in Miami, Florida.

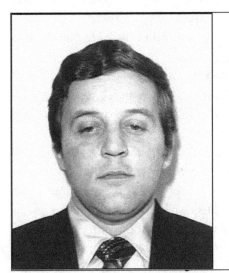

In 1970, Tony Spilotro was listed as an active mob "juice" man when he was indicted on February 26 for gambling, aggravated battery, and resisting arrest. On May 20, 1970, he was indicted on federal charges of making false statements on loan applications.

In September 1972 when Spilotro was arrested for the murder of Leo Foreman, the Las Vegas FBI hoped that Spilotro would go away to prison forever and not return. Since Spilotro arrived out west, he had set up a gift shop at the Circus Circus Casino and Hotel on the Las Vegas strip to use as his "juice" headquarters, and five bodies were found out in the desert, which investigators tried to link to Spilotro's "juice" loans operations. He also set up a shylocking business preying on casino employees in desperate need to pay off gambling losses.

Weeks after the Sam DeStefano murder, information made its way that Tony Spilotro was selected by the Chicago group to arrange for hoodlum interests to obtain a foothold in legalized gambling operations, which were at the time expected to be legalized in New Mexico. It was to be Spilotro's function to make contacts in New Mexico for hidden interests of the Chicago group. Spilotro was to place hoodlum Ronald De Angelis, known as an electronic wizard, of the Chicago mob as his second in command of the New Mexico, operation since De Angelis was living in Deming, New Mexico.

Spilotro became the man to contact in Las Vegas concerning "juice" loans, robberies, and getting rid of stolen loot. A quick summary of a month in the life of Tony Spilotro in the 1970's after he became involved in the West coast rackets is as follows:

"In June of 1974 Spilotro was in Los Angeles staying at a $160 a day cottage on the grounds of the Beverly Hills Hotel located on Sunset Boulevard. He was with his associates Joseph Hansen, Chris Petti, and Fred Sica. Joseph Henson was alleged to be a hit man for hire and one of the best "stick-up" men in the country and would not commit a robbery for less than $100,000 specializing in jewelry.

Spilotro was there meeting with Ricky Manzie, a theatrical agent, and a former minor hoodlum from Chicago, who married nationally known singer Barbara McNair. The reason for this meeting was that Spilotro was becoming involved in the theatrical booking business and had four or five clients in Hollywood for work in Las Vegas.

As FBI Agents listened through a hidden microphone connection, Spilotro talked about returning from Chicago after meeting with mob boss Sam Giancana. He relayed the story of how Giancana told him about how the Mexican authorities suddenly picked Giancana up after hiding in Mexico for three years and put him on a plane back to America. Spilotro said, "*Things are very hot in Chicago and several subpoenas were outstanding.*"

He also talked about how he recently went to San Francisco with Chris Petti and Jack Klausen to look at valuable coins in the old San Francisco Mint. Klausen wanted the coins stolen but after they learned about the physical set-up at the old San Francisco Mint, Spilotro decided he was not interested in the robbery.

The conversation continued with Spilotro stating he was bankrolling football making in the fall with someone named "One Eye" and with a Jasper Speciale who was then the operator of the old Tower of Pizza Restaurant in Las Vegas. He also complained how he purchased $35,000 worth of stolen wigs in Chicago and was unable to dispose of them. He had them sitting in a warehouse in Los Angeles.

He expressed his anger because he said he had to sell his gift shop concession at the Circus Circus Casino upon orders of his "Capo," Joe Lombardo back in Chicago because of the publicity in the newspapers at the time setting forth La Cosa Nostra ties with the Teamsters Pension Fund money. Spilotro complained about the Federal indictment he was facing in Chicago and talked about how he and his companions borrowed the money from the Teamsters union but paid it all back. He said he expected to be convicted and imprisoned.

He then complained about Frank Fitzsimmons who was running the Teamsters Union and that when Allen Dorfman left the Chicago based pension fund that was the end of the Chicago mob's ability to get large amounts of money out of it. Spilotro said he and some of his hoodlum associates were backing Jimmy Hoffa in his bid then to take back the presidency from Fitzsimmons.

The conversation ended with him telling about how he went to Walt Disney World in Orlando, Florida with Ricky Manzie when his wife Barbara was singing there. That was a few weeks in the life of Tony Spilotro."

In 2005, mobster Nick Calabrese became a government stool pigeon spilling mob secrets dating back to the 1950's. He told authorities the truth about Tony Spilotro's end. In 1986, Tony Spilotro's time was done in the minds of Chicago mob bosses, especially Joey Aiuppa. Calabrese said that Tony Spilotro had been sleeping with the wife of Frank "Lefty" Rosenthal, Chicago's man running the Stardust Casino in the 1970's. Spilotro was also said to be involved in moving drugs with a motorcycle gang. Tony's brother Dr. Patrick Spilotro, said that three weeks before the murder he received a phone call from Michael stating he was in trouble with the mob, but Michael never did tell his brother what kind of trouble.

Calabrese testified that he and mobster John Fecarotta went to Las Vegas to attempt a hit but were unsuccessful. Then word was sent out to Las Vegas that Tony was being moved up in the ranks to the position of captain or "Capo" and that his brother Michael Spilotro was to become a "made" man in the Chicago outfit. The two were ordered back to Chicago for the induction. The story until now had been the Spilotro brothers were taken to an Indiana cornfield alive, then beaten with baseball bats and buried alive in a shallow grave. However, according to Nick Calabrese, when the brothers reached Chicago on June 14, 1986, he, Fecarotta, and mob boss Jimmy LaPietra were ordered to go to a shopping center on 22nd Street and wait. According to Calabrese, James Marcello picked up the three men in a fancy blue van.

From there the men drove to a house in Bensenville, Illinois, where they were joined in the basement by mobsters Joe Ferriola, Sam "Wings" Carlisi, John "Bananas" DiFronzo, Louie "The Mooch" Eboli, and Louis Marino. Once the Spilotro brothers arrived, Michael was the first one down the steps. Calabrese said that he extended his hand to Michael and said, *"How ya' doing?"* Before he could answer Calabrese said, he jumped at Michael's legs to restrain him while Eboli put a rope around Michael's neck. Calabrese said that he could hear behind him Tony Spilotro asking his killers for some time to say a prayer before he was killed; they declined and beat the brothers to the ground with their fist and feet. Calabrese said once the two were dead, he took a cloth and wiped up a small spot of blood that had fallen where Michael had been beaten. The bodies were then driven to a cornfield in Newton County, Indiana were they were buried in a 5-foot deep grave only wearing their underpants. Calabrese said he then went for coffee.

On June 22, 1986, a farmer had noticed the freshly overturned soil and thought the remains of a deer shot illegally by a poacher would be found, but he discovered the Spilotro brothers. Three months later the body of John Fecarotta was found for botching the burial.

Anthony Spilotro (signature)

Robert J. McDonnell

Bob McDonnell was given the title of "mob lawyer" when he represented Sam DeStefano and many of Chicago's criminal hoodlums throughout the 1960's.

An Irish man from 82nd and Wood Streets on the south side of Chicago, McDonnell attended St. Ignatius College Prep High school where he played on the football team as a center. He then went to Notre Dame University where he played a year of football before he volunteered to enter World War II. While an infantry squad leader in the Army, he was sent to Italy and was wounded as he stormed a German machine gun nest. He returned to Chicago with a Bronze Star and a Purple Heart award, but he was a different man and when he attempted to return to Notre Dame, he was expelled for organizing a protest against the food that was being served to the students. With his explosive voice and confidence, he finished his law degree at DePaul University in Chicago and became a lawyer.

In the early 1950's, McDonnell spent five years as a Cook County assistant at the state's attorney's office. By 1956, he left that office and became a defense lawyer representing bank robbers and stick-up men.

McDonnell did have some minor incidents with the law. In September 1953, River Forest Police arrested him for speeding, doing 50 miles an hour in a 25 mile-an-hour speed zone. In February 1964, he was arrested and received four more traffic tickets from the Chicago PD. His brother, Gregory McDonnell, told a newspaper reporter that his brother had a weakness for martinis and gambling. It was his heavy horse and football gambling that ushered his path into the way of Chicago mobsters.

In January 1966, Fred Ackerman testified before the Illinois Crime Investigation Commission investigating Chicago's "juice" rackets that Robert McDonnell borrowed money from mobster Lennie Patrick to cover his gambling losses, as well as from a number of other juice operators. That led McDonnell to admit that he was a slave to Sam DeStefano because of $80,000 in "juice" loans owed to him.

Ackerman would also testify that in 1966 McDonnell and four other Chicago mobsters were charged with interstate transport of stolen money orders. Mobsters James "Cowboy" Mirro, Ernest "Rocky" Infelice, Americo "Pete" DiPietto and Frank Santucci were the focus of the scam involving money orders stolen from a Melrose Park supermarket on May 27, 1961. According to Ackerman, Frank Santucci broke into the supermarket and used a cutting torch to break into the safe, gaining access to 148 American Express company checks. Santucci then brought the checks to Mirro, DiPietto and Infelice to distribute. Mirro was said to be the leader of the scam. Ackerman, acting as the "go for" man in the conspiracy, said he went to Robert McDonnell asking for his help in locating a man in Missouri who would cash them. Charles Richard Lent and John Vincent O'Connor were arrested for cashing the checks in Missouri and New York. Santucci, Mirro, Infelice, DiPietto and McDonnell were all convicted of conspiring to pass stolen money orders across state lines.

McDonnell would also go on to plead guilty to tax evasion for not filling his federal income tax returns from 1960 thru 1964, the years he was DeStefano's main lawyer.

The Chicago Tribune reported a story that a going-away party was held for McDonnell at a Northside bar. Allegedly at the party were James "Cowboy" Mirro, Nenos "King" Solomon, and Johnny "Bananas" DiBiase. The article alleged that the hoodlums told McDonnell that all his debts were being wiped out as long as he did not tell the government anything he knew about organized crime.

After nineteen months in prison, McDonnell was released and was listed as being involved in his relatives' construction firm, investing in a used-car lot and helping to set up a South Side medical center. In 1979, he attempted to regain his law license to practice law again. He did regain his license in 1980 but was disbarred once again for trying to bribe a union official.

He would go on to marry the "Mafia Princess" Antoinette Giancana, daughter of mob boss Sam "Momo" Giancana, in 1983, just a few days after meeting her in the lobby of his law offices. Their marriage would end in divorce. Robert McDonnell died at Hines VA Hospital in Chicago of heart failure on October 29, 2006.

The Bastone Group

Carmen, Angelo, and Sal Bastone ran a "juice" operation in the Melrose Park area around the 1960's and once used the old Come Back Inn Restaurant on Lake Street as their "juice" headquarters. The corners they operated at were 15th and North Avenue, and 22nd and Division Street in Melrose Park, and Midwest Road and 22nd Street in Oak Brook, Illinois.

Carmen Peter Bastone was born on April 25, 1931, and listed his address as 1803 Shoreline Drive in St. Charles, Illinois and 7207 Breen in Niles, Illinois. He was arrested on January 6, 1964, by the U.S. Secret Service in Chicago for violation of federal counterfeiting laws. Eighteen days later, the case was dismissed. In 1975, he was convicted of making false statements to the FHA.

Salvatore "Sal" Bastone was born on August 9, 1935, in Chicago and was a huge thug, standing at 6'1" in height, weighing 250 pounds. He was living at 50 Cody Lane in Deerfield, Illinois when in 1987 he was convicted of Federal racketeering, being sentenced to 18 months in prison.

Angelo Bastone was the older brother who was born on April 12, 1921. Angelo was known as an Illinois State Trooper dating back to 1948 before being caught and fired in a towing company shakedown in 1962. Angelo was responsible for getting his two younger brothers, Sal and Carmen, connected with Sam Giancana and Hy "Red" Larner. The Bastone brother's story was laid out in the book "Double Deal" by the onetime mob cop Michael Corbitt and mob boss Sam "Momo" Giancana's nephew also named Sam Giancana. In that book, Corbitt wrote that once Angelo was fired from his state trooper job, Momo Giancana sent Angelo out to Las Vegas to work as a bodyguard for Morris Shenker at the Dunes Hotel. Angelo Bastone once boasted that he was a collector of bad debts for a Jake Gottlieb who was listed as the operator of the Dunes Hotel in Las Vegas, Nevada in the 1960's.

One of their victims told an FBI informant about the situation he was involved in with the Bastone brothers. He said that he went on "juice" with Carmen Bastone for $500 and that his juice payments were $50 per week. After five months of making his payments on time and paying over a $1000, he fell behind. Unable to keep up the payments, he was given a beating by Tommy Tucker, a muscleman for the Bastone's. This victim finally was able to borrow the money from someone else and get off the "juice" with the Bastones.

Another FBI report states that Carmen and Angelo Bastone acquired possession for about two months of the property of the Meadowbrook Swim and Tennis Club located at 8307 West North Avenue in Melrose Park with a man by the name of Harry Brown, who was a mortgage broker and had a percentage of the club. This club was used as the Bastone's headquarters and it became a place for many Melrose Park hoodlums to gather. Carmen and Angelo Bastone would make phone calls from this establishment to their delinquent "juice" victims and made threats if payments were not made on time. An FBI informant came forward and told them that the Bastone's were assisted in their operations by Ralph "Red" Ciangi who was an employee of the City of Chicago working for the Streets and Sanitation Department. Red Ciangi was also listed as the right hand man of mob labor official Anthony "Tony X" Esposito. At the time, it was investigated if Red Ciangi was using money from Esposito or Local 1001 for the purpose of "juice" loans. Ciangi was also very close to members of the Democratic offices of the First Ward in Chicago. One of the men working under Ciangi was Joe Lucente who was known as Ciangi's enforcer.

Information was received that in April or May 1964 that Harry Brown was held captive by Red Ciangi and Carmen Bastone. Any financial deals, which Brown undertook, were taken over by Ciangi and Bastone and any money Brown was able to make was taken from him. Even Brown's two Cadillacs were taken from him and used by Carmen Bastone and Red Ciangi. In that same time, both Ciangi and Bastone became incensed at Brown and beat him several times in which his ribs were cracked and his legs and body were badly bruised. Red Ciangi died in August 1969.

In 1986, Sal Bastone was indicted on charges of using threats of violence to collect "juice" loans with Albert Rabin and John Heckens. At the time, Sal was listed as a lieutenant of mob boss Joseph Ferriola. One report stated Sal was actually a relative of Ferriola's.

Angelo Bastone died on April 27, 1989. Sal Bastone died in Minnesota at the Mayo Clinic in March 1998 and is buried at All Saints Cemetery in Des Plains, Illinois. Carmen Bastone died from pulmonary disease in April 2002.

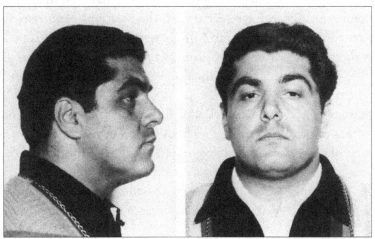

Carmen Bastone

Chapter Twenty-Seven

The Chicago Outfit and "Juice"

This section is to focus on the Chicago mob's "juice" business covering most of their activities in the 1960's and 70's. The Shylocking racket became the mob's second highest moneymaker, next to gambling.

The Chicago Crime Commission report

In December 1964, the New York State Commission of Investigations conducted public hearings on the loan shark racket in New York City. Following New York's lead, the Chicago Crime Commission decided to gather its own information and release a booklet to Chicago law enforcement agencies, alerting them to who was running the juice rackets in Chicago and its outlying areas. Lt. Michael O'Donnell of the Chicago PD made its files and reports available to the Chicago Crime Commission to help formulate this report. Their conclusion as of 1965 was that Fiore "Fifi" Buccieri was the Chicago outfit's headman, personally supervising the juice loans and their collections. The files indicated that Buccieri was getting his orders from mobster Jackie Cerone. Under Buccieri were Joe Gagliano, William Messino, and Joe Lombardi. According to the report, the positions of authority varied in each particular case. An example given was mobster Phil Gazaldo who was under direct orders from Jack Cerone, while the Grieco brothers, Joe and Donald, allegedly took orders from their uncle Ju Ju Grieco who was in federal prison at the time.

In January 1964, the Chicago Police Department issued a confidential bulletin listing eight of the leading mob juice men operating in the Chicago area. The list of names and their information listed in the bulletin are:

1. **Felix "Milwaukee Phil"** Alderisio who had been arrested 35 times and was once convicted of transporting unstamped whisky. He has been

suspected of many murders and was closely associated with Marshall Caifano and Albert Frabotta.

2. **Nick Bravos** who was active on the west side of Chicago. He served seven years for armed robbery and was active in bookmaking. He was seen in the company of Tony Accardo, Sam Giancana, and Gus Zapas.

3. **Lennie Patrick** who was active in the juice racket in the Fillmore Street Police District, especially along Roosevelt Road and in the Rogers Park area where he controlled a great part of the juice loans and gambling. Patrick had been questioned many times about murders.

4. **Albert "Obbie" Frabotta** who was an ex-convict who served 4 years for bank robbery in Indiana and was active in the juice and gambling rackets on the north and west sides of Chicago. Police officers classify him as a low-grade moron with the mental capacity of a 10-year-old child. He had been arrested about forty times and questioned about many murders.

5. **William "Willie" Messino,** who was often seen in the company of Tony Accardo, was an ex-convict who served about 5 years for robbery and had been questioned regarding several gangland murders. He operated a juice racket mainly on the west side of Chicago.

6. **Joseph "Joey G" Gagliano** who was recognized as an underling of Jack Cerone, operated on the west and Northside of Chicago. He could regularly be seen at Moon's Restaurant at Chicago and Hamlin Avenues. He was considered one of the top juice men for the syndicate.

7. **Charles Nicoletti** who frequented the west side of Chicago and was said to be a leader in the juice rackets in the Loop area of Chicago and also in the East Chicago Avenue Police District. He was seen many times in the company of Tony Accardo and on numerous occasions with Phil Alderisio.

8. **William "Potatoes" Daddono** was a Westsider who operated city-wide. He served time for burglary and was discharged in 1946. He was active in the scavenger business and had even tried legitimate

ventures. He was a "juice" man often seen with Sam Giancana, Tony Accardo, and Joey Aiuppa.

Others mentioned as top juice men in this report were Frank Buccieri, Americo DiPietto, Dominic Curtin, Ernest "Rocky" Infelice, Leo Rugendorf, Joseph Spadavecchio, Frank Parker, Irv Weiner, and Joe Grieco.

In 1969, hearings were conducted on the Chicago "juice" rackets and one story was told about pressure the mob was putting on victims. A man by the name of Jack Oak took out a $500 "juice" loan from the mob and had to pay $50 a week in payment. When he became unable to make his weekly payment, he knew he had to get away so he joined the U.S. Navy and asked for a position on a submarine to escape the beatings he was receiving from mob muscle men.

The mob's "juice" men

A confidential source in the 1960's advised that Joseph Gagliano and William Messino were involved in an extensive and lucrative illegal enterprise commonly known as "juice." The informant added that Sam DeStefano was the meanest "juice" man in Chicago, but was not a made mobster. The informant said that Gagliano and Messino were members of the Chicago "Outfit" and, in his opinion, were almost as sick as Mad Sam when it came to attacking their victims. Both Messino and Gagliano were under the direction and control of John "Jackie" Cerone.

John Phillip Cerone Sr.

John "Jackie the Lackey" Cerone was born on July 7, 1914, in Chicago and used an alias of John Cironi and J. Arnold. Jackie Cerone lived at 2000 North 77th Avenue in Elmwood Park and during his life he would achieve the roll as "boss" of the Chicago mob. In 1970 Jackie Cerone was listed as one of the top "juice" men in Chicago. Listed as his areas of operations

were Harlem and Lawrence Avenues in Norwood Park, Grand and 74th Avenue in Elmwood Park, North Avenue and River Road in Melrose Park, and his headquarters at the old Rocky's Drive Inn at 2204 West North Avenue in Melrose Park.

Cerone's arrest record dates back to 1932 with arrests for gambling, robbery, driving while intoxicated and many murder investigations. In 1970 he was found guilty on a federal gambling conspiracy charge and was sent to prison. In the 1980's he went back to prison once again for his roll in skimming $2 million dollars from a Las Vegas Casino. He died in August 1996 from natural causes.

Cerone's "juice" operation was controlled by his lieutenant Joe "Gag's" Gagliano who controlled all of Cerone's organized illegal activities in Chicago during the 1960's. Cerone's territory bordered on Chicago's west side by Austin Avenue, on the east side at Ashland Avenue, on the Northside at Armitage Avenue, and on the south side by Madison Avenue.

William Messino was in charge of all "juice" activity in this territory and answered directly to Gagliano. The "juice" income of Gagliano and Messino was considered their most lucrative source of income and was controlled by the use of extortion, physical harm and threats. Messino was described as sadistic in controlling his "juice" victims and had, in the past, been admonished by Gagliano and Cerone for his beatings of victims, causing police interest affecting all of their illegal activities.

Numerous confidential sources advised that Gagliano and Messino used to meet their "juice" victims at the old Moon's Restaurant at 3756 West Chicago Avenue and at the old 3800 Club, 3800 West Huron, both in Chicago.

Joseph Gagliano

Joseph Gagliano was born on July 21, 1915, in Chicago and had the nicknames of "Gags," "Joey Gags," "Joey G.," "Jack Gailo," and "Pip the Blind." He was also known for the tattoos on his forearms. On one forearm was a tattoo of a girl's head named "Marge" and on the other forearm, a tattoo of "Felix the Cat."

His arrest record dates back to 1926, including arrests for kidnapping, bootlegging, battery and armed robbery. He got his start working as a muscle-man for the syndicate under mobster Joey Glimco.

On April 23, 1933, Joe Gagliano and Gene Kellino robbed Harry Fishman of $57. After his arrest, Gagliano forfeited his $10,000 bond rather than stand trial. Kellino was granted 14 continuances before being found guilty and given one year to life in prison.

There is another report that a Joe Gagliano was arrested in December 1949 for armed robbery but no further details were listed.

On November 26, 1971, Gagliano complained he was having chest pains and was admitted to Oak Park Hospital. On December 12, 1971, Gagliano died due to complications from a heart ailment.

Joseph Gagliano
AKA: Joey Gags
Born: July 21, 1915
Died: December 12, 1971

Known Addresses
1522 Mohawk Street, Chicago (1944)
1731 North Thatcher Road, Elmwood Park (1963)

Known Areas of Operations
Hamlin and Chicago Avenues (Chicago)
Chestnut Street and Wabash Avenue (Chicago)
Achsah Bond and Outer Drives (Chicago)

Joe Gagliano's official 1964 FBI bio listing reads as follows:
"Joseph Gagliano resides at 1731 Thatcher Avenue, Elmwood Park, Illinois. Gagliano is an ex-convict, sentenced in 1934 to one year to life for armed robbery. He was paroled in Illinois in 1940. Gagliano is a family man, however, is known to be amorous with many females.

Gagliano controls an area in Chicago, principally consisting of the Austin District of the Chicago Police Department. In his designated area he controls all organized crime consisting of gambling, bookmaking and "juice" activities.

Gagliano is directly under the domination and control of Chicago hoodlum Jack Cerone. Gagliano is considered an up and coming member of the Chicago crime group and reportedly an active and ambitious individual in organized crime. Information has been received to the effect that Gagliano had been receiving added responsibilities in the overall network of the Chicago crime syndicate.

Gagliano, together with his Chief Lieutenant William Messino and others, recently were tried and found guilty in a state violation. They were charged with kidnapping and beating of a loan shark (juice) victim. Gagliano and others were found not guilty in this case, which was defined as one of the largest miscarriages of justice in Illinois. Gagliano's "juice" operation was described as an operation receiving over $400,000 a year income. The publicity which resulted from the trial of Gagliano and others in this operation resulting in a reprimand on the part of Sam Giancana. Giancana reportedly instructed Gagliano and others to discontinue all 'juice' activity, or insure that in the future no 'juice' victim would testify.

Recently, twelve wire rooms were raided and charged with gambling and failure to possess federal gambling stamps. These wire rooms were in the territory controlled by Gagliano and information was received to the effect that Gagliano delegated the control of these wire rooms.

Gagliano reported income as an employee of Commercial Phonograph Survey Company. Commercial Phonograph Survey is a sister of Recorded Music Service, both organizations existing under the dues paid by juke box operators. Commercial Phonograph Survey is the "muscle" portion of the juke box operators association; in that they are responsible for influencing juke box operators who do not abide by the rules and regulations of Recorded Music Service. Recorded Music Service is an association whereby members of the association agree that they will not infringe upon territories or locations operated by other members.

Gagliano had reported income from Commercial for a number of years and exercised no control over the activities of this organization.

Gagliano, although considered an up and coming member of organized crime in Chicago, is considered a 'playboy type,' and during the summer months spends a great deal of time on his yacht on Lake Michigan."

Gagliano and Messino had a number of individuals employed as their "juice collectors." A few of the most infamous listed were Albert Sarno, a former Chicago Police officer; John DiFronzo, an ex-burglar; Chris J. Cardi, a former Chicago Police officer and Joseph Lombardi, an ex-burglar and thief.

All of these individuals were considered vicious "juice collectors," administering many beatings to their victims at the drop of a hat. These individuals, as well as Gagliano and Messino, were charged with the kidnapping and beating of Joseph Scott Weisphal, a "juice" victim and ex-convict. Weisphal had been arrested by the Chicago PD for passing bad checks in connection with a "juice" loan. It was learned that Weisphal had been dealing with Messino in connection with "juice" and Weisphal had introduced two individuals to Messino for "juice" loans. These persons made their "juice" payments on the loans and then left town with an outstanding balance. Messino told Weisphal that he was responsible for the payment of these defaulted loans and demanded payment. In order for Weisphal to make these payments, he had to try and cash bad checks. Not being able to make these payments, Weisphal went into hiding in order to avoid Messino. However, Weisphal, for some reason, made a date to meet a bondsman. When he met the bondsman, Messino and some of his henchmen were waiting for him. Messino and his men forced Weisphal into his car and then proceeded to drive to the Moon's Sandwich Shop. Moon's Restaurant was owned by Joseph Gambino who took it over from his father, Mike Gambino. Messino, Joe Gagliano and William Daddono all used the shop as a hangout and torture chamber. En route to the shop, Messino began to beat Weisphal over the head with a club. Once at the shop, Weisphal was taken into the back room where a person known only as "Pete" began to beat him. After "Pete" was done, Messino and a man known to him as "Joe Banana" began to kick and punch him in the face. He also added that another man with a rash on his nose took his time punching him in the body. After the beating, Weisphal heard his attackers say that they were going to get Al Sarno because he was an ex-Chicago police officer and that he would have a set of handcuffs. Weisphal was then placed in the trunk of his car and Messino and the boys drove around for an hour. The group returned to the Moon's shop and dragged him out of the trunk taking him back inside to re-start the beatings all over again. After the beating, he was once again placed in the trunk of his car and driven to Mr. Lucky's Restaurant located at 7747 West Belmont, in Elmwood Park. That establishment was operated by James Sarno Sr., the brother of Al Sarno. James Sarno, his son James Jr. and an Albert Alphonse all owned the lounge and were associates of Joe "Gags" Gagliano. Weisphal was taken to the basement of this restaurant and placed in a large meat locker. He was handcuffed to an overhead pipe, then beaten in relays by several young Italian goons. The beating was stopped when they realized that he was almost dead and they still wanted their money back. Weisphal was released but Messino kept his car, made the final payments on it, and obtained the title to the car for himself. Weisphal suffered head injuries, lost most of his teeth, had every rib broken, but managed to live.

After that experience, Joe Weisphal went to the Chicago police for help, William Messino, Joe Gagliano, Al Sarno, Richard "Chris" Cardi, Joe Lombardi, and Pasty DiConstanzo were arrested on December 9, 1963. All were released on $10,000 bond except for DiConstanzo who was released immediately and his charges were dropped. John DiFronzo was later identified as one of the assailants and was arrested and charged. They were all charged with conspiracy to commit aggravated assault, aggravated kidnapping, and aggravated battery, and their bond was changed to $25,000 each.

One of the people reportedly at the time worried about the arrest of Messino and Gagliano was mobster Maishie Baer. Baer was concerned because he believed he was going to possibly be involved in the investigation, exposing his "juice" operations.

At the first trial in March 1964, a mistrial was declared when it was learned that attempts were made to bribe one of the members of the jury.

In May 1964 a new trial began and all involved were found not guilty, acquitting all of the defendants in this matter.

Another incident report showed if a "juice" victim could not pay, it paved the way for these "juice" men to gain control of legitimate businesses. One victim of Messino's was John Esposito who owned the Cross-Country Acceptance Corporation. Esposito went on "juice" with Willie Messino and fell behind in his payments opening the door for Messino to gain control of a legitimate business. Messino had taken over the interest in the Roman Fiesta Snack Shop, which Esposito owned and operated, and used it to show legitimate earnings.

In 1969, The Chicago Crime Commission listed William Messino as the most dangerous gangster in the Chicago crime syndicate.

William Messino, known as "Wee Willie" and "William the Beast," was born on January 7, 1917, in Chicago. The nickname "Wee Willie" was given to him because he only stood between 5-foot-6 and 5-foot-7. It was said that William Messino was once a houseman and gardener, pulling weeds for mob boss Tony Accardo before he graduated to a vicious loan shark. However, someone who knew Messino back then claims he was no gardener but a bodyguard protecting his boss, ready to "kill at the drop of a hat." This informant also called him by the nickname of "Little Shrimp." In a 1965 Chicago Police alert, Messino was listed as one of the most powerful and dangerous gangsters in the Midwest.

His parents, Christ Messino and Bridget Serpico, lived at 1064 Polk Street with their six children; Biagio, Nancy, Julia, Josephine, William, and Christ Jr.

Wee Willie's older brother Biagio "Blessie" Messino, was born on April 4, 1915, and was considered a member of the old "Polk Street Gang." Blessie and William were surrounded by organized crime, making their membership an easy transition. Between 1918 and 1935, Polk Street contained many of the mob's up-and-comers. The Messino's next door neighbor was Gaetano Acci, known as "The Muscler" and "The Wolf." Acci was Polk Street's Italian Black-Hand member specializing in blackmail, extortion, and terrorism. On May 13, 1928, the bullet-ridden body of Acci was found on a roadside in Harvard, Illinois. He had been shot two times in the head and two times in the chest.

Down the street at 1005 West Polk Street was Carmen Castaldo, a hoodlum who was friends with Joseph "Diamond Joe" Esposito. Castaldo was arrested after leaving the funeral of Diamond Joe Esposito in 1928 when he, Cullo Nuggo and Frank Vaia, being intoxicated smashed their car into three parked cars.

On the other side at 1062 Polk Street lived Dominic Marzano. In October 1933 Marzano was arrested for the murder of gangster Gus Winkler. Across the street at 1065 Polk lived Philip Colonero, a gang member who was arrested for armed holdups in 1934. His neighbor at 1063 Polk named Joseph Clementi was a city laborer who killed hoodlums John Palumbo and Jack Prete in March 1927. A few houses down at 1070 Polk lived the Latone family. In 1924, a member of that family named Frank La Macchia was found in an alley riddled with bullet holes. Two houses down was 1074 Polk Street, the headquarters for the Polk Street Gang at the Modern Sanitary Barber Shop, run by the Briatta family. The Briatta brothers, including Lou the Barber, Joe, John, Frank, Ralph, Thomas, and Michael, became a staple on Polk Street being connected to the Chicago Mob. The house was actually owned by top mob boss Gus Alex, but the Briatta's occupied the house and later purchased it.

Across the Street at 1075 lived Paul Ascoli who was listed as a Chicago gang member. In 1935 Ascoli was arrested on rape charges. Next door at 1077 Polk lived Geatano and Marcella Esposito. Marcella, the widowed mother and Geatano, her brother-in-law raised Marcella's two sons and a daughter. The brothers, nicknamed Frankie X and Tony X, both became syndicate labor leaders controlling the street laborers unions in Chicago for over 40 years. Down the street at 1116 Polk Street lived John D'Arco who would go on to become the Chicago mob's man in politics and alderman of the old First Ward.

Next door at 1122 Polk Street lived many hoodlums. In 1913 Frankie "X" Esposito lived there before moving down the street. In 1931, a Thomas Messina was living at the address when he and three fellow 42 Gang members attempted to rob a drugstore on West 13th Street in Chicago. During the escape, a gun battle broke out between the armed robbers and policemen. Thomas Messina was shot and killed, collapsing in a passageway 100 feet from the drug store. The other three 42 Gang members were Sam Surdo, Pasty D'Angelo, and Bennie Maioni. In 1937, a James Payne was living at 1122 Polk when he was arrested as a bookmaker for the syndicate.

In 1928 Rocco "Rocky" Fanelli was living at 1110 Polk Street. Fanelli was the brother-in-law of gangster James Balcastro. Anthony Coduti was listed as living at 1110 Polk in 1932 when he was arrested for armed robbery; police identified him because he was shot in the hand during his escape. Living next door at 1106 Polk Street, was Charles Battaglia who was arrested in 1933 for election fraud.

Also listed as living at the Messino's house at 1064 Polk was a Michael Messino. It is not know what relation Michael was to William but he was a 42 Gang member and was arrested with Michael DeStefano in 1932. In the 1940's Sam DeStefano and his wife would move to 1062 Polk Street mainly so she could be protected while Sam was in prison.

William Messino had already been arrested twelve times when in May 1935 he, Joseph Ippolito, and Hugo Fabrizio were arrested when they forced the attendant at the Vernon Park Place garage to give them a deputy sheriff's automobile that was parked in the garage. The car belonged to their neighborhood friend, Deputy Sheriff Joseph Briatta. After they took the car, a police chase ensued. Messino and Ippolito were arrested and reportedly confessed to over fifty robberies. Eighteen days later, Willie Messino's father, Christ Messino Sr., was arrested with Leonard Tufo for trying to bribe a complaining witness who identified his son. The witness was Fred Brightly, an official of the Standard Galvanizing Company on Van Buren Street, who was robbed on the street on February 23 of that year by three gunmen. He identified William Messino and James Ippolito as two of the three who robbed him. After the alleged bribe, Brightly went to the police saying Christ Messino and Leonard Tufo offered to repay him the $81 he lost in the robbery if he would promise not to identify the prisoners when he took the witness stand at the robbery trial. The elder Messino also told Brightly that he had strong political influence and that he would be able to obtain any political favor for him. When Willie Messino was arrested he too boasted that he had political influence and declared that he would not be convicted and could "beat any rap." Fred Brightly told the press, "*I am going to follow this through to the end to learn whether political influence can keep holdup men and thugs on the street to the menace of decent citizens!*" Oddly enough, Leonard Tufo gave his address as 2827 Polk Street and said he was a family friend to the Messino's.

In connection with Tufo was an incident that occurred a month earlier when a west side gangster named Vito Messino was arrested for attempted kidnapping and extortion. On February 7, 1935, Vito Messino and gangster Tony Pinna tried to kidnap Louis Kaplan, owner of the Kaplan Nash-La-Fayette automobile agency on Ogden Avenue. Messino walked into the auto showroom and dragged Kaplan out the door to a waiting get-away car driven by Pinna. Kaplan was screaming for help as he wrestled with Vito Messino. A constable Edward Dews came out of the back room with a pistol in his hand and shot Messino in the arm and leg. Messino made his escape running down Ogden Avenue, while Dews pointed his gun at Pinna sitting behind the steering wheel of the get away car and shot him in the head, killing him instantly. Messino was later arrested at Mount Sinai Hospital where he was being treated for his gunshot wounds. Kaplan said that Pinna and Messino had kidnapped him in 1930 and let him go when he paid them $500. This time they were there to kidnap him for $10,000. Vito Messino said he lived at 2837 Polk Street, the same house as Tufo.

At the April 1935 trial of Willie Messino and James Ippolito, both were found guilty and given one year to life in prison for the robberies. In 1940 both came up for parole and soon after were released.

In 1941 Wee Willie was arrested for intentionally driving his car over the legs of a fallen man, breaking both legs. He was acquitted of that charge. Thrughtout the 1940's, Messino was arrested and questioned in almost every mob murder in Chicago.

In May 1946, millionaire policy game operator Edward Jones was kidnapped and held for $100,000 ransom. The ransom drop was made and Jones was released the next day. Nine known kidnappers were arrested and questioned about the kidnapping. Among the nine arrested was William Messino, listed as working as a clerk, and Jacob "Polly

Nose" Eisen. Both were questioned and all nine were released on habeas corpus writs.

In April 1953, the Chicago Police raided a bookmaking operation at the building at 3655 Chicago Avenue. The four men running the operation and arrested were Patrick Cerone, brother of Jackie Cerone, Mario Lupo, Ralph Basso, and William Messino. However, the charges were dismissed by Judge Alfonse Wells who ruled that the police lacked a warrant when making the arrests.

In April 1958, Willie Messino turned himself in when he found out the police were looking for him. He was wanted for questioning in the smashing of 23 plate glass windows at the City Auto Sales Company showroom at 2255 Michigan Avenue. The incident caused $18,000 in damage. The owner, Michael Gersh, told the police two men with 2-by-4 inch timbers had smashed his windows. Gersh told police that before the vandalism, Willie Messino had demanded two new automobiles and $100 a month to maintain the cars for him. Gersh also added that he was good friends with Willie's father, Christ Messino, then living at 5263 Jackson Blvd. When Christ was brought in for questioning he told police that his son Willie had been working as a union business agent but refused to name which union. Willie Messino was charged with attempting to extort by threat.

Two weeks before the trial, Michael Gersh was subpoenaed to appear at the trial. The next day, Gersh received a phone call from a man saying, *"Lay off the case or you'll be found dead in an alley."* Frightened, Gersh went to the police for protection while police searched once again for Messino to see if he could shed some light on who made the call. At the trial, Gersh testified that Messino told him he would *"get a lot of protection"* for the two cars and the $100 a month to maintain them. He also added that Messino said *"If you don't, I'll break your legs and you'll be coming to work in a wheel chair."*

Messino took the stand and said that he steered customers to Gersh's auto dealership and that he was owed commission money. He denied making any threats against anyone. The jury deliberated for 6 minutes before returning a verdict of "not guilty." All charges were dropped and veteran court observers believe it was a record for brevity.

Willie Messino's older brother, Biagio "Blessie" Messino, became close with the Esposito family from Polk Street and was referred to, on occasion, as "the right-hand man of Frankie X." His official job with the city of Chicago started out as a foreman which led him to becoming Assistant Superintendent of Street Paving. In December 1956, Blessie was involved in a bribe when a lieutenant of the park district police was shaking down construction companies. Messino was the middle-man in the bribe between the J.M. Corbett Construction Company and Chicago Police officer Robert Hoffman. At the trial the police tried to serve a subpoena for Messino to testify but he could not be found. Blessie Messino died in January 1996.

The 1960's were a step up for "Wee Willie" as his stature in the Chicago mob changed from hood to enforcer. He would make his headquarters at the old Starlite Club in Elmwood Park, Illinois. There he would run his "juice" operations in the company of George Bravos and Joe Lombardi.

Police informant Jack "Hot Dog" Wilensky once talked about the time he had to go out and collect a "juice" loan for a Johnny "Bananas" Di Fronzo who was a member under William "Wee Willie" Messino's group.

In January 1964, Chicago detectives received word that William Messino was marked for death by his mob bosses unless he came up with lost money owed to the mob. He made good on the demand but was warned not to screw up again, or else.

After being acquitted for kidnapping and beating Joseph Weisphal in May 1964, Willie Messino hired a minor hoodlum named John Johnson to set fire to Richard's Lilac Lodge in Hillside. Once again, Messino would walk when Johnson could not support his assertion.

In August 1965, the Illinois Crime Investigating Commission went to arrest William Messino, George Bravos, Joseph Lombardi, Alice Erwin, Sander Caravello, and Sam Mercurio on charges of aggravated kidnapping, aggravated battery, and the Federal usury law. George Bravos and his brother Nick Bravos had been supplying "juice" money to Messino and the Joe Gagliano crew to put out on the streets.

Three businessmen named Jack Chiagouris, George Chiagouris, and Albert Chiagouris took out a $165,000 "juice" loan from the men agreeing to pay 20 percent interest a week. The Chiagouris operated two companies at 127 N. Dearborn Street, George P. Chiagouris & Co., and Chiagouris Builders Company. When they fell behind and couldn't come up with the money, Jack and George Chiagouris were kidnapped from a restaurant on Harlem Avenue, taken to the basement of Messino's home at 2037 N. 77th Avenue in Elmwood Park, beaten and tortured for 15 hours, suffering a broken jaw, knocked out teeth and broken ribs. The brothers were also taken to the apartment of Messino's alleged girlfriend, Alice Erwin. She was charged with conspiracy to commit aggravated assault. According to reports, after the Chiagouris were tortured, they were taken to their brother Albert who was forced to sign over a $200,000 trust agreement to Messino. This, the brothers charged, was security for the remaining balance on the "juice" loan. The brothers also added that they had paid the mobsters back $164,000 but still owed them $124,000 on the "juice" loan. The gangsters operated with extreme caution, and on the day before the payment was due, the victim would be telephoned and told the place for delivery of the money, each time a different location. The brothers went to mob ball-breaker Charles Siragusa, who was the executive director of the Crime Commission at the time, for help.

Bravos, Caravello, Lombardi, and Mercurio were arrested without incident. As for Willie Messino, he would not go down without a fight. Messino was walking down Harlem Avenue with Vito LaPorte, but when he noticed the police walk out of a store, Messino turned and ran the opposite way; a three-block chase ensued through streets, alleys, and back yards. Seeing that Messino was getting away, the officers opened fire, trying at any cost to stop him, but Messino gave them the slip. It was originally believed that Messino was wounded from the volley of gunshots and bouncing bullets.

A week later, Messino, accompanied by his lawyer Harry Busch, turned himself in. Underworld rumors that reached the newspapers said that Messino had been killed during the escape incident. When reporters asked him about the rumors, he laughed and told them *"I was just hiding, nobody's trying to get me."* Messino added that he ran from the agents because they appeared "menacing" as they approached him, and he thought at first they were relatives of his "juice" victims. He also added that he scaled nine backyard fences escaping, cutting his hand on one of them. Messino was released on $10,000 bail awaiting his trial.

In January 1967, Willie Messino, Joseph Lombardi, and George Bravos were convicted on one count of conspiracy, which brought a sentence of 6 months in prison; two counts of aggravated kidnapping for which Messino was sentenced to 10 to 30 years on each count; and two counts of aggravated battery, which landed Messino two 5-to-10 year sentence in prison. Sam Mercurio was found guilty on one count of conspiracy but was acquitted on two counts of aggravated kidnapping. Sandor Caravello was found not guilty due to lack of evidence.

While the trial was underway, information surfaced that Willie Messino's first wife was divorcing him and Willie had moved into an apartment at 426 Wesley, Oak Park, Illinois. Another problem was that Willie's girlfriend, Alice Irwin, was hiding out in fear that she would be subpoenaed to testify in the kidnapping, assault and extortion case. Because of this case, mob boss Gus Alex was reported to be particularly upset with Messino because Alex felt that Messino's problems had been brought about by his "stupid" actions. This was confirmed when the FBI brought in an informant regarding the Messino situation. The informant said that Gus Alex and his associates in organized crime felt that Messino "had it coming to him" and that they had no right in taking action, including violence against the victims of their extortion. Alex felt that had Messino asked whether he could take the extreme measures against his victims, which he did, he would certainly have been advised by his superiors in organized crime that he could not. Alex indicated that Messino had cost the mob a great deal of money in the past in connection with trials in which he was involved and was exceedingly upset with Messino as a result of his stupidity in causing his prosecutions. Gus Alex did not feel that he would take any action whatsoever on behalf of Messino in attempting to receive favorable consideration on appeal. Even though Alex sent word out that Messino was on his own, information was uncovered that allegedly five of the jurors in Messino's case were union members belonging to a Chicago labor union and had been approached by their union leaders, who were under the influence of the mob, to vote in favor of Messino. However, it turned out that it was not enough.

While waiting, the FBI observed Messino going in and out of the old Mary Ann's Pancake Restaurant at 3756 West Chicago Avenue during 1969. There he would meet with George Bravos, Joe "Gags" Gagliano and Chris Cardi.

On February 24, 1970, Willie Messino phoned the Elmwood Park police department and told the police chief that he "wanted to give himself up" since his appeal bond was revoked. Messino, George Bravos and Joe Lombardi arrived at the police station and the State's Attorney's Police were called. From there the three were sent to Joliet Prison to serve their prison sentences. Once in prison, Messino was put to work as a janitor for 60 days until he was placed in a program to learn how to become a barber. Charles Siragusa, then Director of the Illinois Crime Investigation's Commission said, *"I doubt that Willie will ever work at the barber trade, he's worth at least a million dollars and he never has earned an honest living in his life."*

But Willie Messino ran into problems at Joliet Prison. In the good old days he would walk down Chicago and Harlem Avenues as a big-shot

William Messino

File Card
William Messino
AKA: "Wee Willie" "Willie the Beast" Willie
Messina
Born: January 7, 1917 (Chicago)
Died: November 5, 2002

Known Addresses
1064 Polk Street, Chicago (1935)
426 Wesley, Oak Park (1967)
2037 N. 77th Avenue, Elmwood Park (1970)
1714 N. 77th Street, Elmwood Park (1980's)

Known Hangouts
Chicago and Hamlin Avenues (Chicago)
Mayfield and North Avenues (Chicago)
Nagle and North Avenues (Chicago)
Central and Diversey Avenues (Chicago)
Altgeld Street and Harlem Avenue (Elmwood Park)
Greenfield and Mannheim Roads (Franklin Park)
Ruby Street and Grand Avenue (Franklin Park)
19th Avenue and Rice Street (Melrose Park)
Des Plaines Avenue and Roosevelt Road (Forest Park)
Gene's Deli 2202 North Harlem Avenue (Elmwood Park)

mob guy and when he arrived in Statesville, no one cared who he was. In 1970, Willie Messino was attacked by a fellow inmate who punched him in the head. Stunned, but not hurt, Willie was at a loss as to why he was being treated that way by the African-American "Black Panthers" gang. Because of this incident, Messino requested to be transferred out of Statesville.

After almost 10 years in federal prison Messino was released due to poor health. He was suffering from a heart condition and had been hospitalized with infectious pneumonia. William Messino was a different man who stepped back into a different outfit. He had spent the last 2 years of his sentence at the minimum security institution at Dwight, Illinois. He was rewarded by mob bosses for keeping his mouth shut and serving his time and became an advisor for west side mob boss Marco D'Amico.

Around 1997, he was listed as an area boss under then Elmwood Park mob boss Joe Andriacchi. In May 1999, Messino was reported at an alleged meeting of mobsters at Armand's Italian Restaurant in Elmwood Park concerning construction and operation contracts for a casino in Rosemont, Illinois. Other alleged mobsters at the meeting were Joey "The Clown" Lombardo, Peter DiFronzo, John "No Nose" DiFronzo, Rudy Fratto, Rick Rissoulo and Joe "The Builder" Andriacchi.

On November 5, 2002, William Messino died in his Elmwood Park home from cancer. His daughter Bridget said that in the last years of his life Messino drove his grandsons to school every day and attended their Little League baseball games. He spent time with his two sons, Chris and William Jr., and his second wife, Victoria E. Terpening-Messino.

Joseph Lombardo Sr.

Known as Joey "The Clown" Lombardo and Joe Padula, he was alleged to be one of the top mob bosses in Chicago as of 2006. In 1970, he was named as being allegedly connected with the Chicago "juice" rackets. The corners alleged to be Lombardo's were Chicago and Kedzie Avenues, and Lumber and 18th Streets in Chicago.

At the time of the report, he was said to be connected with the International Fiber Glass Corporation in Elk Grove, Illinois. His arrest

record is said to go back to 1954 and allegedly contained arrests for burglary and loitering. He was acquitted in 1963 of kidnapping charges.

In 2005, Joey Lombardo was charged in mob indictments as part of the Operation Family Secrets federal investigation with 13 other Chicago mobsters. The investigation was tied to 18 unsolved mob murders. When the authorities went to arrest Lombardo, he was gone. After nine months of being on the lam, Lombardo was caught in an alley in Elmwood Park, Illinois. He had been staying with an old friend named Dominic Calarco. Lombardo told his friend that there was one more thing he had to do before he turned himself in, that was go to the dentist to have his tooth fixed. The dentist was Pat Spilotro, brother of mobster Tony Spilotro. Pat Spilotro had gone to Lombardo in the 1980's to find out who had killed his brothers and why. Lombardo could not help him and told Spilotro to let it go. In 2005, Pat Spilotro fixed Lombardo's tooth, and then called the feds to tell them where Lombardo was hiding. At the time of his arrest, Lombardo was sporting a beard that resembled the kind of beard that Iraqi Dictator, Saddam Hussein, had grown to hide his identity.

Albert Sarno

Albert A. Sarno was born around 1935 and lived at 2034 77th Avenue in Elmwood Park. He was arrested in 1962 for theft in interstate shipment and in 1963 for aggravated kidnapping. In 1969 he was convicted on contempt charges based on refusal to answer after  being granted immunity in juice investigations. He received 6 months.

The area Sarno was alleged to be active in was Mayfield and North Avenues, Central and Diversey Avenues, Barry and Central Avenues all in Chicago, Bonnie Brea Street and North Avenue in River Grove, and 73rd and Grand Avenue in Elmwood Park.

Rocco Rotuna Aka Rocky Joyce

Rocco Rotuna was commonly known as Roc Rotunno and Rocky Joyce living at 2149 N. Superior Street in Chicago with his wife Mance Rotuno. Known as a "juice" man under Joseph Gagliano in the 1950's and 60's, Rotuna got his start as a prize fighter in the 1920's under his fighter name of Rocky Joyce. During his boxing career, he was placed in the Auto Wreckers' union as an agent under the control of gangster Murray

Humphreys. Under Humphreys, he and his gang would specialize in trailing wealthy couples from night clubs and robbing them.

In January 1929, Rotuna was arrested as a suspect in a stick-up robbery; that arrest led police to discover that he was one of the robbers that robbed the First National Bank in October 1928. He was found guilty of participating in a robbery of a café in which one person was killed and six others were wounded. He was also convicted of stealing $66,000 in jewels from a Dr. Frank Pierce.

On January 29, 1929, Rotuna entered Joilet prison for robbery. His prison record says his parents were born in Italy, he left home at the age of 15, born around 1905 in Illinois, left school after the 8th grade, and was working as a motorman when arrested. During his prison stay he was punished for getting into two fights with inmates Naples and Gavin, was talking in the dinning room, knocked a package of yeast out of the hand of one of the officers, refused to be searched and ran away from the officer. Rocky Rotuna was paroled on June 10, 1942.

Also arrested with Rotuna during the robbery and served time with him in Joliet were Arthur Schaeffer and Edward Cummings. Schaeffer was of German decent but Jewish religion and worked as an office clerk living with his mother Jennie Schaeffer at 1138 N. Monticello Avenue in Chicago when he was arrested. During his prison stay he was disaplined 7 times for neglecting his work, talking in line, being away from his work station without permission, being in the dinning room when it was being checked and being forced back to his cell by gun point and sleeping late and not going to breakfast. He was paroled on December 4, 1942. Edward Cummings, aka Ed Davis, was born around 1902 in Chicago and was of Irish decent. When arrested he was listed as a furnace repairman living at 3238 MayPolk Avenue in Chicago. During his incarseration he was punished over 9 times for fighting, talking back to the officers, throwing his meat at dinner, wearing another inmates pants, taking his cloths to the laundry to be washed, not working, having razor blades, and refusing to get off the grass outside after being told to do so. Cummings was paroled on June 10, 1943.

Chris Joseph Cardi

Born Chris Joseph Cardi around 1933, he used the alias of Richard Cardi. Listed as a nephew of William Messino, Chris Cardi lived at 5241 West Jackson Boulevard and 2025 N. 77th Court in Elmwood Park. He became a member of the Chicago Police Department on October 1, 1957, and resigned on May 17, 1962.

Chris Cardi's height 5'10" and his weight of 225 lbs made him a perfect muscleman and "juice" collector for the mob. He could usually be found around Hamlin and Chicago Avenue or Chestnut and State Street in Chicago; Clinton Place and North Avenue or Thatcher and North Avenue in River Forest.

After his arrest for aggravated kidnapping with Messino in 1963, the Chicago police went to Cardi's home and convinced his wife Renee to turn over all of Cardi's "juice" records to them for safe-keeping. The blunder angered mob bosses, first for turning over the records to the police and second for even keeping records. Some of the mobsters names listed in the records were Sam DeStefano, Joe Gagliano, William Messino and Louis Briatta. The records would help convict several hoodlums.

Cardi was convicted in 1969 for contempt after having been granted immunity to testify but refused. He was sentenced to 6 months in prison. Once out, he reached out to his mob buddies to become involved in the narcotics racket and borrowed $100,000 on a "juice" loan. A few weeks later in October 1971, he was arrested for selling heroin and sentenced to 10 years in prison.

After serving only 3 1/2 years at Terre Haute Prison, he was released on parole. In July 1975, three weeks after his release from prison, two men with ski masks over their heads and black gloves on walked into the Snack Stand at 1620 N. River Road in Melrose Park, which was owned by his wife Renee, shortly after midnight. One stood at the door while the other walked up to Cardi and pointed a gun to his head. Cardi began to run and fell to the floor right in front of the hoodlum standing at the door. The gunman raised his .45-caliber automatic and the two fired 12 shots into the back of Chris Cardi, killing him. The two men walked out of the store while Renee and their two children, Chris Jr. and Christine, dropped to the floor in horror.

Among theories as to why Chris Cardi was killed was the 1963 blunder involving his wife and the "juice" records. Detectives believed the reason Cardi was killed in front of his wife was her punishment for turning the records over to the police. Two other theories were that he got arrested with drugs and was unable to make any payments on his $100,000 "juice" loan, or that mob bosses feared he either had or was going to rat-out his mob buddies.

Joseph J. Lombardi

Sometimes confused with alleged mobster Joseph "Joey the Clown" Lombardo, Joe "Pretty Boy" Lombardi was known as one of the mob's playboy "juice" men in Chicago in the 1950's and 60's. "Pretty Boy" Lombardi was born around 1936 and lived at 621 S. 22nd Avenue in Bellwood, Illinois and was part of the Melrose Park group.

The "click" which Lombardi allegedly ran with included more of the Joey Aiuppa group and the Messino group. He was a very close friend and often in the company of mobster Gerald Carusiello. He was a staple at the mob's Casa Madrid in Melrose Park in the 1960's, and was known to "take out" the younger up and coming mobsters and hoodlums on jobs with him to see if they could pull them off.

When he was arrested in 1963, the newspapers mistakenly listed him as living at 2210 West Ohio Street, which was then the address of Joey "The Clown" Lombardo.

If you needed "juice" from Lombardi, you were either sent to Mannheim Road and Fullerton Avenue in Franklin Park, or Higgins Road and Mannheim Road in Rosemont, or 77th and Belmont Avenues in Elmwood Park for the loan.

In 1967, he was sentenced to 7 to 20 years at Joliet Prison for threatening to kill a "juice" victim. Lombardi spent his prison days as a Statesville maintenance man.

In June 1993, a grand jury indictment for extortion was filed in federal court alleging seven mobsters with running a mob money-lending business. The indictment said that the men running this business treated their customers the same way electric and gas companies treat the people who do not pay their bills--their service is cut off. How did that translate into the mob's versions. You didn't pay your "juice" loan on time, your "breath" would be turned off. One of the examples in the indictment was a borrower who could not repay his $7,100 in loans at a rate of 260 % a year. The seven men charged in this case were Michael Castaldo and Robert Ruscitti of Melrose Park, Salvatore Cataudella, Michael Sarno, John Rainone, John Spizzirri and a Joseph Lombardi living at 7508 S. Octavia Avenue, Bridgeview.

Fioravante Buccieri
a.k.a. Fiore Buccieri, and "Fifi" And the Buccieri Group

Fiore Buccieri was a Chicago-born Italian hoodlum who grew up in a west side Italian neighborhood which has spawned most of the top hoodlums in the Chicago area. Buccieri was a lieutenant or "Capo" of Sam "Mooney" Giancana in the 1960's and was reported to make the arrangements for most of the Chicago area gangland murders ordered by Giancana. Confidential sources related that Buccieri had participated in a number of these slayings in the past. In fact, informants report that Buccieri's wife was widowed in 1954 when her first husband was murdered, reportedly by Buccieri or his then lieutenant Joseph Ferriola. Buccieri used to reside at 3004 South Maple, Berwyn, Illinois, and also had a summer home at Block 14, Birchers Sub Division, Maple Lane Road, Dock #690 in Lake Geneva, Wisconsin. At this property, Buccieri maintained a large shooting gallery and target range so other Chicago hoodlums could practice for further utilization of their shooting accuracy.

Fiore "Fifi" Bucciei was born on December 6, 1907, in Chicago and would move up the crime ladder to control the old 25th Ward and parts of the old First Ward and 27th Ward of Chicago. His arrest record dates back to 1925 when he was a labor goon for the Embalmers Union. His arrests were for murder, burglary, receiving stolen property, carrying a concealed weapon, larceny, disorderly conduct, a suspect in three bombings, gambling, and a conviction of bribery. In 1961 a mob informer told the FBI that Fiore Buccieri was responsible for the killing of John Hennigan in October of that year.

In February 1962, Fifi Buccieri and Joe "Spa" Spadavecchio were listed as partners in the "juice" rackets in Chicago. Buccieri was the owner of Angel-Kaplan Sports Service, which was one of the nation's largest sports handicapping services. This company was operated by Don Angellino who was known as Don Angel.

On October 25, 1963, a confidential source advised that Buccieri was recognized as the kingpin in the loan shark racket for the city of Chicago. This source stated Buccieri supervised, for juice loan purposes, the territory south of Devon Avenue, west of the Loop and south of Van Buren Street. A list of the sections he controlled as of 1970 were Milwaukee Avenue and

Ohio Street, Harlem and Stanley Avenues, Ellen Street and Milwaukee Avenue in Chicago, Roosevelt Road and Cicero Avenue in Cicero, County 12 and Route 134 in Fox Lake, and County Line Road and 91st Street in Hinsdale. In connection with the "juice" loan racket, Fiore "Fifi" Buccieri and Joe Ferriola were both directly connected to Hacking Brothers Loan service. Another confidential source advised that the Buccieri organization had all the juice loan operations in Cicero, Illinois.

In the file cabinets of the Intelligence Section of the Chicago PD lies a case entitled the "Indian Case." This case is based on an individual known as Jack "Hot Dog" Wilensky with the alias of Jack Wilens. Wilensky lived at 9310 North Keystone Avenue in Skokie, Illinois and owned a junk business at Lawrence and Kedzie Avenues. On the side he was a juice collector on juice himself. In June 1964, Wilensky received word from his underground buddies that his life was in danger due to his delinquency in payments on his "juice" loans. Police officers of the Intelligence Division were assigned to guard him until he left Chicago and headed to Los Angeles, California, to stay with his family, fearing they, too, would be in danger.

On August 11, 1964, the Los Angeles Police Department contacted the Chicago PD informing them that Wilensky, known to them as Jack Wilens, was hiding in Los Angeles and had contacted the LAPD for protection. Wilensky received word from his aunt who lived in Skokie, Illinois, that mobster Steve Annoreno passed word to one Solly Lieb, a Skokie bookie at the time, that *they didn't want to kill the kid (Wilensky) but just cut off an arm or leg; it did others more good.*" It was learned that Wilensky worked for the FBI and the Intelligence Division as an informant and at the same time was forced to work for the Buccieri group as a collector of juice. Police learned that Wilensky went to a man known as "Murphy" and borrowed several hundred dollars from him on "juice." This "Murphy" was a partner of Morris Saletko, known as Maishie Baer. Around 1962, Frank Buccieri informed this "Murphy" that he and the Buccieri mob were taking over his and all the juice rackets in Chicago. Buccieri told this "Murphy" that he was to collect all of his outstanding accounts and pay Buccieri the amount collected. This "Murphy" did as he was told and paid Buccieri $40,000; in thanks, his head was blown off. Right after "Murphy's" death, Wilensky was called to Cicero by the Buccieri group and told he still owed $1,000 of "juice" on the old "Murphy" account. Wilensky insisted he paid off his "juice" to "Murphy" and didn't owe any money. The Buccieri group didn't accept his word and threatened Wilensky and his family to pay up or else. A frightened Wilensky made a deal with the Buccieri group and agreed to become a "juice" collector and was assigned to collect on all the remaining "juice" accounts under "Murphy's" old operation. Sometime later a syndicate contract was placed on the life of Wilensky, but the contract could not be executed because Wilensky went under heavy police guard.

Wilensky gave the police a run-down of what he knew of the Buccieri group. He said that Fifi Buccieri and his brother Frank Buccieri were the big bosses of the "juice" mob which they took over after getting rid of "Murphy" around 1962. From the moment the Buccieri brothers took over, the number of killings and beatings increased 100 percent. Angelo LaPeitra was Fifi's right-hand man and acted as a juice racket lieutenant. Steve Annoreno acted as a top enforcer in this group and was described as a manager working under the direction of Fifi and LaPeitra. Annoreno was high in the ranks of the juice rackets and disposed of stolen property for the mob, handled narcotics and was also engaged in legitimate businesses. Wilensky said that there was a high level "juice" man in Annoreno's position by the name of Al Milstein, but Milstein was not strong enough to enforce the rules. Milstein operated a strip joint for some other syndicate big shots while his son Sidney Milstein was a bondsman. Wilensky said he met Steve Annoreno when Annoreno approached him to collect a juice loan that he had with Al Milstein. One time Wilensky said he was talking to Maish Baer and he, Baer, warned him that if Annoreno ever questioned him about loans he should not tell him of any he made.

Another "juice" man by the name of Angelo Buccieri worked around the old Commonwealth Hotel in Chicago. In 1963 a man by the name of John Saccaneno ran the old Bel Air coffee shop on Diversey Parkway in Chicago and approached Angelo Buccieri for a loan of $600. Saccaneno did borrow the money and agreed to pay $60 a week for the "juice" loan. The next day another "juice" man named Irving Dworett walked into the coffee shop and offered Saccaneno $800 in the form of a "juice" loan, he took it and agreed to pay $80 a month. Dworett was listed as a small time "juice" man working out of the Pine Grove Apartment Hotel at 2828 North Pine Grove Road. After Saccaneno paid thousands of dollars in interest, he had yet to reduce the principals on his loans. Unable to pay, Saccaneno filed for bankruptcy and was able to return to operating his coffee shop under the bankruptcy proceedings whereby all of his business was recorded and handled by the bankruptcy court until his legitimate debts were paid off. Saccaneno was threatened by both Dworett and Buccieri, upon thier learning of the bankruptcy, to make his regular juice loan payments, but Saccaneno refused, advising them that under bankruptcy regulations he could not take money out of the business to pay them without receipts. They continued to intimidate him; Dworett visiting the coffee shop in person to threaten him with death and Buccieri sending two of his goons named Larry and Joe to threaten him. Saccaneno was forced to advise the police of this matter. Saccaneno's attorney contacted Dworett and informed him that he could not obtain any more money from Saccaneno. Dworett became extremely angry and said that he was not interested in any bankruptcy proceedings. Later that day, Dworett went to the coffee shop and confronted Saccaneno, telling him he had better come up with the money or he would be asking for an "undertaker." It is not known what became of the situation.

In 1967, Fifi Buccieri made his move to become top mob boss of Chicago, but couldn't pull the trigger because he was diagnosed with cancer. In 1970 a theft indictment was filed against him for leading a theft ring that specialized in stealing heavy construction equipment, but he was so sick that the government never followed through on it. He was found dead in his Berwyn home on August 17, 1973.

Buccieri's interests in the juice racket were watched over by his first lieutenant James "Turk" Torello.

James Torello

James Vincent Torello, known to all as "Turk" Torello, an ex-convict and well known former burglar, controlled loan sharking on the West side of Chicago.

File Card
James Vincent Torello
AKA: Turk
Born: December 15, 1930
Died: April 16, 1979

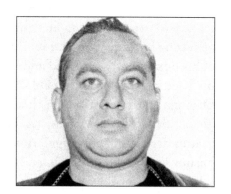

Known Addresses
919 South Marshfield Avenue (1930)
1133 S. Mason Street, Chicago (1940's)
1645 N. Halsted, Chicago (1945)
2727 S. Austin Blvd, Chicago (1950's)
5220 W. Kinzie, Chicago (1950's)
8400 W. Lawrence, Chicago (1950's)
1448 W. Filmore, Chicago (1950's)
2623 Ridgeland, Berwyn (1960's)
1601 South 58th Street, Cicero (1963)
1836 South 60th Court, Cicero (1969)

Vicinities Frequented
Monroe and Bishop Streets in Chicago
Harlem and Stanley Avenues in Berwyn
Cermak Road and 49th Avenues in Cicero
Roosevelt Road and Austin Boulevard in Cicero
91st Street and Countyline Road in Hinsdale

Known Arrest Record
1943	Theft of Auto (Oak Park)
9-18-1945	Auto Theft (Juv Del) (Missouri)
2-28-1945	Fug-Dyer Act (St. Louis)
5-22-1952	Theft from Interstate Shipment (Chicago)
5-27-1952	General Purposes
5-28-1952	Robbery
3-26-1953	Violation FFA & NFA (Louisville, KY)
6-11-1953	Dyer Act and unregistered firearms
6-15-1953	Possession of Burglary Tools (Belleville)
5-22-1952	Violation of Sec. 659 T 18 (Chicago)
11-1-1953	Motor Veh, Theft Act & Nat Firearms

12-19-1953	Transfer to Leavenworth Prison
4-28-1956	Possession of Burglary Tools (Chicago)
2-28-1958	Investigation
5-12-1958	Investigation (Kankakee, Illinois)
7-23-1961	A & B
6-21-1962	Traffic Warrants

Torello's job was to watch over two groups of collectors, one headed by Angelo LaPietra and the other by Angelo "Mustache Angie" Severino.

Angelo "Mustache Angie" Severino was known to have the following collectors working for him; Joe Rossi, Frank "Calico Kid" Tuetonico, Tony Monaco, Angelo Petitti, aka "Little Angie," Anthony Ozzanto, and Freddy Raporto. This group formerly used the 1501 Club at 1501 49th Avenue, Cicero, as its headquarters. In the summer of 1964, they moved their headquarters to the Sportsman's Billiard Parlor at 5142 West 25th Street, Cicero. The last location listed in this report was located on the southwest corner of Roosevelt Road and Blue Island Avenue, Chicago.

This group was considered a smaller group putting out "juice" in the Cicero area. An informant told the FBI that the group was not considered to be "outfit" or syndicate connected, but the individuals were all lifelong associates of Angelo LaPietra and were permitted to operate on a small scale. The group was made up of thieves and highjackers and would make small loans, referring all of their larger "juice" loans to Angelo LaPietra. According to the informant, Joe Rossi, Freddy Raporto, and Angelo Petiti operated as if under the cloak of being syndicate but in fact were not the syndicate but merely sanctioned by LaPietra. In this manner, they were able to flourish under the reputation of LaPietra. This group, as well as the LaPietra group, put out "juice" loans on the basis of 10 percent a week.

Angelo J. LaPietra

Angelo "The Hook" LaPietra was born on October 30, 1920, in Chicago. He lived with his wife Mildred and his two kids Joann and Angelo Jr. in the building at 5303 West 30th Place in Cicero, Illinois, and at 250 W. 39th Street in Chicago. It was said that he gained the nick name of "The Hook" after he hooked a one-time Chicago alderman into a syndicate crap game. Other known names used by LaPietra were Joe Milo, Angelo Petro, and Angelo LaPitia. In his life, he would go from small-time hood to top boss of the old First Ward, Loop District, Berwyn, Chinatown, Cicero, and king of the infamous "26th Street Crew."

In 1938, LaPietra was convicted of a crime and sentenced to 30 days in the House of Corrections. In 1953, he was listed as living at 518 W. 37th Street and working as a bartender at the Red Wagon Lounge at 2134 Michigan Avenue. LaPietra, Joseph Iorio, and Angelo's brother, James LaPietra, were arrested in a raid of the lounge. The raid occurred because days earlier Angelo LaPietra was charged with punching a federal narcotics agent who was conducting an investigation inside the lounge. When arrested, Angelo had a revolver on him. Other arrests listed were for murder, narcotics, and kidnapping.

Another place run by Angelo LaPietra was located at 14th Street near 50th and Cicero. In conection with this place, three stories were told of "juice" victims and other "juice" men. An informant stated that someone known as Andy runs "juice" at 53rd and Cicero where interstate truck drivers stay overnight for Angelo LaPietra. Some of the "juice" payments for Andy used to be dropped off at the Stop Light Tavern which was located at 12th and Cicero. Another "juice" man working under LaPietra was known as "Cadillac Joe" who ran a crap game at 127th Street in Alsip, Illinois. Cadillac Joe controlled all the "juice" at this game.

Some stories concerning Angelo LaPietra listed a victim on "juice" to LaPietra named Chris Mendalis. Mendalis, also known as Chris Dallis, worked as a cab driver who used to hang out at the Stop Light Tavern. The story was that every time Mendalis would show up and bet, the syndicate hoodlums present would hope he would lose his money and have to go on "juice." They were hoping that once on "juice" Mendalis would fall behind on his payments so they could take great pleasure in beating him continuously. Their wish came true one night when Mendalis went on to "juice." Unfortunately, Mendalis became lucky in the Barbout game and was able to pay off his "juice" loan.

Another individual on "juice" was a guy known as "Fat Gus" who weighed around 300 pounds. "Fat Gus" made his living as a trucking dispatcher. "Fat Gus" was a regular at the Stop Light Tavern where he went onto "juice" with LaPietra and was always late on his payments. He received many beatings by the LaPietra group and it was not known if he ever paid his debt off.

In 1977, the mob's stolen auto racket and "chop shop" operations were stripped from mobster James "Jimmy the Bomber" Catuara and handed to Angelo LaPeitra. The racket was pulling in $40 to $50 million a year in Chicago and $1.5 billion a year nationwide. Catuara didn't hand over the racket easily; he was kidnapped, thrown into the trunk of a car, and held prisoner for 3 days before he agreed to step aside and hand it over to LaPietra.

In 1986, Angelo LaPietra was sentenced to 16 years in prison for his role in the skimming of $2 million in untaxed gambling profits from a Las Vegas casino. Two years later, he had some trouble in prison when his associates were smuggling some of his favorite Italian foods in a scene right out of the movie "Good Fellas." He was transferred from a minimum-security prison in Connecticut to a federal prison in Petersburg, Virginia.

Angelo LaPietra died on March 28, 1999, at Rush-Presbyterian Hospital of natural causes. His wake was held at the Blake-Lamb Bridgeport Funeral Home and he is buried at Queen of Heaven Cemetery in Hillside, Illinois.

LaPietra had the following juice collectors and other mobsters listed under his control:

James LaPietra

Steve Annoreno

Carlo Morrelli

Alfred Milstein

Louis DiRiggi

Frank "Blackie" Morelli

Angelo Annoreno

Joe LaMantia

Joe Wing	Carmen Bastone
Sal Bastone	Sam Bills
Wayne Bock	Mike Gurgone
Gino Martin	John Monteleone
August Monteleone	

This group, prior to June 1963, used the S.A.C. Club at 4755 West Roosevelt Road, Cicero, as its headquarters. In June 1963, they moved to the S.A.C. Club at 4907 West 14th Street, Cicero. Other areas of operation listed as under the control of LaPietra in 1970 were Cermak Road and Cicero Avenue and 18th Street and Cicero Avenue in Cicero.

During April of 1964, Sam DeStefano's "juice" collector named Vito Zaccagnini became a rat and spilled what information he knew about the "juice" loan rackets in the early 1960's. During the interview with the FBI, it stated:

"Vito Zaccagnini advised that there were at least two distinct groups operating juice rackets in the city of Cicero, Illinois. The largest and main group was under the management of Angelo LaPietra, also known as "Moustache Angie" and "Nutcracker." Zaccagnini explained that he knew this group as: James "Turk" Torello, Johnny Figuarata, Tony DiRiggi, Blackie Morelli, and a man known as "Salaam."

Zaccagnini explained that approximately around 1962 Angelo LaPietra, Turk Torello, and Johnny Figuarata were close associates and were nearly inseparable. However, changes were made and Turk Torello and Johnny Figuarata had moved up in the outfit.

Tony Di Riggi had a falling out with Angelo LaPietra and no longer associated with him as of 1964 because he was beat up for some reason and dropped out. Frank "Blackie" Morelli was no longer connected with that organization because he became deeply involved in juice and received a beating for not paying his debts off. He went to work as a handyman on Fifi Buccieri's farm. Salaam had been arrested sometime after 1964 and it was believed he appealed his conviction. Zaccagnini added that the people who replaced them in the LaPietra group were Steve Annoreno and Louis Di Riggi, brother of Tony. As of 1964, this operation was the biggest in Cicero and all of the largest loans went through this group. In addition, Angelo LaPietra was known to buy stolen merchandise such as jewelry, trailer loads of merchandise and in general acted as a fence.

Zaccagnini also gave a list of "juice" victims who have obtained loans from the outfit:

Chuck Giangalo   Dave Tinucci
Billy Taglia   Benny Taglia
Bezee Summario   Frank Rinelli
Art Pascucci (was beaten by Angelo LaPietra with a Baseball Bat)

James LaPietra

Known as "Jimmy the Lapper," James LaPietra was Angelo's right-hand man as well as his brother. Born on March 28, 1927, James lived at 7116 West 28th Street in Berwyn, Illinois, and spent time as an inmate at the Illinois State Training School for boys in Kane County, Illinois, as a teenager.

On September 20, 1945, James LaPietra was arrested with Jack Gento on a charge of rape. A 20-year-old woman accused the two men of being part of a gang of six hoodlums who raped her in the garage at 231 W. 24th Place. The victim said that LaPietra was the one who forced her into the garage and then called the other five men.

In January 1952, James LaPietra was arrested with Bruno Frank Bertucci, Salvatore Nugara, and Harold Schubmehl as suspected burglars and safecrackers after a stolen safe was found in their possession while at Bertucci's key shop located at 252 W. Cermak Road. All four had the charges quashed since their constitutional rights had been violated. The police did not have a proper search warrant to enter the key shop. At the time, Bertucci, was on probation in federal court for thefts from interstate commerce. Harold Schubmehl was known as "The Weasel" and was listed as a draft dodger and professional safecracker. Salvatore "Blackie" Nugara was known as a burglar and would be sent to prison in 1957 with Nathan "Fats" Chiarella and Sam "Soapy" Serritella on a heroin conviction. In November 1964 both Schubmehl and Nugara were arrested trying to break into a business. They were charged with burglary and possession of burglary tools. Both admitted to police that they had been arrested over 30 times.

While Angelo LaPietra was in prison in the 1980's, Jimmy LaPietra was in charge of the street crew calling the shots. Jimmy would visit his brother in prison often so Angelo could issue mob orders for Jimmy to take care of. James LaPietra died in September 1993.

Steve Annoreno

Steve Annoreno was born around 1926 and used the aliases of Steve Reno, Steve Brown, and Boxie Brown. He lived at 938 Jackson Street in River Forest, which he also used as the address for his company Annoreno Management.

He was frequently seen at 18th Street and Cicero Avenue and 59th Street and Roosevelt Road in Cicero. In 1954, Annoreno was convicted by the U.S. Army Court Marshal division on desertion charges and was sentenced to one year in prison. In February 1966, a cab driver named Wilbur Barnard told the authorities that Steve Annoreno and George Vertucci made him drive hoodlums to and from robberies and forced him to work as a janitor in mob-owned strip joints to pay off his "juice" loan. Both Annoreno and Vertucci were arrested after the two threatened Barnard that if he didn't come up with $600 in 2 days he would be found floating face down in the Chicago River. When the police went to arrest the two at the Big Top Tavern on Cermak Road, Annoreno ran out of the tavern and down the street in an attempt to flee. While he ran, he also tried to get rid of a revolver that he had hidden on himself but failed. He was caught and the police discovered $2,100 in cash in his pocket. Vertucci and Annoreno were charged with intimidation and Annoreno was charged with illegal use of a weapon.

However, an informant to the FBI told them that there was another "juice" man known to him only as "Steve" who worked as an associate under Angelo LaPietra. This informant said most people tried to get their "juice" loans through this "Steve" because he seemed more lenient on demanding collections and was much better to deal with than LaPietra. It was not known if this was Steve Annoreno.

On September 10, 1969, Annoreno was arrested on a federal juice charge. He was found guilty in 1971 and sentenced to 15 years in prison and a $10,000 fine. The judge made a statement while imposing the sentence, *"You were the leader in the Chicago area of what is unmistakably one of the worst crime situations we have in large cities in America today."*

Tony Annoreno, who was born around 1931, was known as Anthony Reno and was the brother of Steve Annoreno. He was listed as a truck driver for the Spector Motor Freight Company in Hillside. His arrest record dates back to 1946 when he was arrested for auto theft. In 1948 he was arrested for petty larceny. On September 10, 1969, Tony Annoreno was arrested on a federal juice charge and received 3 years in prison.

The Spillone Brothers

Vito Dominic Spillone was listed as Steve Annoreno's lieutenant in the 1960's. Born around 1937, Vito lived at 1639 N. 75th Avenue in Elmwood Park when he was arrested on a federal juice charge. He received a 12-year sentence but only served 5 years before being paroled. The area listed as his section of operations was 29th Street and Cicero Avenue in Cicero, Illinois.

The Chicago loan-sharking operation which Vito was allegedly part of was based in Cicero under the name Family Amusement Center, which was one of the crime syndicate's largest at that time. Spillone was accused of heading the operation that lent as much as $40,000 at one time at extortive interest rates.

Spillone was accused in 1984 in a grand jury's indictment of operating a juice-loan racket behind the facade of a lucrative wholesale food business in South El Monte, California. According to Justice Department sources and news reports, Chicago mob bosses had become fed up with the Dominic Brooklier's California-Nevada group of alleged mobsters, which they said was running a "Mickey Mouse operation" involving "juice" loans. The mob moved to rebuild the bookmaking and loan-sharking satellite after former operators Dominic Brooklier, Louis Tom Dragna and three other Southern California gangsters were convicted. Allegedly mob bosses Tony Accardo, Joey Aiuppa, and Anthony Spilotro replaced Brooklier's group with Spillone's group.

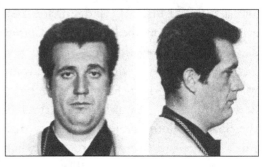

Vito Spillone allegedly set up the new satellite in Las Vegas and Los Angeles. Others involved, according to news reports, were John C. Abel, a bank robber, muscle man, and a member of the white-supremacist Aryan Brotherhood which was once held in the Metropolitan Correctional Center in Chicago; John Meccia, of La Salle, Illinois; and John Barro of Anaheim, California, then owner of a pizzeria chain. It was reported that Spillone allegedly said he would deal with delinquent clients by killing them or breaking their legs.

In 1985, Spillone was convicted on 20 counts of racketeering and faced a maximum sentence of 100 years in prison for loan sharking and racketeering in Southern California and Las Vegas.

Frank Serrao, John Clyde Abel, and Frank Citro were convicted by a federal court jury in Los Angeles of making and collecting loans by extortive means. Three other defendants were acquitted in the case; John Meccia, John Barro, and Joseph Bolognese of Las Vegas. Vito Spillone was released from federal prison on March 3, 1995.

Anthony J. Spillone, brother of Vito, was born around 1932 and lived at 1915 North Broadway in Melrose Park in the 1960's. He was arrested in Chicago on September 10, 1969, on federal juice charges. Tony was given 5 years in prison on that charge.

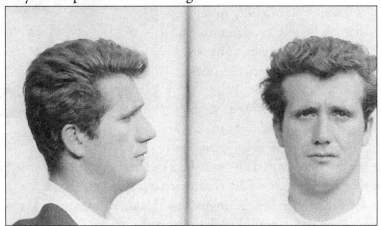

Author's Collection

Martin Bucaro Jr.

Martin Anthony Bucaro Jr. was born around 1941 and went by the alias of Martin Bucard. He lived at 238 N. Parkside in Chicago and worked at Marty's Red Hot's on N. Broadway in Chicago when he was arrested on November 4, 1969, and charged with a federal juice charge. He was listed as a lieutenant of mobster Steve Annoreno when he was sentenced to 12 years in prison in 1971.

Frank Teutonico

Born on November 21, 1909, in Chicago, Frank T. Teutonico also used the aliases of Frank Tonico, Frank Torino, and Frank Tutonico. In the 1960's he listed his residences as 2425 West Taylor Street and 1007 South Seeley Street in Chicago.

His police record contains a conviction from January 30, 1928, for larceny in which he received 90 days in prison. Once released, he was arrested for burglary, gambling and extortion. On August 1, 1956, he was convicted on Federal narcotic charges and was sent to prison for 2 years and fined $1000. Teutonico and Peter Calamia, also known as Jimmy Calamia, plead guilty to selling 8 ounces of heroin on January 28, 1956. Also accused in the crime was a Calumet City gambler named George Barton.

On December 3, 1964, a gambler by the name of Joe Union attended the "Chicago Avenue crap game" to make some money. It turned out to be a bad decision. It was learned that night that Frank "Calico Kid" Teutonico beat the crap out of Joe Union because he had fallen behind on his "juice" loan. At that time, Teutonico was known on the street as Frank Calico as he ran his juice loan business at O'Hare Airport where he would prey on taxicab drivers. Many of the cab drivers were the prey of syndicate-connected guys around the early 1960's because mobster Charles Giancana's brother-in-law, Ronreo Toriello, owned the White Top Cab Company. James "Turk" Torello also used Teutonico as an enforcer for collections.

In 1970, law enforcement agents operating at Jackson Boulevard and Francisco Street, and Roosevelt Road and Austin Boulevard in Chicago observed the "Calico Kid". It's believed he died on November 15, 1993.

Frank Buccieri

A third juice loan group operating under the aegis of Fiore "Fifi" Buccieri was under the supervision of Frank Buccieri, a brother of Fiore Buccieri. Frank Buccieri lived at 1028 South Greenwood and 2020 Arthur in Park Ridge.

Frank Paul Buccieri was born on January 23, 1919, in Chicago and was known by the following names; Frank Bruno, Frank White, "Big Frank," and "Frank the Horse." Buccieri, known as the mob's playboy, spent a considerable amount of time at the old Playboy Club and the bar scene on Rush Street during the 1950's, 60's, and 70's. His area of operation was listed as Milwaukee and Grand Avenues, Rush Street and Delaware Place, Delaware Place and State Street, and Milwaukee Avenue and Division Street in Chicago.

His arrest record prior to 1970 only contained one conviction for petty larceny in 1936, for which he received 6 months in prison.

In 1961 Frank Buccieri and Joe "Spa" Spadavecchio operated a "juice" operation located at 5th Avenue and California Street in Chicago. The building was known as Parker's Restaurant and handled a considerable amount of horse betting for the mob.

Frank Buccieri had the following juice collectors working for him:

Sam "Subbie" Sammarco	Christ Seritella
Michael B. Tenore	Joseph "Spa" Spadavecchio
Anthony "Tony Pine" Eldorado	Andrew Carsello
Frank Beto, aka Frank Parker	Anthony Catalano
Carmen Buccieri	John "Johnny Bells" Sprovieri

John Schivarelli, aka John "Johnny the Bug" Varelli

This group formerly operated out of Frontier Finance Corporation, 5131 West Madison, Chicago, and also out of Moeller Brothers Furniture Company, 1272 North Milwaukee Avenue, Chicago, of which Frank Buccieri was a partner. As a result of the FBI's investigation of the Frontier Finance Corporation, the owners sold the corporation in 1963 to the Mercantile Corporation. Most of the juice operations were then switched to Moeller Brothers Furniture Company.

The five original investors for the Frontier Finance Corp. were John Scherping, one-time Captain of the Chicago Police Department; Edward Moore, one-time Cook County Republican Committeeman; Carl Schrorder, former postmaster of Chicago during the Eisenhower administration, and Frank Buccieri.

When Buccieri was exposed as being a partner in the company, he sold his interest to a Michael Tenore, aka Mike Michell. An informant said that Tenore had taken over Frank Buccieri's interest on paper only and Buccieri remained a silent partner. It was also mentioned at the time that Tenore used the back room of Frontier Finance as his headquarters and used Anthony "Tony Pineapple" Eldorado and Joseph Spadavecchio as his main collectors for delinquent "juice" loans.

In 1963 a convicted felon by the name of Peter James Verri Jr. furnished information to the FBI about Frontier Finance Corp. He said that "Johnny the Bug" Varelli sent numerous "juice" loan customers to Frontier Finance. He said the in 1961 Verri worked as a car salesman for a John Ivanelli at Johnson Motors in Chicago. Ivanelli persuaded Verri to make an $800 loan for him in the name that Verri used as an alias, John Pelligrino, from a syndicate controlled "juice" company. The company turned out to be Frontier Finance Corp. The money was given to Ivanelli after Carmen Buccieri okayed it. Sometime later, Verri did not pay the money back, and a man by the name of "Tony Pine" contacted Peter Verri Sr., his father, and told him that if he did not pay the money back, Verri Sr. would be receiving a *"knock on the head."* Fearing the beating, both Verri's came up with the money and settled the loan.

Another informant stated that Fiore "Fifi" Buccieri and his brother Frank were fighting between themselves because of the publicity Frank received in connection with Frontier Finance Corporation. Fifi believed that Frontier Finance would eventually be his downfall but would not explain why.

Another informant once told the authorities that Frank Buccieri had been given certain "juice" privileges but had to turn over 50 percent of the profits to Angelo LaPietra and Fifi Buccieri. LaPietra was Frank's direct boss since Frank was said not to be intelligent enough to operate on his own, and was required to pay percentages or had to rent a certain section to operate his "juice" racket.

This informant added that at that time Fifi Buccieri used the Leader brothers, Norm and Dave, owners of a liquor store at Irving Park Road and Sacramento Avenue, to solicit "juice" customers for the group. At the time the Leader brothers were known to operate a large bookie operation on the Northside.

Frank Buccieri mostly stayed out of the mob's limelight after his brother's death in 1973. Frank died in March 2004.

Joe Spadavecchio

Joseph "Spa" Spadavecchio was born on February 17, 1928, in Chicago and was listed as living at 4112 Congress Street and 7633 Armitage in Elmwood Park. Also listed under the nickname of "The Spot," Spadavecchio was known to operate at the Onion Roll Restaurant at 6935 W. North Avenue in Oak Park.

In 1962 an FBI informant said that Joe Spa was the weakest member in the Buccieri organization because he was always nervous and afraid of being deeply involved in mob operations.

On May 5, 1963, Joseph Spadavecchio was arrested down the street from Sam Giancana's Villa Venice for driving without a license. Joe Spa, his wife, Theresa, and another couple were leaving a wedding reception for Charles "Chuckie" English's son, Ronald English, who married Diane Altieri. Also arrested that night after the reception was Marshall Caifano.

In February 1976, Spadavecchio was indicted with Dom "Large" Cortina, Donald Angelini, Frank "The Knife" Aureli, Salvator Molose, Nick "Moose" Camillo, and John "Chicky" La Placa for operating a gambling ring on Chicago's west side. It was believed that the gambling ring was pulling in around $1.5 million a month from football, baseball, basketball, and horse betting. Spadavecchio was found guilty in February 1979 and sentenced to 2 years in federal prison and a $20,000 fine.

In 1989 he was charged with another federal gambling violation, which landed him in prison for another 18 months. Joe Spa died on April 19, 1995, in Elmwood Park.

Joe Ferriola

Joseph Ferriola, also known as Joe Negall, Joe DeGaul, The Spooner, Mr. Clean, Joe Nicol, and Joe Nick, was a lieutenant of Fiore Buccieri and would later become top boss of the Chicago mob.

Ferriola was primarily engaged in gambling but was used by Buccieri as an enforcer along with James "Turk" Torello for juice loan problems. Around 1962 Ferriola was handling the book making operations for Fifi Buccieri and was always seen in the company of Buccieri, Al Milstein, and Steve and Angelo Annoreno at the Stop Light Tavern.

The FBI listing of him in 1964 stated, *"Joe Ferriola is generally considered as being on his way up in the Chicago criminal group and was very close to Fiore "Fifi" Buccieri. He allegedly obtained this position with Buccieri by murdering the former husband of Buccieri's present wife. Ferriola had gained his reputation as an enforcer and killer and has been associated with the 'juice' rackets, gambling, fencing of stolen property, and gangland slayings. Recently Ferriola has been running a gambling and 'juice' operation in Melrose Park. Also in this operation was Frank Beto, a Chicago hoodlum."*

In 1958 Joe Ferriola, James "Turk" Torello, Johnny Gattuso, and Jasper "Jay" Campise were linked in the mutilation murder of a Puerto Rican hoodlum involved in the Bolita Gambling games. The man, Santiago Rosa Gonzales, was a leader in Chicago's Northside Puerto Rican community. His body was discovered on February 2, 1958, in an empty parking lot in Chicago where he had been cut and slashed and his intestines were pulled out. Gonzales' influence and power grew to a point where he had a chance to take over and actively oppose the gambling from the Italian mob.

In the late 1960's Ferriola's areas of "juice" were listed as Harlem and Lawrence Avenues in Norwood Park, 74th Street and Grand Avenues in Elmwood Park, Austin Boulevard and Roosevelt Road in Cicero and 91st Street and County Line Road in Hinsdale.

Informant Joe Weisphal told the FBI in the 1960's that the Big Top Snack Shop at 6000 West Roosevelt Road in Oak Park was licensed to a Nick Koronpilas since 1957 and the place was used as a headquarters for Joe Ferriola, James "Cowboy" Mirro, Rocky Infelice, Tony Ozzanto, and Joseph Torella.

In August 1968, Joe Ferriola and Frank Buccieri were arrested by the Clark County Sheriff's Office in Las Vegas; Buccieri said his name was Frank White from San Francisco but later admitted his true identity. As for Ferriola, he told the officers there was no way he would be photographed. When the officers tried to sit him down to take his mug shot, he hit the sergeant in the right eye with his fist. Ferriola was charged with battery to a police officer, photographed, stripped of his clothes and placed in a padded cell.

In August 1969, Ferriola was arrested with Sam "Butch" English, Anthony "Puleo" DeRosa, and Pasquale "Buck" Celementi for interstate gambling. Also charged were James Cerone, Donald Angelini, Frank Aureli, John "Jackie" Cerone, and Dominic Cortina. He was found guilty in June 1970 and sentenced to 5 years.

A July 1986 FBI document stated the following concerning Joe Ferriola; *"Joe Ferriola now appears to be the unquestioned boss of Chicago's LCN in view of the trial, conviction, and incarceration of Jack Cerone and Joseph Aiuppa."*

Joe Ferriola only served as top boss of the Outfit for 3 years. During his rule he suffered from cancer and serious heart problems. He died in March 1989 in a Houston Hospital.

File Card
Joseph Anthony Ferriola
AKA: Joe DeGaul
Birth: March 16, 1927
Died: March 12, 1989

Listed Occupation
Yellow Cab Company (1952)
Chauffeur (1952)
Restaurant owner "2200 West Taylor St." (1954)
Store Keeper "9224 Cottage Grove" (1958)
J&R Cleaners (1970)

Known Addresses
929 Hoyne Street, Chicago (1049)
1645 West 61st Court, Cicero (1950)
2337 West Greenshaw, Chicago (1955)
270 South Cote Road, Riverside (1963)
10730 West Cermak Road, Westchester (1973)

Known Arrest Record

Joe Ferriola	8-23-1944	Disorderly Conduct
Joe Ferriola	8-2-1945	Disorderly Conduct
Joe Ferriola	12-28-1946	Disorderly Conduct
Joe Ferriola	2-2-1946	Traffic Violation
Joe Ferriola	3-29-1946	Disorderly Conduct
Joe Ferriola	4-14-1946	Traffic Violation
Joe Ferriola	6-21-1947	Disorderly Conduct
Joe Ferriola	6-12-1948	Gambling
Joe Ferriola	6-23-1948	Disorderly Conduct
Joe Ferriola	7-5-1948	Disorderly Conduct
Joe Ferriola	7-29-1948	Disorderly Conduct
Joe Ferriola	11-9-1948	Disorderly Conduct
Joe Ferriola	1-31-1949	Disorderly Conduct
Joe Ferriola	7-13-1949	Traffic Violation
Joe Ferriola	9-12-1949	Traffic Violation
Joe Ferriola	12-4-1949	Disorderly Conduct
Joe Ferriola	7-27-1950	Disorderly Conduct
Joe Ferriola	7-16-1952	Vehicle Violation
Joe Ferriola	11-22-1953	No Drivers License
Joe Ferriola	9-16-1954	Investigation
Joe Ferriola	8-12-1958	Gambling
Joe Ferriola	8-3-1968	Vagrancy, Nevada
Joe Ferriola	8-19-1969	Gambling (FBI)

Gus Alex and the old First Ward of Chicago

Gus "Gussie" Alex was born on April 1, 1916, in Chicago and grew up working at his parent's restaurant on Wentworth Avenue right next to Chicago's Chinatown. Other aliases of Alex were "Slim," "Shot Gun," "Bananas," Gust Alex, Paul Benson, Gus Johnson, "Muscle," Martin Ryan, and Michael Ryan.

After a few years of high school, Gus Alex got involved with his brother Sam Alex, a gangster and thug in Chicago's labor field. Gus gained the nickname of "Shotgun" and "The Muscle" because in the 1930's he would cut down his victims with two shotgun blasts. Since he was a non-Italian, he went to work as a bodyguard for powerful gangsters Jake "Greasy Thumb" Guzik and Murray "Curly" Humphreys. It was Tony Accardo who in the 1940's noticed that Gus Alex was being wasted as a bodyguard. Alex had also been running a prostitution ring in a slummy hotel at Polk and State Street; that is when he began to move up the ranks in the Outfit. Alex's superior intelligence about organized crime made him one of the top non-Italian mob bosses in Chicago's history.

File Card
Gus Alex
AKA: Gussie
Born: April 1, 1916
Died: July 24, 1998

Known Addresses
1074 Polk Street, Chicago (1930's)
2604 S. Wentworth Avenue, Chicago (1935)
2319 S. Wentworth Avenue, Chicago
5100 West 25th Street, Chicago (1937)
5816 S. LaSalle Street, Chicago (1938)
4710 West Madison Street, Chicago (1940)
4010 West Madison Street, Chicago (1940)
5703 S. LaSalle Street, Chicago
4000 Washington Blvd., Chicago (1944)
9355 S. Spaulding Avenue, Evergreen Park (1956)
6111 South Lytle, Chicago (1957)
1502 West Jackson, Chicago (1957)
4300 N Marine Drive, Chicago (1958)
1150 North Lake Shore Drive, Chicago (1967)
1300 North Lake Shore Drive, Chicago (1969)

Known Arrest Record
(Original arrest record destroyed on court order in 1945)

9-24-1933	Murder
2-1-1937	Disorderly Conduct
3-20-1937	Traffic Violation
10-10-1937	Murder
10-15-1938	Investigation
2-22-1940	Manslaughter
2-12-1943	Gambling
4-8-1944	Traffic Violation
5-4-1944	Disorderly Conduct
6-5-1944	Disorderly Conduct
9-21-1944	Disorderly Conduct
10-3-1944	Investigation (River Forest)
9-10-1946	Murder Investigation (Regan Murder)

Known Hangouts
Health Club, 400 E, Randolph, Chicago
Playboy Club, Chicago
Mike's Fish Restaurant, Chicago
Michigan Avenue and Wacker Drive (Juice Area)
Rush Street from Chicago Avenue to Division Street (Juice Area)
State and Monroe Streets (Juice Area)
Randolph and Wells Streets (Juice Area)

Other arrests include kidnapping, bribery, fugitive, assault with intent to kill, and gambling. After the death of Jake Guzik and gangster Bruno Roti in 1956, Alex was handed the old First Ward in Chicago and became its boss and political fixer. Also moved up with Alex was his Italian boss Frank "Strongy" Ferraro. In 1993 Alex's lieutenant, Lennie Patrick, turned government witness and helped put his long-time friend behind bars for the rest of his life. Gus Alex died of a heart attack in federal prison in July 1998.

Gus Alex had a hand in every "juice" loan made in the old First Ward. In the 1960's, Gus Alex placed Bruno Roti's son-in-law, Frank Caruso, in charge of mob operations in Chinatown and the south portions of the old First Ward, especially controlling the syndicate's "juice" operation.

Frank Caruso, Known as "Skids"

Frank T. Caruso was born on December 2, 1911 in Chicago, and went by the nickname and alias of "Skids" Caruso and Frank Spino. He listed his residence as 215 West 23rd Street and 234 West Cermak Road in Chicago.

In 1965 the FBI reported that Frank "Skids" Caruso was controlling all of Gus Alex's "juice" operations around 31st and Normal Streets in Bridgeport. At the time, he was working with Jimmy "The Bomber" Catuara and a mobster by the name of "Jimmy the Cat."

In 1969 his area of operations were 31st Street and Princeton Avenue, 26th Street and Princeton Avenue, and 22nd Street and Wentworth Avenue in Chicago. He also used the House of Fong at 2249 S. Wentworth Avenue as his headquarters.

His arrest record dates back to 1935 and contains many arrests mostly for gambling, conspiracy, and larceny. Frank "Skids" Caruso died in November 1983.

A list of Caruso's top men, according to FBI reports in the 1960's, were Anthony "Poppy" Maenza, Joe "Shorty" LaMantia, and Jimmy Cordovano.

In 1963 the big "juice" man in Frank "Skids' Caruso's district, which then ran from 22nd Street to 39th Streets and Wentworth to Ashland Avenue in Chicago, was Jimmy Cordovano.

James R. Cordovano

Jimmy Cordovano, also known as "Cubay," was born on December 18, 1921 in Chicago, and lived at 462 West 28th Place in Chicago. His arrest record dates back to 1951 with arrests ranging from manslaughter, gambling, theft, and burglary. On April 3, 1951, Cordovano received a verdict of justifiable homicide for having shot and killed Robert Gaglione in March 1951. A fight broke out at Cordovano's tavern at 2600 Wallace Street between Gaglione and a Phil Imbergo. Gaglione, who had a long police record including a charge of rape, kidnapping and auto theft, picked up a bar stool and was going to hit Imbergo. Cordovano, trying to separate the two, pulled out his gun and shot Gaglione six times with three of the shots hitting Gaglione's head.

On May 14, 1954, Cordovano was received at Milan, Michigan Correctional Institution after a conviction for dealing narcotics. He would serve 2 years before his release. On December 29, 1962, Cordovano was arrested with Tony D'Amico and was charged with being the keeper of a mob dice game. The game was being held at the Nightingale Social and Athletic club in the old First Ward of Chicago. The game was said to be run by mobster August "Gust" Liebe. The "juice" men at the game were under the control of Morris Saletko, aka Maishe Baer. All 28 persons arrested in that raid were discharged when the judge ruled that the evidence was seized illegally.

The Nightingale Tavern located in the building which Cordovano owned at 26th and Wallace Streets in Chicago was used as Cordovano's headquarters. A informant said that "juice" payments were made in envelopes delivered to the bartender at the Nightingale Tavern who would stack the envelopes alongside the cash register. Cordovano then gave a percentage of his profits to Caruso.

In August 1964, Jimmy Cordovano and Joseph "Spider" DiCaro were driving to the wake of mob boss Frank "Strongy" Ferraro when federal narcotics agents seized them. At the time of Cordovano arrest, an investigation determined that he owned R.C. Cartage Company, which leased trucks to the city of Chicago. Cordovano, DiCaro and two other hoodlums named Sam Garafolo and James Rancatore were charged with the sale and possession of heroin between October 21, 1963, and January 9, 1964.

In 1968 Cordovano was convicted for illegal voting. At the same time, an informant told the FBI that Cordovano made his money peddling narcotics and making "juice" loans. This informant said at the time that Cordovano owned about five buildings and had over a quarter of a million dollars in the bank. Working for Cordovano at that time was Peter Gushi and John Fecarotta as "juice" collectors.

In July 1980, a report asking why a Chicago mobster, who was on the city payroll as a $2,210-a-month masonry foreman for the sewer department and was a precinct captain in the old 11th Ward under the control of Richard M. Daley, was allowed to have his trucking company, R.C. Cartage, provide trucks to the city of Chicago totaling over $90,000 in an 18-month period to do city work. The city sewer commissioner at the time, Edward Quigley, said that the company was not owned by James Cordovano but by his wife Rose Cordovano. Nothing became of the investigation. James Cordovano died in January 1983.

Joseph LaMantia

Joseph Frank LaMantia was known as "Shorty," Rocco Madia, and Rocco LaMantia in the 1960's. Born on February 1, 1934 in Chicago, he has an arrest record containing arrests for burglary, theft in interstate commerce, armed robbery, and shoplifting.

In September 1951, LaMantia was arrested with James Cozzie, Victor Crivilare, and Frank Di Foggio for stealing a truck from the C&C Cartage Company at 2719 S. Quinn Street in Chicago. LaMantia was charged with larceny in the manner of property valued at $10,400 which included two trailers, thirty five cartons of clothing, fifteen cartons of jackets, twenty cartons of shirts and one rug. LaMantia was also charged with stealing freight from the Pennsylvania Railroad Company. Taken were six cases of shirts, eight cases of ties, one case of tablecloths, thirteen cases of shoes and five cases of dry foods. Arrested with LaMantia were Thomas Veraetto, Dominic LaCario, Moratio Fedel, Eugene Blades, and Frank Di Foggio. He was convicted and sentenced to 1 year of probation for tampering with an auto, and 2-to-5 years for burglary.

In February 1958, Joe LaMantia was arrested and charged with robbing Edmund Juzwik at gunpoint. Juzwik said LaMantia and another unknown man took $460 in cash and $4,000 in diamonds that had been laid into a ring and a watch from him. Eight months later, right before Juzwik was to appear as a witness against LaMantia, three men walked up to him and said, "*We want to talk to you,*" and began to beat him. Two of the men held Juzwik while the third punched him. Juzwik was able to get free and dive under a parked car screaming for his life. The three men ran to a getaway car and sped off. Fearing for his life, Juzwik was placed under a 24-hour guard by police. On March 31, 1959, only a month and a half after the 24-hour police guard had been released, Juzwik got into his auto and drove down Nagle Avenue when another car pulled alongside and opened fire. Ten bullets penetrated his car with only one bullet hitting him in the shoulder, knocking him to the floor of his car. Juzwik lived, but LaMantia would go on to be acquitted.

In the 1960's LaMantia was listed as allegedly being connected to the "juice" rackets having been seen by authorities at the corners of 22nd Street and Wentworth Avenue and 26th Street and Princeton Avenues in Chicago. In the 1980's he was seen at the Italian American Club at 268 W. 26th Street with known mobsters.

On May 6, 1979, a frantic 911 call was placed from Joe LaMantia's home at 2812 Shields Avenue by his son Rocco LaMantia. Published reports list Rocco as saying "*I, uh.......* *It was a mistake with a gun. It's a girl. She's young. Come here, please….. she's bleeding, and it's my girlfriend.*"

Rocco LaMantia's girlfriend, Martha DiCaro, was shot in the face, and lying in the kitchen in a pool of blood. Court documents state that before police arrived, Joe LaMantia arrived at the house in a panic and ran inside. By the time police arrived, DiCaro was dead and court records state that LaMantia told them that two men with ski masks and blue jackets broke into the house and shot DiCaro, and then ran off with her purse. A third story given later by LaMantia's lawyer was that Martha DiCaro had found a gun in Joe LaMantia's bedroom and Rocco took the gun away, refusing to show her how to use it. DiCaro attempted to grab the gun away from Rocco when it went off.

The police were confused at first; DiCaro's body was found in the kitchen, but in the bedroom blood was splattered all over the dresser, mirror, and floor, and the bed was soaked with blood. Another report stated that the gun was allegedly pushed up against the face of DiCaro when it was fired. Rocco LaMantia was charged with murder and in the 5-day court trial, DiCaro's family testified that Martha DiCaro had left her family to go over to Rocco's house to end their 5-year relationship. Another friend of DiCaro's allegedly told the police that Rocco had allegedly bragged once that if he caught Martha with anyone else he would kill both of them and have his father pay $20,000 to "get him off." In one of the crime scene photos entered as evidence, a blood soaked item was seen lying on the top of the bed. Martha's best friend looked at the photo and identified the item as a beige clutch purse that Martha often carried. The police officer who investigated the bedroom looked at the photo and said he did not remember seeing the blood-soaked item later that night when he investigated the room. Among other items not found was the gun that killed Martha. The case against Rocco LaMantia was mostly circumstantial and he was acquitted of the crime.

In October 2007, Rocco LaMantia was arrested on an armed robbery charge. The charge alleged that LaMantia and three other robbers robbed the ABBA pawn shop on Roosevelt Road in Chicago.

In December 1982, Joe LaMantia, his adopted son Aldo Pissitelli Jr., Frank "Toots" Caruso, and Fred Bruno Barbara, aka Fred B. Russo, Caruso's cousin, were arrested for allegedly trying to collect $50,000 in "juice" loans. In court it was said that a city of Chicago Water Department clerk named Daniel Borak was an alleged bookmaker and gambler and was $50,000 in debt to LaMantia. Borak was allegedly given the money so he could make "juice" loans in the amount not larger than $500 to his bettors and charge 5 percent a week in interest. However, Borak took the $50,000 and lost it all gambling.

Unable to come up with the money, Borak went to the FBI for help. Wearing a hidden tape recorder, Borak set up meetings with LaMantia explaining that he was unable to come up with LaMantia's money because he loaned $20 to a drug dealer named Bob Johnson. Bob Johnson was no ordinary drug dealer; he was an undercover FBI agent named Rob Elder, set in place to build a case against LaMantia.

LaMantia, Borak, and Johnson met in a south side parking lot on November 17, 1982. Johnson told LaMantia that a drug deal had fallen through and he needed another week to come up with the money. Johnson challenged LaMantia's ability to enforce his ability to collect on the loan, LaMantia pointed to a car parked down the street and told the agent, *"If I just take off my cap, he'll come out with a pistol and drop you right here."* Satisfied with the arrangement, Johnson left the car. LaMantia was recorded as saying to Borak, *"I want you to tell this guy, the guy I'm with, he's a gentleman, but he'll cut your heart out. You scare him cause he don't mean a thing to me. I'll stick him in the head with an ice pick."* He went on to say, *"They talk about how the mob deals with that"* meaning drugs, *"that's a lie, Danny. Not in this town. I don't care what anybody says, the mob don't deal with dope in this town."* All four defendants were acquitted of the charges.

In 1993 LaMantia was indicted with Joe Wing on gambling charges. Joe Wing was listed as the supervisor in charge of gambling operations in Chinatown. In 1997 LaMantia was sentenced to 5 years in prison on gambling charges while Aldo Pissitelli was convicted of running the day-to-day gambling operations. He was given 51 months in prison and released on August 13, 2001. Joe LaMantia died in October 2002 and is buried at Queen of Heaven Cemetery in Hillside, Illinois.

Nicholas and George Bravos

The Bravos brothers have operated throughout the city of Chicago and its suburbs as two of the largest bookmakers in the United States as of 1965. They never operated from any one location and generally moved throughout the entire area handling extremely large bets on the part of prominent individuals who were in a position to make large wagers.

In addition to their extensive bookmaking activities, Nick and George Bravos had operated a successful supply of money to their customers for many years.

The Bravos brothers were not beyond the use of force in the collection of their debts from their "juice" customers who might lag behind in payment. They were closely linked to numerous syndicate hoodlums and had the potential for supplying unspeakable force.

Nicholas "Nick" Bravos was born July 22, 1913, to James Bravos and Kanela Faling. One report states that he was born in Romania but was of Greek origin. James and Kanela had two sons and a daughter, Helen. With both parents dead by 1931 both Nick and George turned to the streets and became burglars. One informant related that the Bravos brothers were distantly related to mob boss Gus Alex in some manner, however, one informant said that the Bravos brothers would tell people that to gain respect, and that the Bravos family was not related to the Alex's, but both families came from the same small town in Greece. One report states that both brothers were bartenders at Andres Restaurant in Chicago, working as heist men when they gained a favorable association with Gus Alex, who raised them to a power in the gambling field.

Nick Bravos was also known as "Nick the Greek," Nick Pravos, Nick Brevos, Nick Bravas, Nicholas Brabas, Robert Marabos, Nick Mattucci, Nick Sovarb, George Nicholas, and M. Brado. He married June Insara and had four children, Kathy, Mary Ellen, James, and Nickie.

One of his first known scrapes with the law came at age 19 when he was arrested in April 1932 for an unknown offense for which he received 1 year of probation. He would be arrested many more times in his life for robbery, larceny, and murder investigations.

In September 1933, Nick Bravos was arrested for armed robbery under the name of Nicholas Bravas with Al Manfucci and Joseph Krupinski. Court records state that one clock, worth $5 and one fountain pen, also valued at $5, were the items stolen. Another report mentions only Krupinski and Manfucci accompanied by another hoodlum robbing four African-American boys of $10 who were playing cards. One of the boys was able to get away during the robbery and call police. When the police arrived, Manfucci and the unmentioned hoodlum fled while

Krupinski engaged the police in a gun battle. Shot and under a storm of bullets in the air, Krupinski managed to make his escape. His freedom was short lived when he was arrested at a hospital after being brought in by his brother, since Krupinski was near death for his wound. There had also been a getaway car waiting for the three hoodlums outside as they robbed the boys, but when the police arrived, the driver sped off leaving his associates behind. The car didn't get very far as it smashed into another police car on its way to the robbery. The report didn't state if Bravos was the driver or the unknown robber.

Joseph Krupinski was already well-known to the police at the time of his arrest. In 1926 he was arrested for stealing an automobile and given probation. In 1931 he was arrested for robbery and sentenced to time in Bridewell reformatory. On January 17, 1933, Krupinski was arrested once again with a Joseph Pick as they robbed a garage at 2943 West Lake Street. After taking $50 from the attendant, they decided to kidnap him and a customer and make a getaway in the customer's car. Once on the street, the car crashed and the two were arrested by River Forest police. The two were later acquitted of the robbery and kidnapping charges.

Al Manfucci was born around 1909 in Chicago under what was listed as his real name, Albert Dini. His arrest record as of 1933 mentioned three terms of probation with an arrest on October 24, 1927, in Cook County for an unknown incident. His prison record listed him as living at 2316 N. Austin Avenue with his father Decil Dini, an Italian immigrant. The record states that Albert left home at the age of 15 and moved from location to location throughout the city of Chicago, working as a laborer. While in Joliet Prison, Manfucci had many marks on his record for punishment. Some listed were defacing state property, talking after lights out, stealing pork chops from the dining area, taking 55 minutes to deliver bread from the kitchen to an officer, having a paintbrush and paint in his cell, having butter in his locker, contraband, and not shaving with his regular line but appearing shaved later in the day. He was paroled in November 1941.

On December 19, 1933, Bravos, Krupinski and Manfucci were sentenced to one year-to-life in prison. Nine days later, Nick Bravos entered Joliet Prison. His prison record listed him as being 23 years old and having the occupation of a city laborer. On February 14, 1934, he was transferred to the Pontiac branch of the state prison. He was released in 1940 and resumed his operations in gambling.

In the 1940's Nick Bravos was known as a political powerhouse in the old 29th Ward of Chicago where he would force restaurant owners to take his "juice" loans when they would fall behind on their gambling debts. In 1945 a police report listed Nick Bravos as a bookmaker who owned and operated the Better Burner Service acting as an oil burner repairman.

In 1950 he was named as a "big shot" in the Miami, Florida, rackets when his name was mentioned by the Senate Crime Investigation Committee investigating organized crime. At that time, he was listed as co-owner with a Harry Russell of the Silver Bar at 400 S. State Street.

On May 17, 1950, detectives raided a racing wire room at 403 Milwaukee Avenue in Chicago and found three homemade switchboards made out of wooden boxes and six telephone lines under fraudulent names. Nick Bravos was arrested and charged with operating a gaming establishment.

In 1954 Nick Bravos was a staple at all Chicago area racetracks working as a mob bookie. He was pulling in so much money that Arlington Park Race Track began to not let him into the park. In 1959 his brother George Bravos was ejected from Balmoral Race Track and in 1962 Nick Bravos, George Bravos, Charles "Chuckie" English, and his brother Sam "Butch" English were barred from Sportsman's Race Track, Arlington Race Track, Washington Race Track, and Hawthorne Race Track---forever.

In April 1958, Nick Bravos and Rocco Collucio were discharged from court after being charged with operating a wire room at the old Santa Fe Hotel on West Polk Street in Chicago.

In the 1960's the FBI learned that Nick Bravos was running a "juice" operation for his alleged cousin Gus Alex and was being placed in a position that if things got too hot about "juice" loans in Chicago, Nick Bravos was set up to be the scapegoat for Gus Alex's "juice" operations.

File Card
Nick Bravos
AKA: Nick the Greek
Birth: July 22, 1913
Death: July 13, 1969

Known Addresses
717 N. Crawford Avenue, Chicago (1931)
714 North Pulaski, Chicago (1950)
2139 South Michigan Avenue, Chicago (1958)
2059 North Newcastle, Chicago (1961)
8831 Kathy Lane, Des Plaines (1969)

Known Businesses
Better Burner Service (1945)
A-1 Industrial Uniform Company (1963)
Roth-Adams Fuel Company (1960's)
Old Brown Laundry (1964) (Front for bookmaking)
Allison's Coffee Shop, Des Plaines (1966)
Grecian Gardens Restaurant and Night Club, Chicago (1966)

Known Hangouts
Athens Restaurant Harrison and Halsted Streets (1960)
Helas Café, Halsted Street (1960)
Bathhouse at Touhy and Western Avenue (1967)

George James Bravos was the oldest of the two brothers, being born on March 4, 1911, and attending Austin High School in Chicago. George was considered a "juice" boss and bookie for the West and Northsides of Chicago. Mostly under the control of mobsters Gus Alex, Lennie Patrick, and David Yaras, he went by the name of "George the Greek."

Officially, George Bravos stated his occupation as a clerk and salesman. He was married in 1931 in Waukegan, Illinois, to Alice Hoffman and divorced in 1943. That same year Chicago police reported that George Bravos was the owner and operator of the Vanity Fair Tavern at 4751 W. Madison Street with a Peter Trakas. It was reported that bookmaking was being conducted at that location.

In October 1951 authorities raided the attic at 2891 Milwaukee Avenue where they found a handbook center and wire room with 19 telephones. Arrested were George Bravos, John Pachon, Erwin Smith, and Joseph Sislon.

The Chicago Police had many complaints regarding investigations for a series of burglaries involving scarce metals. Listed in the investigation was George Bravos who was connected to an Arnold Plating Company.

On November 16, 1955, the Chicago division of the FBI received a phone call from George Bravos saying that his brother Nick had been kidnapped, and a ransom of $75,000 was demanded or his brother would be killed. He told agents that his brother's hat was found on the sidewalk in front of his home at 2059 Newcastle and his brother was nowhere to be found.

During the investigation it was discovered that the ransom demand was made to Nick Bravos close friend Carl Torraco. Torraco was known in the Capone Gang as Charlie Carr. Torraco was one of the "old timers" in Chicago who got his start as an agent for Johnny Torrio in the early 1920's. He would go on to become a private gunman for Al Capone, a bootlegger in Melrose Park, and manager of Capone's Four Deuces Saloon. Torraco was even responsible for providing the guns for the infamous killings of Assistant State's Attorney William H. McSwiggin in 1926 and the killing of 7 Moran Gang members in the St. Valentine's Day Massacre on February 14, 1929. Shortly after that murder, Carl Torraco was found guilty of robbing a bank with gangsters David Taddeo and Carlos Stepina and was sent to Joliet Prison for 5 years. It was there that Torraco and Bravos served time as inmates and became good friends. Once out, Torraco went into semi-retirement running his bookmaking from Harry's Billiards at 2553 West Chicago Avenue.

Torraco had been selected as intermediary in the ransom negotiations. Not breaking any speed records for a known mobster that the FBI wanted to see locked up in prison for life, they began their investigating. However, two days later, the authorities went to Nick's home where they found Carl Torraco, George Bravos, and Nick Bravos all sitting in the living room together unharmed. While being questioned, Nick told the authorities *"The whole kidnapping business is strictly a phony, it never happen."*

A newspaper reporter went to Nick Bravos' house and managed to get him to come to the door to give a comment on this story. Nick told the reporter, *"You know, a lot of people get excited about things. You newspaper people get a lot of rumors."*

All three were placed under arrest and served with grand jury subpoenas to answer questions. All three refused to talk and were eventually released.

But it did happen. Nick Bravos was kidnapped and the $75,000 was paid and Nick was released unharmed. Since the Bravos brothers were listed then as lieutenants of Jackie Cerone, Cerone attempted to learn the identity of the kidnappers but was unsuccessful. Cerone then went to Charles "Chuckie" Nicoletti who "put the finger" on the men who kidnapped Bravos. The three kidnappers only identified as one Greek man and two Italians were found murdered in the trunk of a car near Plainfield, Illinois.

File Card
George J. Bravos
AKA: George the Greek
Birth: March 4, 1911
Death: November 11, 1988

Known Occupations
Vanity Fair Lounge, 4751 West Madison, Chicago (1947)
L&M Disposal Company (1960's)
Atlantic Industrial Uniform Supply, Miami, Florida (1960)
A-1 Industrial Uniform Company (1963)
Parking Lot Attendant (506 West Harrison)

Known Addresses
717 N. Crawford Avenue, Chicago (1933)
920 West Cullon Street (1940's)
715 North Pulaski Road, Chicago (1971)

Known Hangouts
Damen Avenue and Division Street (Chicago)
Mannheim and Higgins Roads, (Rosemont)
Grand Avenue and Thatcher Road (River Grove)
Chicago Avenue and Damen (Chicago)
Chicago and Western Avenues (Chicago)
Golden Bear Pancake House (River Forest)
845 West North Avenue
Logan Square Area (Chicago)
Sportsman's Park (Cicero)
Currency Exchange at 23rd and Cicero Avenues
Chicago Greek Town, Halsted and Van Buren Streets (1966)
Perry's Coffee Shop, (Chicago)
Mary Ann's Pancake House (Chicago)

The FBI learned that the Bravos brothers were running their "juice" loan racket in the Chicago Loop with Gus Alex receiving considerable income from it. What happened was the Bravos Brothers had been instructed by Gus Alex to discontinue their gambling operations in 1962 because both brothers had become two of the most recognizable bookmakers at all the racetracks. They were causing too much heat and it was spilling over to the unknown bookmakers working the races. So they went full force into the "juice" field full time.

Information stated that the reference to the Shylocking business prior to 1961, individuals had been assuming risk of their own in connection with loans, and if they had a bad loan, they handled the situation themselves on an independent basis. An informant said that George Bravos explained to him that there was a clearinghouse which maintained records of individuals applying for these loans. Bravos said that when he loaned money, generally at 20 percent for 10 months, he was told by bosses that when he had a loan outstanding he would generally attempt to have the debtor take out life insurance for the amount of the loan plus interest outstanding.

One unlucky gambler who became a confidential source for the FBI said his story was that in 1961 that he had been heavily engaged in gambling activities in the Chicago area with regard to betting on horses and playing in poker and dice games. His losses were in excess of $15,000 and it became necessary for him to make contact with individuals in the "juice" racket. He was placed in contact with George Bravos who at the time was operating out of a poolroom on Chicago Avenue just two doors west of Western Avenue. Bravos had arrangements where he assumed the debts of the indebted individual and paid them off. These debts were mostly to other "juice" operators and Bravos made his dealings with these "juice" operators. In turn, the indebted individual was required to pay over $300 a week in interest due to this arrangement. None of the $300 was applied to the principal of the loan. He also added that another "juice" collector by the name of "Pete," used to hang out in a saloon across the street from the Bravos brothers' poolroom and was known as a very tough "juice" collector. The two competed for business.

Another source in that year stated that the Bravos brothers moved their "juice" operations to a flower shop located at Chicago and California Avenues in Chicago. The informant said that in the basement of this flower shop, a safe was kept containing all their "juice" records. This informant said that the way the Bravos' brothers worked was that they would loan $1,000 to a borrower and he would have to pay back $100 a week for 15 weeks. If he was slow in his payments, they would go after him in every way.

Another example was that of Mike LaJoy, a nephew of William Daddono's wife. In 1963, LaJoy was the owner and operator of LaJoy Grocery Land on Lincoln Avenue and served as a front for William Daddono at Joy's Liquors at 16th and Kedzie in Chicago. LaJoy had become heavily indebted to Bravos due to his gambling looses and had been taking money out of his grocery store operation to pay the losses. He took so much money out that his grocery store was nearly bankrupt, and he still needed money to pay his gambling debts. LaJoy was taken to George Bravos at the A-1 Industrial Uniform Service where Bravos advised him that he would be given $8,000 for which LaJoy was to pay $400 a week "juice" on the loan for an indefinite period. LaJoy became heavily indebted through his losses to the bookmaking operations of Joe "Caesar" DiVarco and to the gambling losses incurred in the "Chicago Avenue crap game" run by Mike Lupo and Johnny "Bananas" DiBiase.

Information was also given that LaJoy had taken an $8,000 "juice" loan from Joseph "Spa" Spadevecchio. Because LaJoy could not make his "juice" payment, it was reported that William Daddono paid LaJoy's loan off to George Bravos, Joe Spadevecchio and mobster Donald Angelini. As it turned out it was not enough for LaJoy, he was arrested on September 27, 1963, for robbing the Franklin Park State bank.

Another informant told the authorities that the Bravos brothers would also maintain "juice" representatives to make on-the-spot "loans" to any gamblers at the mentioned games and numerous other games in the Chicago area.

Because of their success in the gambling and "juice" business, they started a business known as A-1 Industrial Uniform Service located at 1217 North Oakley, 77 West Washington Street and 3330 West Lake Street in Chicago. Along with the Bravos brothers in this business were Chicago and Miami, Florida, mobster David Yaras, and mobster and President of the Chicago Laundry Workers Union, Local 46, Gus Zapas. A-1 Industrial Uniform Service expanded to four large industrial laundries in the Chicago area and two laundry firms in Miami.

Another person involved in the company was the brother-in-law of outfit Capo Charles Nicoletti. This brother-in-law, known as Tony, was made a boss in A-1's offices. Another individual by the name "Boston" assisted Nicoletti's brother-in-law in running a portion of the business, while Faith Bravos, daughter of George Bravos, worked as an accountant for the firm. At the time, the Bravos brothers had unlimited funds at their disposal to run the business and used their hoodlum and political connections in the City of Chicago to build rapidly expanding business. Among mob labor union bosses listed as steering business their way were Gus "Windshields" Zapas, Sam English, Eco James Coli, Eugene "Jimmy" James, Tom "Juke Box" Smith, Joey Glimco, Al Pilotto, Vince Solano, and Tony "X" Esposito.

The A-1 Company quickly claimed most of the laundry business in the city making other laundry businesses lose most of their business including the Industrial Uniform Company that was owned by mobster Fred Evens. After Evens was killed, the company was sold to a legitimate firm.

In 1964 the Bravos brothers were faced with a problem. The machinery at A-1 was in need of repair. They discussed taking out a $500,000 loan to upgrade the machines but, in mob fashion, quickly switched to the idea of blowing up the laundry building and collecting the insurance to build a new laundry building.

When the FBI investigated the A-1 Company in 1964, they discovered that the Bravos brothers were running a "juice" loan business in connection with the laundry stops. An informant said that when a customer wanted to borrow money, an interest of 10% percent per week was made on the loan until it was paid back in-full. The drivers for A-1 would collect the normal A-1 laundry service payments at the same time they were collecting the principal and interest payments on these loans. They even increased their laundry route among Clark Street restaurant owners where they would try to get the owners "hooked" on juice to them so they could make a delivery and a pick-up at the same time.

One complaint came from a gas station owner who made an agreement with one of A-1's truck drivers to rent uniforms from A-1 for his gasoline attendants. Back in the 1960's when you pulled into a gas station, a service attendant would walk out to your vehicle and fill your gas tank up for you. These men wore uniforms and the owner paid a weekly bill to rent them. The owner stated that A-1 was slow in furnishing the uniforms and that a weekly billing was started immediately for the use of the uniforms before any had, in fact, been delivered. When the owner contacted George Bravos to cancel the agreement, Bravos informed that owner that he was still accountable for the weeks he agreed to pay and had outstanding bills for the uniforms he never received.

Gus Zapas had his hand in other forms of the loan shark racket. Another company connected with "juice" was the Hacking Brother's Company owned by Joseph Panucci. In 1962 Panucci was seen meeting with James "Monk" Allegretti and Dominic Nuccio at Valentino's Restaurant in Chicago. Hacking Brothers had some help from mobster Gus Zapas who would direct his members of his union to borrow considerable amounts of money when they were in need of loans. It was believed that Zapas was getting a kickback from the amount of people he sent. Mobsters listed as being directly connected with Hacking Brothers were Fifi Buccieri, Joe Ferriola, Albert "Obbie" Frabotta, Felix Alderisio, and the Bravos Brothers.

George "The Greek" Bravos was one of the most feared non-Italian "juice" men in the 1960's. He operated his bookmaking operations at the building located at 2406 West Chicago Avenue. This establishment was operated primarily as an incentive for gamblers to borrow from George on "juice" terms. The loans were made at this establishment for the purpose of gambling on horse races and sporting events. Informants enjoyed telling the FBI about George's private life. He lived at 715 Pulaski Avenue in Chicago with his daughter, Faith, and his son-in-law who was an Italian hairdresser. The informant said George was very frugal and very obnoxious, and was hated by most of the hoodlums in Chicago. His girlfriend was named Mary Kelly, who was a partner in a photo embossing firm on North Avenue. The two met when Kelly worked at the old mob hangouts known as Blackie's Restaurant and the Le Bistro in Chicago. While Kelly worked at her job, George dated another girl by the name of Miralla, who was a Greek belly dancer often featured at the old Kismet Night Club in Chicago. Another girl he frequently went out with was named Muriel, who was alleged to be an independent prostitute working out of the old Tony's Cellar on Rush Street.

George and his brother Nick would leave their homes everyday at around 10:15 in the morning and head for the racetracks for business. The informant said that the brothers got along well in their business relations but did not particularly agree on family and social opinions and kept their families, as well as their social lives, separated..

At the racetracks, the brothers utilized many hoodlums to run their racket. Obbie Oberlander and Eddie Gates, listed as two notorious Northside gamblers, were used as runners inside the tracks. Tommy Bova, known as "Big Tony," operated a book under the Bravos control inside some of the parks. Bova was a one-time waiter at the old Ricardo's Restaurant on Rush Street.

The FBI discovered in the 1960's that Nick Bravos was paying Frank Papa, then Captain of the Chicago Police force, $1,000 a week to operate freely inside the tracks. Another report alleged that George Bravos took up a pool of $1,000 at the racetracks from the other bookies to pay off a Mr. Robilowski, listed as the then police chief of Stickney, Illinois.

One of the victims listed in connection with the Bravos brothers and racing tracks was a Tom Downs, who was in charge of security at Sportsman's Park Race Track and Hawthorne Park Race Track in 1960. Downs, also a Chicago policeman, allegedly owed the Bravos brothers $10,000 in bets placed. Instead of paying the owed money, the Bravos brothers let Downs "eat it up," meaning that this amount was reduced every time Downs won. Instead of Downs paying back the money, he was used and expected to handle any problems for the Bravos brothers while they were operating their book inside the parks. When Downs was questioned by the FBI, he denied that he owed anyone any money; he denied that there was any horse books at either race track, and he denied being involved with any hoodlums. He did admit knowing Gus Alex, Murray Humphreys, and the Bravos brothers but said that his association was that they would come and eat at his restaurant called the Singapore Steak and Chop House in Chicago. It was reported that allegedly, before Downs owed money to the Bravos brothers, he demanded they pay him $500 a day to operate their book and an additional $50 for each of the other bookies under the Bravos control at the track.

An incident that occurred in the early 1960's was when George was overheard on a hidden FBI microphone complaining how mad he was at the "Italian" element in Chicago for the way they treated him. He and mobster Rocco Potenza set up a huge crap game in a warehouse-type building across the street from the old Flamingo Hotel in Cook County. Once the game was up and running and began to make large sums of money, Rocco Potenza "kicked out" Bravos and the "Italians" controlled the game. Bravos also complained that he had set Potenza up with the Flamingo Hotel which would house the crap's game when the "heat was on," meaning the police were looking for the game to shut it down. George added that since Potenza was Sam Giancana's man and Giancana was behind the operation, he had no strength whatsoever in the Giancana organization, being more closely associated with the Gus Alex group.

Bravos's connections reached into city hall in Chicago when it was exposed that Nick Bravos was selling most of the coal used by the Chicago Sanitary District. In May 1963 Nick Bravos was found on the payroll of the Roth Adam Fuel Company and was paid over $15,000 in salary. The Roth Adam Firm was owned by Edwin Roth Sr. who received $500,000 in coal contracts from the Chicago Sanitary District controlled by Frank Chesrow, who was alleged to be a relative of mob boss Tony Accardo. Many times Chicago detectives followed the Bravos brothers as they drove from gambling den to wire room in a black convertible bearing the license plate number DM 9921 which was issued to Roth Adam Fuel Company.

Law enforcement reports recorded that word on the streets of Chicago was that George and Nick Bravos went into semi-retirement in Florida where they were becoming more involved in operations with David Yaras in Miami Beach. According to reports, George Bravos was ordered back to Chicago by mob bosses to revise the crime syndicates Northside gambling and shylocking operations. He was back only a few months when he was arrested for kidnapping one of his "juice" victims.

However in 1965, George Bravos was supplying the money that Willie Messino needed to run his "juice" racket, where Messino would split his shares of the profits fifty-fifty with Bravos. It did not last long when in August 1965 George Bravos, Messino, and Joe Lombardi were arrested for aggravated kidnapping and aggravated battery against the Chiagouris brothers.

After the arrest, George Bravos was quickly removed as President of A-1 Uniform Company and Leonard Yaras, son of mobster David Yaras, was installed as President. David Yaras sent orders to the Bravos brothers to stay away from the A-1 company.

At the end of the 1960's, Bravos was once again in trouble when he was charged for beating a West Side restaurateur who fell behind on his "juice" payments. The charge didn't matter. After 5 years of court appearances and appeals, George Bravos was found guilty and arrived at Joliet Prison on February 27, 1970, to start serving his four sentences, three of them for 1-to-10 years and one for 5-to-20 years.

Once released from prison, he mostly remained out of the spotlight. There was mention of George Bravos in investigations here and there. One report from January 1981, involved an investigation into a syndicate bookie ring involving the lost revenue of a racetrack in the southern part of the U.S. The alleged bookies involved were Dick Stevens, Bill Pappas, James Roberts, and Alf Ritroni. When Roberts arrived in Dearborn, Michigan, to visit some relatives, he was searched by law enforcement agents and a plane ticket was found with the name "George Bravos, Chicago" written on it. All of these men were listed as being connected to organized crime in Chicago.

Nick Bravos died of throat cancer at Wesley Memorial hospital on July 13, 1969. His wake was held at Kringas and Marzullo Funeral Home at 5400 W. Harrison and his funeral at Holy Trinity Greek Orthodox Church at 6047 W. Diversey. He is buried in Elmwood Cemetery, Illinois. The FBI stood outside the doors of the funeral home and wrote down the names of most of the mobsters attending. The list included William Messino, Joseph Gagliano, Chris Cardi, Jasper Campise, Charles English, Charles Nicoletti, Jack Cerone, Paul Ricca, George Dicks, Gus Zapas, Felix Alderisio, and Anthony Accardo.

George Bravos lived to the old age of 77 when he died at Rush-Presbyterian-St. Luck's Medical Center of natural causes on November 11, 1988. His Funeral was held at Holy Trinity Greek Orthodox Church and he was entombed at Elmwood Cemetery.

Leonard Patrick, Known as "Lennie"

Lennie Patrick was listed as being very close to Gus Alex and was a "juice" man operating on the west side of Chicago. Patrick was known as an old-time Chicago hoodlum with vast connections to Chicago bookmakers and gamblers. Patrick always had a representative of his in gambling operations which were supervised by other members of the gambling syndicate. In this instance, Patrick would not have direct interest in the gambling activities, but his representative would be in a position to handle many "juice" loans to the gamblers patronizing the bookmaking establishment or the gambling game.

Born in Chicago on October 6, 1913, Leonard Patrick lived at 2820 West Jarlath Avenue and 7425 W. Belmont in Chicago with his wife Lorraine Ordman and their two daughters, Sharon and Sara Lee. He used the nicknames of Leonard Levine, Joseph Cohen, Pete Leonardi, Joe Cohn, Patrick Leonard, Pete Peonardi, and Blinkey.

Lennie was assisted in his operations by his brothers Mike Patrick and Jack Patrick. His arrest record dates back to 1932 with an arrest for murder. He had a conviction in 1933 for bank robbery and received 10 years in prison. In 1947 he was arrested for murder but was released.

In the 1950's a man by the name of Harry Levine was working as a "juice man" and was associated with Lennie Patrick, Davey Yaras, and Jack Patrick. This was an illegitimate operation and to establish a so-called legitimate source of income, Levine started the Reliable Products novelty business. Lennie Patrick, Jack Patrick, and Davey Yaras soon showed an interest in the place which handled novelties, toys, jewelry, and similar general merchandise. This business was more of a front for his more lucrative business of shylocking. Lennie and Jack would actually put up some of the money that was loaned on a 6-for-5 basis but only on the okay from Harry Levine. Levine would never use actual violence in making collections but on occasions he had to resort to threats and similar non-violent means to scare some of his accounts to "pay up."

In the 1960's Davey Yaras and Lennie Patrick began to ease Harry

Levine out of the "juice" business and fearing for his life, he left Chicago. The business was taken over by Patrick who put Rudy "The Mule" Wolfar and a man known as "Solly," a one-time cab driver, in charge. The business made over $100,000 a year in "juice".

One place known to be under the interest of Patrick was the Lawndale Restaurant located at 3700 Roosevelt Road in Chicago. Rudy "The Mule" Wolfer was the "juice" man who

395

could always be found at the Lawndale and usually carried between $5,000 and $10,000 in cash. He supplied the "juice" for the gambling rooms located in the back of the restaurant. He always kept the money to make payoffs in the drawer under the cash register stand.

A man by the name of Maurice "Greenie" Greene, a disbarred attorney, was listed as being under the control of Lennie Patrick and represented Patrick at many mob roulette and major craps games. In the 1960's Patrick had a piece of the "juice" loans from the 6-for-5 money operations at the old J & J Picnic Grove at 159th Street and Wolf Road in Will County.

Other associates seen in the company of Lennie Patrick in 1962 were Gus Alex, Felix "Milwaukee Phil" Alderisio, Joey Aiuppa, Dave Yaras, and Sam DeStefano.

Jack "Hot Dog" Wilensky, an informant, told the police that he knew of an Arthur "Boodie" Cowan who was a "juice" collector and enforcer in connection with Louis Henick. Cowan was a bookmaker on Morse Avenue and worked out of the old Tip Top Hat Tavern. Cowan also ran card games for Lennie Patrick and ran his own handbook in the Morse Avenue Social Club, which was located on Morse Avenue near the El station.

In 1970 Patrick was listed as one of the top "juice" men active in Chicago. Listed as his area of operations were California and Foster Avenues, Lincoln and Foster Avenues in Chicago, Dempster Street between Kostner Avenue and McCormick Boulevard in Skokie.

One of Patrick's "juice" collectors who specialized in collecting special "hard-to-collect" loans was named James LaValley. Also known as an adult bookstore owner for the mob, LaValley one time cut the hand off of a dead beat "juice" victim and threatened to cut the other arm of an amputee who was behind in his payments. LaValley joined the long line of mob rats turning government informant. As of 2007, LaValley was going to testify in the "Family Secrets" mob trial in Chicago, which was charging Chicago's top mob figures for 18 unsolved mob murders.

Lennie Patrick would go on to become a mob rat sending many of his oldest and closest friends to prison. He entered the witness protection program and it may never be known if he is alive or dead.

Sam Cesario

Born around 1919 in Chicago, Sam Cesario was known as "Sambo" and was a known "juice" man in the Taylor Street area of Chicago. He was listed as living at 917 S. Bishop Street in 1966 and later 1070 W. Polk Street.

Listed as a lieutenant under Sam Battaglia, Sambo was well known as a First Ward hoodlum. It was mentioned in 1964 that Sambo was the stepfather to a young girl whose mother was from the Briatta family. It was believed that Sambo and Louis Briatta controlled some of the "juice" in Chicago's Little Italy together.

Sambo was mostly known for controlling mob card games and gambling. On October 19, 1971, while Sambo sat in front of his house on Polk Street with his wife Nan, he was shot to death by two masked mob hit men with white cloths covering their faces. Underworld rumors said that Sambo was killed for two reasons; one, he was expanding his operations into the south end of the Loop section of Chicago without permission; and two, he married the ex-girlfriend of mobster Felix "Milwaukee Phil" Alderisio while Felix was in prison. No one was ever arrested for his murder.

Maishie Baer, Real name Morris Saletko

Maishie Baer, as he was commonly known, was listed as a "juice" man in the Loop area and the South Water Market section of Chicago. According to reports, he had "juice" representatives in many of the crap games in the Loop area, and in this instance, the "juice" rate was on a 6-for-5 basis.

Born as Morris Saletko on June 6, 1914 in Chicago, he was listed as living at 4255 Chase Avenue in Lincolnwood, Illinois. Maishie Baer conducted much of his book making at the old Comiskey Park during the Chicago White Sox baseball games in the 1960's.

Another report stated that Baer was a partner of Frank Zimmerman and Lennie Patrick. Zimmerman controled the H&H Restaurant at 209 La Salle Street in Chicago, which had been a known gathering place for small time hoodlums. Big shot hoodlums seen there were Leslie "Killer Kane" Kruse and Ralph Pierce, both very close friends of Baer's.

Leslie Kruse was listed as being a financial backer of Baer in one of his "juice" operations. Through Kruse, it was believed that Gus Alex had a piece of Baer's shylocking business since Gus Alex controlled the Loop. Also seen at H&H on many occasions were Cook County Judges Anton Wosik and "Buck" Sorrentino who were seen having many conversations with various hoodlums.

One informant said Baer was a very important person to borrow money from, and he continually threatened to send someone out to collect the debts owed to him.

Another report stated that Maishie Baer had financially backed the "juice" and gambling operations of mobster Rocco Potenza in the unincorporated area of Niles, Illinois. In 1962 Baer and his partner known only as "Mannie" handled "juice" operations at a large crap game run by mobster Gus Liebe. This crap game was under the control of Rocco Fishetti and Leslie "Killer Kane" Kruse. It was reported that Maishie Baer was forced to take over the operations by himself when "Mannie" died.

FBI agents went to see Baer on May 13, 1962 to question him about being involved in the rackets. Baer denied that he ever had anything to do with the syndicate and denied knowing Gus Alex, Sam DeStefano, Frank Ferraro, Louis Briatta, or Nick "Mosey" Garambone. He refused to answer if he was the owner or operator of the H & H Restaurant and told the agents *"I don't know anything, all I do is sell sandwiches."* He also informed the agents that he did not have any education and said, *"You're just trying to get me to say something and trap me. I have nothing further to say."*

In June 1962, Maishie Baer was arrested for attempting to bribe Sergeant Raymond O'Malley of the Shakespeare Avenue Police Station in Chicago. Baer offered a $100 bribe to go easy on a George Kambouris who was going to appear in front of the judge in traffic court.

One of the goons reported working for Baer as a muscle man and slugger was Irving Gordon; Gordon was given the nickname of "The Market Master."

In 1967 Baer was found guilty with 12 other men of conspiring to hijack $994,000 worth of camera equipment and silver. However, the conviction was overturned.

In March 1970 Baer was sentenced to 8 years in federal prison in Sandstone, Minnesota, for receiving stolen property from an interstate shipment. After being released from prison in 1975, Baer was shot in the hand while he stood at a fruit stand with hoodlum George "Peacock" Weinberg on Jackson Boulevard. Weinberg, a small-time hoodlum, was shot in the back. Both lived and refused to say why someone wanted to kill them.

It did not matter because on July 13, 1977, the body of Maishie Baer was found in his 1977 Oldsmobile in front of 6505 W. Diversey Avenue in Chicago. He had been shot in the left side of his head. At the time, he had been listed as living at 4255 Chase Avenue in Lincolnwood, Illinois. In 2007 reports came out alleging that Joey "the Clown" Lombardo had something to do with the murder. Which is still unsolved.

James Catuara, Known as "The Bomber"

Known as "Jimmie the Bomber," "The Owl," and James Catura, Jimmy Catuara lived at 9600 S. Kilbourn Avenue in Oak Park. Born around 1906, Jimmie the Bomber was convicted in 1933 on charges of compounding explosives and he received 5 to 25 years in prison.

In 1970 he was listed as one of Chicago's top "juice" men operating at 68th Street and Damen Avenue, 31st Street and Princeton Avenue, Lumber and 18th Streets in Chicago, and Lincoln Highway and Washington Avenue in Chicago Heights.

James Catuara was considered the biggest "juice" operator in the south suburban area of Chicago in the 1960's. According to reports, running these operations for Catuara were Charles Gus Rubino and William Earl Dauber. The major portion of "juice" loans were made in connection with gambling losses, but Catuara was also known to make loans to small taverns.

Charles Rubino once operated the Ace Bonding Company at 139th and Western and made numerous loans to ex-convicts and would then "set up" burglaries for them so they could repay the monies.

In 1964 it indicated that most of the gambling was down in the south suburbs and most of the "action" was in Gary, Indiana. It was reported that Catuara was attempting to determine if he could move his operation to that section to get in on the money. However it was learned that Catuara was at odds with mob boss Frank La Porte over the "cutting-up" of the profits in La Porte's section.

On July 28, 1978, Jimmy Catuara was sitting in his Cadillac at the corner of Ogden Avenue and Hubbard Street when two hoodlums walked up to his car and opened fire. Catuara was shot a few times in the neck. Wounded, Catuara managed to lean over and open his passenger side door where he fell out of his car and fell face first onto the sidewalk. One of the killers walked up to him and shot him in the back to make sure he would die.

Police believed that Catuara's murder was either linked to the mob's "chop shop" operation in which Catuara had some power, or some suspected that Catuara was involved in narcotics deals without the permission of mob bosses. Illinois State Police had been investigating syndicate "chop shop" operations and had been forcing Catuara and other mobsters to close up their operations causing a major strain on the Outfit's cash flow.

On July 8, 1978, the mob placed a bomb at the home of one of the investigators to send a message to back off its investigation into the "chop shop" rackets. The investigator accidentally kicked the bomb that had been placed on his porch and defused it.

Catuara's murder capped off a string of murders that had plagued Catuara's operations for a few years. Catuara's enforcer Richard Ferraro disappeared on June 13, 1977, and has never been found. His chief enforcer Sam Annerino was shot to death on July 24, 1977. A robber and associate of Catuara's named Joseph Theo was shot to death on June

15, 1976. Other men shot to death connected to Catuara were James Palaggi, Steve Ostrowsky, Earl Abereromble Jr., Harry Holser, Norman Lang, and a one-time racecar driver named Robert Pronger Jr. whose body was listed as never being found. James Catuara is buried at St. Mary's Cemetery in Evergreen Park, Illinois.

Guido Fidanzi

Listed as one of Catuara's men involved in the "juice" racket in 1967 was Guido J. Fidanzi. Born on October 15, 1927 in Chicago, Fidanzi was known as "The Weed." Other aliases for Fidanzi were John Arealo and Guido Finanzi. He lived at 220 Arquilla Road in Chicago Heights, Illinois, and was known to be involved in "juice," frequenting 155th Street and Dorchester Avenue in Dolton, Illinois.

His arrest record contained nine arrests with no convictions. In October 1959, Fidanzi was arrested for extorting money from a tavern owner in a scheme to fix a court case against her. In 1968, Fidanzi was convicted of federal income tax evasion and sentenced to 5 years in the Federal Correctional Institute at Texarkana, Texas. He did manage to get released on $10,000 bond while his appeal was being pressed but he quickly had his bond revoked on April 18 when several people complained that he was threatening them.

On April 30, 1969, Fidanzi and a Chicago attorney named Harvey Powers were named in a federal grand jury indictment. The two were accused of operating fraud operations preying on businessmen from 1964 thru 1967. According to the charge, both men used the mail and interstate telephone calls to con businessmen into paying fees for promised loans and then reneging on the promises after obtaining advanced payments from the businessmen. Fidanzi had 4 years added to the end of his prison sentence.

In February 1972, Guido Fidanzi was indicted with mobsters James Catuara, Frank "One Ear" Fratto, Earl Dauber, and Louis "Lou the Tailor" Rosanova for bilking $1 million from colleges, convalescent homes, and more that 70 hospitals. The 19 men indicted used a phony organization called the Church of Christ Manors, Inc. to collect fees ranging as high as $46,500. Other men named in the indictment were Alexander Gaus Jr.,

Stanley Durka, Anthony Gizzi, Daniel Jerome, James Micucci, Robert Ostrander, Stanley Schulman, M.D. Scott, George Stanaszek, Charles Verive, Louis Verive, and Chester Weisinger.

While in prison, Fidanzi became good friends with fellow mobster Richard Cain who was serving time on a conviction. Both were paroled around October 1971. While Fidanzi was in prison he reached out to his boss James Catuara to financially take care of his wife Thelma while he was away, which Catuara did. Once out of prison Fidanzi was in desperate need of fast cash to pay his growing legal fees and began to set up his operations outside of his territory in Cook County.

On August 8, 1972, Guido Fidanzi drove to see his brother-in-law Tony Renzetti at his gas station located at 251 E. 14th Street in Chicago Heights. Fidanzi pulled into the gas station and parked his car. As he walked to the front door he passed his brother-in-law and said some words. Another car pulled in needing service so Renzetti walked to the car to fill it up with gas. Fidanzi walked into the office and waited for Renzetti to finish so he could talk to him. Another car pulled into the station and Renzetti looked over and said *"Be with you in a minute."* Before he could finish, a man got out of the car with a gun and handkerchief over his face and said, *"Get down."* Another man emerged from the car and walked into the gas station, ignoring a telephone repairman and a customer standing at the desk, he walked into the office. Fidanzi noticed the man walking in with a gun in his hand and screamed, *"Oh, God"* as the gunman opened fire from his .22 caliber pistol. The first shot missed hitting the cash register as Fidanzi bolted for the bathroom just feet away. As he tried to close the door to lock himself in, the gunman kicked the door knocking Fidanzi onto his back. The gunman relaxed and smiled as he unloaded his gun into Fidanzi. Once the gun was empty, the gunman calmly placed it back into his coat and took out another revolver and shot Fidanzi two times in the head to make sure he was dead. He then walked out of the gas station and drove away with his masked accomplice.

When it was all over, Fidanzi had been shot 13 times in the chest, groin, and head. Among the theories thrown around as to why Fidanzi was killed was because he was stepping on other mobster's toes while running "juice" in their territory, or he was trying to take over the rackets from James Catuara, or he was holding back on his "juice" collections. One report alleged that James Catuara and alleged mobster Frank Schweihs were seen together not too far from the gas station a week before the killing.

Felix Alderisio, known as "Milwaukee Phil" Alderisio

Felix Anthony Alderisio, real name "Alderizio" was born in Yonkers, New York, on April 26, 1910 or 1912, both dates are listed in his records. He made his way west ending up in both Chicago and Milwaukee. His parents, Domenico (Dominic) Alderizio and Ippolito (Pauline) Materesa, were both born in Italy before coming to America. They remained in Yonkers, New York, with their two daughters Phyllis and Anna.

Having dropped out of school after completing the 7th grade, Felix Alderisio was always considered a smart and tough up-and-coming hoodlum. He held a variety of jobs; in 1933 he worked at Richardson's Grocery Store in Yonkers; in 1934 he worked for Westchester Ice Company in Yonkers, and was listed as a truck driver for Armand Trucking Company in Chicago in 1935. He married Molly W. Prapopke in Miami Beach, Florida in 1935, and the two of them would later adopt a young boy.

He gained the nickname of "Milwaukee Phil" and simply was known to his associates as Phil "Philly" Alderisio. His criminal record dates back to December 17, 1929, in Chicago when he was arrested for disorderly conduct. On December 8, 1930, he was arrested in Yonkers on a charge of third degree assault, which was a misdemeanor. On January 14, 1933, a charge of disorderly conduct was listed; on May 3, 1933, he was arrested for auto theft in Wheaton, Illinois, and on December 6, 1933, he was arrested once again for disorderly conduct.

In 1936 Alderisio was convicted for violation of Internal Revenue laws (possession of illegal alcohol) for which he was placed on probation for one year. He claimed that a man asked him to deliver a package for him in which he was to receive $5. He said he had no idea the package continued bootleg alcohol.

In October 1942, Alderisio enlisted in the U.S. Army serving time at Camp Grant in Illinois. He received an honorable discharge in August 1943, as a private in Miami, Florida, for a disability due to psychoneurosis, constitutional, manifested by hypochondrias, hysterical fixation on symptoms of old injuries, emotional instability with some lack of normal responses, defective ethical and moral outlook, anxiety over health and financial stability, impaired judgment, defective insight with a long history of anti-social behavior and unproductive visits to physicians and hospitals and a defective ethical and moral outlook.

Once out, he resumed his criminal career being arrested on July 27, 1945, in Detroit, Michigan, for an investigation of unlawfully driving away from a police officer. In the years of 1945 and 1946, Milwaukee Phil was observed many times at the residence of Al Capone's Miami, Florida, home. In November 1948 he was arrested at 1073 Polk Street for being the keeper of a gambling house.

File Card
Felix Anthony Alderisio
AKA: Philly, Milwaukee Phil, Phillip Aldi, Phil Gato, Felix Aldrise, Felix Alderessi, Felix Alderist, and Felix Aldrise
Born: April 26, 1912 or April 26, 1910
Died: September 25, 1971

Known Addresses
133 Elm Street, Yonkers, New York (1913)
133 Beech Street, Yonkers (1931)
2453 West Taylor Street, Chicago (1931)
2088 Ogden Avenue, Chicago (1932)
4540 Magnolia, Chicago (1942)
700 Lennox Avenue, Miami Beach, Florida (1943)
813 East Wells Street, Milwaukee, Wisconsin (1945)
725 North 5th Street, Milwaukee, Wisconsin (1954)
4736 West Addams, Chicago (1954)
515 Long Common Road in Riverside, Illinois (1958)
505 Berkeley Drive, Riverside (1964)

Known Business
Hickory House, 750 N. Rush Street in Chicago
Gay-Lur Mercantile Corp. 329 W. 18th Street in Chicago

Vicinities Frequented
Monroe Street and Ashland Avenue
Chicago Avenue and State Street
Roosevelt Road and State Street
111th Street and Western Avenue
18th and Canal Streets
Harlem and Lawrence Avenues, Norwood Park
Bennett Street and Arlington Heights Road in Elk Grove Village

Alderisio's 1964 official FBI bio reads as followed:

"Felix Alderisio has been characterized as a 'hit' man and is said to be an independent operator answerable only to Sam 'Momo' Giancana. Approximately around 1960 Alderisio was considered only a muscleman and was noted for his rough, uncouth appearance. He once appeared at a hoodlum wedding wearing a sports shirt and no tie. As of 1964 Alderisio's rise in stature in the hoodlum element has been meteoric and he has emerged as a dapper dresser who poses as a successful businessman. He invariaby dresses immaculately and on occasion when picked up by Chicago Police has had from $800 to $2,500 in his pocket, it has been alleged that he is considered in some areas as second in command to Sam Giancana, and is considered to replace Giancana when he steps out of the top spot.

Alderisio has a various businessmen operating as a front for him and providing a legitimate source of income. Alderisio also states he is a member of the Central West Dry Wall Company and allegedly draws an income from this business. In addition to these businesses in which Alderisio maintains an open contact, he is represented in various other businesses by Larry Rosenberg. These include a high school for home study and several finance companies which handle financing for the high school.

In addition to his legitimate endeavors, Alderisio is engaged in 'scam' operations, a term denoting a planned bankruptcy. It has been alleged that he has extorted money from local businessmen through set up situations where Alderisio apparently does a favor for the businessman and gets him out of trouble. Various people have been interviewed who have dealings with Alderisio but invariably furnish an untrue story and immediately advised

405

Alderisio of the FBI contact. Alderisio's associates are always in great fear of his potential to either have them beat severely or murdered.

Alderisio was in charge of the Diversey Avenue area of the Chicago Northside which includes the Commonwealth Hotel. All gambling and vice activities which took place in this area were under Alderisio's control and had to be sanctioned by him. Through his lieutenants operating in that area Alderisio received money from any and all illegal sources operating in his territory.

Alderisio is presently under two federal indictments on extortion charges, one in the Miami area and the other in the Denver area."

Concerning Alderisio's "juice" operations, a confidential source advised that the old Twin Food Products Company, which was run by mobster Leo Rugendorf as a rendering company, actually did produce shortening; however, its primary function was a front for "Milwaukee Phil" Alderisio and Albert "Obbie" Frabotta, who through Rugendorf, operated a large "juice" racket at this address. Rugendorf was listed as an operator of a butcher shop at 35th Street and Wentworth Avenue.

By way of background concerning the Twin Foods Products Company, confidential sources said that Meyer Ditlove was the original owner and was involved in the "horse meat scandal" in the 1960's involving the mob. A son-in-law of Ditlove, Lawrence Roseberg, was employed by the firm and actually supervised the shortening business. However, Rugendorf represented the interests of Alderisio and Frabotta and controlled the 6 for 5 "juice" rackets from the establishment. Also involved, according to this source, in this juice racket, was Irwin Weiner, a prominent Chicago bail bondsman. Weiner, as well as being a bail bondsman, was suspected of being a fence for stolen property and also an individual who could put up huge sums of money which a proposed fence could borrow by way of a "juice" loan in order to fence stolen property. Weiner was reputed to have an excellent contact with the local police and represented all of the better-known thieves, burglars, and hoodlums in the Chicago area.

According to this same confidential source, Tony Panzika, a prominent hoodlum from the southern suburbs of Chicago, entered into business with Rugendorf and was well connected with people influential within the higher echelon of the criminal element.

Sam Battaglia who controlled the criminal element in Melrose Park, Illinois, was also associated with Leo Rugendorf in the operation of this "juice" business. Battaglia was a prominent individual in bookmaking activities and other forms of gambling and referred many of his customers to the Twin Food Products Company. Because of newspaper notoriety, the license for the Twin Food Products Company was revoked by the City of Chicago and the shortening business ceased. However, the foregoing had no influence upon the operation of the "juice" racket that was operated out of the company. Profits derived from the "juice" racket moved through "Milwaukee Phil" Alderisio to higher members of the criminal element in the Chicago area.

Chicago informant told the FBI on March 16, 1961, that one Leroy Sterling of the Sterling-Harris Automobile Agency, also had an interest in the Nationwide Acceptance Company located on Diversey Parkway in which Alderisio and Leo Rugendorf had an interest. He advised he also learned that Sterling was making weekly "juice" payments to "Milwaukee Phil" Alderisio, "Obbie" Frabotta, and Leo Rugendorf.

This source indicated that Leroy Sterling was very much afraid of Leo Rugendorf and "Milwaukee Phil" Alderisio. In connection with Sterling's trouble regarding the disappearance of numerous automobiles from the Sterling-Harris Automobile Agency, this source stated he believed that Sterling had over-financed himself with Rugendorf, Alderisio, and other members of the Twin Food Products Company. In order to pay back the money he owed to them, Sterling sold the cars at a ridiculously low price in order to get quick money so that he might get himself out of trouble with Rugendorf and Alderisio. Sterling formerly owned the Howard-Perry Studebaker Sales, 4748 West Fullerton, which had burned down about a week prior to March 16, 1961. He stated that Sterling and Howard were very close friends and contacted each other socially, visiting each other's homes to play cards. In connection with the burning of the Howard-Perry Studebaker Sales, a source advised that the "syndicate" owned this car agency. He further advised that it was his belief that the syndicate burned this agency to realize insurance payments for the loss.

Another informant came forward in 1962 to say that Phil Alderisio, Willie Messino, Joey Aiuppa, and Lennie and Jack Patrick were the biggest syndicate loan sharks around. He advised that these juice men would only kill a person as a last resort. In most instances, they would attempt to obtain their money through threats of bodily injuries and when that failed, the borrower was considered to be a "deadbeat" and was generally eliminated.

In 1963, a confidential source said that Frank Allisio, who was a meat purveyor at the old Fulton Market in Chicago, was heavily involved in juice activities. Allisio was associated with "Milwaukee Phil" in this juice loan activity. Frank Allisio would loan the money and Alderisio would handle the collections from customers who were slow in paying.

Sometimes when a "juice" man's reputation caused fear simply when it was spoken, it became a tool for other less-feared "juice" men to get their money on the streets. In March 1963 a confidential source reported one such story as he learned that mobster Louis Tornabene had received a $2,000 loan from a person known as "Chappie" Bertucci, who used to operate the 51 East Oak Club. This club was closed due to a altercation there with two Chicago police detectives. It was learned that Tornabene was paying Bertucci $100 a week on this loan and during the period of the loan had paid $900 in juice interest. Bertucci had told Tornabene that he obtained this loan from Phil Alderisio. However, according to this source, that could not be true because Bertucci did not know Alderisio personally and could not obtain such a loan. It was not known if Alderisio ever found out that loans were being made in his name to provoke fear so that others would be paid back on time.

One frustrating moment concerning Alderisio came in February 1964 when an FBI informant told them this story. An unnamed woman who was very close to Clarice Accardo, wife of top mob boss Tony Accardo, had taken a European trip with Clarice Accardo. Once back, this unnamed woman had two sons who apparently were inveterate gamblers and had lost large sums of money at the racetrack and in order to sustain their gambling losses they had to go to various juice collectors. They had become considerably in arrears in their juice payments. The juice men involved were not known, however, they were apparently under the control of "Milwaukee Phil" Alderisio. The Alderisio group had been pressuring these sons to make their "juice" payments, and the situation had gotten to a point where they were unable to satisfy their present juice loans and had been receiving considerable pressure from the Alderisio group. According to this source, this unknown female went to the home of Anthony Accardo to plead with Clarice Accardo to intervene on behalf of her sons. Accardo then called a meeting at his River Forest home and summoned Alderisio for a discussion of the situation.

Alderisio was told by Accardo to arrange for the sons to pay back the remaining principal that they owed on their loan without any "juice" interest and to split these payments over a reasonable period of time. Alderisio apparently was not too happy with this situation, however, he agreed to Accardo's wishes. As Alderisio departed Accardo's home he reportedly stated to the unknown female, *"You should not have gone this high to get a favor done for such a small thing as this."* The Alderisio group did not bother the sons again.

Other businesses Alderisio was involved with were the Workmen Savings and Loan Association located at 2724 West 47th Street in Chicago, the Bank of Niles in Niles, Illinois and the Bank of Mascoutah. Control of these institutions was realized through the First National Mortgage Company, a mortgage brokerage business operated by Joseph Stein who was a close associate of Alderisio and a front man for him. Another man was Leonard Stallmann, a Chicago attorney who was closely associated with Stein and was also a front for Alderisio. Stein and Stallmann were on a very friendly basis with various officers of these institutions and would make arrangements whereby the First National Mortgage Company acted as a collection agency for the bank of Niles. Joe Stein had represented himself as a member of the Board of Directors of the Bank of Niles and had given his First National Mortgage Company address as a branch of the Bank of Niles.

In various mortgage brokerage deals, loans were made through the Workmen Savings and Loan and the Bank of Mascoutah. Joe Stein had indicated that several of those loans were not legitimate and would not stand close scrutiny by bank officials. Stein said that substantial fees were earned through those bogus "take out commitments" with no possibility of the commitment ever being fulfilled.

Another was the 1963 story where a Darrel Griffin owned a hardware store named "Griffin's Hardware" in Bridgeview. Griffin once had a U.S. Postal Sub-Station in Bridgeview in conjunction with his store and had misused approximately $20,000 of postal funds on his own behalf. When the postal inspectors discovered this, Griffin was relieved of the sub-station and was told to pay back every cent immediately. Because of this, Griffin went to "Milwaukee Phil" Alderisio and took out a "juice" loan. Because of this loan, Alderisio gained a foothold in the hardware store and used the store to sell stolen merchandise received from cartage thefts and as an outlet for merchandise from numerous Chicago area "scam" type bankruptcies.

In 1965 Milwaukee Phil was convicted in federal court on extortion charges and sentenced to 4½ years in prison. Right around the time he was to be released, he was convicted in 1970 for federal bank fraud receiving a sentence of 5 years to begin when his 1965 conviction was finished. However, it did not matter; on September 25, 1971, while Milwaukee Phil was walking in the recreation yard at Marion Prison in Illinois, he dropped dead of a heart attack.

Leo Rugendorf

Born on September 4, 1914, in Missouri, Leo Rugendorf was known as a syndicate "juice" man and bondsman, living at 4020 Chase Avenue in Lincolnwood. His arrest record dates back to 1934, and in March 1946 Leo Rugendorf was arrested for the murder of Theodore Lee, a meat cutter. The two had been working at the meat market at 3503 Wentworth Avenue, which was owned by the Rugendorf brothers when Lee attacked Rugendorf after a fight with a butcher knife. Rugendorf pulled out his gun and shot Lee 4 times. Rugendorf claimed self-defense and said Lee had threatened him many times prior to the killing.

In 1951, Rugendorf, Joe Bagnola, Harry Widger, and Anthony Maenza were sought for their involvement in the killing of a New Orleans used car dealer named Henry Stern. Stern was beaten to death during a robbery that netted the murderers $76,000. Rugendorf was acquitted of that charge.

In June 1956, Rugendorf was arrested for the murder of his fellow gang member Ralph Rizza whose body was found in the trunk of a car. The two had a fallout a week before Rizza's body was found. Rugendorf was never charged with the murder.

In 1961 Leo was implicated in the disappearance of 300 automobiles from a Ford car dealer agency. In 1968 he plead guilty to conspiring to conceal $228,000 in assets of a Ford Agency from the Federal Bankruptcy Court and was given 6 months in prison.

In 1970 he was found guilty of shaking down Eugene Sorinsky of $15,000 under threat of death. A year later in April 1971 Rugendorf was arrested with Thomas LoDolce for purchasing $50,000 worth of hijacked cigarettes. Also sought in that robbery were Theodore Burnett and Jack Koeller. Rugendorf was acquitted in the case.

In March 1972, Leo Rugendorf was arrested with Henry Solvang for their involvement in transporting $5,000 worth of stolen merchandise from Denver, Colorado, to Chicago in 1967. Rugendorf was also indicted for transporting $100,000 in stolen jewelry from a burglary in Indianapolis, Indiana in 1967. Leo Rugendorf died at Bethesda Hospital on April 7, 1973.

Leo's older brother Sam Rugendorf, born on October 18, 1907 in Chicago, was a partner in the meat business with Leo and was listed as a "juice" man. In March 1962, the FBI raided the home of Sam at 3117 Jarvis Avenue and found in his basement furs from a robbery in which 82 furs were taken totaling over $125,000. Others wanted in that robbery included Frank Schweihs, Tony Panzica, and Mike Condic, all known burglars who were known to dispose of their spoils thru Leo Rugendorf. Sam was found guilty and sentenced to 10 years in prison. Sam Rugendorf died in March 1977.

Chicago's Near Northside
Area Controlled by the
Ross Prio Group

Mobster Ross Prio was identified as one of the top five leaders of organized crime in the Chicago area in the 1960's. Prio was born either on May 10, 1900, or 1901 in Ciminno, Italy. He arrived in the United States on June 21, 1909, and received U.S. citizenship on September 24, 1929.

Prio got his start in the rackets as a bootlegger in the 1920's on Chicago's near Northside and amassed a fortune during the prohibition era. He was also successful in several legitimate business ventures. He had been arrested on several occasions; however, he was never convicted of any crimes. The Prio group was a very powerful group and had a very successful "juice" operation running in the 1960's and 70's.

His official 1964 FBI bio card reads, "Ross Prio is identified as one of the five leaders in organized crime in the Chicago area maintaining control of operations covering the near north and northwest sections of the city and suburbs. Included in this area is the lucrative nightclub section of Chicago, where Prio derives a great amount of income through the utilization of personnel from the Attendant Service Corporation owned by Prio, which provides hatcheck, car hikers, and other concession employees.

In addition, this section of the city provides a further outlet for the installation of machines served by the Zenith Vending Machine Company, also owned by Prio and founded by Kenny Leonard. In addition to the above income from this section of Chicago, it has always been reliably reported that Prio receives a substantial payoff monthly for protection from all large nightclubs in this area. The Playboy club, for one, pays a monthly stipend of $16,000 for protection to Prio and his underlings.

During the height of the racing season, investigations into Prio's activities led directly to the uncovering of information indicating the operation of cheap cleaning house bookmaking offices operated by Prio's lieutenants, which offices were successfully raided by local authorities based on warrants provided by the FBI. As a result of these raids, Prio has greatly reduced his bookmaking operations and recently remarked that, 'I can count the number of employees I have on one hand.' During the summer of 1964, Prio purchased a home at 6485 North Sauganash Avenue in Lincolnwood, Illinois, for approximately $80,000. During the winter season Prio spends considerable time in the Miami, Florida area, where he owns considerable real estate.

His daily activity places him in contact with his Lieutenants, namely, Vince Solano, President of Chicago Local 1 of the International Hod Carriers Union, and also the following, who serve as Prio's chauffeurs and body guards; Dominick Nuccio, Dominick DiBella, Joseph DiVarco, James Allegretti, Anthony De Monte, Frank Orlando, Ralph Scaccia, and Joseph Arnold."

Ross Prio died on December 25, 1972, in Florida and is buried at St. Joseph Cemetery in River Grove, Illinois.

Joseph DiVarco

Prio's top lieutenant in the 1960's was Joseph Vincent DiVarco, born on either July 27, 1911 or December 17, 1910 in Chicago. He lived at 4275 Jarvis in Lincolnwood, Illinois, with his wife Peggy and their two children. Known as Joe "Little Caesar" DiVarco, and Placideo DiVarco, he served a prison sentence for bootlegging during the prohibition era and a one year sentence for counterfeiting in 1937. His arrest record contained arrests for murder, fraudulent voting, and conspiracy to bribe a juror.

Listed as DiVarco's area's for "juice" loans were Rush and Delaware Streets, Fullerton Avenue and Rockwell Street, Rush and Division Streets, Ohio and State Streets in Chicago, and Milwaukee and Harlem Avenues in Niles, Illinois.

His FBI bio card from 1964 reads; "Joseph DiVarco reportedly continues to maintain his number one position directly under Ross Prio in the near Northside area of Chicago. He continues to be the individual who personally passes on all large 'juice' loans. He undoubtedly controls much of the bookmaking operations on the Chicago near Northside and a recent report reflects that he has also moved into the Loop area where he controls some of the bookmaking. He continues to maintain his position as the chief liaison individual between Ross Prio and his various underlings. He also maintains his position as the one who refers anything of note to Ross Prio when it involves Chicago Police Officers. At one time DiVarco's right hand man was hoodlum Charles Hudson.

DiVarco has long been associated in various legitimate enterprises. One of them was the A. Abbot Store Fixture Company, which handles 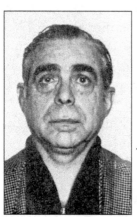 glassware, and the C & B Provision Company, which is a meat purveyor for various hotels and restaurants in the Chicago area. An informant told the Chicago PD that a Lou Sax, son of George D. Sax, then chairman of the board of the Exchange National Bank of Chicago, had some arrangement with his father, which enabled Joe DiVarco to borrow money from the bank whenever he wanted to. DiVarco keeps all his records in a safe at the Abbott Storage Fixtures place which was located at 615 North Clark Street."

After Ross Prio died and mobster Joseph DiBella was suffering from terminal cancer, Joey DiVarco became top boss of the Northside as of 1976. Acting as runner between the DiVarco-DiBella group and the Lennie Patrick group was Benny Goldberg, a Jewish hoodlum, who was a well-known bookmaker. Patrick had the far Northside of Chicago and DiVarco had the near Northside of Chicago. Both respected each other's territory.

In June 1976 DiVarco was "putting the move on" Rush Street, increasing his personal income from bookstores and taverns. The Rush Street tavern owners held a meeting. One of the topics of conversation at this meeting was the fact that DiVarco objected to Rush Street taverns having "barkers" on the street and distributing literature, inasmuch as most of those places used go-go-girls, he felt that type of activity cheapened the area and drew too much police attention to his "juice" operation. DiVarco had every porno bookstore and adult place using go-go girls pressured for protection by the Chicago Northside group.

In 1985 DiVarco was convicted of running a mob sports betting racket accepting up to $200,000 a day in bets. He was sentenced to 10 years in prison. On December 19, 1985, DiVarco was put on a plane and taken to Washington D.C. to speak with staff members of the President's Commission on Organized Crime. Sometime after the plane landed, he complained he was having chest pains and was taken to the District of Columbia Jail and brought to the prison's infirmary. On January 5, 1986, Joseph DiVarco died at the hospital of a heart attack.

James Allegretti

Another top lieutenant in the Prio group was James "Monk" Allegretti. He was born on May 31, 1905, in Naples, Italy, and entered the United States while an infant on May 15, 1906, under the name of Vincenzo Rio, stepson of Lucia Rio and son of Dominic. In 1940 he registered as an alien under the names of James Policheri and registered his name in the selective service as James Allegretti. He also used the name of James Millo.

He was nick-named "The Monk" but undercover microphones recorded mobster Murray Humphreys calling Allegretti "Fat Boy" to his face.

Allegretti received much press publicity for his activities on Chicago's near Northside as a purveyor in prostitution, strip shows, bookmaking, and "juice" activity. He was also the "fixer" for the Northside group with strong police contacts. In 1957 Allegretti was convicted in Peoria, Illinois in a conspiracy violation concerning the possession of whiskey stolen from an interstate shipment. He was sentenced to 7 years on this conviction, but was released on bond when the United States Court of Appeals overturned the conviction and ordered a new trial.

In December 1959 a 16-year old girl named Joanne Rhodes accused Allegretti of paying her $30 to perform certain acts. He was charged with contributing to the delinquency of a minor but it did not stick. He was cleared of all charges and set free.

Another incident involving Allegretti in April 1960 was when he was accused along with Joseph DiVarco of fixing the hijacking trial of mobster Gerald Covelli. A Chicago policeman named Michael Saportino disappeared after he paid his brother Robert Saportino, a juror in the Covelli case, $250 to vote not guilty, which he did.

James Allegretti operated as the ostensible head of the Chicago near Northside hoodlum element from his headquarters at 15 East Ohio Street, Chicago. This address was Valentino's Restaurant in the old Berkshire Hotel. One of the storage rooms in conjunction with Valentino's was used for the sale and distribution of "scam" merchandise. The "scam" merchandise came from businesses bankrupted by the mob, which then disposed of all the assets and without paying the suppliers.

Allegretti was often in the company of Dominic DiBella, Dominick Nuccio, Anthony De Monte, Joe DiVarco, and Joe Arnold.

In 1963 an FBI informant advised that James "Monk" Allegretti had more or less gotten out of the "juice" racket on the near Northside and that Mike Glitta and/or Mike Shore took over and were the main "juice" men in that area. They catered to strippers, prostitutes, and small-time gamblers. This informant said all "juice" loans had to be approved by Mike Glitta personally. The reason for this was because Allegretti's extreme diabetic condition periodically confined him to Wesley Memorial Hospital and made him unable to operate a motor vehicle. From that point on, he was chauffeured buy his lieutenant Joseph Arnold.

On April 25, 1965, Allegretti's brother Ben Policheri was arrested with Carl Pio, Frank Orlando, Larry "The Hood" Buonaguidi, Nick Loard, Nate Zukerman, Frank Loverdi, and John "Herbie the Cat" Libretti in a gambling raid at the Rambler Social Athletic Club at 501 North Clark Street. When the police came charging in, it sent hoodlums scattering out of the building and onto rooftops, with police chasing them. Some mobsters escaped through a trap door but were caught hiding behind garbage cans. Policheri and Pio were charged with being the keepers of the club. A month later another Allegretti wire room was raided and Mitchell Pawlowski and Edward Catie were arrested and charged with gambling and being Allegretti's guys.

A year later Ben Policheri and Frank "Frankie T" Tornabene were arrested in another gambling raid. Tornabene was facing charges in federal court for running a $600,000 a year national vice ring.

Jimmy Allegretti had lost his bid to stay free from his whiskey conviction and was sent to Springfield, Missouri, to serve his prison term. On December 15, 1969, Allegretti was paroled from prison. He and his brother boarded a plan for the flight back to Chicago, but when the plane landed at O'Hare Airport an ambulance was summoned; Allegretti had suffered a heart attack during the flight. By the time he reached the hospital, he was pronounced dead.

His wake was held at the Montclair Funeral home on Belmont Avenue but no mob bosses attended. Only second-class hoodlums and hangers-on paid a final farewell to their one-time boss. Among the guests were Ken Eto, who ran away when a Chicago detective standing outside the funeral home said "Hi Kenny." One car pulled up and an old short Italian man got out saying, "My name is DeGrazio, I'm in the outfit, go ahead and write down my license number."

Joseph Arnold

Joseph "Big Joe" Arnold's career started as an 11-year-old kid when he served time in the Ohio State Reformatory for auto theft. Born on June 1, 1917, he also went by the aliases of Jack Moore, Jerry Boltaire, Joe Aranyos, and Jerome Voltaire. He was listed as living at 2724 Winnemac Avenue in Chicago and 426 W. Briar Lane in Skokie.

He was convicted in 1929 for auto theft in Cleveland, Ohio, and sentenced to 1 to 20 years. He had also served time in federal penitentiaries for extortion and had been convicted on four occasions, receiving sentences amounting to 40 years. He had traveled throughout the United States, and since coming to Chicago in 1957, he was associated with organized crime on Chicago's near Northside.

Since settling in Chicago with his wife, he rose steadily in hoodlum circles from a strip joint operator and "juice" man to that of bodyguard for James Allegretti. Arnold was also close to Ross Prio and formerly handled "juice" loans in the larger amounts. Arnold was observed in attendance at gatherings involving underworld figures and handled "outfit matters" in connection with the police.

In 1965 a mob informant named Jack "Hot Dog" Wilensky told police what he knew about the Northside group. He said Joseph "Big Joe" Arnold was a bookie and "juice" man who could always be found at State and Ohio Streets, Rockwell Street and Lawrence Avenue, Rush and Chestnut Streets, and the old Valentino's Restaurant, where he maintained his records and made his payouts.

In regards to the Northside group, Wilensky believed that a Joe "Yuse" Meyers was among the biggest bookmakers in Chicago at the time and operated in and around the Rush Street nightclub area under Jimmy Allegretti and Joey DiVarco. Wilensky had heard that Meyers handled about $300,000 in bets a day during the football season. During the first month of 1964, Meyers lost about $250,000 in gambling operations and was laying off half of his bets to Frank "Lefty" Rosenthal. Meyers collected and paid off bets at the old Black Angus Restaurant that was owned by Irving Singer. Wilensky added that Meyers spent around $1,000 a week at the Black Angus buying drinks and was a close friend of Jackie Pearlman who owned a Westside card factory.

Wilensky told about the "juice" loans witnessed while in Valentino's Restaurant and gave an example as to the time when a Robert Wolcoff and his brother Burton Wolcoff made a "juice" loan from Joe Arnold and Jimmy Allegretti for $50,000 because the Wolcoff's were close friends of mobster Joe DiVarco.

Wilensky told another story about how Joe "Pepe" Giancana went overboard betting with David Roth at hockey games at the old Chicago Stadium and got into all kinds of trouble with the mob since he was delinquent in paying off his debts. This matter was straightened out by what Wilensky called "Pepe's half brother" who turned out to be mob boss Sam "Mooney" Giancana. Pepe was a staple at Gus' Steak House where he could be found making out horse-betting sheets, but used his home in Berwyn as the base of his operations. Wilensky told about the time he met "Pepe's other brother" Chuck Giancana who introduced himself as being in the real estate business in Oak Park and the western suburbs. Wilensky added that Pepe did not deal in "juice" loans but that he was always crying that he did not have any money but somehow managed to buy three new automobiles each year.

The FBI listed the following as activities involving Joe Arnold:

1) In March 1962 the owner of Marco's Pizzeria on North Clark Street was in debt to Joseph Arnold and was making "juice" payment under threat of bodily harm.

2) In April 1963 Tom Gallagher, formerly with the Diner's Club, was on "juice" to Joseph Arnold for $1,300. He was approached by Arnold near the old Gaslight Club and inasmuch as he could not produce the principal or the interest, he was kicked in the groin and beaten by Arnold. Arnold told individuals connected with the "juice" racket that when roughing up "juice" debtors that if a club or any weapon is used, the victims should not be hit on the head. Arnold indicated that the best procedure is to strike victims on the arm, which will paralyze and make them defenseless.

3) During the summer of 1963, Joseph Arnold frequented the old Fritzels Restaurant at State and Lake Streets, and made money exchanges in connection with his "juice" racket operation. That same summer, "Big Joe" Arnold was alleged to be writing life insurance policies on all recipients of "juice" loans made under his jurisdiction.

4) In October 1963 Joseph Arnold was known as a collector of "juice" on Chicago's near Northside, working for James Allegretti and Joseph DiVarco. He generally handled loans over $500 and was also a muscleman to collect interest.

5) In November 1963 Joseph Arnold had reportedly removed himself from "juice" activity on Chicago's near Northside and Mike Glitta was taking over as the top "juice" man in that area.

6) In February 1964 Lawrence "Hornsby" Moretti was handling some of the "juice" action for Joe Arnold, James Allegretti, and Sam Louis of the More Finance Agency in the Rush Street area. He was primarily making "juice" loans to taxicab drivers.

7) In March 1964 "Big Joe" Arnold was known to control all "juice" action on behalf of James Allegretti on Chicago's near Northside. Arnold also operated as the chauffeur and bodyguard for Allegretti. James Allegretti, along with Fiore "Fifi" Buccieri and Leonard Patrick were known as the three chief "juice" operators in the Chicago area, in their respective areas.

8) In May 1964 Joseph Arnold and Mike Glitta were identified as handling "juice" on Chicago's near Northside. Most of their business had shifted to elevator operators and bellboys in various hotels in that area, as well as individuals working the local bars and strip shows. It was mentioned that not many strippers or prostitutes were on "juice" in 1964 because Arnold decided that they did not have stable employment and could not be counted on to repay loans, since they change their working areas and addresses frequently.

9) On July 28, 1964, a police informer was referred to Joseph DiVarco by the son of a prominent financier who was a gambler and was "hooked" by "juice" men. The police informer contacted DiVarco, who instructed him to meet another party, who turned out to be Joseph Arnold. Arnold agreed to lend the police informer $5,000 if the informer would pay back $6,000 on "juice" rates. The police informer did not meet the regular payments and received telephone calls and personal warnings from Arnold emissaries. The messages were delivered when the witnesses were not present. The informer was threatened with being smashed on the head with a baseball bat and "having the hell kicked out of him."

10) In July 1964 a Tony Monaco was listed as collecting "juice" in the Rush Street area. Although being an alleged member of the Fiore Buccieri group, apparently some arrangements were made so that he could contact individuals on "juice" to this group in the area controlled by Ross Prio.

11) In October 1964 it was reported that Joseph Arnold was "no longer handling juice" as such, but was devoting full time to his association with James Allegretti as bodyguard, chauffeur, and constant companion, in view of Allegretti's illness.

12) In November 1964, it was learned that Arnold, when in charge of "juice" on Chicago's near Northside, was called upon to threaten a

former bellboy who had worked at the Berkshire Hotel and who refused to pay a "juice" loan. Arnold attempted to persuade this individual who told Arnold he would not pay it. The bellboy was a former prizefighter and since it was felt that it might not be easy to collect from him without a problem, Arnold apparently wrote this loan off as a loss.

In 1970, Joe Arnold was listed as one of the biggest "juice" men around and went on to be a player in organized crime. Around 1973 Big Joe Arnold and Joe DiVarco were sent to jail to serve a one-year sentence on federal income tax evasion charges. In 1974, Arnold and DiVarco were charged with racketeering, criminal usury, and conspiracy. However, the charges were dropped when the state's attorney's office said that the witness on whose testimony the case was built on had lied.

In March 1980, Joe Arnold was running his drugstore at 913 N. Rush Street called "Odds 'N' Ends Drugstore" when a Robert Urban rushed in and shot him in the abdomen seriously wounding him. Urban was the manager of the Oldsters for Youngsters social club across the street, of which Arnold was the owner. Urban told the police that he had shot Arnold because the 6-foot, 300 pound Arnold had beat him up in front of his girl friend.

Other individuals working in the Prio group in connection with the "juice" racket were:

Dominic DiBella

Dom DiBella was born on May 10, 1902, in Franklin, Louisiana, and used the address at 2603 Wright in Crystal Lake, Illinois. He was known as one of the "3 terrible Dom's" which also included Dominick Nuccio and Dominick Brancato. The "3 Dom's" were a powerful trio of gangsters who controlled much of Chicago's Northside in the 1940's and early 50's. In the 1960's DiBella met with Ross Prio and Vincent Solano on an almost daily basis at the Old Sunshine's Restaurant in Niles, Illinois. It was reported that any large "juice" loans made by Ross Prio to any individual were personally delivered to the individual by Dominick DiBella.

One example was in August 1964 when Carl Fio Rito, a well-known Chicago jewel thief who was once charged with narcotics violation, contacted Ross Prio at the Sunshine's Restaurant and requested a loan in the amount of about $5,000. Subsequently, Prio granted this "juice" loan which was delivered to Fio Rito by Dominick DiBella. Fio Rito was to repay the loan within 90 days and was to pay about $1,000 interest. It's not known if he did.

DiBella was an avid horse racing fan and had a horse named Becky. He would train racing horses through a stable owned by his son William DiBella, a Chicago attorney. During the winter seasons, DiBella was quite active in Miami, Florida, being involved with horseracing.

DiBella had gone into retirement in the late 1960's but was ordered back by mob boss Tony Accardo in 1972 to take control of the rackets on the Northside. Dom DiBella died in July 1976.

Vince Solano

Vince Solano was considered Ross Prio's right-hand-man and was known to have a "piece" of "juice" loans concerning members of his union. One informant affiliated with Solano and his union told authorities that "juice" loans were available to Local 1 members through any unknown source. He did state that you "did not" go to Solano directly for this loan but you had to go to someone from the Northside group under the control of Prio. In return Vince Solano would receive a "cut" from the "juice" interest from his union members.

Vince Solano's official 1964 bio card on file with the FBI reads as follows, "Vince Solano resides at 161 Andy Drive, Melrose Park, Illinois. He is president of Local 1 of the International Hod Carriers Building and Common Laborer Union, 3942 West Madison Street, Chicago. Solano was raised in the Italian neighborhood on Chicago's near Northside and is acquainted with many individuals from that neighborhood who have been close companions to Ross Prio. Solano serves as Prio's chauffeur. During the past two years, Solano has been a constant companion of Prio and accompanied Prio on his various visits to contacts in connection with the operation of Prio's Northside group.

In view of Solano's association with Prio as bodyguard, chauffeur, and companion, he is likewise associated with Prio's associates and is obviously aware of Prio's responsibility as leader of the Northside Group in the overall picture of the organized crime element in Chicago."

In 1976, Vince Solano was promoted to lieutenant under mob boss Joey DiVarco. According to FBI reports, Anthony Accardo, Joey Aiuppa, and Gus Alex decided to "keep DiVarco out front" in an effort to make law enforcement feel he was the leader of the Northside group. This enabled Solano to handle his responsibilities as actual leader without interference. Vincent Solano died in November 1992 at the age of 72.

Mike Glitta

Michael J. Glitta was an operator for several years with the strip joints on Chicago's near Northside. When Joey DiVarco was made boss of the near Northside, Mike Glitta put up a fight to move up in his position in the group. Glitta at the time was said to be wearing hearing aids in both of his ears when he was promoted to his new job. His job was to call on the operators in the Rush Street area concerning their street tax.

Born around 1921, Mike Glitta lived at 238 N. Chester Street in Park Ridge, Illinois, and 1221 N. Dearborn Pkwy. As a young man, Glitta drove a delivery truck for the Daily Racing Form. He was known as "Fireplug" to his mob buddies because he stood a mere 5 feet 8 inches tall and weighed 200 pounds and used the alias of Frank Ingo. According to a report, Mike Glitta was rumored to be related to mobster John Matassa Sr. who was at one time the bodyguard and driver for mob boss Sam Giancana in the early 1960's.

His arrest record listed a conviction in 1956 on federal charges of possession of stolen goods from an interstate shipment. He would only receive one year of probation. He was convicted on federal charges of possessing six cartons of women's nylon stockings which was part of a $6,000 shipment of hosiery stolen a year earlier from a Chicago railroad freight house.

In the 1960's Mike Glitta was an active "juice" man working the corners of Rush and Delaware Streets, State and Delaware Streets, and Montrose and Broadway Avenues in Chicago. On March 5, 1966, a raid of the Lincoln Baths at 1812 N. Clark Street seized 32 persons engaged in some kind of illegal activity. The establishment was under the control of Mike Glitta and Lawrence Buonaguidi.

Another job of Glitta's in 1976 was his alleged arrangement with a then sergeant La Calamita of the Chicago Police Department Dispatcher's Office to the effect that when a complaint came into the dispatcher's office concerning a Rush Street area tavern, a call was first placed to Glitta prior to any action being taken.

Another position for Glitta in the Outfit in the 1960's, 70's, and 80's was the control of all their obscene literature and pornography bookstore activities with Peter Dounias on the Northside of Chicago. Glitta and his company, JG Corporation, were involved in an obscenity case in the 1980's. In this case, 6,500 charges were filed at one time against Glitta. Agents raided Glitta's warehouse on Milwaukee Avenue and took every piece of material that seemed to be actionable under the State of Illinois statute. The State's Attorney saw fit to charge each piece of material that seemed to fit the statute's elements on obscenity. Glitta avoided jail when he pleaded guilty to obscenity and was placed on court supervision for a year by Judge Leo Holt in the Markham Branch of the Circuit Court.

A Chicago Crime Commission report said, *"B-girls, prostitutes, and pornography have apparently been Mike Glitta's stock and trade for the past 20 years that extended from Rush Street to the Wisconsin border."*

In 1986 Marco Glitta, a former Sanitary District electrician since 1961 and the brother of Michael, was sentenced to 8 years in prison on explosives charges. Marco was arrested after purchasing a remote-controlled bomb so he could blow up a moving car.

In 1988, Michael Glitta was charged with illegally owning two .38 caliber revolvers. As a convicted felon, Glitta was prohibited by federal law from possessing a firearm. However, he purchased two handguns in 1983 and failed to disclose he had a criminal record. The four-count federal indictment alleged that Glitta bought two .38 caliber revolvers at a gun shop in Franklin Park. It didn't matter. Michael Glitta died in his apartment at 1221 N. Dearborn Street from heart ailments on October 5, 1988, while watching the Dan Quayle and Lloyd Bentsen vice-presidential debate. It was reported that Frank "Babe" DeMonte was chosen as the new president of porn for the mob in Chicago.

Lawrence Buonaguidi

Lawrence "Larry the Hood" Buonaguidi was born on December 14, 1915, in Chicago under his real name Lawrence Bradi, and used the aliases of Larry Brady and Lawrence Bounaguide.

In the 1960's Larry the Hood was listed as an enforcer for James "Monk" Allegretti living at 2618 N. Francisco Street, 5235 N. Sheridan Road, and 1446 Larrabee Street in Chicago. He could always be found on Rush Street near hoodlum hangouts or by Valentino's Restaurant in the 1960's.

His arrest record dates back to 1933 when he was sentenced to 60 days in jail for larceny. In 1942, he was sentenced to one year and a day at the Terre Haute Penitentiary in Indiana for federal income tax evasion. In 1946, he was back to prison at Joliet State Prison for robbery, being sentenced to 1–3 years.

In 1970, he was listed as a top "juice" guy in Chicago working the Rush Street area. He worked the corners of State and Chestnut Streets, Ohio Street and Michigan Avenue, and Oak Street and Michigan Avenue in Chicago.

By 1974, Joe DiVarco and Joe Arnold went to prison; Ross Prio and James Allegretti were dead; Mike Glitta suffered a heart attack, which left Larry the Hood the man to run Rush Street for Dom DiBella. But by that time most of the rackets had dried up and were closed down, making Larry the Hood the king of better days. He died in June 1975.

Ken Eto

Ken "Tokyo Joe" Eto, who operated as a lieutenant under James Allegretti concerning gambling matters, went by the Italian nickname given to him by the Prio group called "Bonzaleech." At one time Eto was a front man for Ross Prio when Prio was attempting to set up gambling operations in San Juan, Puerto Rico. He lived at 1034 Grandville in Park Ridge, Illinois.

In December 1964, Ken Eto was handling small-time "juice" in the Rush Street area, working out of the Golden "8" Ball Pool and Billiard Hall. Eto's position in the Prio group was confirmed when on January 4, 1965, Ken Eto and Ross Prio were observed by Bureau agents driving aimlessly about the Morton Grove and Niles, Illinois, areas in Eto's automobile.

In 1983, mob boss Vince Solano ordered Eto's death when Solano became concerned Eto would turn government informant after a gambling conviction. As Eto sat in his car on Grand Avenue, mob hit men Jasper "Jay" Campise and John Gattuso shot Eto in the head three times. While Eto was playing dead, Campise and Gattuso congratulated each other on another mob hit well done. Once they were gone, Eto gathered himself and walked a block to get help. The bullets had bounced off of Eto's skull. With nowhere else to turn, Eto went to the government to save his life and give him a new one. He turned government rat and had a hand in putting many mob figures behind bars.

He was moved to a town near Atlanta, Georgia, where he lived under his new name of Joe Tanaka. There he would live out his final days watching Atlanta Braves baseball games and fishing. He died of natural causes on January 23, 2004.

Victor Musso

On June 22, 1964, Victor Frank Musso of 3501 North Janssen Street admitted to FBI Agents that he was acquainted with mobsters Ross Prio and Joseph DiVarco. He was aware that a numbers racket existed in that area but did not know specifically who controlled it. He assumed it was syndicate-controlled under the Prio group. He indicated that it was general information at that time that Prio controlled all racket activities in that area for the "outfit."

It was discovered that Victor Musso had long been associated with the criminal element on Chicago's near Northside and it was alleged that in addition to being involved in the "juice" racket, he was also a mob-gambling figure.

In 1987, a Cook County jail inmate named Victor Musso told the FBI that he was marked for death as an FBI informant and was left unprotected in the jail's most dangerous area. He was stabbed and seriously injured, receiving 27 stitches.

Musso admitted in published interviews that he was a federal informant and complained of a lack of protection from the FBI. Musso helped the government nab a corrupt courtroom sheriff's deputy who was caught in the act of taking money to fix a criminal case. Musso was listed as a twice-convicted thief and was serving jail terms of up to 9 years at the time. He was moved and placed under government protection.

Mike Albergo

Michael Frank Albergo was born around 1928 in Chicago and was listed as a top "juice" loan figure in 1970 for the mob. Albergo went by the nicknames of "Bones" and "Hambone." During the 1960's he lived at 518 N. Racine in Chicago and could be found at the corners of Campbell and Hirsch Streets, Wells and Randolph Streets, and Sheridan Road and Foster Avenue in Chicago.

Albergo's arrests were for burglary, murder in 1960, grand theft in 1962, and possession of stolen property in 1965. In October 1969 Albergo, Libero "Tony" Ingignoli, and Tom Immerso were arrested and charged with criminal usury for running a "juice" loan operation. The three were said to be preying on city garbage workers making around $250,000 a year in "juice" loans. They were even accused of running credit checks on three victims and making them fill out forms including their social security and driver's license numbers. In November of that year, a tavern owner named Daniel Brown testified that he obtained a "juice" loan from Albergo for $1,400. When Brown was unable to make his payments, Albergo sent hoodlums Sal Romano and Tony Schmidt

 posing as repairmen to steal Brown's cigarette vending machines. It was Albergo's intention to rob every piece of equipment from Brown's tavern until he paid up on his outstanding "juice" payments.

By September 1970, Mike Albergo was a missing man and was believed to be dead. One reason for his disappearance was the belief that Albergo failed to recognize an undercover policeman who was posing as a chronic gambler and made a "juice" loan to him, or, Albergo either was working as a informant or was simply too weak to keep around.

In August 2003, mob turncoat Nick Calabrese told the FBI that Albergo was killed by the mob and his body was buried under an old warehouse at 33rd and Shields streets in Chicago. The warehouse is long gone and the spot it once occupied is now a parking lot at U.S. Cellular Field, home of the Chicago White Sox Baseball team. After days of digging, only a few bone fragments were found and it could not be determined if they were those of Mike Albergo.

Libero Ingignoli

Libero "Tony" Ingignoli was born on January 1, 1920, and lived at 4257 West Fullerton, Chicago. He was the owner of "The Shelter" tavern at 4257 West Fullerton when he was arrested on October 7, 1969, for criminal usury charges. He died in November 1981.

Thomas Immerso

Born around 1922, Tom Immerso was listed as a bus driver in Skokie, Illinois, during the 1960's. He lived at 8716 Georgiana in Morton Grove when he was arrested on October 7, 1969 on criminal usury charges. He was allegedly connected to shylocking in Chicago, being active around the Lincoln Avenue and Wells Street area and the corners of Fullerton and Kostner Avenue in Chicago.

Joseph "Red" Amari

In December 1964 Joseph "Red" Amari was handling the "juice" in connection with the operations of the Zigonette game at the Ramblers Athletic Club, then located at 501 North Clark Street in Chicago. This game only operated on Sundays. It is noted that the Ramblers Athletic Club was utilized by the hoodlum element on Chicago's near Northside as a meeting place and game room and was raided on many occasions.

Chapter Twenty-Eight

Other Outfit Operators

Albert "Obbie" Frabotta

Albert Frabotta used the last name of his wife Santina De Marco calling himself Albert De Marco to hide his identity. He was known as a mob hit man who was considered to be very close to Felix "Milwaukee Phil" Aldersirio and Marshall Caifano. He was sometimes referred to as "The Executioner."

Albert Edward Frabotta was born on August 24, 1911, to Gugliemo and Jessie Frabotta in Steger, Illinois. The FBI listed both parents as "foreign illiterates" residing at 1538 Greenshaw Avenue in Chicago with brothers Joseph, James, Rocco and sisters Theresa, Norma, and Angela. When Albert Frabotta was very young, his mother Jessie was arrested for receiving stolen goods and sentenced to eighteen months in prison.

In the 1920's he joined the 42 Gang in Chicago becoming close with Sam DeStefano and Sam Giancana. He spent some time in jail and was discharged from the Indiana State Prison on May 6, 1938. When World War II broke out and America went to war, Albert Frabotta avoided military service by indicating to doctors that he was a psychotic.

Albert and his brother Joseph L. Frabotta both got their starts as syndicate burglars. In the 1960's Joseph was arrested for stealing cigarettes, resisting arrest and being involved in a $10,000 clothing burglary with a Richard Davis. In February 1964, he was arrested at "The Pad" strip tavern at 937 North State Street as being the keeper of a house of prostitution.

In the late 1950's Albert Frabotta was a known partner of mobster David Yaras in the "juice" rackets operating a portion on the Northside of Chicago.

In January 1962, a confidential source advised that Obbie Frabotta had borrowed money from the Hacking Brothers Company many years prior to 1962 and never paid the money back. An agreement was reached between

Joseph Panucci and Frabotta whereby the debt was cancelled in return for Frabotta's services in collecting "juice" payments for Hacking Brothers. That agreement remained active for many years.

In 1963, Frabotta's operating district was from the Chicago River to Cicero Avenue and Belmont Avenue to Lawrence Avenue. However, syndicate rumor in 1964 placed Albert Frabotta as on the "outs" with the syndicate and financially broke. To add to his problems, it was reported that Frabotta and Alderisio had a "falling out" and were now bitter enemies. It was not known why the two dissolved their partnerships but Frabotta made peace with the syndicate and was observed many times in 1965 playing cards with Sam Giancana. In 1966, he was frequently seen together with Charles "Chuckie" English and other well-known mobsters.

In October 1967, Frabotta was walking his poodle "Susie" on Lake Shore Drive in Chicago when two young hoodlums attacked him. He suffered minor injuries and his dog was kidnapped. Frabotta called in many favors to find out who attacked him. With a vengeance, he discovered who the hoodlums were and the poodle was returned.

By 1972, Albert Frabotta was once again on the outs with the mob. The FBI even closed their investigation on him because every informant said Frabotta was "a nothing and nobody anymore." He spent the last 10 years of his life walking the streets of Chicago on the Northside.

He died on November 20, 1982 of natural causes. His funeral was held at Montclair Funeral home and his mass was at St. Priscilla Church. He is interned at Mount Carmel Cemetery in Hillside, Illinois.

File Card
Albert Frabotta
AKA: Obbie
Born August 24, 1911
Died November 20, 1982

Known Addresses
936 South Marshfield, Chicago (1920's)
1137 South Ashland, Chicago (1941)
3950 Lake Shore Drive, Chicago (1961)
3920 Marine Drive, Chicago (1964)

Known Arrest Record

Chicago PD	6-18-1927	Larceny
Chicago PD	1-30-1928	Larceny
Chicago PD	10-23-1928	Larceny
Chicago PD	11-1-1928	Larceny
Chicago PD	8-29-1929	Disorderly Conduct
Chicago PD	1-1-1930	Burglary
Chicago PD	5-20-1930	Burglary
Chicago PD	8-21-1931	Suspect Burglary
Indianapolis PD	12-24-1931	Bank Robbery
Pendleton PD	2-19-1932	Bank Robbery
Chicago PD	3-11-1941	Robbery
Chicago PD	4-23-1951	G.F., Chicago
Chicago PD	12-4-1951	Murder Investigation of Sam Rinella
Chicago PD	7-19-1960	Disorderly Conduct
Chicago PD	7-12-1962	Battery, Disorderly Conduct

Total amount of known arrests 45 times.

Sam Battaglia, known as "Teete"

According to the FBI Salvatore Battaglia was born on November 5, 1908, in Chicago to Salvatore Battaglia Sr. and Guiseppa Scaletta, both born in Italy. One report lists him as being born on November 5, 1906 in Kenosha, Wisconsin. Battaglia and his brothers Frank and Joseph were members of the old 42 Gang with Sam Giancana and Sam DeStefano. In 1930, Frank Battaglia had made his mark and was considered the leader of that gang. His power came from his two cousins Paul and August Battaglia who were members of the powerful Genna Gang in the 1920's. Many in the Battaglia family met their end by way of the gun. On January 4, 1931, his cousin August Battaglia was killed by assassins on Roosevelt Road; in March 1932 Frank Battaglia was killed by gangsters; in August 1938 Paul Battaglia was dumped out of a moving car on West Monroe Street with two bullet holes in his head and Sam's other brother Anthony Battaglia was shot to death in front of his home in April 1975.

Sam Battaglia was known as a high-ranking member of the Chicago Outfit and was considered by many to be only second to Sam Giancana in importance in the 1960's. He lived at 1114 North Ridgeland in Oak Park with his wife Angela Siciliano and his three children Joanna, Sam

Jr., and Richard. He was the owner of an infamous large farm known as Free Meadows Stock Farm where he would make those on "juice" to him and behind in their payments work off their debt performing manual labor.

Battaglia was in general control of the Western suburbs of Chicago in "juice," prostitution and gambling. His lieutenants at one time were listed as Felix Alderisio and Marshall Caifano but he worked closely with old Capone gangster Rocco DeGrazio at the famous Casa Madrid saloon in Melrose Park. Members of "Teete's" crew in the 1960's were, Anthony Battaglia, Rocco "Bobby Dore" Salvatore, Joe Battaglia, Joseph F. Rocco, Angelo Jannotta, Joseph "Joe Shine" Ambile, Richard Derrico, Guy Cervone, William Del Percio, Elmer "Healthy" Del Percio, Gerald Nargie, Angel Pacheco, Joe Scaccia, John Tarrara, and John P. Zito.

Sam Battaglia was the syndicate overlord for the Melrose Park area and a number of nightclubs and bars in Melrose Park, Stone Park, and the Northlake area. He reportedly gained the bulk of his income from these establishments, gambling operations, and through "juice" loans made by his organization. A confidential source close to Battaglia in 1962 said Sam was considered the most sinister and menacing of the "young bloods" that were replacing Tony Accardo and Rocco DeGrazio, heirs of the late Al Capone.

Some known victims on "juice" to Battaglia were a Sonny Lazarus and Sid Sheridan. Sonny Lazarus was listed as a Public Adjustor for the F. Lazarus Company and was on a $150,000 "juice" loan in 1963. This amount was the result due to Lazarus losing while betting on the horses. In order to afford Lazarus the opportunity to pay off his "juice" to Battaglia, he was being utilized by mobster Marshall Caifano as a public adjustor on many of the organized crime syndicate's fraudulent insurance claims resulting from fire or theft losses.

Another victim was Sid Sheridan, a local contractor who was on "juice" to Battaglia. An informant said that this "juice" loan was paid off by Sheridan boarding horses at Battaglia's farm paying $60 per month for each one of the horses. Battaglia forced Sheridan to buy these horses at an extremely over-valued price and that, on this semblance of a legal transaction, Battaglia was able to issue "juice" loans.

One victim that engaged the wrath of Battaglia was named Lester Bagis who was on "juice" to members of the Chicago mob in the 1960's, including Battaglia. An FBI informant came forward and stated that this Bagis was to be killed by one of Battaglia's men because he was behind on his juice payments. This informant also added that a private detective named Julian Burkman had been utilized on several occasions to locate recipients of "juice" loans for Battaglia who tried to skip out on their debts. It was believed that this detective was used to find Bagis and the informant was not sure if they ever did or what happened to Bagis.

In July 1964, the FBI received word from an informant that Sam Battaglia was "getting out" of the "juice" business because of the order issued from Sam Giancana that "NO ONE" was to use any violence of any kind to obtain collections from "juice" victims. Battaglia, knowing that would be impossible, was handing over his "juice" area to a fellow mobster. Battaglia would go on to assume the role of top mob boss controlling the day-to-day operations for about two years after Sam Giancana fled America in 1966. Battaglia was eventually convicted and sentenced to 15 years in prison for his part in an extortion scheme. Nine days after his release from prison in 1973, Sam "Teetz" Battaglia died from cancer.

File Card
Samuel Battaglia
AKA: Teete, Joe Rock, Sam Rice
Born: November 5, 1908 or 1906 (Chicago or Kenosha)
Died: September 7, 1973

Known Addresses
161 Ewing Street, Chicago (1908)
567 Cabrini Street, Chicago (1942)
1114 Ridgeland Avenue, Oak Park (1961)

Known Arrest Record

12-13-1924	Disorderly Conduct
5-11-1926	Attempted Burglary
1-?-1929	Larceny
7-18-1929	Section 233
9-19-1930	Assault Deadly Weapon

10-11-1930	Suspect in Robbery
11-14-1930	Robbery
1-1-1931	General Principals
6-9-1931	Assault to Murder
6-18-1931	Robbery
5-17-1932	Attempted Murder
8-13-1933	Murder of John Perillo
6-24-1934	Disorderly Conduct
8-1-1935	General Principals
8-17-1942	General Principals
10-2-1944	Suspect in Robbery
2-26-1946	Investigation
6-5-1946	Investigation
7-15-1946	Investigation
10-13-1948	Investigation
6-2-1961	Disobedience to Police
2-1-1967	Murder Investigation of Charles Michelotti
2-17-1967	Interstate extortion

John Varelli, Known as "Johnny the Bug"

John Varelli, real name John Michael Schivarelli but known as Johnnie the Bug, used to live at 1519 Bonnie Brae in River Forest, just down the street from mob boss Paul DeLucia.

The FBI lists him as either being born on May 12, 1926 or May 12, 1930. John Schivarelli and his brother Mike Schivarelli had secured jobs with the city of Chicago through their mob connections. Mike "Ike" Schivarelli was a labor goon for mob union boss Frank "Frankie X" Esposito. At one point Varelli's take on the "juice" rackets was in the form of "life insurance." Being known as an active "juice" man in the 1960's, Varelli was president and a partner in the Granite Insurance Agency Limited, located at 6809 West North Avenue, which was known as an insurance brokerage firm. He would sell life insurance policies to "juice" victims. Business was so good in the 1960's that one time he won the award of "man of the month" by the Associated Life Insurance Company for the high volume of sales over a period.

His viciousness was only doubled by the air of respectability, which surrounded him, and the fact that his name at one point was not often mentioned in connection with the crime group by those outside of that organization.

In December 1955 Varelli was arrested when police raided a floating crap game. Eighty one prisoners were arrested but Varelli was let go once they found out who he was. The papers at the time called him a west side hoodlum known for fencing stolen goods in cartage thefts, an operator of crap games and a mob enforcer.

In 1964 the FBI listed John Varelli as, *"Varelli is generally considered as a young up and coming member of the Chicago crime group and enjoys the respect of crime leaders in connection with his abilities as an enforcer and 'hit' man. Varelli also is reputedly a thief, juice man, bookie, fence, gambler and bank robber."*

In 1961, FBI agents arrested Varelli stealing scrap metal. Since no federal violation existed, he was turned over to local police and charged with robbery. He pled guilty and received 5 years probation but, through his "connections," he was released from probation after only ten months.

One known situation of Varelli acting as a "juice" broker and which mobsters he generally sent his clients to came from an interview by FBI agents in December 1961 with a Theodore Kay. In this interview, Kay claimed to be in debt to mobsters Fiore "Fifi" Buccieri, William "Wee Willie" Messino, George and Nick Bravos, and Rocky Joyce for over $40,000. Kay had lost all of his money from syndicate gambling losses over a 3-year period and was sent to the above "juice" men by John Varelli.

From July 1963 to April 1964 Varelli was President of the Newport Construction Company at 515 North La Salle in Chicago. This company obtained home improvement contracts and arranged for Title 1 loans through a bank. When the FBI investigated, it was revealed that much of the work was of very poor quality and most times was never completed. Numerous completion certificates were forged and submitted long before work was finished, or in some cases even commenced. On some jobs, kickbacks in cash were made along with consolidation of debts.

In July 1964 word on the streets of Chicago was that mob boss Sam Giancana was going to be stepping down as top boss and being mentioned as his replacement were Felix "Milwaukee Phil" Alderisio or Johnny "the Bug" Varelli. The job went to Sam Battaglia.

In 1965 Varelli was charged with conspiring to hijack three truckloads of silver with John Boresllino, Albert Cardenas, Thomas Bambulas, and Max Heckmyer. In 1967 Varelli was convicted and sentenced to Leavenworth Prison. In 1969 he won the right for a new trial and at the hearing Varelli took out a razor blade and cut his wrist as a government psychiatrist testified if Varelli was competent to stand trial. After he was bandaged up Varelli was returned to the courtroom where he sat shaking uncontrollable throw out the hearings. In 1979 Varelli was reported to be a top mob figure taking orders from Jackie Cerone. It's believed Johnny the Bug died in December 1985.

Known Arrest Record

Name	Date	Charge	Agency
J. Schivarelli	07-20-1942	none	SOS U.S. Army
J. Schivarelli	03-5-1943	Unknown	River Forest PD, IL
J. Schivarelli	03-10-1943	Burglary	Chicago PD
J. Schivarelli	01-8-1944	Work Check	Chicago Public Works
J. Schivarelli	08-3-1945	Work check	Chicago Park District
J. Schivarelli	04-22-1948	Chauffeur license check	
J. Schivarelli	02-12-1958	Investigation	Chicago PD
J. Varelli	09-28-1961	GL Investigation	Chicago PD
J. Varelli	09-28-1961	Investigation L	State's Attorney
J. Varelli	03-14-1966	FHA Violation	USH Chicago
J. Varelli	04-19-1966	SKUSM	Cook County Jail
J. Varelli	08-25-1967	15 years	Leavenworth Prison

Morris Goldstein, Known as "Greenie"

Morris Goldstein was known as a "juice" man representing the interests of many Chicago hoodlums, particularly Leslie "Killer Kane" Kruse and Rocco Fischetti. One report stated that the Cook County State's Attorney's police arrested "Greenie" on one occasion when they raided a lounge in Cicero, Illinois. On that occasion when "Greenie" was picked up, he had thousands of dollars on him, which he stuffed into his shirt. The police never found the money.

In December 1961, "Greenie" was operating as a "juice" man at all the major craps and roulette games going on in the Chicago area. Goldstein was known to spend most of his time at the J & J Picnic Grove, a gambling establishment that was being operated by Kruse and Fishetti in Will County, Illinois.

In 1962, Goldstein was handling the "juice" at a gambling game being run by Rocco Potenza on Milwaukee Avenue near Niles, Illinois until "Killer Kane" Kruse opened his gambling joint. Goldstein then switched his allegiance to Kruse and provided his "juice" for Kruse's operations. Goldstein was also listed as providing "juice" at the Vernon Hills Country Club in Half Day, Illinois. However, Goldstein was listed as representing Lennie Patrick's interests even though that game was being run by William McGuire for "Killer Kane" Kruse. McGuire was a former Chicago Police Officer who was a front man for mobsters.

William Daddono, Also known as
"Willie Potatoes" Daddano and William Miller

William Daddono commonly known as "Willie Potatoes" Daddano was born on December 28, 1912 in Chicago. He lived at 8109 West 26th Street in North Riverside, Illinois with his wife Mary and eight children. He had a lengthy police record dating back to March 1938 and on January 24, 1945, Daddono was sentenced to a year and a day for violation of the Federal Bank Burglary statute. He spent one year in Joliet Prison before being released on February 15, 1946. On March 8, 1946, he was sentenced to Terre Haute Penitentiary for one year and a day for entering a bank with intent to rob.

He had been arrested as a suspect in a number of gangland killings in Chicago and reportedly was a syndicate boss of jukeboxes, pinball machines, and coin-operated machines operations in DuPage County, Kane County, McHenry County, and Will County in Illinois. He also had considerable power in the old 24th ward of Chicago where he held interest in many liquor stores. The FBI's bio card listed him as *"a former gambler who developed into a 'muscle man' for the Chicago syndicate and at one time was recognized as the chief executioner for the Chicago organization.*

He is known as a vicious, unreasoning, and sadistic killer who has crimes ranging from burglary to murder."

In April 1957, Daddono's chauffer and bodyguard Salvatore "Sol" Moretti was found shot to death in Will County. An informant stated that Sol Moretti and two other men were given the job of picking up a Chicago banker named Leon Marcus, scaring him, and obtaining papers from him that involved then mob boss Sam Giancana. During the scaring process, Moretti became excited and somehow shot and killed Marcus and then failed to properly clean Marcus' pockets, leaving behind the paper that implicated Giancana. The informant further stated that the two men who were with Moretti during the killing of Marcus were given the job of killing Moretti for the bungling of the job. The informant said that William Daddono was one of the men on both killings.

In March 1960, Daddono turned himself in to police for questioning in the murder of Joseph Albanese. Under questioning, Daddono admitted he knew Albanese since the two were cellmates in the Federal Penitentiary at Terre Haute and had loaned him money but had not seen him for several months.

An informant advised the FBI in 1963 that William Daddono and a group of his associates were using the old Tastee Snack Shop Restaurant located at the northeast corner of Cermak and Central Avenue in Cicero as their "juice" collection headquarters. At this establishment, Daddono worked along with Anthony "Puleo" DeRosa, Pasquale "Buck" Clementi, Frank "One Ear" Fratto, Alex Ross, Vincent "The Saint" Inserro, James "Muggsy" Tortoriello and his nephew John Allegretti, a Chicago Police officer at the time. As the group met at this location, William Daddono learned that the Tastee Snack Shop restaurant was turning a profit. Because of this, Daddono bought into the business as a partner.

A year later in 1964 William Daddono began to meet nightly with a group at the old Riviera Bowling Lanes on North Avenue in Melrose Park, which was once owned by mobster Nick DeGrazia. Daddono would show up almost every night shortly before 10:00 p.m. and stay until almost 5:00 a.m. the next morning. The group was there to do business and no business was conducted unless Daddono was present. Daddono would answer phone calls under the name of William Miller.

The group consisted of hijackers, cartage thieves, and "juice" men. Overheard during these meetings were comments such as *"Either you pay up or we'll send a couple of boys over"* and other similar comments made over the phone and in person to individuals who appeared there in front of Daddono. It was noted in the report that the nightly appearance of these hoodlums ruined business for the 24-hour bowling alley. The then owner was powerless to stop these individuals and the Melrose Park Police Department refused to take any action.

At one point during the late 1960's, Willie Potatoes was mentioned as becoming top boss in the Chicago replacing Sam Giancana. That would never happen since he was sent to prison in the 1970's where he died a natural death.

File Card
William Daddono
AKA: "Potatoes," Daddano, William Russo, William Miller
Born: December 28, 1912
Died: September 8, 1975

Known Employment

Commonwealth Edison Company	(1930's & 40's)
Mc Henry County Tobacco and Candy Company	(1962)
Tastee Snack Shop Restaurant	(1963)

Known Addresses

4053 Lexington Avenue, Chicago	(1936)
4053 West 5th Avenue, Chicago	(1941)
8109 West 26th Street, North Riverside	(1946)
8109 North 27th Street, North Riverside	(1961)

Known Arrest Record (names are spelled as in arrest report)

Under	Date	Charge
William Dado	7-7-1936	Rockford, IL, Investigation
William Daddano	3-4-1938	General Principals (suspect)
William Doddono	1-4-1940	Berwyn, Motor Violation
William Daddano	8-6-1944	Burglary
William Daddano	8-9-1944	Burglary
William Daddano	8-14-1944	Bank Robbery
William Daddano	11-24-1944	Burglary 1 to 14 years prison
William Doddono	1-15-1945	Investigation

William Daddono	1-24-1945	Burglary
William Daddeno	2-15-1946	Larceny, County Jail
William Daddeno	3-8-1946	Attempted bank robbery
William Daddeno	1-15-1947	Berwyn PD, Investigation
William Daddeno	9-17-1947	Investigation
William Daddano	3-6-1960	Murder investigation
William Daddono	4-19-1966	TFIS
William Daddano	12-20-1967	FBI Conspiracy, Misprison of a felony

James Mirro, Also known as "Cowboy" and Vincenzo Mirra

James "Cowboy" Mirro was born on January 2, 1914, and lived with his wife at 1548 61st Court and 1500 S. Austin Boulevard in Cicero. He was known as an off-and-on bookmaker and "made" member of the Chicago mob. In 1947 James Mirro was a member of the Red Hawk Gang which became the Pasczko Gang. The Red Hawk Gang specialized in safe burglaries, theft from interstate shipments and vehicle theft. Also in the Red Hawk Gang with Mirro were fellow organized crime members Stanley Jasinski, John Quinn, Sam Ferrara, James Lubiak and Adolph Starzyk.

Mirro had been arrested as a suspect in many gangland-type slayings, being listed as a hit man. In 1954, he was convicted on federal charges of transporting stolen goods in interstate commerce and sentenced to 3 years. In 1964, James Mirro and James Capezio were using the Allied Park American Legion Post Number 226 located at 2032 West Grand Avenue, Chicago as their bookmaking and "juice" loan headquarters. At this building, Mirro was in charge of the "juice" operations and catered to individuals in need of money in the Grand and Damen Avenue neighborhood on Chicago's near northwest side.

His arrest record contains arrests dating back to 1932 for gambling, robbery, larceny, and loan sharking. He was convicted again in 1965 of interstate commerce of stolen goods and given 5 years in prison. Another conviction came on August 21, 1969, for resisting arrest when he was sent to Terre-Haute Prison in Indiana for 5 to 20 years. He died in April 1982.

The Grieco Family

One of the families linked with the syndicate and "juice" operations in Chicago is the Grieco family. According to law enforcement agents, they controlled the corner of Race and Leavitt Streets in Chicago during the 1960's at their Lu-Lu Snack Shop.

Joseph E. Grieco, born on December 23, 1927, lived at 4600 North Overhill in Norridge, Illinois. Grieco, also known as Joe Emery, was convicted in 1956 for theft from an interstate shipment and receiving stolen property.

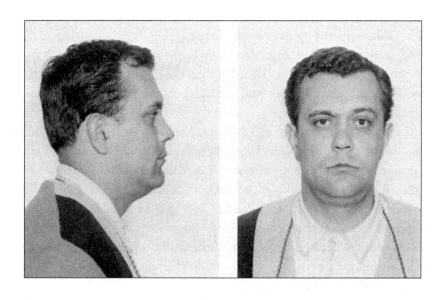

Donald L. Grieco was born around 1938 and lived at 7701 West Wilson in Norridge, Illinois.

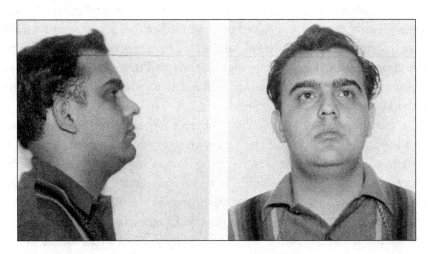

Joseph and Donald Grieco were brothers who operated Nicky's Frozen Pizza located at 2015 North Larrabee in Chicago. Nicky's Frozen Pizza Company was a legitimate enterprise, which sold frozen pizzas to restaurants and groceries in the Chicago area and 26 other states. Also at the address was the Vic Damone Pizza Company. Associated with the Grieco brothers in that venture was Vic Damone, an entertainer, nightclub singer and recording star of some stature in the 1960's. Joseph Grieco was listed as the president and director of Damone Pizza while Donald was listed as secretary-treasurer. However, it was also reported that the Grieco brother were just using that name to hide their involvement. Also located at that same address was the Independent Loan Company and the Independent Factoring Corporation operated by the Grieco brothers, otherwise known as the headquarters for the Grieco's alleged mob "juice" loan business. When police searched the office, they found a check for $3,475 made out to George Buccieri, the brother of mobsters Fifi and Frank Buccieri.

Police contacted Vic Damone in Hollywood to question him about his role in the pizza company. Damone admitted meeting the Grieco brothers when he performed a show at the Sahara North Motel in Schiller

Park in 1962, which was owned by mobster Manny Skar. Damone told the police that he agreed to let the Grieco brothers use his name for the pizza company in exchange for 50 percent of the profits but denied knowing that they were involved in organized crime. Vic Damone would later go on to turn down the role of the Italian entertainer named Johnny Fontaine in Francis Ford Coppola's and Mario Puzo's "The God Father" movie in 1971. He said the role was a slur on the majority of decent Italian Americans.

In February 1964 Joseph, Donald, and Alfred Saigh were arrested by the Chicago Police and charged with aggravated battery. A George Quarnstrom went to the police stating he was on "juice" to the Grieco brothers and had fallen behind in his payments. Because of this Quarnstrom was forced into the washroom of a tavern and was beaten and threatened by the Grieco brothers. Quarnstrom said he browed $500 from the Independent Loan Company because of an illness in his family but only received $375 and agreed to pay back $750 at the rate of $28 a week. Joseph Grieco was convicted of battery and sentenced to six months in prison while his brother Donald was convicted of battery and was put under court supervision for two years. He was not given a prison sentence since he was a bystander in the beating and did not strike Quarnstrom.

At the time, Mayor, Richard J. Daley's office launched an investigation into the Grieco's businesses and found that the Vic Damone Pizza Company had no city license to operate. The city also evoked the city license for the other pizza company. Mayor Daley's office also went after the Buccaneer Tavern at 1653 N. Wells Street to have its liquor license revoked. The license was in the name of Joseph Viola but a police investigation determined that the true owner was allegedly Joseph Grieco. In addition to that investigation, the Chicago detectives reopened an unsolved mob murder that occurred on December 21, 1963. In that case, Dominic "Bags" Bagnulo, listed as a hoodlum and horseplayer, was heavily in debt to the loan shark gang operated by the Grieco's,

Because of the arrest, information not known to police was discovered. Donald Grieco was the son-in-law of northern Indiana mob boss Gaitano "Tommy" Morgano. Morgano acted as underboss for mobster

Anthony "Mr. Tom" Pinelli and controlled gambling, vice and narcotics in Lake County "Gary" Indiana until January 16, 1963, when he was deported back to his home in Calascbetta, Enna, Sicily. A year later in 1964 evidence was uncovered that Morgano was still receiving "his cut" from the Indiana and Chicago rackets he was forced to leave behind. According to the report, a Jennie Scaglione sent a cashier's check to Morgano in Sicily from Chicago for $1,500. Jennie is the wife of John Scaglione who is the brother-in-law of Joseph Grieco. It was clear that the Grieco brothers were operating "juice" for Morgano.

The Grieco brothers were ushered into the business by their uncle Julius "Ju Ju" Grieco.

Julius J. Grieco, believed to be born on May 1, 1915 in Chicago, went by the nickname of "Ju Ju," living at 5324 Crystal Street. In the 1950's Ju Ju was known as a syndicate hoodlum who controlled West Madison Street in Chicago with an iron fist. He was involved in vice and mob liquor distribution. In 1952, Ju Ju joined the lengthy list of mob hoodlums arrested and questioned in the murder of Republican committeeman Charles Gross. Both Ju Ju and a William Lisante were arrested and interviewed about the murder however; both were released on writs of habeas corpus.

In 1959, Ju Ju Grieco was arrested with six other men for running a syndicate check-raising fraud involving call girls. Grieco, David Goran, James Korbos, Amedeo Di Domenico, Nate Schulman, Dom Abbrescia, and Alec Harris ran a scam where convention delegates visiting the city of Chicago would be steered from their Chicago Loop hotels to syndicate bars where they would be force-fed enough alcohol to get them drunk. Then B-girls and prostitutes would be brought in so the delegates could have sex. While the extremely drunken delegates were lead to a private place, their wallets were taken and all the cash stolen. Afterwards, the delegates were approached, told the fee for the prostitute, and asked to be paid. A delegate would reach for his wallet and it would be either gone or empty. Unable to pay, the delegate would be told by the bartender that he could pay in the form of a blank check. The check would be written for $100, and then the bartender would take the check and inform the drunken delegate that he made a mistake writing the check and had to re-write the check for $100. The bartender would pretend to tear up the check in front of the man while he wrote out a new one. Then the first check was taken and an extra zero was added to the $100 making it a check for $1000. Both checks would be cashed totaling $1,100 for the mob. The scam ran from September 1956 and ended in 1957, with over 800 convention visitors scammed totaling over $250,000. Grieco and Schulman were the ones who would cash the checks through their businesses. In April 1960, all seven men were found guilty of mails to defraud and interstate transportation of forged checks.

For this, Ju Ju Grieco was sentenced to 15 years in prison. When Ju Ju was convicted, the judge was amazed that the Chicago Police Department said that Grieco had no police record. But when the FBI ran a check of his fingerprints, they uncovered a long arrest record dating back to 1932. It was discovered that Ju Ju was a very close friend of a Chicago Police Captain who protected vice joints and syndicate saloons. As soon as it was reported in the newspapers that his arrest record was nowhere to be found, all of a sudden it was found by the Chicago Police bureau of identification. His police record contained many arrests, some listed were for a robbery charge in 1932, another on March 5, 1932, for disorderly conduct, another on June 12, 1935 for petty larceny which landed him in the Bridewell Prison for one year, another on December 14, 1944 for defrauding the government of cabaret tax, and one on August 3, 1959, for an investigation.

Ju Ju Grieco was married to Rose Grieco and had three sons named Joseph, Glen and Julius Jr. Among earlier companions linked to Ju Ju was Nan Partipilo, wife of mobster Sam "Sambo" Cesario. It was reported that Ju Ju opened an Oak Park beauty salon for her, which she operated with the widow of William "The Saint" Skally.

On March 20, 1969, the body of Ju Ju's son Joseph Grieco, not to be mistaken for his alleged mobster cousin Joe Greco, was found shot to death in his blue Cadillac in Baltimore, Maryland. He was found in Baltimore's notorious vice area called "The Block." According to reports, three gunmen abducted him outside one of the "Blocks" gambling joints. Baltimore police said they were investigating Joseph's links to an interstate white slave racket involving hoodlums in Cicero, Illinois.

Joseph had moved to Baltimore in the early 1960's with his one-time dancer wife Melba Jean. In his early days, Joseph was listed as a prizefighter in Chicago. A report in 1951 listed that Joseph "Marble-eyes" Grieco was arrested with Joe Galassi when the two were selling drugs and were part of a million-dollar dope ring supplying 1,000 addicts. Grieco's mother told the police that her son was addicted to heroin and had been a patient for 6 months in a federal hospital in Lexington, Kentucky.

His body was found in front of 4200 Vermont Avenue in Baltimore. When the police investigated, they found Grieco leaning against the right door window of the auto with a bullet hole in the left temple of the head and one in the chest. Found on the seat next to him were two envelopes filled with what was believed at the time to be marijuana.

A fingerprint was found on the car and it was compared to Edward Mallon, Gordon Williams, Nicholas Borozzi, and Frank Watts Jr. None of the names match the print but a Leonard Ciaccio was charged with conspiring with certain persons to kill Joseph Grieco and Edward Mallon was charged with solicitation of murder.

After 10 years in Leavenworth Prison Ju Ju Grieco was paroled in June 1971 and returned to Chicago to reclaim his area and re-establish himself among his fellow mobsters. However, what Ju Ju returned to shocked him. It was a different Chicago; his Austin District area had changed. He tried to use the "old" ways of muscling in on tavern owners but learned that the "old" ways didn't work anymore. Ju Ju began to step on his fellow mobsters toes and was paid a visit by mobster Charles "Chuckie" English. As the two sat English told his old friend that the bosses, Tony Accardo and Paul Ricca had sent word that Ju Ju was to close down his operations and get out of town. Ju Ju even tried to reach out to his old business partner and friend Charles Nicoletti for help but was told there was nothing he could do. So Ju Ju packed up and moved to Margate, Florida, right outside Miami. He died in Hollywood, Florida in August 1984.

Reported working for the Grieco brothers Joe and Donald was Alfred Saigh who was known as a two-hundred-and-fifty-pound enforcer noted for his terrorist tactics.

Alfred "Big Al" Saigh was born around 1919 and lived at 10843 S. Western Avenue in Chicago and 1219 S. Elmwood Avenue in Berwyn. In 1964, Saigh was arrested on battery charges based on a "juice" racketeering case.

Saigh's area of operation was listed as Polk and Dearborn Streets, Taylor Street and Racine Avenue, Lexington Street and Racine Avenue, and Polk Street and Racine Avenue in Chicago's Little Italy.

It was believed that the Grieco brothers allegedly operated their "juice" business under the protection of Fiore "Fifi" Buccieri. One report alleged that Joe Grieco was so involved in getting money owed to him that he was one of the Chicago hoodlums who went to New York City in August 1963 in an attempt to intimidate a Daniel Segal into paying the "juice" and gambling debt incurred by his brother, Alan Segal, who operated the Trade Winds Night Club on Rush Street in Chicago. Segal was listed as a front for syndicate figures that took over after Arthur Adler was killed.

In July 1966, information reached the Chicago Police that; Donald Grieco was using the Mr. Richard's School of Beauty Culture at 5603 Cermak Road in Cicero as a front for his "juice" operations. During the investigation, detectives witnessed William "Wee Willie" Messino, Joe "Gags" Gagliano, and Chris Cardi coming and going from the beauty school. The investigation discovered that the beauty school was in the names of Theresa Grieco, Donald's wife, Carmella Grieco, Joseph's wife, and Patsy DiConstanzo who was using the alias of Pat Longo. Informants had told detectives that Di Constanzo had told his associates that the Grieco's wished to buy the school as a front. But when detectives went looking for DiConstanzo to question him, they found out he had fled to Indiana because allegedly Joe "Gags" Gagliano was seeking DiConstanzo's son because he allegedly owed $29,000 to mob loan sharks and gamblers. However, that story was just a rumor.

Later that year an Illinois Crime Investigation commission announced they were launching an investigation into the Chicago "juice" rackets and were ordering 30 mob figures to testify. Donald Grieco gathered up his family and left Chicago to hide out in Florida. He had his neighbor turn on the lights in his home every night to try and throw off the police, making them believe that he had not left town.

In 1968, public hearings of the Illinois Crime Investigating Commission on Organized Crime were held and Dorothy Franchina testified how in 1966 her husband Anthony Franchina obtained a $400 loan from the Grieco brothers. After making the payments, the Grieco brothers squeezed and demanded more and more money out of Franchina. When he fell behind once in his payments, the Grieco's told Dorothy she was "*a young and good-looking girl*" and should return to prostitution to pay off the loan. Soon after, Franchina's 6-year-old son didn't return from school one day. Dorothy jumped into a taxicab and began to search the streets looking for him. She finally drove to the Vic Damone Pizza factory and confronted Donald Grieco making a "juice" payment and demanding her son be returned. Grieco assured her that her child would be waiting for her when she returned home. The young Franchina was at home when she returned, telling his scared mother that two or three guys identified themselves as friends of his father and took him for a ride for awhile. Soon after, Anthony Franchina could not take the constant pressure of making the "juice" payments so he killed himself. Joseph Grieco was questioned in the hearings, invoking the Fifth Amendment 51 times.

In November 1982 Joe Grieco, Charles Cesario, John Manzella, and Samuel Malatia were arrested on charges of conspiracy to collect a debt by extortionate means. Also arrested were mobster Ernest "Rocky" Infelice, Salvatore DeLaurentis, and Louis Marino, all charged with using terrorist tactics to collect sports bets. Steve Hospodar lost $11,000 in bets and was unable to pay his loses so he went to the FBI and became an informant wearing a wire. The jury acquitted all six of their charges. Grieco went to the jury box and began to shake the hands of the jurors, thanking them. One juror refused to shake his hand.

His victory was short lived. In 1985, Joe Grieco was sentenced to 5 years in federal prison for obstruction of justice. The charges were loan sharking and extortion. Grieco and mob boss Joseph Arnold threatened Ralph Carazzo and promised to wipe out his $15,000 "juice" loan if he would not testify against the two in a grand jury investigation into loan-shark activities. Carazzo once worked as a parking lot attendant in the Rush Street area for Arnold and was called to appear several times since 1979 to testify against the mobsters. He refused to testify after he was granted immunity and was found in contempt of court and sent to prison for 18 months. The charges were based on tape recordings from a hidden wiretap placed in Arnold's Odds 'N' Ends Drugstore on Rush Street. On the tapes Grieco, Arnold and Carazzo were heard discussing strategies to throw off the grand jury. Also heard was Grieco promising to pay Carazzo's legal fees telling him *"to become an actor, grow a beard, wear coveralls, tell them you're tired and you need a drink of water. The government won't protect you because the government can't shadow you for the rest of your life. You know where we're coming from. It's either us or them. Let's call a spade a spade."*

Carazzo disappeared after he was released from prison and could not be found. During the trial, Grieco denied being a member of organized crime but the government alleged him to be an enforcer for the mob.

In a 1990 Chicago Crime Commission chart on the Chicago mob, Joe Grieco was listed under the west side group being controlled by Dom Cortina. Joe Grieco was paroled from prison in March 1990.

Nick D'Andrea

Nicholas J. D'Andrea, born around 1932, was known as a mob vice boss under mobster Al "Caesar" Tocco. A 1965 report lists Chicago Heights, Illinois as the area under the control of the D'Andrea brothers. Nick D'Andrea and his brother Armand D'Andrea were listed as main lenders and collectors in that area. Nick D'Andrea's persuasion tool was a baseball bat that he used to convince the people who were delinquent in their payments to pay up. Nick D'Andrea owned and operated the Chicago Heights lounge and a motel in Manteno where prostitution was available.

On September 13, 1981, a burning car was discovered near Crete, Illinois. When the flames were extinguished, the charred body of

Nick D'Andrea was discovered in the trunk of the auto. Eighteen days later Nick's brother Mario D'Andrea was killed after a firefight with undercover DEA agents at a gas station in Chicago Heights, Illinois. In 2007 mob turncoat, Nicholas Calabrese told the government that some of the people allegedly responsible for D'Andrea's murder were Sam "Wings" Carlisi, James Marcello, and Angelo LaPietra. They believed that D'Andrea knew something about an attempted murder on mobster Al Pilotto and was trying to use the situation to "move up" in the chain of command. Mob bosses turned out to be wrong and D'Andrea was killed for nothing.

Calabrese said that he was ordered to a garage in Chicago Heights and was told that when a tall man and a short man came walking into the garage he was to hit the smaller man with a baseball bat until he was dead. When the tall man, later identified as mobster Sam Guzzino, and the short man walked into the garage, Guzzino began to run, the short man, D'Andrea, had to be overpowered and subdued until he was killed. Weeks later, Guzzino himself was killed.

Joseph E. Walan

Chicago Police learned that Joseph Walan was an alleged gambling overseer for mobster Ralph Pierce and controlled gambling operations on the Southside of Chicago and in southern Cook County, specifically in the Calumet City, Illinois area. Walan had been arrested 10 times by the Chicago PD between 1936 and 1951. In 1940, he was sentenced to 90 days in prison for rape and on July 15, 1940 was given one year of probation on a charge of manslaughter, reduced from a charge of murder.

Informants stated in 1964 that Walan had allegedly attempted to spread his bookmaking and "juice" activities into the Hammond-Gary Indiana area. With that, Walan allegedly used a John Montagna as his main "juice" man. It was Montagna's job to make most of the contacts with "juice" victims for Walan. Most of the loans made and collected by Montagna for Walan were the results of gambling debts owed to Walan through his handbook operations and personal gambling.

One person listed as being on "juice to Walan was Dempsey Arnett, described as an alleged pimp from the Grovertown, Indiana area. It was reported at the time that he was behind on a $40,000 "juice" loan.

Louis Spear

There is a government report containing information given during an interview to the FBI in 1962 concerning a Louis Spear, then listed as the General Manager or Business Manager for the Chicago Sun-Times newspaper in Chicago. Spears, who had his offices close to Marshall Fields Jr. in the Sun-Times building, was one of the larger "juice" operators in the Chicago area. Spears was considered one of Marshall Field Jr.'s right-hand men in the operation of that newspaper at the time.

This informant stated that Spears allegedly only loaned large amounts of money at 20 percent interest and preferred to loan money to bookmakers and prominent gamblers. This individual only dealt on a high level and generally for extremely large sums of money. This informant advised that Spears's activities in the "juice" business went through a Tony Tornabene who operated a notorious strip club called Eddie Foy's Club on Wabash Avenue in Chicago. This informant also added that Tornabene once borrowed $10,000 from Spears.

Sam Farrugia

In 1961, Sam Farrugia was singled out as one of the top mob "juice" men operating in Chicago. According to reports, he was considered a veteran loan shark in the jukebox industry.

In 1978 an FBI report said, *"Information was obtained that Sam 'Little Sam' Faruggia was involved in a large scale 'juice' operation which was connected with the vending machine industry in Chicago."*

Samuel S. Faruggia was born on July 11, 1920 in Chicago. Faruggia was arrested for the hold-up murder of Hyman Hymovits on May 24, 1941, with Guy Esposito, Sam Spina, and Peter Scardina. In May 1981, Sam Faruggia's body was found in the back seat of his 1980 Oldsmobile, which was parked in front of the house at 758 N. LeClaire Avenue. His throat was slit and he had been stabbed in the chest many times.

Sam Lewis

One FBI informant said that Sam Louis was one of the most vicious "juice" racketeers in Chicago in the 1950's and 60's. Sam Lewis got his start back in the 1920's when he was a member of the 42 Gang with Sam DeStefano, William Daddono, and Sam Giancana. He had three sons who all worked for the Chicago police department at one point. He controlled the Parr Loan Company as a front for his "juice" operations up until the time they found William "Action" Jackson murdered in 1962. The Parr Finance Company located at 507 South Oak Park Avenue in Oak Park was owned by the politically connected Donald Parrillo. The listed officers of this company were, President Donald W. Parrillo, Secretary William J. Parrillo, and Registered Agent Joseph Ungaro.

The Parrillo family gained its wealth through William Parrillo who served as the Assistant Attorney General for the state of Illinois under Republican Governor Dwight Green. William Parrillo was a known "fixer" for the Capone gang during Al Capone's rule. After Capone went to jail, Parrillo's power continued through his close friendships with mob bosses Paul Ricca "DeLucia," Sam Giancana, Tony "JB" Accardo, and Sam Louis. When William Parrillo died, he left several million dollars to his family and his wife purchased part of the Parr Loan Company for her son, Donald Parrillo, so he could be a partner with Sam Lewis. The Parr Loan Company made legitimate loans to gamblers in debt, hoodlums, and other individuals unable to obtain loans through legitimate sources. The interest charged then was 20% yearly.

Listed as working for Sam Lewis as "juice" collectors in the 1950's and 60's was William "Action" Jackson, Joseph Lombardi, Carmine "Carmie" Francis and Tony Sisto. Sisto had been arrested with mobster Sam "Sambo" Cesario for bookmaking activities in the Taylor and Halsted area of Chicago. After Action Jackson was killed, the police hounded Lewis at every corner so he decided to leave Parr Loan and open his own company which was called The More Finance Company located at 754 North Leamington, Chicago. This time it was reported through an informant that Sam Lewis was allegedly using his son Robert Lewis as his muscle and main "juice" collector. It was learned that Sam Lewis was allied with Leonard "Needles" Gianola and Felix "Milwaukee Phil"

Alderisio. The three had a great deal of hoodlum influence in the Diversey District of Chicago and had interest in most of the illegal operations conducted in that area.

Harry Aleman

Harry Sam Aleman was born on January 19, 1939 in Chicago, and went by the names of Harry Mustari, and Tony Romano.

In 1970, Aleman was allegedly involved in "juice" when he was listed by law enforcement officials as working around Taylor and Bishop Streets area, Taylor Street and Racine Avenue, and Ninth Street and Wabash Avenue in Chicago.

According to reports, some of Aleman's arrests were for aggravated kidnapping, battery, theft and in 1960 for malicious

Author's Collection

mischief, in 1962 for reckless conduct, shoplifting on June 30, 1966, and armed robbery on January 1, 1967. As of 2008 Aleman was serving time in prison and has denied any and all reports that he is connected to the Chicago mob.

Salvatore Angileri

Sam Angileri was born around 1935 and was alleged to have operated "juice" loans at the corners of Austin Boulevard and Fullerton Avenue in Chicago and Main Street and Broadway in Melrose Park in the past.

Angileri was associated with the Fit-Right Plastic Covers Incorporated located at 5613 West Chicago Avenue in Chicago. His arrest record listed a conviction for gambling in 1968 for which he received 2 years probation.

Sam Ariola

Born around 1926, Ariola was known as "Big Sam" Ariola and was a staple at Chicago area racetracks. He ran his "juice" business out of his Villa Rose Pizza place located at 2672 River Road in River Forest, Illinois. In 1970, he was listed as a top "juice" man in River Forest living at 9759 Franklin Avenue in Franklin Park.

In September 1961, Sam Ariola was arrested with mobsters Guy Crevone and Louis Eboli for aggravated battery for beating two pinball players named Melvin Kent and Peter Gothard with a baseball bat. Also charged were Roland Letcher, Herman Bingham and Robert Tobin, three River Forest Police officers who allegedly turned Kent and Gothard over to Ariola to be beaten.

Michael Biancofior

Mike L. Biancofiori was born on October 2, 1925, and lived at 2803 Oak Street in Bellwood, and 1507 Hawk in Melrose Park, Illinois. Biancofiori was arrested in 1945 for larceny and was given one-year probation. In 1969 he was convicted on a Federal juice violation, extortion and racketeering. He was sent to the penitentiary at Sandstone, Minnesota on a 7-year sentence. He died on February 15, 1996, in Melrose Park.

Herbert Blitzstein

Herbie Blitzstein, born on November 2, 1934, was known as Herbie Blitz. His area of operation was around Grand and Wabash Avenues and Rush and Delaware Streets in Chicago.

Herbie Blitz was listed as a Chicago area "juice" man living at 7334 N. Ridge in Chicago. His arrest record contained one arrest on a gambling charge. In 1981 Blitzstein, Tony Spilotro, John Spilotro, and a one-time Las Vegas Metropolitan Police officer were indicted by a federal grand jury on racketeering charges. At that time, Biltzstein had been in jail for contempt for refusing to give the grand jury a handwriting sample in connection with the investigation. Blitzstein died in Las Vegas on January 7, 1997.

Frank Calabrese

Frank James Calabrese could never have imagined the situation he was in as of 2007. His trusted brother Nick Calabrese and trusted son Frank Jr. had both sold him out to the feds. Born on March 17, 1934, Calabrese is known by the nicknames of "Frankie C" and "Breese."

In 1970, Frank Calabrese was listed as an alleged "juice" man in Chicago. The alleged places that "Frankie C" operated, according to law enforcement officials, were the corners of Delaware Place and Rush Street, and Belmont and Central Avenues in Chicago.

His arrest record indicates that he was convicted in 1954 in federal court for possession of stolen cars in interstate commerce. He was also convicted in 1954 for going AWOL and was incarcerated in a U.S. Army Stockade in Missouri. Other listings on his arrest record are for robbery, larceny, and illegal possession of firearms.

In September 2007, Frank Calabrese Sr. was found guilty of murdering mob associates in one of Chicago's biggest mob trials of all time, the Family Secretes trial. During the trial, Calabrese took the stand and admitted that he made millions from illegal street loans but said he had no time to kill anyone. He admitted doing business with people in the Outfit and paling around with mobsters, especially mob boss Angelo "The Hook" LaPietra, but said he, himself, was not a mobster. When the prosecutors played the secret tape recordings his son Frank Jr. made while the two were in prison together, Frankie C said he just told his son made-up stories to "win over his son" and have him think his old man was a big shot for the mob. Calabrese said that he got his "mob" knowledge from magazines, books, and from movies like the Godfather, parts 1 and 2.

Calabrese's street crew according to published reports consisted of:

Philip "Philly Beans" Tolomeo, was a one-time Chicago Police officer and Calabrese collector who entered the witness protection program. In the 1970's and early 1980's, Philly Beans was paid 25 percent commission on the "juice" loan payments he collected until he had a falling out with Calabrese in 1988. Tolomeo was accused of stealing money and operating his own "juice" racket with money that belonged to Calabrese. For this Philly Beans's nose was broken by Calabrese and he was forced to sign to place the title of his mother's home in Elmwood Park in the name of Nick Calabrese's father-in-law, Salvatore Tenuta. Tolomeo was forced to give up his "accounts" to other members in the crew. In 1990 after leaving Chicago, Philly Beans found himself in on the East Coast in the District of Delaware allegedly supplying "loans" for John Stanfa, Larry Veach and Ronald Mazzone. The three men allegedly gave Tolomeo $100,000 for his operations.

Philip J. Fiore, known as Pete, was listed as an alleged "juice" loan collector, troubleshooter and in 1997, a low-level supervisor.

Terry "T J" Scalise was an alleged "juice" collector.

Louis J. Bombacino, known as John Lordo, was an alleged juice collector who once called Philly Tolomeo and Louis "The Mooch" Eboli his mentors.

Frank Calabrese Jr. was a "juice" collector and son of Frank Sr. who turned government witness against his father.

Kurt Calabrese, Frankie C's other son and was listed as an alleged member of the Calabrese crew.

Robert Dinella, who was listed as an employee of the Celozzi-Ettleson Chevrolet dealership in the 1990's, made arrangements with Calabrese to bilk the dealership and customers for fraudulent or inflated repair charges.

Jasper Campise

Known as Jay Campise to his mob buddies, Jasper Campise was born on March 14, 1916 in Chicago. He lived at 3011 N. Keating in Chicago, and 1631 N. Newland. He was known to operate at the corners of Belmont and Harlem Avenues in Chicago, and Belmont Avenue and River Road in River Grove, Illinois. His arrest record states he was arrested in 1963 on an aggravated battery charge and in 1966 for murder. Also in that year, the FBI reported that Nick and George Bravos put up a considerable amount of the principal money for Campise to run "juice" operations so the Bravos brothers didn't have to be directly involved in the operation. Jay Campise was found murdered in July 1983.

John Carr

Known by the alias of John C. Carr, Kaspar J. Ciapetta was a known police bagman and "juice" man for the mob. He was born around 1918 and lived at 2 S 746 Orleans Street in DuPage County, Illinois and 22 W. 326 Glen Park, Glen Ellyn, Illinois. Listed as his areas of operation were Cermak Road and Austin Boulevard, 18th Street and Cicero Avenue, 49th Street and Cermak Road, 26th Street and Austin Boulevard in Cicero, and Ogden and Center Avenues in Lyons. His arrest record contained an arrest for bribery in 1965.

Sander Caravello

With many aliases such as Sam Sanders, Jim Marino, Santo Caravello, Sanders Caravello, and Sam Caravello, Sander was listed as a mob "juice" man in the 1960's. Born on July 23, 1908, Caravello lived at 814 East Kimber Lane in Arlington Heights, Illinois and was listed with the Elk

Grove Village business called Shak-Ur-Corn and B-G Builders at 5420 North Harlem Avenue in Chicago.

His arrest record contains a conviction in 1928 for armed robbery and in 1937 for conspiracy, which carried a 1-to-5 year sentence. In 1965, he was charged with theft of checks and money orders. In 1967, he won an acquittal for aggravated kidnapping. Sander Caravello died in January 1981 in Sun City, Arizona.

Ralph Casale

Born around 1910, Ralph Casale lived at 1210 N. Long Street in Chicago. Casale was named as an alleged "juice" man when he was arrested on April 12, 1969 in Chicago for conspiracy to violate criminal usury laws.

Mike Castaldo

Mike Sam Castaldo was born on August 8, 1929, and lived at 925 Park Street in Melrose Park. In 1970, he was a "juice" man frequenting the corners of Ninth and North Avenues in Melrose Park and Thatcher and North Avenues in River Forest, and Gene's Deli at 2202 N. Harlem.

In 1956, Castaldo was convicted for extortion, being sentenced to 4-to-7 years in prison. In 1963, the FBI discovered that Mike Castaldo was one of the "guys" representing Gus Alex in the "juice" rackets. Castaldo was listed as a partner of mobster William "Wee Willie" Messino in two nightclubs and was the financial "front man" for Alex in those clubs.

In November 1969 when an Illinois crime investigation into criminal usury rackets was conducted, a former businessman named Morton Golden went to mobsters Mike Castaldo and Tony "Radio" Renallo to get a "juice" loan for his business. He was forced to sign a promissory note for the money and after time lost his business because he couldn't keep up on the "juice" payments. He continued being active in "juice" into the 1990's when he was charged with loaning money at a 260 percent-a-year interest rate to his loan shark victims. Michael Castaldo died in August 2005 and is buried at Queen of Heaven Cemetery in Hillside, Illinois.

Sam Castonzo

Samuel A. Castonzo used the aliases of Tony Certo, Sam Sarno, Sam Borelli, Sam Castonza and Sam Costanazo. Born on June 11, 1921, Castonzo was listed as living at 9275 Clancy Drive in Des Plaines, Illinois. His arrest record contained a conviction in 1952 for burglary, receiving 3 years of probation. In 1939, he was arrested for possession of burglary tools. Other arrests included charges for pimping, burglary, auto larceny, and keeper of a house of prostitution.

His areas of operation were listed as Halsted Street and Lawrence Avenue, and State and Division Streets in Chicago. He was the owner of the Bella Via Coiffures Beauty Shop at 8811 N. Milwaukee Avenue in Niles, Illinois. Sam Castonzo died in January of 1975 in Des Plaines, Illinois.

John Cimitile

John Cimitile was known as "Big John" Cimitile but used the aliases of John Amola, John Cimity, and John Cimatie. Born on December 4, 1906, "Big John" lived at 1025 N. Parkside in Chicago. In 1965 and 1966, he was arrested for gambling and in 1967 was convicted on a gambling charge. His base of operations connecting him to "juice" was said to be

around 17th Street and Ashland Avenue in Chicago. In March 1963, the FBI reported that John Cimitile was alleged to be engaged in gambling and active in the "juice" racket on Maxwell Street for Gus Alex. When the FBI approached him, he denied any connection to the mob except his friendship with Gus Alex's gambling Lieutenant Louis Briatta. He died in March 1986 in Las Vegas, Nevada.

Anthony Cirignani

Anthony Vito Cirignani was born around 1929 and lived at 1501 West Erie Street in Chicago. In 1945, he was arrested for burglary and sentenced to six months in prison. Other listings on his arrest record were for battery, contempt, and murder. He was listed as being allegedly connected to the "juice" loan rackets in 1970.

Pasquale Clementi

Pasquale Clementi was known as "Buck" Clementi and "Patsy" Clementi. Born around 1909, he lived at 1681 N. 5th Avenue in Melrose Park. His brother Louis Clementi was a Capone mobster during the 1920's while Patsy was a member of the 42 Gang, being close to Sam Giancana and Sam DeStefano.

Buck Clementi operated around 15th and North Avenues in Melrose Park and Roosevelt Road and Austin Blvd. in Cicero during the 1960's. He was listed in 1966 as being under the faction directed by mobster Leo Manfredi and in 1967 working for Willie "Potatoes" Daddono. That same year the police launched a manhunt to find Patsy to have him testify in hearings being held on Chicago "juice" rackets. Clementi had left Chicago to hide out while the hearings were going on. The police were not the only ones looking for him. His wife was looking for him because she needed money to run the house and hadn't seen or heard from him in over a month.

His criminal record contains arrests in 1941 for larceny and conspiracy to violate U.S. Internal Revenue Liquor Laws. After a year in jail, he was arrested in 1958 for assault and battery.

Frank Covello

Known as Frank B. Martelli, Frank T. Santi, and Frank Canella, Frank Covello was listed as being allegedly connected to the Chicago "juice" rackets. Covello's alleged locations of operations in the 1960's were North and Central Avenues, Princeton and 31st Streets in Chicago and Harlem and Lawrence Avenues in Harwood Heights. His arrest record contains arrests for gambling, a conviction for burglary in 1955, and a charge of conspiracy to violate criminal usury laws on April 12, 1969.

Marco D'Amico

Marco D'Amico, born on January 1, 1936, was alleged to be connected to the "juice" rackets operating around Foster Avenue and Sheridan Road in Chicago. In 1968, he was arrested on a gambling charge and in the 1980's was known to hang out at the Elmwood Park Social Club located at 7520 W. Diversey.

Billy Dauber

William Earl Dauber was born on June 30, 1935, in the Appalachians and was murdered on July 2, 1980.

He got his start with James "Jimmy the Bomber" Catuara, becoming a trusted mob hit man involved in more than 20 mob murders. He

participated in the "chop-shop wars" in Cook County in the 1970's, selling his stolen goods from Paoli Auto Parts.

Billy Dauber was connected to the "juice" rackets, listed as working around the corners of Mackinaw Avenue and 88th Street, Baltimore Avenue and 85th Street in Chicago, and Dixie Highway and U.S. Route #54 in Hazelcrest, Illinois.

Among his arrests were charges of larceny of an auto and malicious mischief. In 1973, Dauber was convicted of mail fraud and interstate transportation of a stolen car that had been used in another murder. After his release from prison in 1976, he went to work for mob boss Albert Tocco as an enforcer.

In July 1980, Dauber was charged with having hidden large quantities of cocaine and weapons in his suburban home. As Dauber and his wife Charlotte drove from the courthouse after a hearing was conducted, a van pulled alongside of their car and opened fire with shotguns. Both were killed as the car ran off the highway hitting an apple tree. Police found the van one mile down the street as it went up in flames; the hitmen set it on fire to hide any evidence.

According to reports, Dauber's wife Charlotte had been vocally expressing her un-happiness with the mob and the way her husband was treated by his fellow mobsters. She began to talk in public complaining that Dauber should not stand for it. Between his wife's outspokenness and the fear that he may turn government witness, Billy Dauber and his wife were taken care of.

Anthony Del Gallo

Anthony Del Gallo changed his name to Tony Gallo sometime after being born around 1926. He lived at 2801 S. Austin Blvd. in Cicero, Illinois. On September 10, 1969, he was arrested on a federal juice charge stating that he was operating "juice" around Cicero Avenue and 18th Street in Cicero. He was found guilty and sentenced to 5 years in prison.

Louis De Riggi

When Louis De Riggi was arrested on September 10, 1969 on a federal juice charge, he was listed as a "mob enforcer" living at 3614 West Grand Avenue in Chicago. Born around 1925, De Riggi was also known as Louis De Rilli around 18th Street and Cicero Avenue in Cicero. He was alleged to have been connected to the Buccieri group. On June 16, 1945, Louis De Riggi was convicted by the U.S. Military Court for desertion during a time of war. He was also convicted at the same time for auto theft and was sentenced to 3 years in a naval penitentiary. He received 8 years in prison on his "juice" indictment. In 1974, De Riggi was fired from the payroll at Chicago's McCormick Place for his alleged mob ties.

Peter DeStito

Peter P. DeStito was born around 1935 and was mentioned as allegedly being connected to the "juice" rackets in Chicago. DeStito could be found at 9th and North Avenues in Melrose Park and was always seen at Sportsman's Park Race Track in Cicero, until he was barred from all Illinois racetracks as of October 29, 1969.

John Difronzo

John "No Nose" Difronzo Sr. was listed in the 1970 "Juice" rackets report for his alleged involvement in the 1964 "juice"-related kidnapping case in which he was acquitted. It was alleged that DiFronzo frequented North and Cicero Avenues in the 1960's in connection with "juice." The Crime Commission listed DiFronzo as allegedly using the alias of John Franzo and his criminal record includes a conviction for burglary in 1946 and 1950.

Charles English

Charles Carmen English was one of the mob's top capo's in Chicago during the 1960's, being a lieutenant under Sam Giancana. Known as Chuckie or Chuck to his mob buddies, he was mostly known as a gambling king with his brother Sam "Butch" English at most of Chicago's racing tracks. Controlling gambling at the racing parks lead to lending money to gamblers so they could bet.

Chuckie English's "juice" racket in the 1960's was listed as being operated at Lathrop Avenue and Roosevelt Road in Forest Park, Austin Boulevard and Roosevelt Road in Cicero, 34th Street and Laramie Avenue in Cicero, and all Illinois race tracks, from which he was barred on October 29, 1969. In 1967, a Marvin Browning operated a store at 1550 West 43rd Street in Chicago then called "George's Store for Men." In hearings held before the Illinois Crime Commission, it was disclosed that Browning had been making and accepting "juice" loans for Charles English for over 20 years. In the 1970's and 80's Chuckie English fell out of favor with many of the mobsters in Chicago. In February 1985, he was killed in Elmwood Park as he walked to his car.

Anthony Eldorado

Anthony Eldorado, known as "Tony Pineapples" and "Tony Pine," was born on August 23, 1914 in Chicago. He used the aliases of Tom Mackay, Ron Eldorado, Frank Eldorado and Tony Elodado. He lived at 6107 S. Knox Street and 5643 W. Madison in Chicago. He was known to be active in "juice" around Madison Avenue and Long Street in Chicago and Harlem and Stanley Avenues in Berwyn. His arrest record contained a 1936 conviction for armed robbery, for which he received 3-to-20 years in prison. Another arrest came in 1963 for battery. He died in August 1975.

Frank Fratto

Frank "One Ear" Fratto was named as a top "juice" boss in 1970. Also known as Frank Farrell and Frankie Frappo, he was born on March 3, 1915 in Chicago. His arrest record contained arrests dating back to 1941 for assault, assault to commit murder, theft and being a fugitive. In 1951, he was convicted on federal charges of interstate theft of whiskey and received 3 years probation. In 1957 he was picked up and questioned in the murder of Willard Bates and once again in 1963 for the murder of Chicago Alderman Benjamin Lewis.

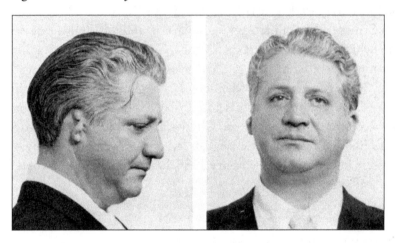

Fratto was listed as living at 6300 W. 25th Street and 8517 Winnemac in Chicago. One report stated that Fratto was related to mobster Felix Alderisio. Fratto's "juice" territory was listed as Higgins Road and Cumberland Avenue in Chicago. Frankie Fratto died on May 25, 1996.

John Fecarotta

John A. Fecarotta Sr. was once asked by government officials who his enemies were; he replied with, *"Only my wife."* He was born around 1929 and grew up around the West Ohio Street area. There he went by the call name of "Big John" and John Fecarotta. He lived at the addresses of 212 N. Hamlin Avenue and 201 Michaux Road in Riverside in the 1960's, with his wife Alice and their five children. He was also known to use the aliases of Frank Pica, Anthony Fecaret, John Ferrotta, Anthony Fecarotto, and Tony Feceret.

John Fecarotta was a "ghost" business agent for Chicago Local 8 of the Industrial Workers Union until he was exposed in 1982 as being a mob capo. His arrest record listed a conviction in 1944 for robbery and was sentenced to 2-to-4 years in prison. In 1952, he received 3-to -6 years in prison for trying to steal the safe from the National Tea Store on 63rd Street in Chicago with Sam Castonzo and Joseph DeMarco. Other arrests were for larceny, assault with intent to kill and  several other burglaries. In 1965, he was listed as an alleged "juice" man working for Fiore "Fifi" Buccieri when he was arrested in the O'Hare Field parking lot for threatening an Alphonso Branch with a gun. In 1970, he was listed as operating his "juice" racket in the Laramie Avenue and 47th Street area of Forest View.

On September 14, 1986, John Fecarotta was chased by a mob hitman until he was shot dead in the doorway of the Brown's Banquets Bingo Hall at 6050 W. Belmont Avenue. He had been shot in the side, the back, the arm, with the final shot in the head. He is buried at Queen of Heaven Cemetery in Hillside, Illinois.

Robert Filippelli

Robert Alfred Filippelli was born around 1934 and had a conviction for gambling in 1967. In 1968 he was convicted of violating his probation and sent to prison for 40 days. Living at 1746 N. Natchez in Chicago, Filippelli was listed as being allegedly connected to the "juice" rackets in 1970. Listed as places he could be found were Broadway and Lake Street in Melrose Park, Austin Boulevard and Fullerton Avenue, and Central and Chicago Avenues in Chicago.

Mike Filishio

Michael J. Filishio was born on December 1, 1916, in Chicago and died on November 3, 1990. His arrest record dates back to 1950 when he was convicted in Federal Court and was sentenced to 5 years in prison for counterfeiting. In 1970, he was listed as being a "juice" man around his home at 6430 Fairfield in Berwyn and was active around Mannheim Road and Soffel Avenue in Stone Park, Illinois.

Anthony Genna

Anthony C. Genna was known as a truck driver for the Chicago Park District. Born on September 12, 1924 in Chicago, Genna was arrested and convicted of using force and threats of violence to collect on a "juice" loan from a James Reese on September 7, 1964. Reese, an unemployed bookkeeper at the time, went to Genna and a Joseph Sarillo to borrow $1,000. After Reese had paid back almost $2,500 on his loan, he was told he must pay an additional $900--or else. Genna was sent to county jail on January 25, 1965, to serve 6 months on his conviction.

Once out, Genna was placed back in his $609 a month job as a truck driver for the Chicago Park District and was assigned to drive a grass-cutting tractor in Humboldt Park, in Chicago. Irwin Weiner, then a Chicago Park District general superintendent, said that Anthony Genna had been an excellent worker since he started working for the park district in 1949. That year Genna was placed into civil service through his First Ward connections. In 1966, it was discovered that Genna was using the address of 1067 Taylor Street in Chicago so he could work for the city when he was actually living at 501 S. 22nd Avenue in Bellwood, Illinois. He died in December 1982 in Addison, Illinois.

August Giovenco

August "Gus" Giovenco, born around 1910, was a cab supervisor for the Checker Taxi Company on West Washington Street in Chicago. His arrest record contained an arrest in 1926 for murder and an arrest for disorderly conduct. Listed as living at 4849 West Catalpa Avenue in Chicago in the 1960's, he was mentioned as being involved in shylocking around Diversey Avenue and Halsted Street and Walton and Rush Streets in Chicago.

Tony Granito

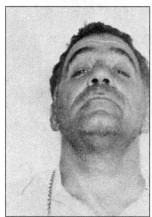

Anthony James Granito was believed to be born on January 9, 1918 in Chicago, and died in February 1983. Known as "Tony the Head," Tony Genero, Anthony Marino, and Tony Granato, Granito was said to operate in shylocking around North and Major Avenues in Chicago and Mannheim and Higgins Roads in Des Plains.

In the 1960's Granito gave two different addresses as his place of residence, 1722 N. Mannheim Road in Stone Park and 5946 W. 25th Street in Cicero.

He was convicted in 1941 for armed robbery and served 3 years in prison. In 1964, he was listed as the manager of a syndicate gambling and vice joint when he was arrested and served 6 months in Bridewell Prison on a battery conviction. In May 1968, Granito was listed as being a member of the Joey Aiuppa group collecting "juice" loans at O'Hare Airport when he was being investigated for illegally selling land on the Grand Bahamas Island. In this business venture mobsters Joe Mirabelli and Gildo Secco accompanied Granito. Mirabelli was listed as an associate of Joe "Gags" Gagliano and was arrested in 1933 for rape, spending nine months in Bridewell Prison. Secco had an arrest for gambling and was seized by police in 1963 as a receiver of stolen property from an interstate shipment.

Granito and Secco were offering free plane rides to Grand Bahamas Island as a lure to people to purchase lots offered at prices ranging from $1,050 to $23,000. Gambling and disorderly conduct charges were added to Granito's record and on May 20, 1970, he was charged with making false statements on loan applications.

William Hickok

William Charles Hickok was born around 1931 and went by the aliases of "Bart" and William Clayton Hickox. His identification sheet contains information that he was an auto mechanic who lived at 1612 Herbert Street in Rockford, Illinois in the 1960's. In 1968, he was arrested on robbery charges and sentenced to 1-to-10 years in prison. In 1969, he was convicted of charges for transporting stolen autos in interstate commerce and was sentenced to Terre Haute prison in Indiana. In 1970, he was listed as allegedly being connected to the "juice" rackets in Chicago.

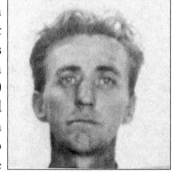

Peter Karyginnis

Peter S. Karyginnis, alias Pete Karigiannis, was born around 1937 and lived at 4709 N. Virginia Street in Chicago. He was associated with Pete's Dinner at 6936 N. Clark Street when he was arrested in 1969 on federal charges of extortion. He was sentenced to 5 years in prison. Other criminal arrests were for burglary, theft, and arson.

John Joseph Kobylarz

Known as John "Slim" Kobylarz, he was arrested on September 9, 1969 on federal juice charges. He sometimes used the aliases of John Hobylooz and lived at 5219 S. Linder Street in Chicago. In May 1966, Kobylarz was arrested by the FBI and charged with stealing $65,000 worth of television sets. In 1968 he was convicted of possession of goods stolen in interstate shipment and was sentenced to 6 years in prison. He was known to operate at 18th Street and Cicero Avenue in Cicero. In

1971, Kobylarz was sentenced to 5 years in prison on his "juice" charge. In 1974, he was fired from his job at Chicago's McCormick Place because of his mob ties.

Gust Korovesis

Born on May 16, 1928, Gust Korovesis lived at 2311 W. Arthur in Chicago in the 1960's. His arrest record dates back to 1962 with arrests for gambling, theft of lost property and theft by deception. Gust Korovesis worked at a used car lot known as Stardust Motors on Ogden Avenue in Berwyn when he was reported as a "juice" man operating at the corners of Lincoln Avenue and Wells Street, and Diversey and Pine Grove Avenues in Chicago. In 1969, he was convicted for deceptive practices and received 5 years probation. He died in Roselle, Illinois on January 17, 1985.

Henry Kushnir

Henry "Red" Kushnir was born on December 4, 1908, in Chicago and lived at 850 N. DeWitt. He was known as a Northside crime syndicate figure who specialized in gambling and "juice" loans during the 1950's, 60's and 70's. Concerning his "juice" operations, he frequented the areas of Chicago Avenue and State Street, Ohio and State Streets, Milwaukee and Grand Avenues, and Roosevelt Road and Wabash Avenue in Chicago.

There is a mention that a Henry Kushnir living at 5819 N. Washtena Avenue in 1951 when he was arrested for being the owner of the Gold Coast Lounge on Rush Street. Kushnir was arrested for allowing call girls to work out of his lounge. In 1966, Red Kushnir and Mike Glitta appeared before an Illinois crime investigation commission and Kushnir hid behind the Fifth Amendment 113 times to every question posed to him.

His police record contained an arrest in 1969 for failure to file assumed name certificate. In April 1973, he was called before a federal grand jury investigating bribery of public officials and possible payoffs to the police in the Foster Avenue District in Chicago. He was granted immunity from prosecution but was charged weeks later for perjury. Kushnir denied making certain loans at 20 percent that the government knew he made. He denied having dealings with mobster Joseph DiVarco and denied introducing alleged "juice" victims to hoodlum Herbert Blitzstein. Red Kushnir died in December 1979.

William Lamnatos

William Lamnatos gained the nickname of "Fat Man" and used the alias of William Reno. Born on June 10, 1929 in Chicago, he lived at 609 Strafford Place in the 1960's. He worked at the used car lot known as Stardust Motors on Ogden Avenue when he was convicted in 1969 for deceptive practices. Other arrests were for gambling and possession of theft of lost property. Locations that were said to be Lamnatos area were Diversey and Pine Grove Avenues, Lincoln Avenue and Wells Street in Chicago, and Ogden Avenue in Berwyn. He died in November 1990.

Sebastian Licato

Sebastian "Buster" Licato used the aliases of Benjamin Licata, Saul Licarto, Sebastian B. Liscoto and Sebastian Licata. Born on March 22,

1908 in Chicago, Buster lived at 6643 Ogden Avenue in Berwyn. Buster was listed as a part-time worker for Mark's Heating Company in Berwyn and was known to be connected to "juice" operations around Diversey Avenue and Neva Street, and Maxwell Street and Halsted in Chicago.

In 1939, he was convicted of grand larceny and was sentenced to 10 years in prison. In 1959, he was convicted of receiving stolen goods, and in 1963,

he received one-year probation for theft. Other arrests listed were for burglary, theft, and shoplifting. He died in August 1981.

Leo Manfredi

Leo John Manfredi, also known as Leonard Corbini and John Dubois, lived at 1833 and 1873 S. Austin Boulevard in Cicero. He was known to operate around Polk and Aberdeen Streets, and Carpenter and

Arthington Streets in Chicago. He also operated from the Bella Rosa Restaurant at 1302 S. Cicero Avenue in Cicero. This building was once owned by Mario DeStefano and was sold to Manfredi in 1966, with Mario still owning a small piece of it.

His arrest record dates back to 1932 when he, Angelo Falco and Frank Damore were arrested for robbing a bakery shop of $400. During their trial, Manfredi and Falco walked out of the courthouse during recess and a manhunt was under way. The two were captured and found guilty of robbery and sentenced to 5 years. In 1942, he was convicted in Los Angeles, California on armed robbery charges, being sentenced to 5-years-to-life in San Quentin prison.

In 1966, he was described as a mob hit man and professional killer who charged $10,000 a hit. In 1969, Manfredi was listed as being spotted devoting most of his evenings visiting the home of a city payroller. It was learned that Manfredi was in good with the old First Ward group in Chicago.

In the 1970's Manfredi was observed from time-to-time meeting top mob boss Joey Aiuppa in a used car lot, handing over envelopes stuffed with money from his loan shark operations.

In October 1982, Manfredi was living at 1833 S. Austin Blvd in Cicero when the police received a phone call from his family. They were concerned because they had not heard from Manfredi and wanted the police to check a pizza parlor that was owned by Manfredi's nephew. The Berwyn pizza parlor at 6233 W. Roosevelt Road was known as "Leo's Toy." There he would hold high-stakes card games for the outfit. Police arrived and found the place closed and locked, and no signs of forced entry could be found. A police officer climbed through an unlocked window to search the place and found Leo Manfredi face down in the basement. He had been shot four times in the head, but was still wearing his trademark fedora. Police believed that the murder was linked to his operations in the drug business. Information was uncovered that Manfredi had been using mob "juice" money to finance short-term narcotics deals without the permission of mob boss Joey Aiuppa. After some of the deals fell through and the money stopped falling into Aiuppa's hands, Manfredi was killed.

Abraham Milstein

Sometimes known as Albert Milsten, Abraham had his 1960's address listed as the Federal Penitentiary in Sandstone, Minnesota. He was arrested on October 10, 1969, on federal juice charges, being connected to the areas of Roosevelt Road and Cicero Avenue in Chicago, and Cermak Road and Cicero Avenue in Cicero. In 1968, he was convicted on federal alcohol charges receiving over 3 years in prison. In 1971, he was sentenced to 8 years in prison on his usury charge.

Sam Mercurio

Samuel A. Mercurio lived either at 3257 or 3357 N. Nottingham in Chicago and was listed as being born on November 19, 1921. His parents, Joseph and Margaret Mercurio, both died one year apart in 1958 and 1959. Joseph was born in Italy and lived his life as a glasscutter. His family consisted of three brothers Michael, Paul and the name of the third not known, and three sisters Clara Patti, Ann Quattrocki and a third, who died at a young age.

A young Sam made his connections while attending Washington Elementary School on the near west side of Chicago. He went on to Wells High School before transferring to Lane Technical High School where he received his diploma at the age of 17. In 1942, Mercurio was drafted into the United States Army and reached the rank of Captain. He was sent overseas to Germany and Belgium where he would receive a Bronze Star for his actions in war. He was discharged in 1946, heading back to Chicago where he worked for various businesses, which ranged from steel equipment to insurance. On November 6, 1943, Sam married Marilyn Parotti in Chicago and the two had a son named Robert and a daughter named Joan.

Sam Mercurio was known as a normal man who became a scoutmaster with the Boy Scouts of America and was involved in youth work, helping towards the betterment of juvenile delinquents. Some jobs listed were a director of a service and Loan Company, an insurance company, a sales broker, and a stockholder in various corporations.

On August 17, 1967, he was arrested and convicted of conspiracy to commit aggravated kidnapping and sentenced to 30 days in county jail with 5 years probation.

Authorities discovered that Sam Mercurio had connections to the "juice" racket located around Chicago and Hamlin Avenue in Chicago, and American Lane and Devon Avenue in Elk Grove Village, Illinois. Sam Mercurio died in June 1987.

Frank Micelli

Francis Anthony Micelli was born around 1928 in Chicago and went by the aliases of "Chi Chi," Fred Mios, Frank Miceli, and Frank Michelli.

Listed as living at 1137 West Paulina, Oak Park in the 1960's, Micelli had an arrest record dating back to a conviction in 1957 for larceny. That case stemmed from a September 1957 arrest with Dominic Contursi and Joseph Altiere where a golf bag, twelve golf clubs, one sweater, one jacket, and ten golf balls were stolen from an Arthur Hagey. The three were going through the parking lot at Chicago's Midway Airport robbing cars when airport security caught them. Other arrests were for criminal damage to property and grand larceny.

In 1959, Micelli was listed as a labor goon and a member of Frank "Frankie X" Esposito's crew. An informant told FBI agents in November 1966 that he had been told that Frank Micelli was at one time a "runner" for Louis Briatta either for bookmaking or collecting "juice" loans put on the streets by Briatta.

In 1970, he was listed as being active in the Chicago "juice" rackets operating around North Avenue and Austin Boulevard, Polk and Aberdeen Streets, Rush Street and Delaware Place in Chicago, and North Avenue and Bonnie Brae Street in River Forest.

Joseph J. Maiola

Joseph Maiola was born around 1919 and lived at 3058 N. Central in Chicago. Maiola was mentioned as being connected to the "Only the Lonely Lounge" at the same address. His arrest record contained a 1964 arrest for contempt of court and a 1967 arrest for selling liquor to a minor. Joseph was listed as being involved in shylocking in the 1960's. In 1970 Joseph's son Frank X. Maiola was mentioned in a 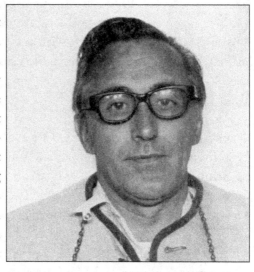 "juice" report. His occupation was that of a taxi cab driver in Elmwood Park. No criminal record was found but it did list the areas that Maiola was spotted by authorities in connection with "juice" loans. Those areas mentioned were Central and Barry Avenues, Belmont and Central Avenues in Chicago, and North Avenue and Roy Street in Northlake, Illinois.

John Manzella

Born around 1924, John L. Manzella was listed as being arrested several times for gambling. His business was Kedzie Korner Drive-In Pizza at 4201 South Kedzie in Chicago and was listed at living at 4503 N. Kedzie. He was alleged to be active in "juice" loans around Harlem and Stanley Avenues in Berwyn.

Joe Nero

Joseph W. Nero Jr. was born around 1947 and lived at 14725 S. Homan in Midlothian, Illinois. Nero made the 1970 "juice" investigation because he was seen at every local horse racetrack company in the 1960's and 70's, associating with and in the company of many known Outfit "juice" men. No criminal record was listed.

Peter Ori

Peter Ori was born around 1929 and worked as a dock foreman in Bridgeview. Ori could always been found at Irving Park Road and Kolze Street in Schiller Park. Living at 3817 Scott Street in Schiller Park, Illinois, Peter Ori was listed as being involved in alleged "juice" operations in the 1960's.

Myron Patrick

Sometimes known as Mike Patrick Myron, he was born around 1912 and lived at 6148 N. Francisco Avenue in Chicago. Patrick's hangouts were listed as Lawrence and Kedzie Avenues, Damen and North Avenues and Devon and Western Avenues in Chicago. Police advised that Myron Patrick was allegedly involved in "juice" in the 1960's.

Andrew Paulo

Andrew M. Paulo was born around 1921 and lived at 5949 S. Kolin Avenue in Chicago. He was convicted in 1943 for burglary being sentenced 3 to 5 years in Joliet prison. Listed, as his vicinities frequented in connection with "juice" were Kedzie Avenue and 42nd Street, and Pulaski Avenue and 55th Street in Chicago.

William Petrocelli

William J. Petrocelli Jr., also known as "Butch," lived at 923 S. Aberdeen in Chicago's Little Italy and 342 Forest Avenue in Hillside.

His arrest record contained a conviction in 1957 for a stolen auto in which he received 2 years probation. In 1967, he was arrested for armed robbery and in 1969 for aggravated kidnapping.

Petrocelli's mutilated body was found in March 1981 in the back seat of his car at 4307 W. 25th Place. His body was stuffed into a sleeping bag with just his feet hanging out. His mouth was stuffed with paper and taped shut. His wrists were taped to his chest and his ankles were bound with a rope. His face had been burned off by a blowtorch and two stab wounds were in his throat. The coroner said Petrocelli had died from suffocation and his body had been left in the car for months decomposing.

Ronald Polo

Born around 1937 Ronald J. Polo lived at 5853 S. Natchez and had an arrest record dating back to the 1950's. In 1953, he was convicted of armed robbery and placed under the supervision of the Illinois Youth Commission. Other arrests for being a peeping Tom and unlawful use of a weapon were listed. In 1962,

he was convicted for accessory to murder and given an indeterminate sentence in the security hospital at Menard Penitentiary.

Samuel Pullia

Sam M. Pullia was arrested on September 11, 1969 on a federal juice charge. At the time he was picked up, his arrest record ranged from aggravated battery, strong-arm robbery, contributing to the delinquency of a minor and homicide. He was sentenced to 3 years in prison in 1971.

Anthony Renallo

Anthony "Radio" Renallo lived at 4107 N. McVickers Avenue in Chicago in the 1960's. Born around 1935, he was arrested for disorderly conduct, resisting arrest, gambling, and paternity. "Radio" could be found at Sol's Food Mart at 1156 W. Taylor in the 1960's. Other places were Taylor Street and Racine Avenue, Ohio and State Streets, and Chicago Avenue and Rush Street in Chicago. There it was alleged that Radio was involved in the "juice" rackets.

Patrick Ricciardi

Also known by the names of Pat Ricardi and Patsy Rich, Ricciardi was mentioned in the 1970 "juice" investigation. He was listed as allegedly being active on Bryn Mawr Avenue and Clark Street, and State and 10th Streets in Chicago.

Mike Romano

Michael J. Romano lived at 845 S. Miller Avenue in Chicago and was the lock tender for the Metropolitan Sanitary District of Chicago River Control Works at the mouth of the Chicago River. He was believed to be born on December 28, 1919 in Chicago and was arrested in 1969 for kidnapping and criminal usury. It's believed he died on May 27, 1978.

Andrew Sargis

Andrew J. Sargis was born around 1931 and went by the alias of Chuck Sargis. He lived at 7732 S. La Vergne in Oak Lawn and allegedly operated "juice" around 4800 West Street and 10300 S. Cicero in Oak Lawn. In 1949, he was convicted for a robbery and sentenced to 2-to-4 years in prison.

Joseph Sarillo

Born around 1937, Joseph F. Sarillo had an arrest for gambling before being convicted of battery and intimidation in 1965. He would receive a six-month sentence on that charge. Also known as Joe Riccardello he lived at 4826 W. Thomas in Chicago and was known to frequent 14th Street between Cicero and Laramie Avenues in Cicero. It was there that Sarillo was alleged to engage in "juice" operations.

Joseph Siciliano

Believed to been born on November 22, 1917, Joseph Siciliano was also known as Joe Stiff, living at 4844 Hull Street in Skokie, Illinois. Working from Aldino's Restaurant on Oakton Street in Skokie, he had an arrest record dating back to 1952 for robbery. In 1954, he was convicted on bribery charges and sentenced to 2-to-5 years in prison for his part in the mob horsemeat scandal. Hoodlums and their friends were peddling horsemeat as beef, with the help of bribes, to state food inspectors. It's believed he died on July 11, 1991.

Frank Tenuta

Frank John Tenuta was arrested in Chicago on April 12, 1969, on criminal usury charges. Areas listed as Tenuta's were Paulina and 31st Streets and Central and North Avenues in Chicago. However, on June 15, 1970, his criminal case was dismissed and charges were dropped.

John Valsamoulis

John W. Valsamoulis, also known as John Vale, was born around 1934 and lived at 4738 North Karlov in Chicago. Some arrests listed under Valsamoulis were unlawful use of a weapon and possession of theft of lost property. In 1969, he was convicted of deceptive practices and received 5 years probation. He was listed as being allegedly available for "juice" loans at the corners of Lincoln Avenue and Wells Street, and Pine Grove and Diversey Avenues in Chicago in the 1960's.

George Vertucci

George Vertucci was believed to be born on April 4, 1923, and was listed as living at 1339 Home Avenue in Berwyn at one time. He was a  staple at Cermak Road and 47th Street in Cicero in the 1960's. Vertucci was arrested on September 10, 1969, for federal juice charges. In November 1947 George Vertucci, Nick Vertucci, Albert Testa, and Pauline Gartin were arrested while trying to pass a counterfeit $20 bill. In 1948, he was convicted on that charge of counterfeiting and was sentenced to 2 years in prison. In 1966, he was arrested and charged with usury and intimidation related to a "juice" loan. He received a 5-year sentence that was short lived; he died on March 25, 1973, and is buried at Queen of Heaven Cemetery in Hillside, Illinois.

Joseph Volpe

Joe D. Volpe was convicted in 1968 for deceptive practices, receiving 3 years probation. Born around 1944, Volpe lived at 1301 S. Gunderson in Berwyn and was once employed as a painter. He was said to hang out around the Rush Street area in Chicago in the 1960's. According to reports, Volpe was convicted of burglary in 1966 and received one year of probation.

In Closing

Sam DeStefano will live on being known as one of Chicago's sickest jokers who killed for the rush of power and declined to be part of the Chicago syndicate. He didn't need to be, he had a mob of his own. In 2001 one of mad Sam's relatives calling herself Helen DeStefano spoke of her great, great uncle saying, *"I think what he did was cool. You know, it's not all the time part of your family gets famous like Sam."*

Mad Sam DeStefano will remain Chicago's "king" of the "juice" rackets in Chicago for the rest of time. The "juice" racket is alive and well and functioning in today's world, much like it has since the Romans ruled most of the civilized world. There will always be someone who needs money who is desperate enough to agree to pay a crazy percentage to obtain a loan. Whether it be a criminal or a bank, either way, you're going to pay!

File Card

Sam DeStefano
Born: September 9, 1909
Died: April 14, 1973
AKA: David Triner, Mike Step, Mike DeStefano, Jack Neapolian
Nicknames, Mad Sam, Mad Dog, The Mad-hatter, Dyno, Sammy Dee
I.R. # 67388   FBI # 67388

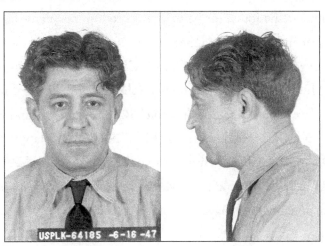

Description
White, Male, 5 feet 10 inches, 165 lbs., fair complexion, brown eyes, grey hair dyed black, wears glasses, 3 abdominal surgical scars, 1 scar form bullet wound.

Hangout
Postl's Health Club
Bella Rosa Bar B.Que, 1304 South Cicero Avenue, Cicero

Listed Addresses
2229 W. Taylor Street, Chicago (1930)
1025 South Winchester Avenue, Chicago (1931)
913 S. Miller Street, Chicago (Dec. 1944 to April 1945)
526 S. 6th Street, Columbus, OH (July 1945 to Sep. 1945)
2430 East 120th Street, Cleveland, Ohio (April 1945 to July 1945)
1062 West Polk Street, Chicago (1945 to 1950's)
1656 North Sayre, Chicago (1960's to 1970's)

Special thanks

This book is dedicated to Linda Rose. I would like to thank the following people for all their help, Nonnie and GramMar-inator who without your help this book would not be possible. I like to thank Mar for all her help in sharing her extensive research and files. Special thanks to Frank Menalocino for all his help. Thanks to Jim "last name blacked out by the government," Nickie Paiezano, Kimmie Sunshine, Joe, Chrysse, Zac the Lego maniac, Waldo, Shawn, Gloria "I'm finally on the wall", Brittany "how did he know my name," John, Denise, Dawn, Little Tony T, Bobby "we named the dog Indiana," Ralph, Cindy, Brandon, Jamie, Joseph, Cindy, Kristen "Dominic's chick," Nick, Ron Happy, Jef Deth, Chew, Deem, Mike Turtle Brown Kozuh, Knarf, Ynot and Peon. Lynn, Sam and the boys, Mr. and Mrs. M, Boku, Yoda, Jill Wagner, Johnny V, Mad Sam and anyone I may have forgotten, sorry!

ALSO AVAILABLE FROM TONY DARK

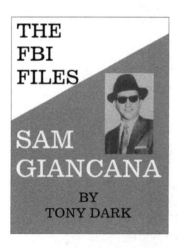

The FBI FILES

SAM GIANCANA

ISBN 0-615-12720-7

Appendix

Newspapers

Chicago American
Chicago Daily News
Chicago Evening Post
Chicago Herald & Examiner
Chicago Herald-American
Chicago Sun
Chicago Sun-Times
Chicago Times
Chicago Today
Chicago Tribune
Fra Noi – Italo-American News
Illinois Police and Sheriff's News
Melrose Park Herald
Rockford Morning Star

Reports and Documents

Chicago Police Arrest Record Mario DeStefano I.R.# 66794
Chicago Police Arrest Record Leo Forman I.R.# 13200
Circuit Court of Cook County, Mario DeStefano Case # 23350 (1966)
Circuit Court of Cook County, Mario DeStefano Case # 74955 (1935)
Circuit Court of Cook County, Mike DeStefano Case # 41798 (1926)
Circuit Court of Cook County, Mike DeStefano Case # 58946 (1930)
Circuit Court of Cook County, Sam DeStefano Case # 61356 (1931)
Murder case 818, Joseph Grieco, Baltimore Police Department
State of Illinois Vs. Sam DeStefano and Charles Crimaldi Case # 64-2672 (1964)
State of Illinois Vs. Mario DeStefano Case # 64-1441 (1964)
State of Illinois Vs. Sam DeStefano Case # 64-1436 (1964)
State of Illinois Vs. Charles Crimaldi Case # 50-1733 (1950)
State of Illinois Vs. Anthony Crimaldi Case # 51-1555 (1951)
State of Illinois Vs. Anthony Crimaldi Case # 51-1677 (1951)
State of Illinois Vs. Sam DeStefano, Mario DeStefano, Anthony Spilotro # 72-2309 (1972)
State of Illinois Vs. Anthony Crimaldi Case #51-1677 (1951)
State of Illinois Vs. Nicholas Bravos Case #71134 (1931)

State of Illinois Vs. Sam Gallo, Vito Zaccagnini, Al Zaccagnini, Robert O'Casey Case #63-153 (1963)
State of Illinois Vs. William Messino, George Bravos, Sam Mercurio, Joseph Lombardi Case #65-2880 (1965)
State of Illinois Vs. Sam Ariola, Louis Eboli, and Guy Cervone Case #61-2464 (1961)
State of Illinois Vs. Sander Caravello Case #65-1313 (1965)
State of Illinois Vs. Joseph DiVarco Case #64-1442 (1964)
State of Illinois Vs. Leo Foreman Case #54-2056 (1954)
State of Illinois Vs. Julius J. Grieco Case #63495
State of Illinois Vs. Joseph LaMantia, Frank DeFoggio, James Cozzi Case # 51-1768
State of Illinois Vs. Joseph LaMantia Case #58-854 (1958)
State of Illinois Vs. James LaPietra, Schubmehl, Nugara and Bertucci Case #52-0179
State of Illinois Vs. Frank Micelli Case #57-2212 (1957)
State of Illinois Vs. Frank Santucci Case # 57-324 (1957)
Division of Corrections Wisconsin State Prison Sam DeStefano # 21284 (1933)
Division of Corrections Wisconsin State Prison Mike DeStefano # 54402 (1934)
State of Illinois Joliet Prison Records # 2089 (1928)
U.S. Penitentiary Leavenworth, Kansas Records, Sam DeStefano #64185-L (1947)
Report of the Illinois Legislative Investigating Commission 1967
Report of the Illinois Legislative Investigating Commission 1972
Report of the Illinois Legislative Investigating Commission 1973
Juice Racketeers, Report on Criminal Usury in the Chicago Area 1970
United States of America Vs. Anthony Esposito Jr. # 71 CR 980 (1971)
United States of America Vs. Anthony Esposito Jr. # 72 CR 706 (1972)
United States of America Vs. Sam DeStefano and Edward Speice # 72 CR 178 (1972)
United States of America Vs. William Hanhardt, Joe Basinski, Guy Altobello & William Brown # 02-2253
Winnebago County Illinois Vs. Sam Destefano Case 4-9
Organized Crime in Chicago 1990, Chicago Crime Commission

Books

Dark, Tony, *The FBI Files Sam Giancana*, Chicago: HoseHead Productions, 2004.

Demaris, Ovid. *Captive City: Chicago in Chains*. New York: Lyle Stuart, 1969.

Kidner, John. Crimaldi: *Contract Killer*. Washington, D.C.: Acropolis Books LTD, 1976.

Roemer Jr., William F. *Accardo: The Genuine Godfather*. New York: DIF INC. 1995.

————Roemer: *Man Against the Mob*. New York: DIF INC., 1989.

————*The Enforcer – Spilotro: The Chicago Mob's Man over Las Vegas*. New York: Ive Books, 1994.

FBI Files

Adler, Arthur 72-80
Alex, Gus 92-3182
Bombings of Restaurants 62-9-9-1163
Bravos, George 179-24
Bravos, Nick 92-1297
Cappelletti, Pete 87-72688
Crime in Chicago Area 62-9-9-1616
DeStefano, Mario 179-199
DeStefano, Sam 92-7456
Fosco, Peter 122-1460
Gallo, Sam 29-1977
General File 62-9-9-1616
Giancana, Sam 92-3171
Humphreys, Murray 92-348
Patrick, Leonard 92-374
Shylocking Chicago 62-9-9-1655

INDEX

Alterie, Louie 19, 20,
Alterie, Joseph 476,
Altobello, Guy 278,
Amabile, Alphonso 192,
Amadeo, Agostino "Gus" 233,
Amari, Joe "Red" 429,
Amatuna Gang 18,
Amatuna, Samuzzo 17, 18,
Ambile, Joseph "Joe Shine" 433,
Amola, John 460,
Anco Insurance Company 46, 169,
Anderson, Andy 206,
Anderson, Kenny 208, 210, 260,
Anderson, Rodger 205, 206,
Andriacchi, Joe "The Builder" 346,
Angalone, Joe 55,
Angel-Kaplan Sports Service 352,
Angel, Don 352,
Angelini, Donald "Wizard of Odds" 369, 371, 389,
Angellino, Don 352,
Angileri, Salvatore 454,
Annereno, Angelo 359, 370,
Annoreno, Anthony 353, 363,
Annereno, August "Genero" 12,
Annereno, Johnny "Peppi Ganero" 12,
Annerino, Sam 400,
Annoreno, Joe 21,
Annoreno, Steve 354, 359, 360, 362-363 (Main bio) 365, 370,
Annunzio, Frank 46, 168, 243,
Anseline, Albert 18,
Anselmi, Albert 12,
Anton, Ted "The Greek" 12,
Anixter, Julius 12,
Anzalone, Joseph 308,
Applequist, Ben 19,
Applwquist, E. 19,
Aranyos, Joseph 417,
Arasso, Tony 12,
Arealo, John 401,
Arena, Mike 309,
Ariola, Samuel 18,
Ariola, Sam "Big Sam" 455 (Main bio)
Arlington Park Race Track 383,
Armand's Italian Restaurant 346,

Armanetti, Frank 243,
Armidano, Robert 315,
Armoado, John 12,
Armondo, Johnny 20,
Armory Lounge 141, 221, 227, 288,
Arnett, Dempsey 452,
Arnold, J. 330,
Arnold, Joseph 413, 416, 417-421 (Main bio) 426, 450,
Arnstein, Nicky 12,
Art Institute Chicago 137,
Aryan Brotherhood 364,
Ascoli, Paul 10, 337,
Aston, Joseph 190,
Atlanta Braves baseball team 427,
Atlas, Morris 206,
Attlomionte, Diego 17,
Aureli, Frank "The Knife" 369, 371,
Aurelli, Joseph 59,
Austin, Mary 105, 106,
Austin, Richard B. 249, 250, 252, 253, 254, 257,
Auto Wreckers' Union 347,

B

Baer, Maishie 79, 335, 397-399 (Main bio)
Bagis, Lester 434,
Bagnola, Joseph 410,
Bagnulo, Dom "Bags" 444,
Bailey, Steve 287,
Bakes, Mike 55,
Bakes, Ned 12,
Balaban, Arthur 80, 81,
Balcastro, James 338,
Baldelli, Ecola 17,
Balistreri, Frank 80,
Baldelli, Ecola 18,
Ballo, Dominick 12,
Balmoral Race Track 383,
Balsommo, Mario 10,
Bambulas, Thomas 437,
Barbara, Fred 379,
Barbaro, Joseph 311,
Barbe, Lewis 222,

Blakely, Charles 12,
Blasi, Dominic, "Butch" 112, 189,
Blaudins, Giovanni 17,
Blitzstein, Herbert "Herbie Blitz" 455-456 (*Main bio*) 472,
Bloody 20th Ward 46,
Bloom, Ike 12,
Bock, Wayne 360,
Bolognese, Joseph 364,
Boltaire, Jerry 417,
Bolton, John 10,
Bolton, Red 19,
Boltz, Leonard 21,
Bombacino, Louis 457,
Boniakowski, Casey 185,
Boniakowski, June 184, 185,
Bonnano, Joseph 161,
Borak, Daniel 379, 380,
Borelli, Sam 460,
Boresllino, John 437,
Borowski, Bob 241,
Borozzi, Nicholas 447,
Boshes, Harry 209,
Boulihanis, George 208,
Bounaguide, Lawrence 425,
Bova, Tommy "Big Tony" 391,
Bowe, Chief Justice 217,
Boyle, John 101,
Boy Scouts of America 476,
Brabas, Nick 381,
Bracco, Alfonso 18,
Bradi, Lawrence "See Lawrence Buonaguidi"
Brado, M 381,
Brady, Larry 425,
Brancato, Dominick 421,
Brancato, Dom "Nags" 12,
Branch, Alphonso 467,
Brandt, Henry 18,
Braseth, James 247, 248, 249, 251, 252, 253, 255, 290,
Bravas, Nick 381,
Bravos, Faith 389, 391,
Bravos, George "George the Greek" 147, 148, 175, 242, 299, 341, 342, 344, 380-394 (*Main bio*) 436, 458,

Bravos, Helen 381,
Bravos, James 381,
Bravos, June 381,
Bravos, Kanela 381,
Bravos, Kathy 381,
Bravos, Mary Ellen 381,
Bravos, Nicholas "Nick the Greek" 175, 242, 329, 341, 343, 380-394 (*Main bio*) 436, 458,
Bravos, Nickie 381,
Brevos, Nick 381,
Briatta, Antoinette "See Antoinette D'Arco"
Briatta, Frank 337,
Briatta, Joseph "Pep" 47, 92, 337, 338,
Briatta, John 92, 337,
Briatta, Louis "Lou the Barber" 10, 46, 47, 48, 91, 92, 97, 337, 349, 397, 398, 461, 477,
Briatta, Mike 10, 47, 92, 337,
Briatta, Mike Jr. 92,
Briatta. Ralph 337,
Briatta, Thomas 47, 92, 337,
Bridewell Prison 89, 382, 446, 470,
Bridgeport Chicago 375,
Bridgeview Illinois 351,
Brightly, Fred 338, 339,
Broadview Illinois 172,176, 177, 178,
Brodkin, Michael 103, 192,
Bronge, Joseph 165,
Bronge, Peter 18,
Brooklier, Dominic 354,
Brooks, Joe "Dynamite" 16,
Brown, Al "See Al Capone"
Brown, Albert 241
Brown, Boxie 362,
Brown, Daniel 428,
Brown, Harry 12, 326, 327,
Brown, Kenneth 314,
Brown, Ralph 12,
Brown, Steve 362,
Browning, Marvin 465,
Bruno, Albert 64,
Bruno, Frank 366,
Bucaro, Martin Jr. 365,
Buccieri, Angelo 354,

Buccieri, Carmen 367, 368,
Buccieri, Fiore "Fifi" 10, 89, 148, 185, 186, 187, 188, 311, 312, 328, 351-355 *(Main bio)* 366, 368, 369, 370, 370, 391, 436, 443, 448, 464, 467,
Buccieri, Frank "The Horse" 185, 330, 353, 354, 366-369 *(Main bio)* 370, 420, 443,
Buccieri, George 443,
Bucher, George "Spot" 16,
Buglio, Ralph 12,
Buonoguldi, Larry "The Hood" 181, 416, 424, 425-427 *(Main bio)*
Burbatt, Joe 28,
Burke, Fred "Killer" 12,
Burke, John C. 30,
Burkman, Julian 434,
Burnet, Theodore 411,
Burns, Henrietta 108, 109, 113, 115,
Burns, John 301,
Busch, Harry 274, 342,
Butero, Mike 12,
Butler, Benjamin 21,
Byrne, Lt. 198,

C

Caefonie, John *"See Marshall Caifano"*
Caifano, Marshall 10, 159, 160, 161, 164, 165, 167, 168, 169, 170, 222, 238, 329, 369, 430, 433,
Cain, Richard 145, 271, 272, 402,
Calabrese, Frank "Breese" 456-457 *(Main bio)*
Calabrese, Frank Jr. 456, 457,
Calabrese, Kurt 457,
Calabrese, Nick 322, 428, 451, 456, 457,
Calabrese, Joseph "Little Joe" 17,
Calamia, Jimmy 366,
Calamia, Peter 366,
Calarco, Dominic 347,
Calico, Frank 366,
Callahan, Gerald "Cheese Box" 12,
Caltro, Christine 33,
Camillo, Nick "Moose" 369,

Campagna, Louis "Little New York" 12, 232,
Campagna, Tony 12,
Campanelli, Fat 10,
Campanille, James 18,
Campbell, Joseph Dr. 169,
Campione, Frank 21,
Campise, Jasper "Jay" 370, 394, 426, 458 *(Main bio)*
Canadian Mob 130,
Canale, Salvatore 12,
Canella, Frank 462,
Cannavino, Mike 308,
Capezio, Anthony "Tough Tony" 12, 17,
Capezio, James 441,
Capise, Samuel 10,
Capone, Al "Scareface" 2, 9, 10, 46, 47, 157, 167, 294, 404, 433, 453,
Capone Gang 9, 385, 433, 453, 461,
Capone, Frank 12,
Capone, John "Miami" 12, 47,
Capone, Matt 12,
Capone, Ralph, "Bottles" 12, 157,
Capone, Ralph Jr. 157,
Caporale, Frank Dr. 125, 127,
Capozzi, Archie 10,
Cappalario, Mat 12,
Capparelli, Louis 183,
Cappelletti, Carla *"Peter's daughter"* 301,
Cappelletti, Clara *"Peter's sister"* 300,
Cappelletti, John *"Peter's brother"* 301,
Cappelletti, John *"Peter's son"* 301,
Cappelletti, Joseph *"Peter's brother"* 300,
Cappelletti, Joseph *"Peter's son"* 301,
Cappelletti, Marge 300,
Capelletti, Michael *"Peter's brother"* 300,
Capelletti, Michael *"Peter's son"* 301,
Cappelletti, Paula 301,
Cappelletti, Peter "Cappy" 4, 5, 69, 76, 102, 209, 212, 260, 280, 300-310 *(Main bio)*
Cappelletti, Paul Jr. 301,
Cappelletti, Verna Mae 301,
Cappy's Bail Bond Service 76,
Caravello, Sam 458,

Cotroni, Mike 130,
Cotroni, Rosina 131,
Cotroni, Vince "The Egg" 130, 131,
Coughlin, John "Bathhouse" 13,
Covelli, Daniel 157,
Covelli, Daniel Jr. 157,
Covelli, Gerald 416,
Covello, Frank 462 (Main bio)
Cowan, Arthur "Boodie" 396,
Cowen, Louis 13,
Cox, Tom 202,
Cozi, Sam 10,
Cozzi, Emil 191,
Cozzi, James 377,
Cozzie, James 64, 377,
Cozzi, Lawrence 17,
Cozzo, Sam 272,
Craig, Andy 13,
Crevone, Guy 455,
Crimaldi, Anthony "Tony" 134, 245, 246, 280, 281, 282, 283, 284, 285, 286, 317,
Crimaldi, Antonio 281,
Crimaldi, Charles "Chuckie" 3, 4, 3, 109, 110, 112,113, 126, 127, 128, 130, 134, 139, 152, 153, 175, 221, 222, 223, 224, 225, 226, 227, 228, 229, 230, 231, 245, 246, 247, 248, 249, 252, 253, 254, 255, 258, 260, 264, 265, 266, 272, 273, 274, 275, 276, 280-292 (Main bio) 317,
Crimaldi, Frank 13,
Crimaldi, Guy 280, 281,
Crimaldi, Janine 283,
Crimaldi, John "Cuono" 280, 281,
Crimaldi, Louise 280, 286,
Crimaldi, Madeline 281,
Crimaldi, Rose Mary 283,
Crimaldi, Roxanne 283,
Crimaldi, Theresa 281,
Crivilare, Victor 377,
Cuba 289,
Culicchia, Carl 94,
Cummings, Edward 348,
Cunningham, David 57,
Curingione, Tony 13,
Curtin, Dominic 330,

Cusick, James 13,

D

Daddono, Mary 438,
Daddono, William "Potatoes" 10, 70, 74, 77, 78, 79, 86, 92, 180, 181, 214, 240, 329, 334, 388, 389, 438-441 (Main bio) 453, 461,
Dakoff, Mike 98,
Daley, Richard J. 213, 245, 444,
Daley, Richard M. 377,
Dallis, Chris 358,
D'Amico, Anthony 376,
D'Amico, Marco 346, 462,
Damone, Vic 443, 444, 449,
Damore, Frank 474,
D'Andrea, Anthony 17,
D'Andera, Anthony C. 13,
D'Andra, Armand 450,
D'Andrea, Mario 451,
D'Andera, Nick 450-451 (Main bio)
D'Andera, Phil 13,
Dandre, Joseph "Dandriacco" 309,
D'Angelo, Pasty 338,
D'Antonio, James 278,
D'Arco, Antoinette 46,
D'Arco, John Sr. 10, 45, 46, 112, 168, 184, 337,
Darrice, Frank 13,
Dauber, Charlotte 463,
Dauber, William Earl 400, 401, 462-463 (Main bio)
Davino, Mary "See Mary DeStefano"
Davis, Angela 260,
Davis, Ed 348,
Davis, Richard 430,
DeAmato, James 13,
DeAngelis, Fred 18,
DeAngelis, Roland 320,
DeAngelo, Robert 64,
DeAngelo, Pasty 10,
DeBartola, Tony 10,
DeChristoforo, Louis "Cadoodles" 10,
Deckman, Alfred 17,
De George, Jim 80,

Dohner, Bob 206,
Domico, Sam 10,
Donovan, "Stick Bomb" 21,
Doody, Willie 10,
Doran, James *"See Robert Whitlock"*
Dorfman, Allen 321,
Dorfman, Paul "Red" 80,
Dorherty, James "Red" 13,
Dougherty, Charles 24,
Dounias, Peter 424,
Downs, Tom 392,
Doyle, Donald 297, 298, 299,
Drake, James 190,
Drake, John 191,
Dragin, Robin 172,
Dragna, Louis 365,
Druggan, Terry 19,
Drury, William 92, 232,
Dubois, John 473,
Duffy, James 16,
Duffy, Tom "Red" 16,
Duffy, William 208, 209, 212, 214, 218, 313,
Dunes Hotel 326,
Durcci, Vincent "Schemer" 20,
Durka, Stanley 402,
Duty, Leda 89,
Dworet, Irving 354, 355,

E

Eboli, Louis "The Mooch" 322, 455, 457,
Echeles, Julius 113, 128, 258,
Egan, Edward 210,
Egan, Edward Officer 210,
Egan, William "Shorty" 16,
Eggleston, Billie 108,
Eisen, Jacob "Pollynose" 339, 340,
Eisen, Maxie 13, 20,
Elder, Rob 380,
Eldorado, Frank 465,
Eldorado, Ron 465,
Eldorado, Tony "Pineapples" 367, 368, 465,
Elkin, Sheldon 308,
Eller, Morris 13, 46,

Elmwood Cemetery 317, 394,
Elmwood Park Illinois 284, 285, 295, 317, 318, 330, 331, 332, 335, 341, 342, 344, 345, 346, 347, 349, 350, 363, 369, 370, 394, 457, 462, 465, 477,
Elodado, Tony 465,
Embalmers Union Chicago 352,
Emerling, William 13,
Emery, Joe 442,
English, Charles "Chuckie" 10, 159, 240, 369, 383, 394, 431, 447, 465 *(Main bio)*
English, Roland 85, 369,
English, Sam "Butch" 10, 85, 240, 371, 383, 389, 465,
Epping, Ted C.
Epsteen, Jane 170,
Epsteen, Peter 170,
Epstein, Joseph 209,
Epton, Saul 261,
Erwin, Alice 341, 342,
Esposito, Anthony "Tony X" 10, 168, 172, 175, 245, 257, 326, 337, 389,
Esposito, Anthony Jr. "Sonny" 168, 172, 173, 175, 176, 177, 245, 246, 247, 248, 255, 257, 290, 316, 317, 477,
Esposito, Frank "Frankie X" 13, 45, 46, 47, 48, 66, 67, 92, 107, 173, 185, 233, 245, 257, 337, 341, 435,
Esposito, Frank Sr. "Butch" 172, 245,
Esposito, Gaetano 13,
Esposito, Gaetano "Guy X" 257, 337,
Esposito, Guy 452,
Esposito, Joe 125,
Esposito, John 336,
Esposito, Joseph "Diamond Joe" 13, 42, 337,
Esposito, Marcella 257, 337,
Esposito, Mary 47,
Esposito, Shirley 257,
Epping, Ted C. 76,
Estes, Frank *"See Ed Piranio"*
Etck, Van 191,
Eterno, Joseph 309,
Eto, Ken 417, 426-427 *(Main bio)*
Eulo, Frank "Sharkey" 75,
Evens, Fred 389,

F

Fabrizio, Hugo 338,
Fahey, Pat 32,
Falco, Angelo 474,
Falco, Anthony 48,
Falcone, Joe 131,
Falcone, Sal 131,
Faling, Kanela *"See Kanela Bravos"*
Fahey, Pat 32,
Fanelli, Rocco 13, 20, 338,
Fanello, Dan 10,
Fanning, Richard 238,
Farino, Sam 18,
Farley, Fred 13,
Farley, James 19,
Ferrari, Joseph 13,
Farrell, Frank 466,
Farrell, James 295, *"See Robert Whitlock"*
Farrugia, Sam 79, 452 *(Main bio)*
Faulk, Geraldine 237,
Faulk, Shelby 237,
Fazio, Louis 188, 271,
Fecaret, Anthony 467,
Fecarotta, Alice 466,
Fecarotta, John "Big John" 322, 333, 377, 466-467 *(Main bio)*
Feceret, Tony 467,
Fedel, Moratio 377,
Fein, Vernon 79,
Ferlic, Frank 55,
Ferrara, Sam 441,
Ferraro, Frank "Strongy" 103, 374, 376, 398,
Ferraro, Joseph 13, 327, 369,
Ferraro, Richard 400,
Ferri, Nick 209,
Ferriola, Joseph "De Gaul" 322, 352, 353, 369-372 *(Main bio)* 391,
Fidanzi, Guido "The Weed" 401-403 *(Main bio)*
Fidanzi, Thelma 402,
Fields, Marshall Jr. 452,
Figuarata, Johnny 360,
Filippelli, Robert 467-468 *(Main bio)*
Filishio, Mike 468 *(Mail bio)*

Filisho, James 55,
Fillichio, Frank 10,
Fillichio, Pete "Mibs" 10,
Finalli, Anthony 17,
Finanzi, Guido 401,
Fine, George 79, 282,
Finn, John 305,
Finnehan, Judge 114,
Finkelstein, Henry 20,
Fiore, Alphonse 17,
Fiore, Frank 27, 112,
Fiore, Joe 13,
Fiore, John 10,
Fiore, Philip "Pete" 457,
Fiori, Alphonse 17,
Fio Rito, Carl 189, 192, 422,
First Ward Chicago 45, 46, 47, 48, 103, 111, 168, 170, 184, 326, 337, 352, 358, 374, 375, 376, 397, 468, 474,
Fischetti, Charles 13,
Fischetti, Joe 170,
Fischetti, Rocco 13, 170, 437, 438,
Fisher, Joe 22,
Fishman, Harry 332,
Fitzgerald, James 228,
Fitzgerald, Richard 124,
Fitzgerald, Sgt. 198, 199,
Fitzsimmons, Frank 321,
Fitzsimmons, Michael 251,
Fligelman, Hy 155,
Fogarty, Bozo 13,
Foley, John "Mitters" 21,
Foley, Tom 21,
Fontaine, Johnny 444,
Fontana, Carl 13,
Fontana, Ernest 13,
Foreman, Leo 82, 83, 84, 89, 197-231 *(Murder)* 260, 263, 265, 266, 271, 274, 275, 276, 299, 320,
Foreman, Ruben 205, 220,
Foreman, Ursela 202, 205,
Forsyth, James 13,
Fosco, Peter 44, 45,
Fosco, Vito 10,
Foster, Frankie 20,
Four Deuces Saloon 385,

George, Albert 149,
Gersh, Michael 340,
Ghee's Brother 149, 150, 151,
Gheto Gang 20,
Giancana, Antoinette 325,
Giancana, Charles 419,
Giancana, Joseph "Pep" 75, 418, 419,
Giancana, Sam "Mooney" 10, 55, 74, 75,
76, 85, 93, 103, 114, 117, 118, 130, 141,
142, 145, 147, 159, 164, 183, 184, 192,
221, 227, 233, 265, 271, 272, 276, 277,
288, 289, 290, 291, 294, 321, 325, 326,
329, 330, 333, 351, 352, 366, 369, 392,
405, 418, 424, 430, 431, 432, 434, 436,
439, 440, 453, 461, 465,
Giangalo, Chuck 361,
Gianola, Leonard "Needles" 10, 93, 94,
159, 453,
Gianotti's Restaurant 278,
Giglio, Sal 131,
Gilfone, Michael 10,
Gillette, Ralph 13,
Ginnis, Hy 157,
Ginnis, Ruth 157,
Ginsburg, James 309,
Gioe, Charles "Cherry Nose" 13,
Giordgno, Louis 18,
Giovenco, August "Gus" 469 (*Main bio*)
Gironda, Anthony 48,
Gironda, Sam 46,
Gistenson, Leo 16,
Gizzi, Anthony 402,
Glimco, Joey "Little Tim Murphy" 13,
141, 149, 287, 291, 332, 389,
Glitta, Marco 425,
Glitta, Mike "Fireplug" 416, 419, 420,
423-425 (*Main bio*) 426, 472,
Gloriana Gang 19,
Gnatek, William 282,
Gnolfo, Phil "Abbate" 17,
Goggins, Edward 155, 156,
Gold, Bill 79,
Goldberg, Benny 414,
Golden, Morton 460,
Golden, Red 17,
Goldsmith, Solly 10,

Goldstein, Bummy 19,
Goldstein, Morris "Greenie" 437-438
(*Main Bio*)
Gonzales, Santiago 370,
Goodman, Oscar 227,
Gordon, David 445,
Gordon, Irving "The Market Master"
170, 398,
Gorman, Simone 13,
Gorney, Walter 19,
Gothard, Peter 455,
Gottlieb, Jake 326,
Grabiner, Joe "Jew Kid" 13,
Grabowy, Ted 309,
Granata & Massey Funeral Home 277,
Granata, Joe "Machine Gun Joe" 13, 21,
Granata, Peter 13,
Granato, Tony 469,
Granito, Tony "The Head" 469-470
(*Main bio*)
Greco, Nick 64,
Green, Dwight 453,
Green Bay Wisconsin 179,
Greenberg, Alec 13,
Greene, Carl 79,
Greene, Maurice "Greenie" 396,
Greenholt, Mr. 32,
Greenlease, Bobby 68,
Grieco, Carmella 448,
Grieco, Donald, 328, 442-450 (*Main
bio*)
Greico, Glen 446,
Grieco, Joseph 328, 330, 442-450 (*Main
bio*)
Grieco, Joe "Marble Eye" 446, 447,
Grieco, Julius "Ju Ju" 160, 215, 328, 445-
447 (*Main bio*)
Grieco, Julius Jr. 446,
Grieco, Melba Jean 447,
Grieco, Rose 446, 447,
Grieco, Theresa 448,
Griffin, Darrel 410,
Grimaldi, Anthony "See Anthony
Crimaldi"
Grimaldi, Charles "See Charles
Crimaldi"

Probst, Marlene 240,
Probst, Ralph 240, 241,
Pronger, Robert Jr. 401,
Proszowlicz, Robert "Whitey" 236,
Pugh, James 110,
Pullia, Samuel 480 (Main bio)
Punchard, Francis 58,
Pupillo, Monk 11,
Puzo, Mario 444,

Q

Quaglia, Emil 11,
Quan, Dinky 19,
Quarnstrom, George 444,
Quayle, Dan 425,
Queen of Heaven Cemetery 89, 273, 277,
300, 317, 359, 380, 460, 467, 483,
Quigley, Edward 377,
Quinlan, Mike "Bubs" 19, 21,
Quinlan, Walter 19,
Quinn, Arthur 15,
Quinn, John 441,
Quirk, Frank 15,
Quirk, Martin "Sonny Boy" 15,
Quirk, Mickey 16,

R

Rabin, Albert 327,
Rabin, William 131,
Rabiolo, William 192,
Ragen Colts Gang 19,
Ragan, Frank 19,
Ragan, James Sr. 19,
Ragan, Mike 19,
Ragucci, Anthony 161,
Rainone, John 351,
Ralph Sheldon Gang 21,
Rancatore, James 376,
Ranelli, James 309,
Raporto, Freddy 357,
Rappaport, John 16,
Raymond, George 18,
Red Bolton Gang 19,
Red Hawk Gang 441,
Reese, James 468,

Regan, Rob 172,
Reilly, Michael 16,
Reimann, Frank 69,
Reinke, Ralph 189.
Renallo, Anthony "Radio" 460, 480
(Main bio)
Reno, Steve 362,
Reno, Tony 363,
Reno, William "Fat Man" 472,
Renzetti, Tony 402,
Restagno, Joseph 294,
Rhodes, Joanne 415,
Ricca, Paul "The Waiter" 15, 447, (Also
see Paul DeLucia)
Riccardello, Joseph 481,
Ricciardi, Patrick 480 (Main bio)
Ricco, Diego 11,
Riccio, Fat 11,
Rice, Peter 285,
Rice, Sam 434,
Rich, Pasty 480,
Rider, Morgan 66,
Ries, Fred 14,
Rinella, Frank 118, 361,
Rinella, John 26,
Rinella, Sam 432,
Rinelli, Pete 14,
Rio, Dominic 415,
Rio, Frank "Kline" 14,
Rio, Lucia 415,
Rio, Vincenzo 415,
Rissoulo, Rick 346,
Rito, John "Billken" 17,
Ritroni, Alf 394,
River Forest 91, 134, 136, 141, 189, 189,
324, 349, 362, 382, 409, 435, 437, 455,
458, 459, 477,
River Forest State Bank 68,
Riverside Illinois, 438, 440, 466,
Riviera Bowling Lanes, 439,
Rizza, Ralph 411,
Robarge, Henry 58,
Robarge, Joseph 58,
Robert, Rene 131,
Roberti, Joe 11,
Roberts, James 394,

264, 271, 274, 275, 277, 280, 317, 319-323 *(Main bio)* 347, 364, 455,
Spilotro, John 275, 455,
Spilotro, Michael 278, 322, 323,
Spilotro, Nancy 227,
Spilotro, Patrick Dr. 322, 347,
Spilotro, Victor 227, 271,
Spilotro, Vincent 227,
Spingola, Henry 17,
Spingola, Joseph 17,
Spingola, Peter 17,
Spino, Frank 375,
Spiotto, Michael 208, 209, 212,
Sportsman's Race Track 383, 387, 393, 464,
Spranze, Mike 15, 85,
Spritz, Walter 159,
Sprovieri, John "Bells" 367,
Stallings, Claude 15,
Stallman, Leonard 409,
Stamas, Louis 283,
Stamos, John 99,
Stamper, George 244,
Stamps, Anthony 282,
Stanaszek, George 244, 402,
Stanfa, John 457,
Stanley, Pollock 15,
Stanton, Danny 15, 16, 19,
Stardust Casino 322,
Starzyk, Adolph 441,
Stasin, Manny 168, 172, 173,175,
Stathatos, George 191,
St. Valentine's Day Massacre 385,
Steffanelli, Pasty 11,
Stein, Ben 209,
Stein, Joseph 216, 409, 410,
Stein, Morris 309,
Stein, Teddy 20,
Stepina, Carlos 18, 385,
Stepp, Helen 189,
Sterling, Leroy 407,
Stern, Edward 282,
Stern, Henry 410,
Stevens, Dick 394,
Stevens, Walter 15, 17,
Stiff, Joseph 482,

Stoloski, John 282,
Stompanato, Pat 253, 254,
Stone Park Illinois 108, 287, 319, 433, 468, 469,
Stone, Sharon 234,
Stopee, Joseph 17,
Storino, Mary *"See Mary DeStefano"*
Storino, Sam 7,
Stryker, Louis 21,
Suba, Andrew 297, 298,
Suburban Refuse Disposal
Sullivan, Frank 101,
Sullivan, John 57,
Sullivan, Paddy 16,
Sullivan, Ted 316,
Sullivan, Tom 15,
Summario, Bezee 361,
Summerfield Gang 22,
Summerfield, Lewis 22,
Summerfield, Max 22,
Surdo, Sam 11, 338,
Sutherland Hotel 163,
Swain, Paul 15,
Sweeney, Matthew 300, 301,
Swinarski, Matthew 301,
Swinarski, Theodore 301,
Sylvestro, Antonio, 131,
Symonds, Joe "Kline" 19,
Szymanski, Walter 309,

T

Taddeo, Aniello 18,
Taddeo, David "Tadders" 18, 385,
Taddeo Gang 18,
Taglia, Benny 361,
Taglia, Billy 361,
Taglia, Sam 172,
Taglia, William "Billy Goat" 15,
Tagonti, Tony 15,
Tam-O-Shanter Golf Club 167,
Tanaka, Joseph 427,
Tancl, Eddie 16,
Tanel, Eddie 16,
Tarallo, Joseph 190,
Taranto, Anthony 64, 65,

CPSIA information can be obtained
at www.ICGtesting.com
Printed in the USA
BVHW041809140521
607367BV00012BA/1752